EDWARD GORDON CRAIG

Contemporary Theatre Studies

A series of books edited by Franc Chamberlain, Nene College, Northampton, UK

Please see the back of this book for other titles in the Contemporary Theatre Studies series

EDWARD GORDON CRAIG
A VISION OF THEATRE

Christopher Innes
York University, Ontario, Canada

 harwood academic publishers
Australia • Canada • China • France • Germany • India
Japan • Luxembourg • Malaysia • The Netherlands • Russia
Singapore • Switzerland • Thailand

Amsteldijk 166
1st Floor
1079 LH Amsterdam
The Netherlands

Every effort has been made to trace the ownership of all copyrighted material in this book. In the event of any questions about the use of any material, the author, while expressing regret for any inadvertent error, will be happy to make the necessary acknowledgment in future printings.

British Library Cataloguing in Publication Data
Innes, C. D. (Christopher D.)
    Edward Gordon Craig: a vision of theatre. – 2nd ed. –
(Contemporary theatre studies; v. 28)
    1. Craig, Edward Gordon, 1872–1966 – Criticism and
interpretation
    I. Title
    792'.092

ISBN 90-5702-124-2

Cover illustration: "Wretched Lovers," *Acis and Galatea*. Courtesy of the British Library.
Title page photograph: Gordon Craig with his model stage, Moscow, 1910.

CONTENTS

INTRODUCTION TO THE SERIES

Contemporary Theatre Studies is a book series of special interest to everyone involved in theatre. It consists of monographs on influential figures, studies of movements and ideas in theatre, as well as primary material consisting of theatre-related documents, performing editions of plays in English, and English translations of plays from various vital theatre traditions worldwide.

Franc Chamberlain

LIST OF ILLUSTRATIONS

ACKNOWLEDGMENTS

The original version of this study could not have been completed without the active cooperation of many institutions and individuals. It was undertaken while some of Gordon Craig's collaborators and colleagues were still available as a resource. Their information and insights were invaluable; and the present book is no less indebted to their assistance. In particular, Edward Craig opened his personal archives to me, answered many questions about his father's work, and was generous in offering advice and criticism. He also provided many of the photographs, which are reproduced again here. Peter Fozzard gave me the considerable benefit of his experience in organizing the centennial exhibition of Craig's designs, while Arnold Rood not only allowed me to work with his Craig collection (now in the London Theatre Museum) but also shared his wide knowledge of Gordon Craig. I remain deeply grateful for their help and encouragement.

Since the documents and visual materials relating to Craig's life and work have been widely dispersed, neither the original nor subsequent research for this book could have been accomplished without the support of the Social Sciences and Humanities Research Council of Canada, as well as York University. In addition, the directors and staffs of the Bibliothèque Nationale in Paris, the Harry Ransome Humanities Research Center at Austin, Texas, and the University of California at Los Angeles were unfailingly helpful.

My thanks are due to the following for permission to reproduce photographs and designs as illustrations: the Bibliothèque Nationale, the Harry Ransome Humanities Research Center, the British Library, UCLA, the Novosti Press Agency, the Lincoln Center for the Performing Arts, and Helen Craig, as well as both Edward Craig and Arnold Rood. For the original version Robert Craig generously gave permission to use copyrighted material in the Edward Gordon Craig, CH, Estate; and with equal generosity Ellen T. M. Craig has given permission to include additional material in this new edition – to both of whom I am, and remain, extremely grateful.

Christopher Innes
Toronto, 1995

Gordon Craig with a marionette, Florence, 1914.

1

PROLOGUE: THE ARGUMENT

Gordon Craig is one of the key figures in the development of modern theater. His influence in the early decades of the century was crucial; and his vision of what theater might become continues to inform the work of some of the leading theater-artists today. But, in addition to the intrinsic significance of his ideas, any attempt to explore Craig's visionary concepts offers a particular challenge in terms of theater-studies.

In a physical art such as theater, theory does not exist independent of the object, and can only be validated on the stage. Yet performance is notoriously transitory and evanescent. If theory depends on practice, how can it be evaluated when there is no opportunity to experience the stage-performances on which it is based? In a very real sense the past is unavailable; and Craig's case is particularly difficult, since he mounted relatively few productions. However, for these there happens to be a considerable amount of detail that has been preserved. This is partly because Craig was intensely aware that he was attempting something completely new, which meant that he recorded his aims and made notes on his rehearsals – partly because he was continually attempting to find financial backing for his ideas, and so commented extensively on what had been achieved – partly because he became involved in writing and publishing theatrical journals, which led him to keep any material that might serve as a resource for articles – and partly because of the centrality of design in his work (costume and set designs being one element of theater that does provide physical evidence). In addition, since Craig had persuaded the theater-world of the time that his work was revolutionary, reviews of his productions were remarkably detailed. Thus it becomes possible to reconstruct to a large degree what actually occurred on the stage, and even (taking into account not only reviews, but correspondence with and by his collaborators) audience response.

One of the intentions of this study is therefore to demonstrate how productions from the past can be reconstructed, by combining evidence from promptbooks, designs, rehearsal notes, stage-photographs, programmes, correspondence and newspaper reviews. The aim is to show what Craig achieved on the stage, and to relate this to his theories, in order to evaluate his vision of theater – but also to provide a model for theater-studies: what might be called an archeology of performance.

At the same time the task demonstrates some of the problems in doing this even for modern theater, since such material tends to be scattered. Indeed, in the case of Craig this is particularly acute. Although he collected and preserved so much of the necessary evidence, historical circumstances have spread it widely across the world. Craig not only worked in Germany, Russia and Italy, as well as England, but he also spent the latter part of his life in France. And when in old age and impoverished, he was negotiating the sale of his collection with American University libraries, the French government declared his work a "national treasure" and forced a sale (for a considerably lower price) to the Bibliotheque Nationale in Paris. As a result, Craig would offer pieces from his collection to the admirers who visited him at his house in Venice. These included American scholars such as Arnold Rood, and enthusiasts such as Norman Philbrick. In addition, Craig had two families of children – one legitimate, although he had abandoned them at the turn of the century; and one from a "common-law" marriage – and he died without making a will. The children of his second marriage, who had participated in his work and cared for him in his final illness, but would have had no legal claim to inheritance, packed up several trunkloads of material; and shipped them out of France before declaring Craig's death. These papers and documents were then sold piecemeal to various archives in the U.S. So, although the Bibliotheque Nationale claims to hold "the Craig Collection", in actuality a large amount of important material, particularly relating to Craig's theatrical plans, is in the Humanities Research Center at Austin, Texas, or at the University of California in Los Angeles. Other material created by Craig is at the London Theater Museum (to which the Rood collection has also been donated), in the British Library, in the Harvard Theater Library at Boston, or in Stanford (where the Philbrick collection has gone). There is also a collection of Craig's designs in Japan, and material relating to his work with Stanislavski in Moscow. This means that in order to build up a picture of any given production, material must be collated from widely separated sources; and the task is further complicated because Craig recorded his ideas in three different series of hand-written books: "Daybooks" for general thoughts and plans, "Notebooks" for specific concepts, and "MS books" as well as Sketchbooks. For instance, the prompt book, original set and costume designs for, say, Craig's 1901 production of Handel's Acis and Galatea are at the BN. However, the "Daybook" for that period is in the HRC, while the "Notebook" is at UCLA, who also have stage photos. Other photos are in London, together with newspaper reviews and background material on the theater of the time, while related correspondence is in three of the different archives.

This, in a sense, is quite appropriate, since Craig was an internationalist, as well as having a diverse career, which covered almost every area of theater.

In 1890, at the age of eighteen, Gordon Craig was hailed as the most promising young actor in England. Ten years later he had turned his back on the conventional stage and devoted himself to a vision of theater so radical that it seemed to have no place for the actor at all. His work as a director established techniques that have become axioms of modern stagecraft, but his theories were so extreme that they had little chance of being accepted or even understood. He was an enigma from the first, and for almost a century has been one of the most fought-over names in world theater. He was one of the innovators who shaped the development of modern theater, yet the exact extent of his influence is almost impossible to measure. His early productions introduced revolutionary techniques of lighting and new principles of grouping and scene design that are now accepted without question. Yet these productions had little direct impact. Practically no other theatrical reformer saw them and the information to reconstruct them has only recently become available. Craig was a leader without clearly identifiable followers, yet a magnet for almost all who reacted against realistic staging; a director with only seven mature productions he could call his own, who denied that even these were true examples of his theatrical concept. He was a founder-member of the new movement that included Copeau and Jouvet, Appia and Reinhardt, Tairov and Vaktangov, Poel and Granville-Barker – but unlike those others, who have won general recognition, Craig has never commanded any critical consensus. From the first, his work either attracted exaggerated praise or was rejected out of hand.

On the one side, artists such as Yeats hailed him as a theatrical messiah. Indeed, by 1931 his early collaborator, Martin Shaw, could fairly claim that Craig was "acknowledged by most people on the continent ... to be the most significant force in the theatre today." On the other, standard source books on twentieth-century staging tend to dismiss his work (together with Appia's) as representative of a "synthetic movement." Because it "produced no new plays and no new actors," it is taken to be merely a superficial "scenic reform in which suggestive simplicity covered with 'a veil of light or darkness' the clumsy literalism of the naturalists' 'tasteless parlour' ..."[1]

This tendency to see Craig solely as a scene designer, and therefore to dismiss his vision as an attempt to substitute visual spectacle for drama, is an all-too-common error. Even Isadora Duncan, whose dancing inspired Craig and confirmed his belief that the essential element of his art had to be movement, referred to his work only as "the perfect setting" – which led Craig to exclaim that "even after 20 years...she thought I was thinking of scenery!"[2] The unfortunate fact is that, having no steady income from productions, Craig lived mainly by exhibiting and publishing his designs. Because designs can be easily reproduced, this is the sole aspect of his work that became generally known, apart from one collection of essays. So it has been all too easy to assume that his theatrical reform was limited to stage settings, whatever Craig himself claimed. This is also partly because his drawings have such artistic merit, partly because he misleadingly labeled one of the prototypes for his new theater as "Scene," and partly because innovations are easier to carry out in scene design than in any other element of staging. Indeed this mistaken emphasis has made it possible to ignore the real implications of Craig's theories, because (as the commercial theater repeatedly demonstrates) a style of setting or lighting can be used completely independently of any aesthetic values it was created to express. But Craig always insisted that he was a director, a *metteur-en-scène*, vehemently rejected the view that he was primarily a designer of scenes, and denied that scenery was anything more than one of many elements in his concept of theater. For him, the essential qualification for a director was acting experience, and he defined a "designer" as anyone with a specifically theatrical vision.

As evidence about the other aspects of his theatrical work has emerged, the critical pendulum has swung more in Craig's favor. However, by now so much time has passed since Craig's major involvement with the stage that his ideas are usually treated as historical curiosities, rather than as the inspiration to the present that he intended them to be. This is reinforced by the way he presented his work – stressing the continuity with tradition as well as the decisive break with it – and by the number of elements in his productions that in fact harked back to the nineteenth-century theater, which they were designed to replace. The paradox was summed up in one of Craig's obituaries, which labeled him "the last Victorian of the English stage and the first prophet of a new order in the theatre, an order still in the making, and, some would add, incapable of being made."[3] As such, however, his vision not only helps to illuminate a past turning point in stage history, out of which our modern theater evolved. It also offers a continuing challenge, one that the post-modern movement in contemporary theater has picked up. Indeed the ideas that Craig formulated lead directly to the work of a designer–director like Robert Wilson. As we go into a new millennium, Craig's concept is again at the cutting edge of theatrical innovation.

The case against Craig was perhaps put most trenchantly by Lee Simonson in 1931, and the terms of his attack deserve note if only because they have been picked up unthinkingly and repeated frequently. But his criticisms also bring out unintentionally the real issues that shaped the unusual course of Craig's career: How much can be achieved by working within an established tradition, when the aim is to change it so radically that in effect it will become a new art form – and how can the true qualities of this new art be understood, when the terms that might be used to describe it can only be drawn from the form it is meant to supersede? Simonson's argument was that it is absurd to extol someone (as Craig's converts did) "as the source of every important innovation in designing stage settings" over the past twenty-five years when that person had not staged any work he could call solely his own during that whole period. Craig's withdrawal from practical theater is explained as "a flight from reality" following the shock of "defeat" in his early productions, which led him to make extravagant demands – a specially constructed stage and sole artistic control – in order to avoid any test of his theories. This "fear of failure" is then taken as support for the contention that Craig's designs are – and perhaps at least subconsciously were even intended to be – unrealizable on the stage, and his essays are dismissed as "a maze of suggestions...a mass of evasions and contradictions." The fact that Craig never managed to put his ideas into practice, even though this was at a time when a wide range of experimental art theaters was able to find support, is offered as proof that those ideas are incoherent and impracticable. The only way his apparent importance can then be explained is by characterizing him as "a demagogue ... an exalted mountebank."[4]

Ironically, the passion of this denunciation itself indicates how dominant Craig's influence is felt to be. But, leaving that aside, from a different perspective the qualities singled out as flaws are precisely what gives Craig's work much of its value. His retreat from the stage was a refusal to compromise with existing conditions that would have destroyed the integrity of his ideas. So was his demand for autonomy and complete control of anything he produced. This assertion of the right to be in sole charge of every element in a production – orchestrating light, music, movement, the setting, and the actors, so that a performance became the work of a single artist – was hardly new. Dramatists such as Goethe and actor-managers such as Macready had called for it up to a century before as the only means of achieving artistic unity. The need for integrating the diverse elements of an increasingly spectacular and technically complex theater was the reason for the rise of the director, and it was largely Craig's claims that legitimized the modern director's position. A generation before, the Duke of Saxe-Meiningen, able to exercise autocratic control because of his social position, had demonstrated what was possible. But it was Craig who provided the theoretical justification for the preeminence of the director as the only way to implement synaesthetic ideals of theatrical performance in which all the different art forms are integrated to create a single emotional harmony. On this level at least he could be said to have shaped one of the determining factors of twentieth-century theater. At the same time, in his own case this claim ruled out what might otherwise have been potentially valuable collaborations with better-established directors such as Reinhardt, even when they shared many of the same principles.

Because Craig saw his work as the antithesis of all accepted theatrical standards, even critical acclaim became suspect, because it meant that his productions fulfilled those conventional expectations he rejected. So it was hardly surprising that, at the very time he was writing his first major theoretical statement, "On the Art of the Theatre," he remarked, "The nearer I come to success the more form and beauty I see in what's called failure."[5] His series of early operatic productions between 1900 and 1902 in fact did correspond to the type of experimental "art theatre" Simonson claims he avoided because of the impracticability of his theories. But Craig moved beyond that possibility as his ideas developed. He came to see that such a framework could only promote partial reforms reforms: that represented innovations in technique and presentation, rather than a completely new art form.

If so many of Craig's ideas seem negative, it is because his concept of what theater might become could not be realized (as Isadora Duncan noted in the margin of "On the Art of the Theatre") until "the great incubus of the present theatre is destroyed . . . leaving CLEAR SPACE." If his essays seem impressionistic and imprecise, exaggerated and enthusiastic, that is because they were intended as a fundamental challenge to all preconceptions. It is true that there is a strong vein of mysticism in Craig's vision, yet on a practical level any coherent manifesto would have been too limiting. The value of Craig's theories, like those of Antonin Artaud a generation later, is precisely that they free the imagination instead of providing a specific program. Indeed this can be seen as one reason why Craig deliberately turned from producing tangible examples of his new art of the theater – although he continued to experiment privately on model stages – and instead turned to writing.

In a critical commentary on one of the early books dealing with his work, which described him as one of "the three giants who led the charge" against realism (the others being Appia and Reinhardt), Craig made the distinction between visionaries such as himself, who acted as catalysts for change, and "organizers" like Reinhardt or Stanislavski, who put new artistic ideas into practice at the expense of popularizing them. At the same time Craig was alive to the contradictions inherent in the attempt to revolutionize the most physical of all art forms, which in a sense only exists in performance, by moving into abstractions. Finding himself labeled as "fundamentally a theorist," he insisted that practical experience was the basis of all his work: "I acted and produced long before I dreamt of enunciating any theory." Even while formulating his theories he had noted that though knowledge of stage history, paradoxically, was a prerequisite for meaningful change, "the more an artist studies the theatre the further he finds himself from the theatre."[6] So in one sense the critics who labeled Craig's work impractical were correct. Even the towering monoliths and shifting architectural shapes, the stairs and skies leading to infinity in his scene drawings, were not designed for the conventional stage, but were attempts "to record what is seen in the mind's eye." Yet his theater of the imagination was always conceived in concrete terms and precise dimensions that generally corresponded to those of a regular proscenium – apart from the single exception of a festival theater he envisaged with a stage opening 170 feet high. He demonstrated the "infinite sky" effect in his early productions, and frequently created scale models to show how designs would be translated into stage terms. Commenting on seventeenth- and eighteenth-century costume designs, he picked out technical drawings that showed the construction rather than the effect for spectators – "Is not one such plate of more true value to us than a hundred fantastic whirling designs by some studio painter?"[7] – and many of his own costume designs include detail on cut, texture, or fastenings. This combination of practical concern (taking all the conditions of the stage into account) and fantasy that breaks out of conventional limitations is characteristic of Craig's work as a whole.

When he came to write his autobiography, *Index to the Story of My Days*, Craig originally planned to focus on his stage work. The first section would "describe the conditions of 1899...so you may see what it is I thought I would change and how I would change it... Secondly my first seven productions... Then must come a break in the story and we must see what others are doing."[8] The final section was to be a description of the forms he had evolved to embody his vision of a new theater: the abstract choreography of moving geometrical shapes that he called Scene, and the production plans for festival performances of *The St. Matthew Passion*. He admonished himself to "write only of the *mise-en-scène*." But, despite all this, his autobiography turned out to be a chronological diary concentrating on personal relationships, beginning on January 16th, 1872, the day of his birth, and breaking off in 1907 before he started publishing *The Mask*, the journal that became the major vehicle for his ideas, and before he developed his theories in such essays as "The Actor and the Übermarionette" and "The Artists of the Theatre of the Future."

Craig – passionate, improvident, mercurial, a self-taught genius who mastered almost everything except self-discipline and who scattered his energy among multitudinous projects; dogmatic yet secretly self-doubting, whimsical as well as visionary – comes across in his *Index to the Story of My Days*. His personality is also described by Edward Craig in his biography of his father, where all the details of his life can be found. The only biographical facts that need mention here are those relating to his theatrical background. The son of Ellen Terry, Henry Irving's leading actress, Craig was practically raised on the stage. His only (in)formal education was exposure to drama under the close personal attention of the greatest Victorian actor–manager. Acting was thus the only conceivable profession for him – and one at which he excelled. He first appeared on stage when only six years old, and even after he gave up performing in 1897 at the age of twenty-five, passion and role-playing remained central to his personality. He fathered almost as many illegitimate children (including two by the dancer Isadora Duncan, and at least one by an actress in Stanislavski's company) as the number of pen-names he took – 17 in all – when he started publishing his own quarterly "Illustrated Journal of the Art of the Theatre" in 1908. Significantly this was titled *The Mask* which relates not only to his concept of non-naturalistic theater, but to his own public persona. Even "Craig" was a stage-name, adopted to distinguish his role as founder of a new form of theater (and possibly echoing the Apostle St. Peter as "the rock" of Christ's new church) from his previous incarnation as the actor "Edward Carrick," an equally made-up name. Theater was his life. So this study concentrates solely on his theater: his theories, his productions, and his plans. The primary aim is to reconstruct and document his stage work, and to analyze how it relates to his developing vision of a new art. It is therefore appropriate to adopt the broad framework that Craig himself never carried out, and to begin with an overview of the late Victorian stage – in particular, Irving's Lyceum Theater, where Craig received his training and against which he reacted.

The next chapters analyze the burst of creative energy between 1900 and 1903, when Craig produced and directed no less than six productions, with his own set and costume designs. These were no more than the initial steps in a lifelong campaign to revolutionize the stage, yet they reveal both his approach and his practical commitment. Although still containing many of the conventional elements from which Craig gradually freed himself, it was in these early productions that he worked out the principles of what was to become his "Art of the Theatre." Craig himself recognized that these represented his most significant work in the theater, although he always undervalued the contribution of his next production, the 1912 *Hamlet* at the Moscow Art Theater, and overestimated his first independent venture as a director, the 1893 staging of *No Trifling with Love*. He liked to see *No Trifling* as the start of his theatrical revolution, despite the fact that it contained few hints of what was to come, whereas he tended to dismiss the *Hamlet* – a landmark production by anyone else's standards – because he had not had complete artistic control and believed Stanislavski had compromised his conception.

In fact, *Hamlet* embodied the new theatrical concepts that emerged from Craig's early stage experiments, and thus has particular importance. Later stage work, like his Copenhagen production of *The Crown Pretenders* in 1926 or his designs for a New York staging of *Macbeth* in 1928, mainly recapitulated his turn-of-the-century stage achievements. Craig's approach in *The Crown Pretenders* was essentially the same as in his first staging of Ibsen's work, *The Vikings*, over two decades earlier – indeed it exactly repeated set-details – while his designs for *Macbeth* were dismissively signed C.P.B. (for "Craig Pot-Boiler").[9] A response to pressing invitations from other directors who admired his work without understanding that it had already gone far beyond the bounds of conventional performance, these productions literally represented a step backwards; and the incompetently executed staging of *Macbeth* in New York undoubtedly fuelled Lee Simonson's attack on Craig just over two years later. At this point in Craig's evolution, the ideas he had been exploring over the preceding two decades simply could not be incorporated in a standard production. They were incompatible with ordinary theater.

This new vision, which preoccupied Craig for the last half of his active life from 1913 to around 1940 (at the age of 62, by which time he had effectively ceased to produce new work or ideas), has been largely ignored. Even if some of its elements appear archaic and Craig himself was never able to put it into practice, this vision still has considerable potential as a catalyst for artistic innovation, and therefore forms a major focus of the later chapters in this study. However, as Craig always emphasized, "I was practising [as a] *metteur-en-scène* long before I wrote about *l'Art du Théâtre* – and I *did* then what I wrote of later – the theory came after the practice."[10] And, as the concluding chapter suggests, some of his core principles have been adopted by one line of contemporary theater. Craig's ideas are by no means a dead issue, or merely historical curiosities. They have a continuing relevance.

2

SCENE CHANGES: VICTORIAN THEATER, AN ACTING CAREER, AND POINTS OF DEPARTURE

The theoretical nature of Craig's published writings and the tendency to abstraction in his designs, many of which are unrelated to any specific play, give the misleading impression that he was a reformer working from outside. In fact, he always asserted that his aim was to revolutionize the theater from within. One characteristic that could almost be said to define contemporary drama is its continual process of rejection. Directors jettison whatever stage conventions have been established by the previous generation or movement as "culinary" (Brecht) or "deadly" (Brook) in order to create new forms through a *"via negativa"* (Grotowski). Craig was no exception. But he, far more than other revolutionaries of the stage, was a part of the theatrical tradition he came to reject. With Ellen Terry as his mother, and the most famous actor-manager of the late Victorian period, Henry Irving, as his mentor, he could be said literally to have grown up in the nineteenth-century theater. Indeed, in some ways he never completely freed himself from it, which occasionally gives his work the disturbing flavor of old wine in new bottles.

Craig was very much a man of his time, and although he lived until 1966, his time was the turn of the century. He was twenty-seven when he started the production of *Dido and Aeneas*, a work that marked his emergence as a director in 1900, and it was at the same time that he first began sketching ideas for *The St. Matthew Passion*, which was to be his final, unstaged work. He continued to write and design until after the Second World War, but his career could be said effectively to have ended with his production of *The Crown Pretenders* in 1926. He always referred to his new Art of the Theater, which he began to define between 1902 and 1905, as an integral part of the wider European movement that he associated with Appia, Diaghilev, Meyerhold, Reinhardt, and Stanislavski. But he also claimed that in attempting "to revitalize our European theatre from within" he was directly following Irving, who epitomized so much of the nineteenth-century theater that his movement opposed.[1]

Henry Irving established the Lyceum as the foremost London theater, and himself as the leading English actor, with a single production in 1871. This was *The Bells* by Leopold Lewis, still in the Lyceum repertoire thirty years later and performed so many times that the scenery literally disintegrated. Adapted from a French original with a plot that recurred in several other plays (including *Paul Zegars, or The Dream of Retribution*, which failed in London just two weeks before *The Bells* opened), this was a psychological melodrama based on the idea of poetic justice: A guilty conscience alone is enough to betray secret crime behind the front of respectability and to destroy the criminal. The dialogue is full of clichés and the dramatic situations are remarkable only for the openness with which the villain – always the active agent, but usually presented as a stock figure, motivated by a simple desire to do evil – is recognized as the true focus of Victorian melodrama. Indeed, all the other characters are little more than symbols of his desires, representing the family happiness and social acceptance that Matthias committed murder to secure, or projections of his fears in the forms of an imagined mesmerist who could hypnotize him into admitting his guilty secret and judges who would condemn him. It was Irving's acting alone, therefore, that was responsible for the success of the play, and Craig's description of his performance vividly evokes some of the key elements in what became known as the Lyceum style. At the same time, his retrospective enthusiasm for the effects Irving achieved reveals something of the qualities he was searching for in his own art.

The only function of the other actors was to support Irving in the main role: to prepare his entrances, to take up groupings that would focus the audience's attention on his figure. Indeed, according to Craig the necessary qualities for a Lyceum actor were those of "the leg of a table," so that "to obtrude would have been out of the question"[2] – and in this overstatement we can see Craig defending his own concept of acting. But this was very different from our modern conception of ensemble performance, and the way Irving organized productions around himself is amusingly illustrated by an anecdote about the rehearsals for another standard Lyceum piece, *The Corsican Brothers*. Running through the duel scene, the actor fighting with Irving broke off and asked, "Don't you think, Guv'nor, a few rays of the moon might fall on me – it shines equally on the just and the unjust." In this case Irving agreed to share the limelight a little. But behind this personal dominance was an ideal of artistic unity, as his remarks about the costuming of *Faust* show: "I have studiously kept as yet all the colour to that grey-green. When my dress of flaming scarlet appears amongst it – and remember that the colour will be intensified by that very light – it will bring the whole picture together in a way you cannot dream of."[3]

Clearly the effect attempted was one of balance as well as contrast, and the subordination of all the other figures to the leading role was one

Scene changes   13

way of achieving harmony. In contrast to Charles Kean, the other great
nineteenth-century actor-manager, whose productions set the earlier
theatrical fashion and stressed visual variety as well as historical accuracy, Irving required an atmospheric unity in scene and costume design
that carried through the whole play. In 1881 the Meiningen company had
appeared in London. The way it integrated acting with the setting
through a discipline directed at building a single and consistent impression, even in mob scenes, was a revelation. The Duke of Saxe-Meiningen's
complete control of the smallest details of costuming, lighting, and gesture gave every element interpretative value. It made the human figure
in movement the primary pictorial unit. Irving immediately took up the
challenge, and the Meiningen influence was already clear in the 1882
Lyceum production of *Much Ado*. Unlike the Meiningen ensemble, in
which every actor took his turn as a supernumerary, Lyceum actors
remained fixed in subordinate positions around their star, but Irving's
rehearsals became meticulous in their attention to precise timing and positioning. Groupings, moves, and gestures were rhythmic, planned, and
measured. As Craig commented, Irving "was forever counting – one,
two, three – pause – one, two – a step, another, a half, a faintest turn,
another step, a word."[4] This detailed precision was the most obvious sign
of the change in Irving's methods after the Meiningen visit. However, in
the Meiningen performances the aim was primarily realistic, whereas
Irving emphasized the aesthetic quality of their techniques. In his hands
their approach created a symphonic totality. For the audience it produced
an emotional unity of vision and atmospheric effect, although it was
almost solely concerned with the external aspects of performance, such
as intonation and attitude, rather than the psychological interpretation of
character, and was therefore highly artificial.

   In their own terms, however, the results achieved were strikingly
powerful. For instance, during the low-key opening of *The Bells* suspense was slowly built up to such effect, leading up to Irving's first
entrance, that the audience always burst into spontaneous applause when
he appeared. This allowed him to demonstrate his control by breaking
character and intensified the energy of his performance by showing a
sharp distinction between the actor and his role. "The shout of applause
going up, he lowers his arm, he lowers his head, he relaxes his force
all over, seems to turn it off to an almost dead calm . . . and then as the
applause dies away . . . the actor clips it off by a sudden gesture
of awakening from his long and patiently endured ordeal – flings cap
and whip to right and left." In his lectures entitled "The Art of Acting,"
Irving defined the actor's approach to a role as "a double consciousness,"
wherein the actor gives his emotions free rein while simultaneously remaining aware of all the expressive techniques by which these

emotional states can be communicated. In doing so, he provided a solution to the debate over identification versus objectivity. Diderot's paradox – that an actor can portray emotions effectively only if he does not experience them, but instead analyzes his role intellectually – had been restated by Coquelin, the leading French comedian, in the 1880s. In reply, Irving synthesized the two poles of the argument in a way that anticipated Stanislavski's theories, although his style of performance was very different. For him, the primary aim of the actor was "the representation of passion."[5] This stress on extreme emotional states was essentially Romantic in that it equated greatness with depth of feeling, and it led in fact to a highly idiosyncratic, exaggerated, and even grotesque form of acting.

The intensity with which Irving expressed emotion often seemed to give a spiritual dimension to his performance, and his interpretations of characters frequently contained striking insights. Hamlet became an introvert whose habitual self-contemplation had the effect of fostering and aggravating his own emotions to hysteria. Shylock became a Jew with a genuine cultural background whose depth of psychological suffering compensated for his crimes and whose forlorn dignity made all the Christian society that baits him seem contemptible by comparison. At the same time this magnification of every trait into passion reduced everything, even *Macbeth* and *Othello*, to melodrama (a simplified view of Shakespeare's tragedies that Craig himself was never able to break free from completely), and neither the intention nor the effect could be called naturalistic.

As Craig pointed out, in his characterization of Matthias "Irving set out to wring our hearts, not to give us a clever exhibition of antics such as a murderer would be likely to go through." So terror was always abject, anguish never less than infinite, hatred or love all-consuming. Drama, for Irving, meant the opposite of the society problem play with its restrained drawing-room conventions of acting. Craig, who heartily agreed, neatly characterized this genre as a form of pseudorealism in which "the villain of the play comes onto the stage smiling: he is quite alone; and although he remains alone for five minutes, he does not dare to tell us that he is 'the villain' – has not dared to let any tell-tale look escape him." By contrast, Irving never sacrificed any potentially dramatic moment to verisimilitude. As a result, his acting was overtly artificial and highly mannered. His hands became talons, his face was transformed into a mask by muscular tension, his movements were either extremely dynamic or tended toward cataleptic stasis at points of extreme intensity – all comparable in some ways to the "schemata" of classical Greek tragedy. In many ways Irving's approach was a prototype for the ecstatic style of expressionist acting. They had similar aims: to communicate emotions directly and in a pure state to the audience. So Bernard Shaw's unsympathetic description of "the condition in which he works" as "a somnambulist one: he hypnotizes himself into a sort of dreamy energy, and is intoxicated by humming of words in his nose" parallels Strindberg's claim that the actor should function like a spiritualist medium in a trance, or the typical expressionist statement that "the actor who knows his inner strength goes onto the stage as someone sleepwalking."[6]

Craig's description of Irving's performance as Matthias is a sensitive illustration of these qualities and their effectiveness, though he shows his characteristic disregard for plot detail or dialogue in conflating two separate points in the scene. Take the commonplace business of Matthias unlacing his boots while the talk turns to the storm during which the Jewish traveller disappeared. According to Craig,

> The way Irving did it had never been thought of till he did it, and has never been done since.
>
> It was, in every gesture, every half move, in the play of his shoulders, legs, head and arms, mesmeric in the highest degree...We suddenly saw these fingers stop their work; the crown of the head suddenly seems to glitter and become frozen – and then, at the pace of the slowest and most terrified snail, the two hands, still motionless and dead, were seen to be coming up the side of the leg...the whole torso of the man, also seeming frozen, was gradually seen to be drawing up and back...
>
> Once in that position – motionless – eyes fixed ahead of him and fixed on us all – there he sat for the space of ten to twelve seconds, which, I can assure you, seemed to us all like a lifetime, and then said – and said in a voice deep and overwhelmingly beautiful: "Oh, you were talking of that – were you?"...Time seemed out of joint, and moved as it moves to us who suffer, when we wish it would move on and it does not stir.
>
> And the next step of his dance began...He glides up to a standing position: never has anyone seen another rising figure which slid slowly up like that: with one arm slightly raised, with sensitive hand speaking of far-off apprehended sounds, he asks, in the voice of some woman who is frightened, yet does not wish to frighten those with her: "Don't you...don't you hear the sound of sledgebells on the road?"[7]

In the actual performance, Matthias spoke of the mesmerist while changing his footwear, and his consternation was caused by the word "conscience." The comment about "the Polish Jew's Winter" occurs later, when he is about to drink some wine. Treating both moments as a single emotional unit may simply be a slip of Craig's memory, but the change is still significant. It reflects the way Craig himself treated dramatic material, simplifying action to create clear emotional progressions and substituting physical movement for speeches. Equally significantly, his description evokes a simultaneous impression of calculated preparation and psychological automatism. The meticulous timing and rehearsed precision, which made Irving's acting an art in Craig's terms, allowed him to draw directly on emotions from a subconscious level. Perhaps because of this, Craig associated stylization with intensity, and his description is dramatized to bring this out.

Irving treated dialogue in much the same way, and his delivery was as mannered as his movement. Words were distorted for musical or emotional effect – "Cut thrut dug" for "cut throat dog" (Shylock), "Tack the rup frum mey nek" for "Take the rope from my neck" or "Ritz" for "Rich" (Matthias) – or elided for ejaculative force, like Matthias's opening speech, "It is I," which Irving transformed into an exclamation: "'t's I!" Critics who supported Ibsen and the new naturalism, such as William Archer, found it easy to be amusing at Irving's expense. "Not a vowel but has undergone a change into something new and strange, not a consonant but is jerked out with a convulsion of the throat or a spasm of the under jaw, while every dental at the end of a word is prolonged into an unmistakable sneeze . . . Trained elocutionists have assured me that, considering Mr. Irving's ignorance of the art, the effects he produces are marvellous." But what some critics condemned as the screeching and staggering style, Craig admired. In his eyes the harsh flattening of vowels gave a graphic register of the character's emotional tension. The stress on sibilants gave the thrilling impression of a hissing serpent. "In short, his tendency was to enrich the sounds of the words – to make them expressive."[8]

Craig served a long apprenticeship at the Lyceum, with Irving's example continually before his eyes. He made his first public appearance on stage at the age of six, started learning his craft (as he put it) at the age of twelve with a walk-on part in *Charles I* and a small speaking role in *Eugene Aram* during Irving's 1885 American tour, and joined the Lyceum company in 1889. From then until 1897 he acted the "juvenile lead" roles in a repertoire of Shakespeare, melodrama, historical romance, restoration comedy, and farce: Cromwell in *Henry VIII*, Richmond in *Richard III*, Arviragus in *Cymbeline*; Henry Ashton in *Ravenswood* (an adaptation of *The Bride of Lammermoor*), Cavaradossi in *La Tosca*; Arthur St. Valéry in *The Dead Heart* (a story of the French Revolution), Caleb Deecie in *Two Roses*, Moses in *Olivia* (based on *The Vicar of Wakefield*); Charles Surface in *School for Scandal*, and Abel Quick in *A Regular Fix*. As early as 1890 he won recognition as one of the most promising young actors – a newspaper cartoon of all the great stars included Craig, representing "the stage of the future" – and he began touring the provinces between Lyceum engagements. This was the traditional training for an actor, and Irving, who himself had started his career in a provincial stock company playing 429 different parts in two-and-a-half years (or a new part every two days), personally selected the roles the young Craig was to play.

At the Lyceum the old established ways of producing a play were disguised by technical sophistication and spectacular realism. In these touring companies Craig experienced them in a pure form, and his reaction against this particular type of traditionalism can be seen as motivating much of his later work. When he joined the W. S. Hardy Shakespeare Company in 1894 at Hereford, for instance, he found that almost the whole stage area was taken up by a huge tank filled with water:

> This was because Miss Ida Millais – probably related to the great painter – was performing in some melodrama called, I imagine, *Ida's Escape or the Last Leap;* for in the last act she, the heroine, had to jump from a big rock into this tank of water, which splashed up, of course. And then the villain jumped in after her and the hero jumped in after the villain, and finally she came up drenched and the body of the villain floated down to the green room. I think we were all fairly brave, looking at this damnable tank and realizing that we only had a yard or a yard and a half of stage in front of it in which to go through all the hither and thither of the five acts of *Hamlet* and the five acts of *Romeo and Juliet.*[9]

Quite apart from the sacrifice of all but the simplest possibilities of blocking and movement in the whole repertoire to a single spectacular climax, the Hardy company's approach to a text had severe interpretative limitations. It was traditional practice for the leading actor to control the tone and set the pace of a production, and when they began rehearsing *Hamlet* Mrs. Hardy, who was playing Gertrude, asked Craig to "tell us exactly what you want, and we will fit in." In addition, as was usual at the time, no member of the cast had the complete text. Each was given only a copy of his or her own words and cues. This was traditional practice as early as the Renaissance. Indeed, cue scripts were still widely used in provincial repertory theater as late as the 1950s, having clearly practical advantages for any actors performing a continually changing repertoire of short-run plays. But, with the large Victorian casts, this had become an almost universal phenomenon, and it had far-reaching effects for nineteenth-century dramaturgy. According to Craig, it was not until much later that he himself came to realize that a play was written as a whole, instead of as the series of fragmented parts that he was accustomed to acting from: "I forget exactly when this illumination came, but it surprised me exceedingly." What this meant was that the emphasis was solely on portraying individual character, with little concept of central ideas or through-lines in a play, and that – just as in the Lyceum under Irving – everything would inevitably be arranged to make the leading figure the focus of a production. Such an approach also meant that remarkably little time and expense were required for rehearsing, as most of the moves and business were bound to be traditional. And indeed the W. S. Hardy Shakespeare Company completed what rehearsals were thought necessary for *Hamlet* in three days, and for *Romeo and Juliet* in two. As Craig later remarked, such productions merely rearranged old bits: "The actors between 1800 and 1900 never made new bits – it was ever the same old show done differently." What the audience saw was "the same Hamlet sitting in the same chair, with no marked sign of difference from any Hamlet seen before."[10]

When Craig founded his own touring company in 1894, however, its repertoire was exactly the same as any other stock company of the time.

Mr. GORDON CRAIG'S COMPANY.

Repertoire:

"HAMLET." — "A BLOT IN THE 'SCUTCHEON." — "FANTASIO."
"TAMING OF THE SHREW."   (From the French.)

"LADY OF LYONS." — "SHE STOOPS TO CONQUER." — "RAISING THE WIND."

The Costumes for all the Plays have been kindly lent
BY
MR. HENRY IRVING.

Letterhead for the Gordon Craig Company, 1894. Courtesy of the Edward Craig Collection, Bledlow.

And when he first brought his own production of *Hamlet* to London in 1896 it was basically conventional. His death scene was accompanied by melodramatic music, and his costume was the one used by Irving himself when he first played Hamlet at the Lyceum twenty-two years earlier. Reviewers certainly saw Craig's own performance as an example of "the new school of acting," on which opinions were sharply divided. One praised his "endeavor to be natural and unstagey…as opposed to the stilted, ranting delivery and often mechanical methods of the old." Another found him "altogether too 'modern' in style" and advised him "to work within the limits of convention… There is danger in being too original."[11] But the reviewers had also described Irving as an exponent of the "modern" school because his style was equally different from the stock rhetorical gestures of the traditional theater. The psychological focus of his characterizations of Shylock and Richard III had also been taken, however incongruously, as "naturalistic."

Craig the actor, as Hamlet at the Olympic Theater, 1897. Courtesy of the
Victoria and Albert Museum.

Craig was greatly influenced by Irving, both as an actor and in his later ideal of a theatrical form that would be an "Art" rather than an imitation of life. The stress on patterned and precise movement and the use of color harmonies to create atmospheric effects were primary elements in his early operatic productions. He compared Irving's acting to the "noble artifice" of Nō drama because it transposed diction into "song," movement into "dance." He believed its overt artificiality was a way of portraying essences instead of appearances – and demanded a similar style for his Moscow production of *Hamlet* with Stanislavski. The harmonic integration of all the elements of a performance into a unified vision under the sole control of a single artist became the fundamental principle in his new theory of theater, though everything was to be subordinated to the central idea of a play and not (as with Irving) to the personality of the central figure. Above all, his much-misunderstood image of an ideal actor came from Irving. What he singled out was the way Irving's elimination of chance or apparent spontaneity in movement and diction made "each moment significant" because "all was sharp cut at beginning and end, and all joined by an immensely subtle rhythm," thus creating a true synthesis of passion with controlled expression. "Indeed," he remarked, "Irving was the nearest thing ever known to what I have called the Übermarionette."[12]

It is this close connection between Craig's principles and the Lyceum conventions that helps to explain the curiously anachronistic quality of some of his work. By the time of the last Lyceum production, Sardou's *Dante* in 1903, Irving's acting seemed very dated. As Craig himself realized at the time, Irving's style had become set at the very beginning of his career and his most effective roles were those he had created thirty years earlier. In addition, Irving's repertoire conditioned Craig's dramatic taste. Craig's earliest attempts to prepare scripts for production followed Irving's practice in cutting dialogue to enhance the more striking plot situations or in transposing and rewriting whole passages to achieve more spectacular effects – and toward the end of his career Craig was still announcing that "it is only the more melodramatic plays and operas which appeal to me as a producer."[13]

Two other elements of Irving's staging also deserve mention: his use of lighting and the type of setting employed at the Lyceum. The Lyceum was the first London theater to keep the houselights dimmed throughout a performance. This was purely for reasons of atmosphere – to create a sense of magic and to draw the audience emotionally into the production – rather than to shift emphasis toward the "fourth-wall" naturalism of Antoine or Stanislavski. It was the importance of this quality that led Irving to insist on gas lighting – and to take his own lighting equipment even on his American tours – long after electricity had become standard in the theater. This gas lighting, with its individual limelight spots used to reinforce the emotional tone of each moment in a play by subtle changes in color, was highly impressionistic. It provided all the suggestiveness of semiobscurity, and Ellen Terry summed up Irving's reasons for retaining it when she commented that "the thick softness of gaslight, with the lovely specks and motes in it, so like *natural* light, gave illusion to many a scene which is now revealed in all its naked trashiness by electricity."[14] At the same time he was prepared to use electricity for elaborate stage tricks, as in *Faust*, where live plates were set in the stage floor and wires ran from the actors' shoes to their gloves for the duel scene, so that blue flashes sparked from sword to sword as the electrical circuits shorted at each contact.

A similar stress on visual spectacle was characteristic of Irving's scenery. This was two-dimensional and painted, rather than architectural, but the pictorial realism was historically accurate and meticulously detailed. To prepare *Faust*, for example, Irving took his scene painters, costume designers, and property master to Nuremberg to collect materials and make drawings. Elaborate scenes could be changed quickly

Scene drawing (by B. Partridge) of Irving's 1888 *Macbeth*, with Craig's commentary. Courtesy of UCLA.

(with the help of no fewer than ninety stage-hands, thirty gas men to handle the flexible hoses and the lights, and fifteen property men). They were painted on a combination of front cloths, back cloths, and "cut" cloths, which unrolled from the flies, and flats, which could be pushed on from each wing, or split horizontally, one half of the set ascending as the other dropped through narrow openings in the stage floor. Thus, in *The Corsican Brothers*, an exact mirror image of the Lyceum auditorium could be dismantled behind a cutcloth during a short banquet scene. This in turn was changed in under forty seconds behind a front cloth that rose to reveal a forest with free-standing (though two-dimensional) trees, among and behind which the actors could pass, and thick snow (salt) covering the whole stage floor. It was only occasionally that the settings were three-dimensional. Then the effects tended to be even more elaborate: The scenic auditorium in *The Corsican Brothers* had practicable boxes seating a whole stage audience in perspective, with children representing adults at the rear. But sometimes a simpler architectural quality was achieved, as in Macbeth's castle – a scene that directly influenced many of Craig's designs, with its steps winding round a broad column, and its steeply mounting staircase, up which the characters climbed to their beds.

As an actor, Craig found the two-dimensional Lyceum sets fake and incongruous, although for the audience the illusion would have been complete, with the softness of the gas lighting blurring joints and hard edges and giving depth to the trompe l'oeil highlights and shadows painted on the flats. Yet the continual and almost instantaneous transformations of scene that such sets allowed remained central to Craig's later ideas and formed the basis of both his screens and Scene, though in very different terms. Similarly, although he turned to the new medium of electric lighting, his principles for illuminating the stage remained much the same as Irving's – the atmospheric or symbolic use of "natural" light. He later commented that "few actors have acted in darker scenes than Irving...It was from Irving that I learnt to plunge my scenes in a good deal too much gloom."[15] Where Craig differed radically from Irving, however, turning all the elements he adopted from the old Lyceum upside down and transfiguring them, was in his complete rejection of spectacular realism. But this came later.

His very first attempt at production was indeed almost a straight copy of the Lyceum style. This was a gothic historical romance, Alfred de Musset's *No Trifling with Love*, which he staged at Uxbridge in 1893. He was still a member of the Lyceum company, and most of the costumes came straight from its wardrobe, with additional headdresses and decoration copied as usual from Viollet le Duc. The scenery (kept simple only because of Craig's slender finances) – damask curtains for interior

*a well built up scene fn
that period in England   a
first class effort.* (1888)

*This abrupt mounting
I am sure was very
good – by Irving's
this scene when they go to
bed*

(A)

*This is an exceptionally poor interpretation of what is really
the best scene in the play – The tower & seemed thicker than
here & the figures much smaller in proportion –*

Scene drawing (by B. Partridge) of Irving's 1888 *Macbeth*, with Craig's commentary. Courtesy of UCLA.

settings, a painted backdrop, a front scene – was representational and in period. The program announced, "We intend giving as *thorough* a performance as possible." The interpretation was equally conventional. The text was "adapted by Mr. Gordon Craig," which meant that he had reorganized the scenes to strengthen melodramatic effects and had cut the dialogue by about one-third. (Looking back on it fifty years later, Craig acknowledged that for "adapted" one should "say 'mutilated,' but I adopted one of the many theatrical conceits of those days.") The plot was reduced to its basic situations. Perdican's father arranges for him to marry his cousin Camille. Each has long loved the other in secret, but Perdican mistakes her modesty for coldness and Camille interprets his bashfulness as rejection. They quarrel, and at a peasant festival to celebrate their engagement, which Craig transformed into an elaborate dance, Perdican sees Rosette – in this version the stock figure of a "simple yet lovely village maiden." He pursues her to spite Camille, who overhears him proposing to her. Camille discovers that Rosette's innocent, trusting nature would be heartbroken if she were to be abandoned.

So when she meets Perdican, who is now suffering from a crisis of conscience, she decides to resolve his dilemma for him by disguising her true feelings and withdrawing into a convent – though in Craig's over-heated interpretation, "Camille gets frightened at his words and at his face and hot breath as he whispers his soul out." She goes to pray – in "despair absolute" reads Craig's direction – and faints on the altar steps, where Perdican finds her. Believing she is dead, he acknowledges his true passion, and the shock of finding he has never loved her kills Rosette, who had followed him secretly to the oratory. This climax Craig heightened with every means at his disposal, replacing lengthy poetic sentiments with exclamations and sound effects.

> PERDICAN: Mine, mine!
> (*He kisses Camille. A great cry is heard from behind the altar. A rush of wind extin-guishes the candles – wind continues to sigh to end of scene [blowing the curtains behind which Rosette lies] . . . Thunder. A big drum. Lightning.*)
> She is dead![16]

Craig's acting was appropriately Irvingesque. As the only review commented: "With frenzied passion he invokes the deity to restore [Camille] to him . . . in fervent tones tells of his *passion tendre*." Yet within this conventional treatment there are certain elements that point forward to Craig's later work. Perhaps not altogether surprisingly, the plot of his adaptation was found "somewhat weak," but it was recognized that sacrificing the story gave "opportunity for many graceful tableaux." The action was restructured to gain a lyrical progression, beginning with the hopefulness of early morning and the ripening warmth of a summer day, and following through a symbolic natural sequence in which sophisti-cated lighting effects were used to shape the audience's emotional response. "Evening stars and sinking sun – the sun sinks deeper and as it sinks it darkens and gets deeper red. *Always changing.*" This was intended to have spiritual significance, and Craig's notes refer to "the setting sun as a suggestion or sign of the promised land." Then came full night, and for the final scene the ghostly light of a rising moon. In addition, the weight Craig later gave to movement as the key element of theater can already be glimpsed in the emphasis placed on the dance, which the reviewer singled out as "certainly bizarre, and what with the delicately hued costumes, altered in tone from time to time by the changing limelight and backed by the deepest shades of foliage, [it] presented the prettiest scene in the play."[17]

When he became aware that his ideas were leading him to a radically new form of theater, Craig labeled his work "the revolution that started in Uxbridge." But looking back over his career as a whole, he dismissed the production as "really... of little significance" because it did not reflect any of the other influences to which he had already been exposed, influences that were to act as catalysts for his theatrical vision.

Until 1897, when he left the acting profession altogether, Craig hardly seemed to be on the verge of any revolutionary breakthrough. The productions he planned were as conventional as those he staged. When he prepared the play-within-a-play scenes of *A Midsummer Night's Dream*, his sketches show a naturalistic setting for both the carpenter's shop, with a rear wall parallel to the proscenium and a beamed roof, and for the wood, with a hawthorne brake for Snug to fall backward into when the "translated" Bottom appears. There were to be several additional non-speaking actors simply "to convey *bustle* and excitement," and much of the "business" was to be left up to the actors, indicating that the production was traditional. The only unusual touch was that in acting the Pyramus and Thisby piece the mechanicals would each wear "a real Greek tragedy mask."[18] Similarly, the last play he actually mounted with himself in the lead role was a melodrama from his stock repertoire, with all the usual wind effects and "hurry" music, and a villain (François Villon, played of course by Craig) turned from his evil path by the kindly treatment of a priest. This was part of an impromptu evening's entertainment, arranged practically on the spot to raise money for a stranded theatrical troupe. The other half of the program, a sentimental recitation, contained one element that was to recur in Craig's later work, the simple white costume and bold black pom-pom buttons of a Pierrot. Yet, despite the freedom offered by the improvisational nature of this performance, it held nothing that suggested anything new.

But beneath the surface, fresh ideas were clearly taking shape. Craig had already come across what he later listed as his three major sources of inspiration. And although his decision to give up acting may have been precipitated by the breakup of his marriage, behind it was a growing realization that the theater in which he had served his apprenticeship was on the wrong track.

The first of these influences came in the shape of magazine articles. These articles, which reflected the growing interest in theater history at the time, made Craig aware that radically different and nonnaturalistic stage conventions had not only existed once, but could still be viable. One in particular that impressed him was an imaginative reconstruction of "A Christmas Mystery in the Fifteenth Century." It emphasized the sacred nature of medieval drama, its links with the liturgy, and its status as a communal "ceremony of public worship." It drew a picture of a sumptuous and symbolic performance: Even those playing beggars were dressed magnificently, and "solemn" aesthetic qualities took the place of realistic illusion – to the extent, it was claimed, that actors chosen solely for their beauty mimed the parts while "the real players and singers were hidden behind the scenes." In short, mystery plays were described as a visionary representation of spiritual existence, the opposite of any naturalistic copy of life: "The stage was...the materialization of all those medieval frescoes and bas-reliefs where we see represented in different planes of the same expanse the different phases in the life of man...The upper floor was open to the sky and in the middle was a golden throne surrounded by golden rays, in which God sat, an attentive and permanent spectator of the play."[19]

Another article, which gave a different example of much the same elements and which Craig claimed had "more positive influence on my scenic work than any other," described the performance of *Oedipus* and *Antigone* by the Comédie Française in 1894 in the ruins of the Roman theater at Orange. This description stressed the effectiveness of visual simplicity and the absence of any representational scenery in contrast to the elaborately carpentered settings for the mystery plays. It portrayed this simplicity as "a direct reversal of the ordinary effect in the ordinary theatre," where a proscenium, stage lighting, and the machinery of illusion "compels us to perceive that the palace is but painted canvas. The palace at Orange – towering up as if it would touch the very heavens and obviously of veritable stone – was a most peremptory reality." The stateliness of this facade was described as reducing light comedy or social problem plays to insignificance, while amplifying the noble passions of high tragedy or grand opera "in keeping with the devotional solemnity of the early theatre...when the play itself was a religious rite."[20]

It was only after seeing the illustrations of the permanent scene (330 feet wide by 120 feet high) in the Roman theater at Orange, Craig later said, that he "realized the possibilities which are opened by height, space and background to the stage."[21] But the other qualities praised by these articles were also to be reflected directly in his work. His idea of a "rich theatre" with costumes created out of "exquisite and precious" materials can be traced back to the description of mystery plays. So can his plans to separate mimed action from vocal accompaniment in *The St. Matthew Passion*, and his ideal of performance as a public ceremony. His concept of architectural settings, with light playing on scenery like the gradually changing light of the sun, the visual simplicity of his later designs, and his clear preference for tragedy and opera paralleled the elements of the Roman theater. In particular, the stress on the religious and spiritual nature of both medieval and classical drama struck a chord in him. But two other influences were of even more immediate importance to Craig's development. One was the experiments of Hubert von Herkomer; the other the stage work of his father, Edward William Godwin.

Perhaps it was precisely because Craig never knew his father, who had separated from Ellen Terry and their two illegitimate children when Craig was only three, and knew relatively little about his work, that Godwin became a focus for his dreams, an ideal to emulate, and an imaginary rival. By profession, Godwin was a successful architect of the Victorian gothic school, but began to write occasional drama criticism in Bristol in 1857, and after meeting Ellen Terry was gradually drawn into theater production. In his early reviews, Godwin criticized Charles Kean's productions for their lack of historical accuracy, and by the 1870s he was writing articles on how the background to Shakespeare's plays should be presented. He was opposed to the popular drama of the time, dismissing melodramas such as *The Wandering Heir* (even with Ellen Terry in the cast) as "stagey" productions with "altogether complicated and uninteresting" plots. He proposed instead that unity and realism be the guiding principles of the theater, that the scenery should be an "exact representation" of the location of the action, and that the actors should discard rhetorical histrionics.[22]

When Bancroft produced *The Merchant of Venice* in 1875, the program acknowledged Godwin's "invaluable aid in archeological research." The reviews singled out the "attention to minute details" in the elaborately carved arches of the Doge's palace, with a panorama of canals and medieval buildings beyond, which put Venice "on the stage with a completeness and picturesque beauty of scenery, costumes and other accessories rarely equalled." Whatever the historical justification, this was pure spectacle, and even the critics who praised it recognized that "extravagance of decoration has a natural tendency to subordinate the action," particularly when a cast "underact ... in the approved drawing room style." Productions like *The Cup* by Tennyson, on which Godwin advised Irving in 1881, or *Claudian*, which he designed in 1883, were perhaps more suited to his principles. Roman architecture called for severe lines, which threw into relief not only the proportions but also the figures of the actors by the absence of distracting decoration, and Godwin was thereby able to gain a type of visual unity that reinforced the emotional tone of the action. In *The Cup* it was noted that the harmony among the actor's poses, their costumes, and the scenery achieved the effect of elevated solemnity, with Ellen Terry's "snake like draperies" falling "into the exact folds of the garments of an ancient Greek statue or a Pompeian fresco."[23] In *Claudian* Craig himself was vividly impressed by the destruction of a temple in an earthquake that brought columns and cornices crashing down around the protagonist.

When Godwin turned to directing, it was this emotional unity – an integration of all the visual elements of a production in order to bring out the essential quality of the action in such a way as to envelop the audience in the dramatic experience – that became his primary objective. Accuracy of historical detail, though of scholarly importance, was now theatrically significant only insofar as it contributed to this unity. But to achieve such an ideal, Godwin had to move out of the conventional theater. The plays in three of his four productions – *As You Like It, The Faithful Shepherdess*, and Tennyson's *Fair Rosamund* – called for natural settings. These were mounted in woodland glades at Coombe or Wimbledon, where there was no "scenery" or "stage illusion" as such. The audience shared the environment with the actors, who passed in and out of the trees, a historically neutral background that could be given any "period" by details of costume.

There were, of course, many different kinds of outdoor theater at the time, from popular entertainment to high culture. At the seaside pierrots played on platforms rather like the traditional booth stages. Festivals were held in special auditoriums, like the Roman amphitheater at Orange. But this totally natural type of open-air performance was an innovation in the 1880s. It was not, of course, new in itself, as Jacobean masques like *Comus* had been specifically written for exactly the same kind of performance. However, Godwin's experiment soon became almost standard practice in England. After the turn of the century there was Ben Greet, of whom it was once remarked: "Just as Mr. Wemmick said in effect, 'Holloa! Here's a church! Let's have a wedding!' So Greet would say, 'Here's a lawn! Let's do the *Dream!*'";[24] and such open-air productions reached their apogee with Reinhardt's 1933 *Midsummer Night's Dream* outside Oxford.

Godwin's only other production applied the same principles in a very different way, though again outside the limits of the conventional stage. This was *Helena in Troas*, John Todhunter's highly lyrical compression of the Homeric legends about the Trojan war into a single day's action and nineteen pages of dialogue carefully structured into the classical strophe/antistrophe/epode pattern. To bring this highly stylized drama to life, and to involve the audience in such an unfamiliar theatrical form, Godwin accentuated its ritualistic qualities. He staged it in 1886 in a large arena, Hengler's Circus, which he altered to create an archeologically correct "Greek arrangement of Pro-scenium, Orchestra and Thymele." (Not perhaps altogether coincidentally, the production was "performed for the Benefit of the British School of Archeology at Athens.") In the center a large circular space, enclosed by a low wall and covered by a floor cloth that was painted to represent a tessellated marble pavement, separated the audience, seated in semicircular tiers modeled on the well-known amphitheater below the Acropolis, from a long, narrow upper stage. The panels covering the front of this structure were reproductions of friezes at the Temple of Phigalia. The arrangement of columns that formed the permanent set of Priam's palace, through which a backdrop of clear blue sky appeared on either side, was copied from the Temple of Empedocles. Incense burned in the altar to Dionysus that took up the center of the orchestra. This aspect of the production was imaginatively effective, particularly when the whole was bathed in "a dim religious light." It was described as "elevating, imposing and very beautiful, full of exquisite grace and refinement." Its impact on the audience was compared to that of a performance of *Oedipus* in another reproduction of a Greek theater at Harvard five years before, when the spectators "dispersed afterwards as if they were leaving a religious ceremony" rather than a theatrical entertainment. This response was attributed "in great part to the fact that the tragedy appeared in its own dignified surroundings and as far removed as possible from the flimsy and artificial accessories with which the modern playgoer is too easily satisfied."[25]

Indeed the visual spectacle must have been exceptionally powerful to achieve anything like this effect, as so many other elements in the

E. W. Godwin's production of *Helena in Troas*, Hengler's Circus, 1886. Production marked by archeological accuracy and aesthetic grouping. Courtesy of the British Library.

production were working against it. According to Beerbohm Tree, who played Paris, there were only two rehearsals of the principal scenes. The amateur chorus moved clumsily and had to be restricted to aesthetically decorative but undramatic groupings, which did little to offset the static nature of the play. The script itself transformed passion into rhetorical clichés:

> PARIS (*to Helen*): Immaculate womanhood...O river of bliss
> Where deeper plunged than vexèd Tantalus
> I stand, and gape with my deluded lips
> To assuage the thirst that fills me at thy sight!

It also reduced the fall of Troy to a purely personal level, with little of the ethical questioning or religious significance of the Greek tragedy it was copying. As one reviewer commented, "For a noble scene we must have a noble art, but to strive after it is at least something."[26]

In his emphasis on historical accuracy, and also in this archeological attempt to reproduce a theater of the past, Godwin stood for much of what Craig rejected. But Craig's psychological need for a father figure led him to adopt Godwin, as he had adopted Irving, as an artistic progenitor, translating Godwin's approach into his own terms, stressing any parallels with him, and ignoring the very real differences. Thus, even after he had established his own antinaturalistic style and had left England for Berlin, Craig believed that he "could create great interest [there] in my father's work for the stage...it bears on mine, and the [two] things together would make for strength." It was specifically his own principles of visual unity, the creation of an emotional harmony out of all the elements of a performance, the bridging of the stage/auditorium division to involve spectators more immediately in the dramatic action, that Craig saw reflected in his father's work. The notion that directing as such was an activity comparable to architecture, as well as the consistently architectural quality of his designs, relates to Godwin; and even Godwin's realism carries over into Craig's work, though in an anti-illusionistic form, in his rejection of scenic artificiality. Above all Craig saw his aims as a continuation of his father's, for one of Godwin's obituaries had described him as motivated in all his stage work by "the absolute necessity for a reform in the usually accepted notions of theatre design."[27]

Irving had acted as Craig's artistic godfather. In Godwin, his biological father, Craig believed he had found a forerunner whose parentage might also legitimize his revolutionary theatrical concepts. He was to pay homage to both of these father figures, writing the book on Irving that has, perhaps more effectively than anything else, preserved interest in his acting achievements, and rescuing Godwin's ideas from oblivion by reprinting his articles on staging Shakespeare in *The Mask*. Yet on a practical level the influence of Hubert von Herkomer, which Craig never directly acknowledged, was even more decisive.

Born in Bavaria in 1846, Herkomer became part of the English artistic establishment. He exhibited at the Royal Academy, lectured at Oxford as the Slade Professor, and founded an art school at Bushey, then a village just outside London, in 1883. The work produced by the students was in the Pre-Raphaelite and Victorian gothic tradition, but they were taught that "dramatic expression – any outward, visible sign of any possible emotion – is proper pictorial matter; and movement is such in a special degree." For Herkomer, therefore, the theater was a logical extension of the easel, and he constructed a small stage for his students to experiment with lighting effects, perspective, figure grouping, and the creation of emotional mood through story situations, "unfettered by tradition, or by the demands of a paying public."[28] Only two productions were finally mounted there: *The Sorceress* in 1889 and *An Idyll* in 1890. But these attracted a great deal of interest because of the novel scenic concepts they displayed. A select audience of leading theater artists was invited to each performance, and in 1892 Herkomer gave a public lecture entitled "Scenic Art" at the Avenue Theater in London.

At first glance these productions seem unlikely material for the seeds of Craig's ideas. They were lyrical rather than dramatic, and reflected the careful balance and sentimental detail of the popular genre painting of the period. The subjects were medieval, and the treatment was realistic to the highest degree. But Craig, who attended all three events, found Herkomer's stage techniques fascinating. He described the performances as "most moving," and commented on the potential value of the ideas put forward in the lecture, regretting that "the Profession" showed no signs of adopting them.[29]

Herkomer always denied that his aim was to reform the theater. Instead he presented his ideas as *improvements* on standard practice. But because neither he nor his students knew anything about traditional stagecraft, they started with a tabula rasa, and although the effects they wanted were basically conventional, the means they invented to achieve them led Herkomer to reject all established practices. In particular he criticized the flatness of two-dimensional scenery, the unnatural shadows thrown on an actor's face by footlights, and the perfunctory nature of stage illusion:

> It is quite safe at present to let your moon rise perpendicularly up the sky, very quickly, until your mechanism is exhausted, and then let it stop. Further, that

the moment this red, rising moon appears over the horizon, it shall send rays of blue light from the opposite direction from which it rose. It is safe to let down a "wobbly" sheet of canvas, close to the footlights, with a scene painted thereon representing [static] breakers dashing over the cliffs, and perhaps a sinking ship in the distance, to which the actor may have to refer in his speech. It is safe to have layers of canvas hanging from the "sky," like so much washing hung on a line; and certainly nobody has ever questioned the prerogative of the "firmament" to come together at right angles in the corners.[30]

By contrast, in his school's productions all the scenery was built-up, footlights were replaced by lights set back on either side of the auditorium, level with the actor's faces and boxed in so that the audience was unaware of them, and the "sky" was an unbroken, seemingly limitless expanse. In addition, a simple mechanism allowed the moon to rise naturally.

Herkomer's lighting was so effective that many in his audience were convinced he had opened out the rear wall of his theater so that what they were seeing was the real sky. The only way to dispel this mistaken but flattering belief was to take a group (which included the young Craig) behind the scenes at the end of the performance and physically demonstrate how the impression of distance had been achieved. Across the back of the stage was a canvas painted in graduated shades of blue. In front of this a sheet of gauze was stretched, angled so that the gap between was two feet at the bottom and twelve

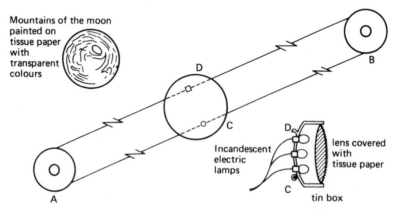

Herkomer's "Moon-mechanism." Two wires stretched between wheels attached to the rear wall of the stage at A and B carry the "moon-box," fixed at either D or C, which is moved by a stagehand slowly pulling on the wire. The mountains of the moon are painted on the tissue-paper cover, illuminated by three "incandescent lamps" with a transformer to reduce or increase the electric current.

feet at the top. Lights were set behind as well as in front of it, so that the surface could be made opaque or transparent, and projections were used to throw moving clouds onto it. As Herkomer described the effect:

> With but little hastening of nature's time – the forty minutes of the act would be long enough to represent the last rays of the sun, casting its long shadows from the different objects on the distant slopes – time enough for the land to darken into that bewitching colour which is to be seen between the setting of the sun and the rising of the moon. Then for the moon to increase in strength as it rises (correctly) into the sky, showing a halo of ever-increasing brilliancy [through the reflection of the lights in the "moonbox" on the gauze in front] as the whole scene darkens almost into night.[31]

When, eight years later, Craig came to mount *Dido and Aeneas*, the first production in which he broke away from the conventional theater, he copied exactly this method of creating an "atmospheric" sky, together with the technique of positioning lights on either wall of the auditorium. In fact it was Herkomer's techniques that made the greatest impact in that performance, and Craig's obvious debt in stage lighting has been recognized for some time.[32] What does not seem to have been realized is how pervasive Herkomer's influence was on Craig's artistic principles in general, and how specifically it shaped many of the other elements in *Dido* and the group of productions that followed.

Herkomer realized that this sort of "stereoscopic" illusion could be created only if all the spectators viewed the stage from the same perspective. The theater he constructed was modeled on a scaled-down version of Wagner's theater in Bayreuth and was limited to an audience of 150 people, all of whom were seated on one level. This was an ideal that Craig also called for and carried out in his early productions, though Herkomer was aware – as Craig apparently was not – that "a non-subsidized theatre constructed in this way would not pay its way." He also outlined plans for an adjustable proscenium, so that the "frame" could contract to accommodate interior scenes or, when a single actor was on stage, to make "the human figure...duly prominent." In addition, he emphasized that design and proportion in the relationship of figures to a group or to objects in the setting could transform the scale, apparently magnifying an actor's stature or making him recede into the distance – ideas that Craig later picked up and expanded. He believed that scenic illusion could be created only if the stage floor were made as three-dimensional as the setting, and in *An Idyll* it was built up into an uneven surface of cobbles (for a village street) and curving slopes. As he noted, this had the additional advantage of preventing "my young performers from attempting the so-called stage-walk." In

PROFESSOR HERKOMER'S MODEL STAGE WITH CONTRACTING PROSCENIUM.

FIG. 1.—Back of Proscenium, partly in section : A, A, Opening, normal size ; B, B, Opening, reduced ; *a*, Sky Piece ; *b, b*, Sliding Wings ; *c, c,* Right and Left-handed Screws, respectively ; *d, d, d, d,* Toothed Pulleys ; *e,* Handle ; *f, f,* Rope for raising Sky Piece ; *g,* Rope for lowering same ; *h,* Guide ; *i, i,* Pulleys ; *j, j,* Counterbalance Weights, working over Pulleys *k, k; l,* Shaft connecting Pulleys *d, d.* FIG. 2.—Section on line c, c : *a,* Sliding Sky Piece ; *b,* Sliding Wing ; *h,* Guide ; *i,* Pulley. FIG. 3.—Front View of Toothed Pulley *d,* and Connecting Chain. FIG. 4.—Greatest Size of Opening. FIG. 5.—Least Size of Opening. FIG. 6.—Method of Raising and Lowering the Curtain ; the dotted lines represent the Curtain lowered ; *m, n,* Pulleys. FIG. 7.—Elevation and Side View of Pulleys *m, n,* and *i* respectively.

Herkomer's plans for an adjustable proscenium, illustrating the "screw" mechanism (*The Magazine of Art*, 1892). Courtesy of the British Library.

his production of *The Vikings* Craig used the same device for precisely the same practical purpose. But he accentuated the slopes, partly because instead of dealing with amateurs he was attempting to break down the long-established acting habits of professionals, and in place of Herkomer's subtle details he substituted steep cliffs in the bold lines that were characteristic of his art. Later, divorced from Herkomer's realistic context, this was to become one of Craig's most challenging concepts – transforming the stage floor into an active dramatic element. Even the darkness of the scenes in *The Vikings*, which followed Irving's practice, could equally be traced to one of Herkomer's suggestions: "Pictorial brilliancy is obtained by the very *economy of light*...leaving some parts of the stage-picture suggestive and indistinct."[33]

Herkomer corresponded to Craig's ideal of the theater artist. He not only acted the leading role in his own productions, directed, and rehearsed the cast, but also designed the scenery, wrote the dialogue, and composed all the music, and even drew the plans for his own theater as well. Like Craig, he emphasized that even "if a thousand people are needed to carry out an art scheme, it must be planned and directed by the *one man* who stamps it as his work." Craig later pointed to what he considered an essential distinction between Herkomer's intentions and his own, not mentioning him by name, but referring specifically to the natural moonlight effect that had become a symbol of Herkomer's improvements in scenic art: "The reproduction of nature's lights is *not* what my stagemanager ever attempts," and the aim should be "not to *reproduce* nature, but to *suggest*." Yet, beneath Herkomer's surface of extreme and detailed realism, the principles on which his work was based were remarkably similar to Craig's. He stressed that "natural phenomena must always be expressed through art," which by definition was subjective, and that "the very foundation of scenic art is *artificiality*." Like Craig, he believed that movement, not dialogue, should communicate meaning (though he was referring to representational mime rather than abstract dance), and that the function of every element in a performance was to contribute to "the 'mood' or, as the Germans say, 'stimmung' of the scene." In *The Sorceress* he had experimented with contrasting the moods of juxtaposed scenes in a way that was very similar to some of the effects Craig was to gain in *Dido*. "Heathen worship...song and dance...[and] incantations of the queen sorceress" during the night were set against the calm "peacefulness" of daybreak and shepherds. In Herkomer's scenarios the plots were little more than visual situations (developed out of his own paintings); and for every speech or song there were ten pages of musical score accompanying and illustrating the actions of the characters. Craig went further, composing "masques" without any dialogue at all – where the stage-action was to be derived from a series of drawings, each expressing a specific "mood." Indeed, the dramatic "visions" that Craig created for his Scene corresponded precisely to Herkomer's definition of a "pictorial music-play. The first word denotes the plastic picture; the second, the musical sounds that are to attune one to the picture; and finally, the word play, to give sufficient motive for the display of the two arts – painting and music."[34]

However, Craig emphasized the qualities of overt artifice and impressionistic suggestion to an extent that made his debt to Herkomer almost unrecognizable. Whereas Herkomer's plasticity tended to stasis, Craig made movement the key element in his theatrical theories. In addition, his representationalism was highly stylized from the first and quickly moved toward abstraction. His demand that every facet of the stage be transformed, from the architecture of the auditorium and proscenium, to the scenery, lighting, stage floor, and even the actor, may have been a response to Herkomer's call – more all-embracing than Godwin's – for reforms. Yet his vision of an Art of the Theater was qualitatively different from Herkomer's Scenic Art, not just an extension of it.

Nonetheless, even in its urgency to find new theatrical forms for a new age, Craig's work has to be seen as a direct development of the theater at the end of the nineteenth century, retaining some of its most traditional aspects as well as building on those new techniques of staging that were already available. His aim of totally renewing the theater was to some extent characteristic of the time, and his first productions after he parted ways with Irving and left the Lyceum were at least partly a logical continuation of well-established trends, with Herkomer's experiments as their starting point.

3

A RISING ACTION:
DESIGN AND MOVEMENT

In 1900 Craig proposed for himself a characteristically far-reaching scheme of work: designing "Scenes, Costumes, Props, Movements and the rest" for seven of Shakespeare's plays (including *Hamlet*, *Macbeth*, and *The Merchant of Venice*), for romantic poetic dramas such as *Peer Gynt* and *Faust*, for "pantomimes and masques," and for musical productions ranging from "Symphonies by Mozart and Beethoven" and Bach's *Passion* to three Wagner operas and Purcell's *Fairy Queen*.[1] This "list of things to be prepared and done" ends with the note, "Prepare slowly my book on the Theatre and its Art," and the fact that this is the final item is significant. Productions precede theory. In a sense the main outlines of all his works for the conventional theater are contained in these early notes. He was later to design *The Merchant of Venice* for Ellen Terry, *Macbeth* for Beerbohm Tree in 1909 and then for Tyler in 1928, and *Hamlet* for Stanislavski. One of Ibsen's romantic plays was the first straight drama he directed, and another closed his stage career; and he worked on masques and *The St. Matthew Passion* off and on over the next thirty years. The fact that, right at the outset of his career as a director, so much of his future program was already articulated in outline gives unexpected consistency and coherence to his development, which otherwise seems so full of fresh starts and new directions. What the list also indicates, however, is a simultaneous preoccupation with such a wide diversity of projects that the odds were against any single production ever being completed – and this scattering of energy is indeed one of the reasons why Craig achieved relatively little on the stage.

But at this point he had someone who helped him focus his ideas: Martin Shaw, whose interest in early opera led him to found the Purcell Society. So Purcell became Craig's starting point. As he later said, "I rang up the curtain on my work in *Dido and Aeneas*" (a more modest and therefore more practicable choice than *The Fairy Queen*), although "without Martin Shaw I should never have thought to do this or done so."[2]

Martin Shaw, unlike Craig's later collaborators, was not another director, but a composer. So his approach complemented Craig's ideas, rather than competed with them; and over the next three years they mounted six productions in which Craig worked out the principles of his theatrical art. *Dido and Aeneas* was repeated in 1901, together with *The Masque of Love* (built around the ballet and incidental music composed by Purcell for Betterton's adaptation of Beaumont and Fletcher's *The Prophetess, or The History of Dioclesian*). *The Masque* was performed again with Handel's *Acis and Galatea* in 1902, followed by Laurence Housman's nativity play, *Bethlehem*. Then in 1903 came Ibsen's *The Vikings at Helgeland* and *Much Ado about Nothing*. For various reasons – the use of amateur performers, the choice of a theater too far off the beaten track, censorship that restricted *Bethlehem* to "private performance," or the general public's lack of comprehension about something so different from their theatrical preconceptions – none ran for more than a few performances. Yet, perhaps because this was the era of new movements, Craig's work was immediately recognized as "the first step of a new movement which is destined to revolutionize the poetic drama." So *Dido* was hailed as "the way for which we have looked so long – the way in which we may see Shakespeare and Maeterlinck in all their poetry...the middle way between ugly pedantry [Poel's Elizabethan Stage Society] and superfluous detail [Irving and the Lyceum]."[3]

For this first production, Craig was literally forced to design his own stage, as the only available space the Purcell Society could afford was the Hampstead Conservatoire. This concert hall – forty-four feet wide, and with a fixed series of steplike platforms built across one end to seat an orchestra – was at first sight an unpromising theater. But the compromises forced on Craig by this shape and structure became characteristic features of his work. The ceiling height was the same throughout the hall, and to use Herkomer's techniques of overhead lighting and sky effects, he had to construct an exceptionally low proscenium to hide not only the frames for back cloths and gauzes, but also a bridge above the stage for a lighting man and his equipment. At the same time, to fit a cast and chorus that together numbered forty-two (swelling to seventy-five for the second production) onto an exceedingly shallow stage area, he had to use almost the entire width of the hall. The effect was strikingly panoramic, and he reused it not only for *Bethlehem*, which was presented in a similar though larger hall, but also in the Coronet and Great Queen Street theaters, where he lowered existing prosceniums by as much as twelve feet to create an impression of width. He also found (as Jessner was later to do in Germany) that stepped platforms made three-dimensional groupings and movement possible, and promoted as well a symbolic ranking of characters. So he designed a series of six steplike platforms for *Acis* (though in the actual production this was reduced to a single low rostrum across the rear, broken in the middle) and planned steps leading down to the orchestra for *The Masque of Love*. Similarly, in

The Vikings, "instead of the stage level" he created "a slope of broken ground . . . to assist proper grouping" and to prevent all the actors from gathering downstage center and facing the audience – as they had become accustomed to doing with the footlights that he was responsible for abolishing.[4]

Two further factors imposed by the concert-hall structure also had a decisive influence on Craig. With four different scenes to mount in *Dido*, six set-changes, and no space for wings or flies, there could be no conventional settings. So the only physical scenery consisted of three or four poles hung with ropes to represent Aeneas's ships in act 3, and Dido's throne, arched over with a dome supported on four slender columns and flanked by six-foot trellis fences covered with dark green vine leaves and purple clusters of grapes. All of these could be easily moved and stacked flat against the side walls. This simplicity of scene, remarked on by almost all the reviews as responsible for much of the beauty of the production, became one of Craig's main principles. As he later noted:

> Remember generally to seize one property . . . and round that conceive and build your scene – accompanying it always with its like a cross [*sic:* i.e., giving it the status of a symbol such as the cross, in order to make the scene] a place for PRAYER, an *emblem*. When you do this, you are able to help the theatre – [and it will be] full of spectators.[5]

The second factor was the unified, single-level seating in the hall. There were no side boxes, parterres, or galleries. This allowed all the spectators to see the play from the same perspective. Craig found it so effective that while working on *Venice Preserved* for Otto Brahm he even tried to persuade him to remodel the Lessing Theater along the lines of the Bayreuth auditorium, and accompanied one of his designs with the declaration, "I would not propose such a scene for any theatre except one of a special form – that is to say, with all the seats on an inclined floor."[6]

These qualities of simplicity and unified effect, together with exceptional possibilities for movement, were already present in Purcell's score. Originally commissioned by a dancing master for his Boarding School for Girls in Chelsea, the libretto calls for no less than seventeen dances and was modeled on the plan of Lully's operas, with choral scenes of spectacle linked by ballet dances and a minimum of narrative. As a result, Virgil's original story is reduced to five basic situations. Dido recognizes that she has fallen in love with Aeneas, who woos and wins her with only token resistance. All join in a "Triumphing Dance." The Sorceress and her witches plot to destroy Dido by sending an evil spirit in the shape of Mercury to command Aeneas to leave Carthage. Then

PURPLE green . vermilion dot .

From red dot to red dot stands a green hedge of green . Purple flowers a thay trellis upholds the green . it is semi transparent the chorus are behind, it dressed ready for the witches scene ; _____ . (more b)

At the end of this scene on page 23 on removal of the hedges 1 & 2 everyone behind must come down close to curtain at the word "Downstage" . This will be done noiselessly & in order .

———

Properties ontstage . Throne . Canopy . Steps . 8 cushions R of 5 red side up 3 black .

Offstage (L) (1) Wreath of purple & green .

    " (2) Crown on silver cushion & robe .

    (R) (3) 2 Cornucopiae . 8 Spears &: SPQR's 8 Shields . Shield & Spear for Æneas .

Lights . 4 Blue & Purple from top on backcloth 3 Ambers from top on to stage xxx 2 ambers from front on people only .

⊕ Girls in Green & purple .

:: Two little black boys sit in corners . green & black .

▢ men with Æneas . Purple & black

Craig's stage plan and lighting notes for act 1 of *Dido and Aeneas* from the promptbook, showing the shallowness of the stage and the tight grouping of the chorus. Hampstead Conservatoire, 1900. Courtesy of the Bibliothèque Nationale.

comes an "Echo Dance of Furies." Dido and her maidens, resting by a fountain during a hunting party, are forced to take shelter from a storm, during which the false Mercury appears to Aeneas. He promises to obey the demands of fate, and the witches dance at their success. Aeneas prepares to sail, while the witches delight in the coming destruction of Carthage. A second "Witches' Dance" follows. Aeneas offers to disobey the gods and stay, but Dido rejects him for being capable of intending to abandon her, and throws herself on a funeral pyre when he leaves.

Craig simplified this schematic story still further by a subtle shift in the opening situation. In the libretto Dido's "torment not to be confest" refers to the passion she is refusing to acknowledge, although Aeneas's pleas make her "eyes confess the flame her tongue denies." In Craig's version Dido was assumed to have acknowledged her love before the opening of the opera. Her inner conflict became "a Presentiment that her love for Aeneas will end in Disaster," and Aeneas's declaration of love a reassurance that "revives her." This gave an even greater emotional unity to the opera and increased its powerful concentration still further. In addition, Craig's synopsis makes quite clear that the emphasis is not on plot. After a bare outline of the Sorceress's plan of deception, the whole action of the last two acts is given a single sentence: "This has the desired effect; the Witches exult, and Dido is left alone to mourn her Loss." The subtitles given to the scenes stress specific moods and indicate that Craig changed the original set-descriptions to produce a structure of emotional tones, even at the expense of verisimilitude. Instead of a palace we are given "The Arbor," with its connotations of a lover's meeting place and cultivated garden. Instead of a cave, the Witches were set under water in a "long, low waste of dunes to which had drifted all the wreckage of the world."[7] The hunt took place in "Moonshine," and the scenes of act 3, with the witches divided from the sailors by a set change, were labeled "Departure," "Under the Ground," and "Death." The effect is both of chiaroscuro and emotional progression. A cultivated garden as "the Morning breaks" is contrasted with a dark wasteland of dashed hopes. The sylvan innocence and tranquillity of a moonlit grove – brought out by Craig's opening stage direction: "A laugh. R two fawns leap out startled and race off to L" – are set against the violence of a storm and Aeneas's anguish.[8]

The reviewers found the unity of the whole amazing as "a new and distinct art." They praised in particular what they (mistakenly) called "decorative scene painting" and pointed out that the settings were "as inseparable from the movements as from the robes of the players and from the falling of the light," all of which "mingle with the tones of the voices and with the sentiments of the play without overwhelming them

Th[...] ze and cut cloth to create ghostly effects in the Witches' scene. Courtesy of
the [...] ary.

un[...] alien interest."[9] This was clearly not a single-tone unity,
however, but a higher type, the synthesis of opposites. Even the colors of
the first scene were deliberately strong, jarring, and discordant to contemporary taste: vivid green, deep purple, black, and light scarlet cushions
on Dido's throne, against purple and black side cloths and a background
modulating from sky blue to lilac during the scene. The same colors were
carried over into the costumes: a red wig, and a green robe with a yoke
of purple for Dido, green drapery with purple gauze veils for her
maidens, and purple and black for Aeneas.

    There were equivalent contrasts between the color schemes of
each scene. The vibrant brightness of the arbor switched to blacks and
whites in the Witches' scene, and the color of the stage floor changed too,
with a green floor cloth replaced by a gray one. Even the textures of the
scenes were set against one another. The clarity of shape and color and
the impression of immense depths – Craig used Herkomer's combination
of light thrown onto a plain back cloth from both behind and in front of

a gauze for scene 1 – were followed by muted indistinctness. With cloth draped over the platforms so that all contours were lost and camouflaged in gray rags against the floor, the Witches seemed to rise out of nothing. Behind a gauze over the proscenium, surrounded by a cut cloth representing driftwood and wreckage, the figures seemed distanced and ghostly, and Craig's lighting notes underline that this was the effect he intended:

> *Black snow is falling as curtain rises. One lime moon. One lime on Sorceress. Rest black.*
> *Keep light away from side cloths at edge and bottom edge. During this scene huge*
> *shadows sweep across the floor and people on the floor (not on the side or back cloth*
> *though).*
>   SORCERESS: Appear! Appear! Appear! Appear!
> *Everyone else flat on ground, heads covered. Their dresses and floor cloth same tone:*
> *mixed green and grey.*[10]

Two further types of contrast also deserve mention because they challenged the audience's imagination in a way that was to become characteristic of Craig's work. On one hand the production was openly theatrical, with obviously imitation vine leaves and grapes on the trellis of the arbor, a crude papier-mâché boar's head on the end of a spear in the hunting scene, and oversize bright pink paper rose petals for the death scene. On the other hand, as critics noted enthusiastically, the deliberate avoidance of conventional realistic detail and the "simple effects of colour... leave the imagination free" – achieving a suggestiveness that Craig underlined in the program for the second production by announcing that he had "taken particular care to be entirely *incorrect* in all matters of detail." This reminded one reviewer of the more delicate friezes of Pompeii, or, as Yeats wrote, "created an ideal country where everything was possible, even speaking in verse or in music, or the expression of the whole of life in a dance" (a phrase Craig was later to repeat).[11]

Similarly, the heroic was set against the grotesque. Craig's costume list emphasizes the "grand plumes" of Aeneas's helmet and the "large spears" of his men, and his prompt notes for the hunting scene deliberately echo seventeenth-century paintings of classical picnics: little black boys with turbans carrying trays laden with fruit and cakes, one holding up a cluster of grapes while a half-reclining maiden stretches up after the fruit, a loving cup ceremonially handed round. At the other extreme the witches were half-animal, half-vegetable, or half-human: deformed shapes with extravagantly fantastic accoutrements. One male witch

> *...wears a fool's headdress and seaweed, green grey and black (velvet). The one black*
> *note.*

Strong handles to be attached to [the 1st and 2nd female] witches as if their hair.
The rest have twigs with green leaves which seem to sprout from their fingers about 8 inches ...
Two have a skull between them (extra large. White).
A model of a child. A bleeding head.
The 5 men who cross after dance – owls' heads (Rosetti?)[12]

Like the Jacobean "antimasque," the effect of juxtaposing two such contrasting scenes heightened the essential quality of each. At the same time the introduction of overtly theatrical elements, as well as the unhistorical approach and a high degree of artifice in the patterning of movement, increased the audience involvement. They raised the imaginative stakes, challenging any too-easy suspension of disbelief by requiring the audience to assimilate discordant and unrealistic elements, and to create a synthesis for themselves in their own minds. (Equally, of course, this stylization ran the danger of making the whole seem absurd if spectators were not capable of taking the imaginative leap. In the second production at the Coronet Theater, which attracted numbers of the regular and less artistically inclined patrons of Notting Hill Gate because of the presence of Ellen Terry in a crowd-drawing curtain raiser, there was raucous laughter from the gallery and heckling at some points.)[13]

However, the general consensus of the reviews was that Craig's *mise-en-scène* harmonized with the dramatic emotion of the opera, creating a remarkable unity of figures, scene, music, and mood through "simplicity both in colour and form." "For the first time perhaps, those present saw operatic singers using gestures of real dramatic significance." In addition, "the main idea was never lost sight of, no detail was allowed to detach itself from the picture, and every touch was of importance in the gradual development of the tragedy."[14] It was the lighting and the movement – the two elements that were to become central to Craig's concept of "a new theatre" – that contributed more than even the colors and costumes, to this unified effect.

Craig never prepared a full *mise-en-scène*, but by collating his notes for both productions a fairly complete picture emerges, as the second reproduced the first with only relatively minor variations. For instance, a special backdrop of hills and woods arched by a rainbow was painted for the hunting scene and Craig noted that it was "to become more mysterious. More moonlight." Similarly, for the opening scene he noted that "Dido *must* stay near or under the canopy. In 1900 she moved too much."[15]

By removing the footlights and replacing them with lights concealed in boxes at the sides of the auditorium and above the stage, not only could the figures be lit naturally, but also a wide range of shadow

A. Two backcloths—one blue, one grey.   B. Grey gauze on a stretcher.
C. Temporary Proscenium-cum-spotting rail, faced with grey canvas.
D. Slender scaffold poles and thin rope to suggest ship's masts.   E. Battery
of 5 electric lamps with coloured filters.   F. Floor lamps on either side of
Proscenium.   G. Auditorium lights concealed in boxes.   H. Permanent
platform of concert hall.   I. Orchestra.   J. Grey curtains.   K. Auditorium.

Edward Craig's reconstructions of the pictorial effect with massed choruses and minimal
scenery and the lighting system for *Dido and Aeneas*. Courtesy of Edward Craig.

effects could be created. By using a single-color back cloth with a gauze stretched at an angle in front of it onto which light of another color was projected, "an astoundingly three-dimensional effect was achieved" which, to Yeats, seemed "like the edge of eternity."[16] The lighting was coordinated with the music, as at the opening, when "drums, lights swell and fall. Lights fall as drums fall." It was also largely responsible for giving an overall unity to the contrasting scenes. For the Witches' chorus "in our deep vaulted cell," Craig intended "a lime light under stage to come through 6 or 10 holes in the floor and steam which ascends as cigarette smoke in heavy atmosphere" (at least for the second production; such an effect was not possible in the Hampstead Conservatoire). This would have provided a parallel to the death scene, where rose petals fluttered gently down onto Dido's body in a vertical shaft of sharply focused white light against the gradually darkening purple sky as the chorus sang, "Scatter roses on her tomb." Perhaps more obviously, the rising dawn of the opening – darkness, with purple, then blue light thrown on a pale indigo back cloth from the top, gradually strengthening amber light on the stage and the green and purple figures – was balanced against the close. There Dido, robed in black on black cushions, and her surrounding maidens, now entirely covered in their purple gauze veils, were bathed in green light, while blue light was thrown from the top onto the indigo back cloth, yellow onto the gauze. The yellow gradually dimmed, then the blue, leaving the sky deep purple, which darkened until the chorus was lost against it and only their waving arms could be seen.

Craig's first reaction once *Dido and Aeneas* was suggested had been to visualize not the scenery, but patterns of movement and grouping to bring out the mood of the music. This final effect was one of his earliest concepts: "One dance I'll make a dance of arms – white, *white* arms – The rest of the scene dark – and out of it the voices – with arm accompaniment."[17] While Shaw rehearsed the members of the cast musically, Craig insisted that from the first they should be required to move around as they sang so that eventually they would be able to follow his direction to "walk with or counter to music. Continuous movement." As he later noted, "It is the large and sweeping impression produced by means of...the movement of figures which is undoubtedly the most valuable means" for transmitting the essential meaning of a drama. So his production notes dictate a highly formalized style of groupings and gesture, which one critic found too "rigidly...decorative."[18] For instance, on the last line of Aeneas's recitative on entering in the first scene – "Let Dido smile, and I'll defy/The feeble stroke of destiny" – the elaborate procession of his attendants with cornucopias, trophies, gold and ivory trays laden with gifts, and spears and shields, makes "a descending

Patterns of mood and movement: the Mourners' dance of white arms. Courtesy of the British Library.

movement. All spears slope on the syllable 'destiny.'" With the next line, "Cupid only throws the dart," the chorus of girls "go[es] off slowly, fingers to lips then slowly extend [arms]. Four men move into a group [downstage R]. Stand still. Heads up. Two slaves carry fruits, presents in golden baskets and lay them each side of Dido. The 4 [men] sink." At the final line of the chorus, "boys [put] fingers on lips. On last 3 notes the 2 slaves move arms and swirl cloaks around (sticks in cloaks)." Frequently the movement directly illustrated Craig's principle of building a scene round a single emblematic property, as at the end of the Triumphing dance, when the girls, grouped in pairs, pick up the flowers that Aeneas's attendants have scattered across the floor,

> filling their hands and scarves with them.
> One girl finds the shield left by Aeneas. Trying to lift it. It falls on her. She puts up one arm – the others, 3 or 4, run to help. They get under it slowly and

with difficulty raise it – a slow movement – everyone throws their flowers into it and exeunt.
　　All the girls who raise it must be same height from head to wrist.

This way of indirectly building up Aeneas's heroic stature risked ridicule, as the shield was barely large enough for six girls to stand shoulder to shoulder beneath its rim. But an accompanying sketch emphasizes the graceful draping of the group holding the shield, piled with blossoms, at full stretch above their heads, and the movement is carefully broken down into beats.

　　1.2.3. lift/hold shield with left hands.
　　1.2.3. wait/throw up with right.
　　1. throw high. Shield is heavy.
　　[Others] run off.

　　By far the most complex patterning of movement comes in the witches' scene. There are effective arrangements at other points, particularly at the thunderstorm of act 2, when the chorus gathers round Dido in a swirling group, the maidens taking shelter under the soldiers' upheld shields at the extreme left, then dashing diagonally across the whole width of the stage in a linear movement to exit with the words, "Haste, haste to town." But the orchestration of the large numbers of witches

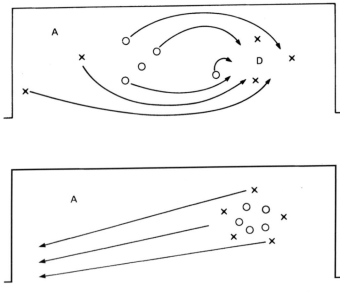

Blocking diagrams for *Dido and Aeneas*, act 2, scene 1.

shows Craig's choreography at its best. As the witches appeared, writhing in the shadows sweeping across the floor, structural patterns of sound were created. First "ah," which was picked up person by person across the stage from left to right. Then one wail at the right and a sigh traveling around from the left, then "whine (one) – 2 gutteral noises and wail. Whine." The line rose silently up, starting at one side, "arms slowly out and up." Singing "Harm's our delight," they advanced one pace and sank a little at each line, to gather in a half circle with the tallest in the center, until "on the end of the last note the hands sweep round from R to L near floor."

Chanting "Ho! Ho! Ho!," the half-circle then advanced inward "swaying, clawing and singing," while from the center the figure of the fool, flanked by the two most grotesque witches with "handlehair," marched straight toward the audience. With a shriek on the last "Ho!" all sank waving toward the sides of the stage. But the effect was not so much one of careful patterning as of threatening confusion, with the orchestrated gestures embedded in passages of "general movement, commotion, no one to be still for an instant." This reached a choreographed climax in the Echo Dance of Furies. The chorus accompanied the music with sung chords, with the girls echoing the men one bar later, and with sharp laughs, with the men echoing the girls. The dancers were divided into two groups of five to create "echo in movement also," and at the end of the sequence the performers in the first group "throw themselves back R and men go off 3 strides at [bar 3]," while those in the second group

at echo go up 3 strides, leap and turn sharp on [bar 5]. They start making circle, 2 one way 2 the other. They get into the right arm and leg position. Move round. [bar 15]. As the dancers begin to go off [re]enter first group. Mysterious steps. Owls' heads.
Noise...echo noise...laugh...echo laugh.
The lights die out. Circle. Enter others hold[ing] long sticks with rags and heads on them...all raised at end in centre.[19]

Throughout, the (male) Sorceress towered almost motionless at the rear.

As the number of notes relating to choreography and gesture indicates, movement was already one of Craig's primary concerns in the first of his mature productions. Another touch that foreshadows one of his central concepts was the use of masks. For the Sorceress and the two leaders of the chorus Craig noted: "Masks for witches – see Japan play." This was his earliest reference to the Nō drama, which was to become one of the models for his new theater. But the influence was limited to a type of stylized distortion. The features remain Western rather than becoming copies of specific symbols from a foreign tradition, and it was the impression of masking – not the masks in themselves – that was significant. As Craig noted in one copy of the program opposite the woodcut of a mask, "Wig and beard in one. Rest *can* be painted on face...nosepiece needed." At first sight his designs seem merely ideal conceptions. But he was dealing with broad effects, which made their realization easier, and was always concerned with the practical details of how his vision could be represented on stage. Opposite the drawing of a skeleton, for example, there are detailed directions for constructing the costume: "This figure wears a cloak of net over garment, bones painted on the under dress." Alternatively, the dress was to have a cage of wire beneath representing the ribs, while the upper part of the skull was to be "painted on old bowler hat" and "the lower jaw to be worn under the chin (the chin to be blackened)" to form the gaping mouth of the drawing.[20]

Craig always selected the most economical means of creating visual effects, and some of these masks were almost as simple as the modern burglar's nylon stocking: "Costume of witches. Net – black. Masks cut to mouth or gauze [stretched] over the upper part of the face. Very scarlet mouths. The gauze passing behind neck and swathing body. Tightly fixed at girdle." Even so, not all of his technical innovations were fully controlled. On the first night, as Martin Shaw recalled, "The limelight men supplied us with two moons; one of them was obviously excessive, but as neither of them would give way, both remained to the end of the scene." Indeed, some of Craig's ideas for this production were clearly beyond the resources of even the professional theater of the period, let alone the Hampstead Conservatoire. There are suggestions for making illusion more complete by involving the audience's sense of smell, as well as their eyes and ears, by filling the hall with the odor of sulphur during the witches' scene, and with "rare perfume" as the rose petals fall on Dido's corpse. And one note suggests something that Craig was later to experiment with in his search for a totally flexible theater form: "Proscenium to alter in size."[21]

With *Dido and Aeneas* recognized as the first step toward a significantly new kind of theater, Craig's next productions can be seen as extending and refining the principles he had established in that work. *Dido* had appealed to him because of "its directness and unconventionality of expression."[22] His subsequent vehicles were even less conventional, and allowed Craig even more latitude for interpretation. Although *Acis and Galatea* had been rewritten in the nineteenth century to conform with the theatrical taste of the period – Galatea being provided with a sister as mate for Damon and a father en route to the Trojan war, which allowed for the introduction of Ulysses and a scene adapted from Shelley's

Rich imaginative effects gained by economical means: costume designs for a witch and a skeleton for the "wreckage" scene of *Dido and Aeneas*. Courtesy of the Bibliothèque Nationale.

Prometheus Unbound – Craig returned to the original version, with its undramatic title "A Serenata." According to Handel's 1732 advertisement, "There will be no action on the stage, but the scene will represent, in a Picturesque Manner, a rural prospect, with rocks, groves, fountains and grottos, amongst which will be disposed a chorus of Nymphs and Shepherds, the habits and every other decoration suited to the subject." As for *The Masque of Love*, removed from the context of *The Prophetess* it had neither story nor situation to limit Craig's imagination, only a series of choral songs, music for a "Furies Dance," a "Chair Dance," and a "Butterfly Dance," and the emblematic characters of an Arcadian Shepherd and Shepherdess, Cupid, Bacchus, and Bacchanals. Perhaps because of the freedom these librettos allowed, Craig later rated both far higher than either *Dido* or *The Vikings*, and called *The Masque of Love* "the best thing I ever did on a stage."[23]

Needless to say, Craig ignored Handel's picturesque prospect in *Acis and Galatea*. For one scene, "The Shadow," he used the three-dimensional effect of limitless sky – blue darkening through deep purple to black at the base – as a backdrop for the lovers, who were seated in a vertical circle of pink light on a small mound of cushions and roses in the center of the stage. Behind them stood "a long dim line of cloaked figures melting into the gloom, yet seen; a row of faces peering from out the black, now a white arm uplifted, now the mass swayed and bent like human reeds." But this was the only scenic effect repeated from *Dido*, and even here he added a new technique. When the chorus bade the "wretched lovers" to "behold the monster Polypheme," a wire frame behind the gauze was illuminated and the impression of "a towering castle emerged in golden outlines."[24] A similar, but even more spectacular piece of theatricality closed the opera, when the dead Acis was transformed into a "Water God." A figure formed out of sparkling drops of water, which appeared to rise and fall like a fountain, appeared against a sheer blue sky. The effect was so magical that one reviewer believed he was seeing an entirely new technique of projected light. But, as Edward Craig has pointed out, this was an old pantomime trick used by Charles Kean: The light from lamps with large perforated discs revolving in front of them shines from behind through holes pierced in the back cloth.[25]

Apart from such spectacular effects, which show the links between Craig's new art and the artifice of traditional theater, the major scenic development in both this production and *The Masque of Love* was toward suggestiveness, simplicity, and austerity. One aspect of this movement, as in the earlier representation of Witches, was Craig's use of indistinct forms and semidarkness to allow each spectator to fill out a

An artist's impression of the "Wretched Lovers" duet in *Acis and Galatea*: in the original the lovers appear light purple against the wall of black figures behind, harmonizing with the deep blue sky. Courtesy of the British Library.

Craig's design for the moment immediately following the lovers' duet: chorus and castle fade away, to be replaced by a gigantic shadow projected onto the back cloth. Courtesy of the Bibliothèque Nationale.

picture of horror with his own imagined fears. But in *Acis* this became pure suggestion, without grotesque accoutrements. When Polyphemus was first introduced, it was only as an enormous shadow projected on the back cloth to tower threateningly over the lovers, a tableau that gave

Craig his title for the scene. When Polyphemus appeared in the next scene, "The Giant," at first only "one single fold of a vast purple mantle, sweeping down from the darkness" could be seen. Then, as the light grew, all that stood revealed was "a huge, brooding form upon a throne of heaped shadows, a haunting shape, barely seen, yet difficult to forget," and it was precisely this allusive bareness that led Max Beerbohm to call Polyphemus "the only real and impressive giant ever seen on any stage."[26]

Even more significantly, the first scene, "The White Tent," showed that Craig could move beyond the easy suggestiveness of semidarkness. Instead of displaying the romantic Arcadian landscape of Sicily, Craig hung a bar right across the stage toward the rear, over which he draped a complete row of long two-and-a-half-inch-wide strips of upholsterers' webbing. At the front these were attached just above the sight lines behind the proscenium to form a gently curving roof, through which light filtered from above. At the back they hung down like a curtain, striped with the narrow gap between each one. This gave an effect of transparency, with the strips swaying and opening as the actors moved past and through them, and the rough material appeared so delicate that one reviewer believed the tent to be made of silk. Behind was a black cloth with circular clouds at the base of a sky that went from white through pink to indigo at the top. (Craig had actually designed this three years earlier in 1899 – the first example of the way he created generalized scenes that could then be incorporated into any production to establish mood rather than representing a specific place, as in more conventional settings.) On either side of the stage two slim columns of trelliswork entwined by vines appeared to be supporting the roof and emphasized the tentlike form. As in *Dido*, the colors of the costumes echoed the background – white, pink, and silver here; brown and black in the later tragic scenes – and in addition gave the effect of shimmering movement. Made of inch-wide tapes, cream outside and colored on the reverse, they looked like drapery when the figures were motionless, swirling ribands of red or blue when they moved. These techniques were intended to convey the floating evanescence of a dream and, as Craig noted, "the strings" of the scene were "to wave now and then as if in the mind." Out of these simple materials and light, a completely original world of poetic fancy was created.

> "O the Pleasure of the Plains!" sang the chorus, and the fierce mid-day light beat down, tempered softly by the draperies of the white tent under which they lay. Of scenery, in the ordinary sense, there was none; all was suggestion, but such skillful suggestion that into the cool, white shadow came the very heat and glare of midsummer's meadows under a burning sun.[27]

Stage plan for *Acis and Galatea*. R and L stand for the two trelliswork columns; the inner frame represents the webbing of the "tent" and the outer frame the back cloth. The large circle shows the position of the "mound" for the lovers. For the opening scene brightly colored cushions are spread on the platforms at the rear, and the only props listed are two "long sticks with Honesty," a bunch of bells, and balloons. Courtesy of the Bibliothèque Nationale.

The action Craig created to accompany this effect was equally simple and fanciful. Among the drowsy nymphs and shepherds, white-frocked children danced beneath pink and white penny balloons that were tied to a hoop above their heads. These they handed out, one to each dreamer as a symbol of their desires, until the whole scene was filled with dancing figures and floating balls.

The setting for *The Masque of Love* was even simpler: plainness carried to austerity. Instead of using suggestion, Craig reduced the scenery to a neutral ground for the imagination – three monotone gray

The transparent "tent" with cloud backdrop, and the effect of tapes in the costumes of the chorus (white outside showing red reverse when swirled apart) in the opening scene of *Acis and Galatea*. Courtesy of the British Library.

Stylized movement and simple toylike props: the ring of balloons against the transparent "tent" in the opening scene of *Acis and Galatea*. Courtesy of UCLA.

canvas walls, a gray floor cloth patterned in squares, and a double gauze front curtain, one ribbed with a grille of dark gray bars, the other hatched with white squares, for "The Prison of Love." Craig found this sort of grille (derived from Inigo Jones) so effective that it reappeared when he designed *For Sword or Song*, in which it was used as a semitransparent "front scene" with dark ragged figures outside toward the audience, and warm candlelight and song behind. He used it as well in the *Caesar and Cleopatra* designs he did for Max Reinhardt. In both productions it was clearly a distancing device, a way of creating the separation between art and "the pushing world" that a symbolist poet like Yeats believed essential if an imaginary vision were to keep its integrity. But in *The Masque* there was also an element of optical illusion directly anticipating the "op art" of later painters such as Vasarelli. The spacing between the bars grew narrower toward top, bottom, and sides, and curved into the corners, so that the grille appeared to bulge out toward the audience, giving a dreamlike effect. Initially Craig had contemplated using elaborate stage properties, and one of his drawings shows Cupid seated on a towering throne, arched with a dome very reminiscent of Dido's arbor. A flight of steps lead down to an elaborate two-tier altar, flanked by ten massive candles, and Craig's notes alongside suggest the full deployment of such pantomime techniques as the "Water God":

> A golden rain descends as the curtain rises.
> Inside dome is a white light – hidden.
> Altars... incense bowls from which smoke ascends in a quite straight line, silver rain descending on same.

In the actual production, the only parts of this used were the candelabra, a pair of which was set on each side of the stage. (The bowls of incense were transferred to *Acis*.) Instead there was an almost toylike simplicity. Cupid's throne was transformed into a small wooden play cart, drawn around the stage by small children, in which a real infant was set as Cupid (with the soprano singing the role offstage – the first use of a technique that was to be developed in Craig's later, unstaged work). Even the costumes were plain and muted. A chorus of Pierrots was clad in loose white smocks with black chiffon scarves hanging from simple headdresses, Harlequins wore surcoats of dark gauze over the traditional pattern of lozenges on their tight-fitting costumes, and a group of Kings and Queens was robed in long sweeping cloaks painted with large patterns in faint gold. But these neutral tones set off the bright yellow of crowns and candelabra, the floral wreaths carried by the Harlequins, and "touches of red, the more brilliant for their rarity," while the "white figures and greys and greens" took on different hues as they moved

through the pools of colored light that covered each area of the stage –
blue and green and red and yellow.[28] At the same time this plainness also
set off the occasional grotesque touches (like the masks worn by Comus
and Silenus and the elaborately beribboned loops and furbelows of the
gray-and-black dress of the Shepherdess), and Craig's costume notes
bring out the diversity within this overall unity. Kings were

Contrasting costume designs for *The Masque of Love*: Pierrot and Harlequin. Courtesy of the Bibliothèque Nationale.

to look as dignified and gorgeous as the costume can manage. Crown gold and crystal with turban – underdress reaching to ground to be cross and dot pattern, yellow and dark grey – overmantle: long train, with pattern round shoulders and bottom edge in dark grey – overmantle to be of heavy stuff. Lining of mantle, yellow and white.

Bacchanals, in contrast, wore skintight "green costume, with leaves down seams of legs and sleeves, at wrists and in ruff at throat. Headdress of leaves and red berries, carrying branch with leaves and berries."[29]

This was all in such stark contrast to the conventional theater's tinsel-and-pretty-lace treatment of imaginary visions (the best example being the usual nineteenth-century gossamer fairyland of *Midsummer Night's Dream*) that at least one reviewer "found a dream that had come true."[30] In a sense it could be called minimal art, gaining richness from a simplicity that made each detail full of significance; and the austere straight lines of the box set, the neutral tones brought alive by complex lighting effects, form a basic prototype for later developments like Craig's use of screens.

Yet this apparent artlessness was achieved only through considerable technical complexity which, like anything complicated, was prone to accidents – and the slightest of mishaps was enough to endanger such a delicate emotional tone. There was laughter from the gallery, for instance, when a dancer brushed against one of the high candles, making it wobble, and on the first night of *The Masque*, according to Martin Shaw, "the children upset the infant in his car and while the unlucky babe (where was the L.C.C.?) hung perilously downward, howling, his attendants shrilly disputed the question who was to blame for his ungodlike position." Similarly, although *The Masque* had only a single set, changing even the apparently almost nonexistent scenery for *Acis and Galatea* caused all-too-obvious problems. After the opening night, one of Craig's friends and supporters, the critic Haldane Macfall, commented:

> Between the acts you lose your public whom you have captured … is there no bridging over this gap? … of course, I quite allow that your bawling behind the curtains was wholly delightful; but while vibrant with suppressed emotional intensity it was not in the picture. You very nearly got an encore once, all the same. It was when you told the carpenter he was ruddier than the cherry.[31]

This was the more potentially damaging because the key factor was not scenic effect, but movement: movement not only within each act in the form of dances, choreographed gestures, and groupings, but also movement between one act and another through developing parallels and contrasts on all levels, gradations of light and shade or color scheme, and variations of human mood and movement.

Preparing for *Acis*, Craig noted: "The stage movement to be far more elaborated, and simpler than 'Dido and Æ' Conventionalize the actions and retain the general one – movements of the crowd."[32] Working on this principle, Handel's single tableau had been transformed into a series of orchestrated groupings, stylized moves, and symbolic positions. This was even more the case in *The Masque*, in which Craig had effectively created a wholly new work around the bare indications of action contained in the lyrics. Here the movement was so central that he later tried to create a vocabulary of notations based on the choreography. A single downward stroke indicated the posture of the body, a triangle the head (tilted for various positions: to one side $\vee$, back $\triangle$, down $\triangledown$, or with a line through it for closed eyes $\triangle$), and an inverted "t" for whichever leg was "pointed" or not bearing weight ($\triangle$). A horizontal line represented three arm positions (raised to the shoulder $\ominus$, to the ears $\ominus$, over the head $\ominus$). A circle stood for a complete turn, with segments of the circle for one-quarter, one-half, and three-quarter turns. Lines and dots showed the direction and number of steps, as well the type of pace (walking on flat foot ----, on toes | | | |; running on flat foot --. --. --., on toes ...). A square stood for an unmoving figure, and $\boxtimes$ indicated a figure holding a fixed posture. These symbols may seem crude. After all, Craig was to some extent pioneering a new field, and a satisfactory system of dance notation still has yet to be developed. But the fact that the range of things that can be recorded by these signs is limited is not accidental. It corresponds to the type of movement in his productions. Obviously this had very little to do with conventional ballet, and that there are no symbols for leaps and pirouettes is significant. Craig's system of symbols is based on ordinary gestures and ways of moving, which are restricted and standardized – three clearly differentiated arm positions, four basic steps – and which can be built up into easily perceived visual patterns. This simplification would be more effective for group movement than for a solo dance, and the tendency is toward geometric abstraction.

Even if the program defined the masque form as "a link between the medieval pageant and the play proper," Craig clearly thought of *The Masque of Love* as "a ballet."[33] Indeed, any outline of its contents is a description of dances and symbolically choreographed movements rather than of dramatic actions.

> In the vague and mysterious depths of a hall, very empty and very spacious...is trod the first measure of the Masque of Love. We see, but only darkly as yet, through the bars of an immense window, that Love for all his great power is a very little god. The children surrounding Love are behind these prison bars, not as captives of the invincible captor, but as his fellow-jailers. They, impersonal little beings, are as gods, and do the god's bidding unvexed by whip or chain. These are the orders which Cupid gives them:
> Cupid. Call the Nymphs and the Fauns from the wood.
> Children... The Nymphs and the Fauns from the wood.
> Cupid. Call the Naiads and Gods of the Floods.
> Children... The Naiads and Gods of the Floods.
> Cupid. Call Flora and Comus...
>   Silenus and Momus...
>   Call Bacchus and his merry fellows...
>   Silvanus, Ceres, and Tellus...
>   All leave for awhile their abodes.

Children...Leave for awhile their abodes.

The children run out swiftly, and return as swiftly, dragging a car full of masks and disguises. In pageantry it is the habit which makes the god or goddess, and Cupid's will is done when the messengers have assumed the guise of the gods whom they were sent to find. As they put on their divine cloaks they sing exultantly: –

 "Come, come away;
 No delay, no delay.
 All bow to his will,
 And all show their skill,
 To grace Love's triumphing day."

The hour has struck for the coming of Love's captives. Darkness falls, and a solemn prelude ushers in the procession. Between sleeping and waking heralds of its advance tread a grotesque measure. Here now are the prisoners of Love. They enter in three groups, from the east, from the west, from the north, and the names of these groups are Rank, Riches, and Poverty. They enter at no visible doors,...

Splendid victims...their wrists are bound, their step is slow. They are here, but chained to a rod of captivity; they are here, but dragged by one only less powerful than Death. As these shapes pass, they sing: –

 "Behold, O mightiest of gods,
 At thy command we come –
 The gay, the sad,
 The grave, the glad,
 The youthful and the old all meet,
 As at the day of doom."

Hardly have they finished their stately declaration of allegiance to Love, than their master, with sweet duplicity, will have them think that their slavery is perfect freedom. Love's little fellow-jailers enter, and strike the fetters from the wrists of the captives. A sprightly "Paspe" (passe-pied) strikes up.

The barred window fades and vanishes. The rod to which the "splendid victims'" wrists were tied by long lengths of cord becomes "a maypole of merriment," and "deliverance is symbolised by a dance," after which "a solemn movement" gives visual expression to the simple descants of "Hear, mighty Love!" that end the second section.

At the conclusion of this high invocation, a mysterious rustling and a trampling of feet are heard outside. The worshippers of Love are filled with mingled consternation and curiosity, which give place to open fear. They flee like startled fawns when a company of Bacchanals rush in with uproarious merriment.

The joy of living, as symbolised by Bacchus and his train, at first astounds and shocks the devotees of Love, but step by step they draw nearer, fascinated by the gay green god and his wild followers...Very soon the two parties mingle. Bacchus and his men sing a rollicking chorus of the vine, which is followed by a chorus and [an interweaving] dance even more full of joy and movement, and delight in living. This prepares us for the coming of Mirtillo and Corinna, the only names in this crowd of nameless wooers and wooed. The man woos, the

Craig's notes for movement at "Behold, oh mightiest of gods" in the promptbook of *The Masque of Love*. The strings are attached to a long stick held by one of the Harlequins above his head. Courtesy of the Bibliothèque Nationale.

woman hesitates; he entreats her reason – Tell me why? – she has none. It was ever thus, even in dreamland. She yields at last, and her winning is the signal for all the maskers to move in a courtship dance. This gives place to another dance, and yet another, this time the "contre-danse." All the dancers except the children are blindfold. Could these blind ones see, their chorus in praise of Love might be a shade less triumphant.

> "Triumph, victorious Love,
> Triumph o'er the universe."
> During this exalted song the maskers resume their chains; but now through the magic of the masque we dream a marvellous dream. It is their persecutors, not they, who wear the fetters. Triumphantly free, they lead captivity captive – and are gone.[34]

Beneath his copy of this summary Craig wrote the words "well described," and what the description brings out is the symbolic nature of the performance. The characters are not simply mythical or metaphoric – even the two figures individualized by names are those traditional fictions, of the Arcadian shepherd and shepherdess. They are also imaginary and overtly theatrical, created by donning masks and costumes in full view of the audience, and similar in many ways to the Commedia dell'Arte (even though at this point Craig knew nothing about this Italian theatrical tradition). Relationships and emotional reactions are communicated by groupings and postures, so that the stage presentation was almost equivalent in its abstraction to the music. Many of the audience found all but the most obvious references obscure, and as one reviewer admitted,

> I could not quite follow all the inner meanings of the show – some were a trifle cryptic. But the triumph of Love was clear enough, and it even caught up a timid nun hovering round the edge of forbidden joys. In the end she too secured one of the strings which hung from the maypoles and followed in the train.[35]

However, the general moods were clear enough, communicated by blending the choreography of the players, the patterns of color and light, and the musical orchestration into a single, unified form of expression – the basis for Craig's new art of the theater.

In *The Masque of Love*, even more clearly than in the two operas, the dominant element was the movement. In *Acis* the dances visually reinforced the scenic effects, as with the transformation at the end, when the flow of the fountain was "echoed in the bending, swaying forms, floating scarves and waving arms of the chorus" so that "music and singers alike seemed to melt together and ripple in a silver flood round the feet of the new-born Water God." But the essence of *The Masque* was in the "ballet," and in an advertisement of 1904 Craig offered to perform "his unique entertainment...at Town or Country Houses, either in the open air or in a large hall." So little in fact did he consider it dependent on the technical apparatus of the theater, or on the conventional relationship between audience and actors, that he even suggested performing it on railwaystation platforms as a traveling show.[36]

In both these productions reviewers noted a "large display of symbolic suggestion in posture and grouping" and an "unconventional conventionality." At the same time, in the dance steps, as with the masks in *Dido*, Craig deliberately used indigenous forms for their familiarity, rather than copy foreign traditions, and he replaced Purcell's original pavanes and minuets with English country dances. The choruses were divided into groups of three and four so that movements could be counterpointed, or a balance created in stylized groupings. Other positions and gestures were deliberately copied from seventeenth-century paintings. For instance, the dance illustrating "the sweet delights of love" in *The Masque* was modeled on a reproduction of Fra Angelico's *Dance of the Angels* that Craig pasted into his promptbook. The gestures for the chorus in the death scene of *Acis* were described as "hands above head, fingers open and bent back – grief: Rubens." Other patterns of grouping were designed to create a geometry of movement – sometimes in three dimensions, as when children with bells climbed up into the trellis columns of *Acis* – each move in a pattern being carefully coordinated with the words and music. This was emphasized in *The Masque*, in which the different groups were all instructed to take "a step on the first beat in each bar" and to move forward and sink "on the word 'Down'...", and the geometrical effects were particularly striking.[37] Repeated parallels were set up. A circle of children moved around Cupid, a circle of dancers around the maypole; first the Poor from the left, then the Kings from the right, each led in on their knees by a Harlequin who held the ends of the ribbons tied around their wrists high over his head. Symmetrical patterns were duplicated on each side of the stage, with groups dancing from the center diagonally down to the right and left, or curving out down from a line along the back to return up the center in a double circle. At one point eight Bacchanals flanking three Harlequins in a long line across the stage pranced forward through a second line of eleven Pierrots in a series of three strongly marked moves. Diagonal movements were executed by triangularly shaped groups. Marchers formed rectangles. The impression of rigid structuring was so strong that Arthur Symons (the chronicler of the symbolist movement) described Craig as working

> in squares and straight lines, hardly ever in curves. He drapes the stage into a square with cloths; he divides those cloths by vertical lines, carrying the eye straight up to an immense height... he sets squares of pattern and structure on the stage; he forms his groups into irregular squares and sets them moving in straight lines which double on themselves like the two arms of a compass... He prefers gestures that have no curves in them: the arms held straight up or straight forwards or straight sideways. He likes the act of kneeling in which the body is bent at a sharp angle; he likes a sudden spring to the feet, with the arms

Craig's blocking for "Behold, oh mightiest of gods." The large concentric circles represent the positions of the candlesticks. The triangles show the starting points and movements for the "Torches," and the groupings of dots those for the Kings and Queens (st. R), the poor (st. L), and the Pierrots (upstage); the squares stand for the Harlequins. Courtesy of the Bibliothèque Nationale.

> held straight up. He links his groups by an arrangement of poles and rib-
> bons...each figure is held to the centre by a tightly stretched line like the spokes
> of a wheel. Even when, as in this case, the pattern forms into a circle, the circle
> is segmented by straight lines.[38]

A description like this brings out the essential unity of Craig's theatrical vision over his whole career. It could be applied, almost without change, to the final stage of his development that is represented by his notion of Scene. At the same time, although the effect from the eye level of the stalls may have been linear, this was an illusion. In the ground plans that Craig drew, curving and circular movements predominate. These diagrams are tangible indications of the link between *The Masque of Love* and Craig's later work. Completed more than two years after the production itself, the patterns still follow the sketches for movement in his promptbook in their general outline. However, they are even more schematic than the

An illustration from Moynet's *Trucs et Décors* (1890) showing the system of ballet notation used by Craig for *The Masque of Love*.

actual dances performed, as they were exercises modeled on a system of ballet notation Craig had discovered in Moynet's *Trucs et Décors*, exercises through which he was working out the principles of a more abstract, completely formalized theatrical art.

For Craig – again looking forward to Scene – this geometry contained symbolic, almost mystical meanings, and as he noted in 1907, "movement can be divided into two distinct parts, the movement of two and four which is the square, the movement of one and three which is the circle. There is ever that which is masculine in the square and ever that which is feminine in the circle." In this metaphysical perspective "perfect movement" came from combining these masculine and feminine elements, which would (supposedly) unite a stage performance with the universal rhythms of nature. The choreography of *The Masque of Love* is clearly an attempt in that direction. When Symons commented that "Mr. Craig aims at taking us beyond reality; he replaces the pattern of the thing itself by the pattern which the thing evokes in the mind, the symbol of the thing," Craig noted in the margin, "Right, right so!"[39]

4

PROBLEM DRAMA: TEXTS AND PERFORMERS

In his early operatic productions Craig achieved a remarkable unity of acting, music, scene, and costume that became his standard for subsequent work. To some extent the circumstances that allowed this were not repeatable. Arguably, it was his success under such special conditions that made him dissatisfied with his next productions. It may explain to some extent his insistence on founding a school instead of on giving practical examples of his theories on the stage, and perhaps even contributed to his eventual abandonment of the theater. The prime characteristic of Craig's style was neither the often-referred-to purple or blue of his apparently infinite skies, nor the reform of stage lighting that followed his removal of the footlights. Nor was it the imaginative use of masks, the color harmonies, or the move away from realistic settings toward a simplification that liberated the audience's imagination – though Craig, considered solely as a scene designer, may be credited with the invention of scenic impressionism. The vital quality was Craig's symbolic choreography of patterned movement and stylized gesture. As any careful examination of his notes and directions for *Dido, Acis*, and *The Masque of Love* show, it was this that preoccupied him and gave his work its characteristic style as well as much of its powerful imaginative effect.

Three of the factors that created these special conditions for his early operatic productions were inherent in the material. For Purcell, "as poetry is the harmony of words, so music is that of notes," and the continuous musical accompaniment, the frequent reprises and refrains, gave a clear structure around which Craig could orchestrate sweeping or repeated movements. At the same time the simplicity of the librettos and the absence of any stage directions (or even, in Handel's case, of any intention that the music should be accompanied by illustrative action) allowed Craig almost complete imaginative freedom. He could create ideal forms to express pure emotional states, corresponding to and reinforced by the music, with minimal constraints of story and characterization. (Indeed, the absence of characterization was one of the criticisms voiced against his first production, in which Aeneas had seemed so much an echo of Dido's visual environment that it was hardly credible he should ever contemplate abandoning her.) In addition, subliminal forms of communication – visual patterns, expressive gesture, sound rather than verbal sense – could legitimately be emphasized at the expense of the more intellectual qualities of dialogue. Quite apart from their share of belcanto arias or reprises that add little to the meaning, as Martin Shaw pointed out, "the libretto of both these pieces is such sorry stuff that it is amazing that Purcell could have written such inspired music to much of it. In *Dido & Aeneas* particularly one meets with such absurd phrases as 'Let Dido die!' and 'Thus, on the fateful banks of Nile/Weeps the deceitful crocodile.'"[1] In short, the operatic form not only gave Craig the scope to move toward a new concept of theatrical art, transforming the mimetic nature of conventional stage representation into something nearer to the abstract qualities of music and architecture, but also encouraged this development and provided a framework for it.

Equally significant was a fourth factor: his use of amateur actors. Because they had no previous stage experience at all, they had no preconceptions, no conventional techniques of characterization, and no established mannerisms and ways of moving that might conflict with Craig's vision. On one level, their lack of expertise (together, of course, with the fact that all had other commitments) meant an inordinate – and commercially impossible – length of time had to be devoted to rehearsing them, starting at the most basic level. As Craig later commented, "These ladies and gentlemen not being dancers (never having had a day's training) were made to walk – to run (now and again a few steps)" and were "given discreet exercises to execute." Preparing *Dido and Aeneas* took six months, all for only three performances. Four months went to rehearsing *The Masque of Love*, whereas it took barely two weeks to mount Craig's production of *Much Ado* with a professional cast. At the same time, if Craig were to create model productions for an entirely new kind of theatrical experience, it was essential for him to return to first principles, which this work with amateurs forced him to do. As he said, they became "excellent in their stepping out – and far better than ballet dancers would have been – for they and I together expressed something and what we said was no echo of what the theatres were at that time repeating over and over like parrots."

In addition, this lack of previous training meant that, however complex Craig's choreography, its components – the actual gestures, groupings, and dance steps – had to be *"simple every way"* (as Craig reminded himself on the opening page of his promptbook for *The Masque*). It also meant that the actors had to be willing to submit themselves totally to his directions, so that every movement and position corresponded to his vision. The same applied to the cast as singers. As Martin Shaw remarked, "There was hardly a trained voice among them," so they accepted being required "to sing their choruses crawling, leaping, swaying, running – any way that Craig fancied."[2] Most professionals would have considered that such demands would cramp their singing and would have refused to do such things. Even with the large numbers in his chorus, the long rehearsal times allowed him to elaborate separate roles for each individual within the overall structure, and the absence of any "stars" accustomed to center stage made it possible for him to go a long way toward his ideal of a unity in which scene, music, and actors harmonized. At the same time, because most of his original cast for *Dido* also acted in *Acis, The Masque of Love,* and *Bethlehem,* by the second or third production he possessed a chorus fairly expert in his requirements. They were capable of reaching a high performance standard – even if filling the major roles satisfactorily continued to be a problem – and it seems probable that working with the particular limitations of this group both contributed to making simplicity one of his guiding principles, and led him later to his ideal of the actor as "Übermarionette," totally under the control of the artist-director.

In many ways *Bethlehem* can be seen as an extension of the earlier productions. Again there was a strong musical element. Laurence Housman had commissioned Joseph Moorat to compose arrangements for the lyrics – a score to which Craig and Shaw, who looked on Moorat as "an amateur composer... nothing but a stumbling block" added passages of Palestrina, Bach, Mozart, and others.[3] A proscenium was

Suggestive simplicity and chiaroscuro in the opening scene of *Bethlehem*. Courtesy of the British Library.

constructed in the same shape as for *Dido*, and there were similar orchestral platforms on the stage to aid in creating effective groupings. There were the same indigo skies and simple but striking visual effects, such as twinkling stars (reportedly achieved by lights behind a pierced back cloth – as in the "Water God" – but in fact created by hanging chandelier crystals on black thread). These struck the only reviewer as inspiringly apt: appealing "to the imagination as the boundless sky of God" and "night as it had never been made before – night, simple as the

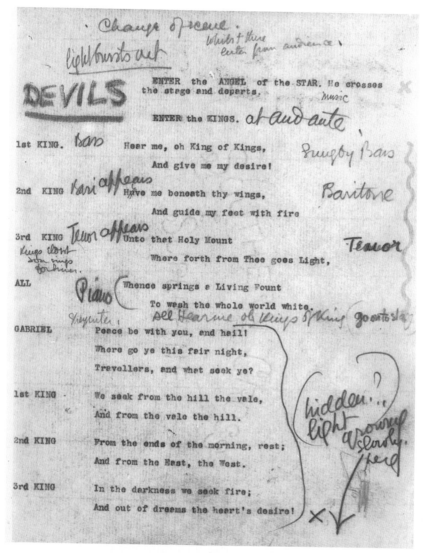

Craig's notes from the promptbook for *Bethlehem*, showing alternatives for lighting the procession of the kings and the positions on the side stage, the vocal orchestration, and the replacement of dialogue by visual effects. (The last four speeches on the page were cut.) Courtesy of the Bibliothèque Nationale.

Shepherds, sublime as the angel host and vast as the message delivered."[4] There was a similar use of suggestion instead of visual statement in the impression of the Shepherds' flocks conjured up out of sacks filled with wood shavings and tied off at the corners for ears. The cast was even larger – seventy-five performers are listed in the

program – but its movements and groupings were equally tightly orchestrated. At the opening the Shepherds were all seated in two basic
positions, bent forward, "hat over eyes. Chin in necktie. Both hands on
knees. Heels drawn back," or stretched out against a hurdle, "hat back of
head. Arms crossed. Legs right out." Then, as Gabriel enters stage left,

> *all move to end in fright.*
> WATCHER: Ay – oh!...
> *Out come heads. Silver bells. Music. From all the shepherds crescendo growl like dogs*
> *roused...*
> ANGELS: Glory be to God – *chorus*
>   In the highest – *semi chorus...*
> *The Angels disappear. Shepherds stretch their hands to heaven – 3 steps forwards. Pause.*
> *Hands up slowly. Swing down, dazzled. "Redeems man's fall": Shepherds stretch out*
> *arms after them as if wanting them back. Advance after them – 3 steps, one step.*[5]

The Masque of Love had concluded with a ceremonial procession.
Here, the entire second scene, "The Coming of the Kings," was transformed into a procession. A King in black headed a retinue in black and
purple, a gray-clad King had followers in purple and green, a white King
led a train in ragged gray. These last provided a grotesque contrast with
the pomp of the other groups and represented "the grave, the sad, the
poor, the bad" as "lepers, idiots, a murderer with red head and beard
who never kneels, a travelling marionette showman, a musician, beggars...," who moved onto the stage to form a half circle around Gabriel
on a central mound.[6] These costumes and props were far more elaborate
than any Craig (helped by his sister, Edy) had designed before: richly
embroidered, fur-edged, and vividly colored robes of medieval cut;
ornate crucifixes and shrines, fantastical lanthorns and offerings; extravagantly different crowns for each of the Kings. The richness of detail
here, to be extended in Craig's next production, *The Vikings*, anticipates
his later demand for a "rich theater," which he associated with the
earliest form of Christian drama, the celebration of the Mass: "In place of
vulgar materials such as canvas and wood, papier masche [sic] and paint,
I want more *precious* material made use of for a durable theatre: ebony
and ivory – silver and gold – copper and brass – silk and the rarest
dyes – marble and alabaster – and fine brains."[7] Indeed, all the props for
The Vikings were made by craftsmen in real wood and metal. But
although this richness was to become one of Craig's less realistic ideals,
it was in no sense whimsical or arbitrary here. It sprang naturally from
Bethlehem's thematic connection with church ceremonial, which Craig
emphasized in his direction – so much so that there were complaints
from Roman Catholic members of the cast who felt that the representation

was verging on blasphemy, and Housman had to intervene. "The Madonna seems to them to take too priestly an attitude in the words of the blessing, especially if the symbols of bread and wine are to be introduced," he contended.

The procession of Kings and their colorful retinues had originally been conceived as "The Pageant of Our Lady, which precedes the nativity play," and was therefore to some extent extraneous. In other respects the costumes repeated effects from previous productions. Housman had wanted Craig to make the Angels "as invisible and like blue night air as possible," and his "first notion was to dress them in sky colour and have only silver faces and silver hair showing out."[8] Craig rejected this as too conventionally pretty and reused the swirling white strips from *Acis*, which appeared even more ethereal in contrast to the Shepherds. These wore cloaks and slouch hats of rough hessian which, with the sacks representing sheep, created a textural unity surpassing the color echoes of scene and costume in *Dido*, while the neutral tones had the same suggestive effect that freed the imagination in *The Masque*.

This production also introduced technical innovations that show the way Craig's ideas were developing. At one point Craig intended to use a double proscenium, with an upper stage behind a row of arched windows above the ordinary acting area. However this, like his plan for reflooring the whole hall to bring the audience's eyes to the right level, could not be carried out because it was too expensive. Housman had envisaged a tangible Christ child, a baby whom Mary would raise from the cradle and hold out to the adoring multitudes, making the sign of the cross with him over their heads – though he was obviously aware of the danger of humanizing what his text had built into a transcendent symbol, and warned Craig that "it is God himself she carries in...all dazed and wondering – so no playing with his toes I beg of you!" In a brilliant stroke of imaginatively suggestive simplification Craig cut all physical representation of the Christ child. Instead he placed a powerful light in the cradle and reduced all other lighting to a minimum. When Mary raised the cloth covering the cradle, it was the radiance from within that illuminated the surrounding faces, and their gestures and expressions alone made the presence of divinity felt.

Still more significant as an advance were attempts to integrate the audience into the performance. Housman's epilogue (which Craig wanted to cut) tried to bring the meaning of the play home to the audience in a rather overly obvious way:

> Oh Maid and Holy Child, where have ye gone?...
> Gentles, O ye that here have watched our play,

Tell me, I pray you, did He pass *your* way?
Say, have ye Him safe, each one, in his breast.

Instead, Craig, anticipating the ideas of Artaud and the work of such directors as Barrault and Schechner, brought the action and environment of the play out into the auditorium to gain relevance on a more subliminal level. To some extent this effect was accidental. It was because the acoustics of the hall at the Imperial Institute were so poor that Craig initially thought of hanging cloth on the walls. But to solve this practical problem, he created the impression of a simple tent, in which the blue of the cloth draped around the auditorium merged with the skies in the stage picture, while the cloth's coarse weave echoed the texture of the Shepherds' costumes.

At one point too, he contemplated spreading "lots of sacks to sit and lie on" instead of ordinary seating for the public. This would have placed the audience in the same physical posture as the Shepherds they were watching. However, in order for them to see the stage from a prone position, it would have been necessary to raise the floor level. Housman, who was personally financing the production, refused to consider "re-flooring the hall from end to end" out of his own pocket. So this particular part of the experiment in environmental staging, which the LCC (London City Council) would never have sanctioned in any case, had to be abandoned. Instead Craig constructed a platform with steps that ran the whole length of one side of the auditorium and up onto the stage, so that the processions – first Angels, then Kings – entered from behind the audience and made their stately way through them. This manner of breaking down the separation of audience and action was felt by Craig to be so important that he insisted on retaining it, even though it drastically reduced the number of places in London where the performance could take place and led to continual complaints from Housman: "You don't seem prepared to cut down one plank of your platform to meet the exigencies of plan or space. No wonder then the Hall takes so long to find."

Yet Craig was careful to keep this sense of involvement on an imaginative rather than a purely physical level. The platform was lined with a gauze on its outer side to preserve an aura of mystery around the figures that passed in such close proximity to the spectators. To strengthen this further, Craig emphasized that the "orchestra must be hidden. Not a single one of the *works* must show... The whole thing must be free from effort and machines." To complete the illusion he equipped one group of Angels and one group in the Kings' procession with their own musical instruments: lutes, cymbals, and bells. He also had Housman write a short extra scene "outside Bethlehem," with lines spoken by a Pilgrim. There was a front curtain with a narrow opening in the center to represent the gates of the town, and just behind – borrowing directly from the medieval staging of passion plays – a miniature two-dimensional cut-out of domes and roofs backed by a second curtain of black with "spangles here and there." As one of the actors noted, "The purpose of the scene is an introduction... the 'Chorus' invites the audience to follow him... to enter by the lower gate and pass through to the cradle."[9] In addition, to preserve the unity of mood and to remove the performance further from the conventions of traditional theater, the program specifically requested the audience not to applaud but "to keep silent throughout and after the performance" – an injunction that later directors were to repeat for similar reasons, as the German director Piscator did in 1965 when staging Peter Weiss's documentary "passion play" about Auschwitz *The Investigation*.[10]

In some ways, working with straight dialogue in *Bethlehem* – for the first time since *No Trifling with Love* – and with a story that was part of his audience's immediate cultural background made Craig's style of representation more effective. Patternings of movement and grouping were given instantly recognizable symbolic resonance by their contexts. As the central figure in Housman's play was the Madonna, one aspect of "the eternal feminine," circles dominated. The semicircular formation of the kings around Gabriel, stepping forward crown in hand, prefigured the emotional climax in Bethlehem. There was no scenic representation of the manger. The figures that were massed in concentric lines on curving platforms, rising up around Mary and the cradle, themselves formed a living scenery. A floor cloth continued the circles of the steps round in front, and the movements emphasized the pattern. The Shepherds entered

> to the music, form in a semi-circle on top step and descend all to gather [round Mary]. End on knees...
>
> Shepherds give gifts – bread, milk, cheese, nuts, wine, a lamb and a song [a reprise of the opening Shepherd's song]. A circle and close so as to hide V. M. then let V. M. speak (when not seen)...
>
> "Angelus." All are kneeling up straight – then heads go down – they sink backwards, hands before clasped chest-high – sink to ground – fingers touching ground... Joseph stands several tiers up – and apart always from the mother and child.
>
> JOSEPH: Stand near in faith, behold...
> Here shepherds, is your fold.
> Mary raises the veil from the cradle, keeping it covered for audience but open for shepherds. All the shepherds make signs to cries of wonder [which substituted for several whole pages of speeches cut by Craig]: Some are dazzled by the light from the cradle. The light grows.

The floor plan and elevation for *Bethlehem*, showing the step construction of the side stage (with the gauze indicated along the inner edge) and the position of the light on one side wall. Courtesy of the Bibliothèque Nationale.

The production received little critical attention because it had to be given as a "private performance" – the Lord Chamberlain refused to license the representation of the Holy Family on a stage. Its only review stated that it was a striking "example of the symbolic element in Mr. Craig's staging" because the circles directly represented "the divine, the perfect figure."[11]

In other ways, however, working with a dramatic text was alien to the style Craig had developed. Craig later commented that he hadn't done Housman's play full justice because "after Purcell and Handel the words of his piece (good as I find them now) then did not move me." His autocratic handling of the material provoked continual conflict with both its author and the composer. His earliest notes to Martin Shaw had emphasized that this production "must in no way be an OPERA," and initially he even thought of separating the singing from the dramatic action by keeping all the singers offstage (extending into a general practice what he had been forced to do by having an infant Cupid for *The Masque of Love*).[12] Yet he clearly felt the lack of continuous musical accompaniment. In his previous work music had inspired and controlled every movement. Here his inability to find a satisfactory equivalent in Housman's rather static poetry was indicated by the amount of music eventually added. This super-imposed a kind of formal organization on the play that was qualitatively different from the structure of the text. The first scene, for instance, became an allegretto, followed by two solos (a Shepherd and Gabriel) and two choruses (Angels, then Shepherds); the final scene was transformed into a counterpoint of chorus and solo, framed by offstage choruses at the beginning and the end. Not surprisingly, Housman complained that Craig's "exquisite Allegros" were "swamping my Penserosos."

Certainly the thrust of Craig's production brought out some of Housman's intentions: for instance, "by symbolic action to quicken the imagination of the beholder so as to make the beauty of holiness more evident" or, instead of simply representing the events of Christmas, "to realize their appeal to the hearts of all to whom they convey a living truth." But Housman's almost daily letters during the rehearsal period are a record of desperate, and almost always vain, attempts to preserve the integrity of his text. Craig cut away at many of the speeches, which he found too long, and omitted several entirely. Housman in turn suggested that Craig see Poel's historically accurate Elizabethan Stage Society production of *Everyman* for an example of how "devoutly" an audience could be brought to accept even longer speeches.[13] Craig criticized "the pompous note" in the dialogue, which he set to music to disguise; Housman protested that what he was obliterating was the note of "restraint and wonder and adoration...quiet and natural." Craig called Housman's Madonna "a prig," omitted several of her speeches, and gave others to Joseph; Housman complained that "the rollicking note of 'Tis Christmas Morn' comes too close and abruptly on the offerings of the Kings and the music of the Adoremus... [because of Craig's] overcutting and bringing things, which were schemed to be separated, too closely together."

  In fact, almost the only element that Housman managed to reinstate was the epilogue. Craig himself epitomized his approach when he referred to the play as "a recipe." Housman's – or any playwright's – position was summed up in his plaintive question, "You do see, don't

Laurence Housman's graphic expression of his feelings about working with Craig. Courtesy of UCLA.

you, that there is this inner unwritten text to be thought about which is the author's own? And the recognition of it leads to unity, not diversity of effect."[14]

In a play of just over 600 lines (before cuts), yet with a performance time of almost two hours, the musical and visual elements of the production clearly overwhelmed the poetry. Hardly surprisingly, Housman regarded this as "a beautiful perversion" of his work, though according to one member of the audience his attitude in fact was one of "resigned complacency – he was sorry so much had to go, but – *que faire* – another effect and a beautiful one had been attained." In this case Craig's autocratic disregard for the text was due to a basic lack of sympathy for its theme. As he commented, "I am nearly suffocated by the halos and holiness of this play. The unbelievers and the no church people *ARE* the only true believers, and the sincere religionists there are only eye and voice lifters."[15] But Craig's treatment here of a dramatist's theme and words, subordinating all elements to a sometimes idiosyncratic vision, was to become characteristic of his approach. At his request Housman had cut all stage directions from the text of *Bethlehem* to leave Craig more freedom for visual invention. Three years later Craig was dispensing with the dialogue too – even that of such a verbal playwright as Bernard Shaw, who liked to say that the basis of his work was "the argument" rather than the plot or action – in order to bring out the symbolic essence of a drama.

In fact his description of the way he arrived at his designs for *Caesar and Cleopatra*, which Reinhardt commissioned from him in 1905, provides an excellent example of both his creative method and his belief that the stage could communicate most powerfully on the subliminal level of mood and metaphoric suggestion. First he cut

> the author's stage directions... And as I read the words, I wanted to omit these too... When I had got the words out of my head I looked to see what was left of the First Scene and I found this First Scene to be like a great rat trap in which figures were hurrying and scurrying to and fro like so many squeaking animals, one real figure standing out in a comic tragic mask – Ftatateeta.[16]

When working on *The Vikings at Helgeland*, too, he asked Ellen Terry to cut out all the stage directions before sending him the text. But on this occasion there was no author in the wings and the public had little knowledge of Ibsen's early plays. So Craig was almost as free to interpret the text here as in his earlier operatic productions, though at least one critic complained that his grouping of the actors seemed solely for aesthetic effect and bore little relation to the dramatic action, which therefore became meaningless. Instead he came into conflict with the

A reconstruction of the stage layout for the four scenes of *The Vikings*, showing the way the built-up pieces might be stacked for the "bare stage" of the last scene, even in the confined space of the Imperial Theater. *Top left*, act 1. The cliff construct. (The curtains, unlit, would be invisible.) *Bottom left*, act 2. The banquet tables. *Top*, act 3. Curtains forming the interior walls of a hall, with the brightly illuminated back cloth visible through the opening. *Bottom*, act 4. The cleared stage and the optical illusion of a mound. (Created by lighting effects alone.) Based on a diagram by Edward Craig.

acting profession. Working with amateurs had presented only one difficulty: lack of expertise. This was one of the reasons why he reduced the importance of the focal figure in *Bethlehem*, cutting her speeches or transferring them to others because "I see Madonnas every day and none knows how to speak... Have now tried 5 Marys, but none can do it."[17] Here his problem was very different. For the first time each member of his cast was a trained performer. Most of his principals were established theater figures. His protagonist, Ellen Terry, was a traditionalist, the leading lady of Irving's Lyceum melodramas, and she was used to playing on the romantic sentiments of her enthusiastic public, who expected her to be the dominant focus of each scene. All of the cast's experience ran directly counter to Craig's concepts, in particular to the visual unity and ensemble acting he demanded and to the ritualistic style of movement he had developed.

To some extent he was able to impose these concepts through the inanimate elements of the production – lighting, setting, costume – that were completely subject to his control. He thus reversed the relative significance of the actor and the visual background in a way that looks forward to his later, more theoretical development. In *Towards A New Theatre* Craig contrasts two scene designs: one that any actor could dominate, even if with difficulty, and another (with the actor dwarfed by towering geometric masses) that would need "a Hero" to dominate. *The Vikings* production was somewhere between the two.

In the first scene a gauze was stretched across the proscenium opening, blurring outlines so that shadowed parts of the figures shaded into the background, and distancing the actors from the audience. As one reviewer described the effect, 'Behind the thin gauze curtain they flashed out and faded away like the strange and gorgeous fish of some aquarium." The costumes were all tonal variations of a single neutral colour, gray, with each of the principals merged into a particular group – Ornulf and his six sons in gray picked out with white, Sigurd and his ten men in gray and green – and Ellen Terry's dresses echoed the emotional tone of each scene. Her robe of blue was covered in the first act by a surcoat of green and gray strips and a white bearskin that hung from her shoulders, in the third act (where Hjordis weaves a magic bowstring from her own golden hair) by an ash-colored cloak bordered with dull yellows, and in the final act of death and transfiguration by a surcoat of black strips patterned with a network of silver. These costume designs alone were enough to create a unified visual effect, but they also harmonized the figures with their backgrounds. In the first act this was misty black with a sinister purple light playing over dull gray rocks. In the third act, ash-gray curtains suggesting the walls of a hall flanked a huge window through which streamed the cold, pale yellow daylight of the far north. In the final act, the blackness of night surrounded a central snow-covered mound under which Ornulf has buried the dead bodies of his seven sons and on which Hjordis stands to shoot Sigurd.

As Craig later remarked,

> Obviously...it is a sensible thing to place a white costume against a dark background and a dark costume against a light background. It makes the figure stand out; but what should you do when you want the figure to be merged in the scene, if not lost in the scene? Macbeth roaming around his castle at night-time seems to be part of his habitation; and I remember that when Irving played the part he was dressed in a costume almost the same colour as the walls.[18]

But this appeal to tradition in the form of Irving is misleading. At the Lyceum this sort of effect was rare, and when it occurred the scene became an extension of a central figure's consciousness. Here, actors and setting together reflected an abstract mood symbolizing the underlying tone of that point on the emotional scale of the drama as a whole. Even in the banquet scene of the second act, where the assembled characters wore bright cloaks of multicolored squares and stripes, the same unity was achieved by setting them against a curtain striped in the same colors. This formed a huge half circle, dark gray at the edges and the center, with a spectrum of vermilion, purple, blue, green, yellow, and crimson on each quadrant. The curtain was made of gauze, and through it the flames of torchbearers could be seen dimly as they moved behind. This linked the actors still more fully with their background, as Craig also used torches in the hands of the servants around the tables to transfer the focus from one speaker to another. In fact the flickering light of the torches held over one or another actor's head drew the eye so effectively that several reviewers believed they illuminated the actors' faces, while those of the rest were shadowed by the general overhead lighting for the scene. (In reality, these torches – long rods with small metal cups at the top holding cotton wads soaked in methylated spirits – could never have acted as a light source.)

The actors were also grouped into a single unit, with no one dominating position, by the shape of the banquet tables around which they sat. These formed a raised circle with a downstage opening, which echoed the shape of the curtains behind and of a massive circular candelabrum suspended above. This concentric amphitheater form clearly repeated the configuration of the manger scene of *Bethlehem*, but there it had been designed to focus all attention on Mary and the crib. Here the central position was empty – and to ensure that no actor take it, Craig placed a fire there in a circular brazier.

A torchbearer in the banquet scene for *The Vikings*. Courtesy of the Bibliothèque Nationale.

Craig's design for the circular banquet table and candelabra for *The Vikings*. Courtesy of the Bibliothèque Nationale.

Even those props and details of costume that distinguished one character from another were designed to cloak the actor's individuality. The shields (as in *Dido*) were large and, with their sharply etched Celtic designs, tended to attract attention away from the persons who carried them. So did the torches, five feet high with the lower one-and-a-half feet weighted ribbons, and the necklace worn by Käre's wife, which was a pre-historic fantasy of teeth, beads, and wild birds' skulls. Similarly, each of the protagonists, including Hjordis as a warrior–maiden, wore a sharply different helmet crested with horns, seabirds' wings, or porcupine quills. With the top lighting, these threw deep shadows on the actors' faces, making it almost impossible to see any emotion that might have been expressed by their features. According to Edward Craig, this was an un-desired consequence of the attempt to recreate the lighting effects of *Dido* in a procenium three times as high with the primitive equipment of the time, which could not project an intensive enough light so far. There is some truth in this, but in fact the height of the proscenium opening at the Imperial Theater was not much more than half again as high as the one Craig had constructed in Hampstead (twenty-seven feet as opposed to sixteen), and Craig himself claimed that the darkness was deliberate – to correspond to "a gloomy subject."[19] A further reason for thinking it intentional is that Craig's initial designs for the helmets had shown them coming down over the actors' faces and in two cases almost completely covering them. Protests from those who wore them forced Craig to alter these, but the male protagonists were given thick beards instead, which served much the same purpose. The major complaint against the produc-tion was that in all acts except the third (titled "Light" by Craig in the pro-gram) the stage was too dark to discern the faces. Yet, as Max Beerbohm pointed out, this was a way of transforming individuals into symbols of passions or elemental forces: "In the case of a play demanding subtle interpretation this complaint would be justified. But *The Vikings* is a play in which nothing would be lost if all the characters wore masks. Indeed, it would be all the better, if the masks were sufficiently grotesque."[20]

As for the ritualistic movement, the steeply angled platforms constructed to represent the rocky cliffs of act 1, with uneven ledges sloping at an angle of thirty to forty degrees, were designed as obstacles to the actors' acquired habits of movement on the traditional flat stage. These platforms also made it impossible for the cast to take their customary turn-of-the-century positions in a line downstage along the footlights Craig had removed. Edward Craig recounts how, when Oscar Asche and Holman Clark, as Sigurd and Ornulf, refused to fight on this rocky incline because it made the fast footwork, slashing, and parrying of the standard Shakespearean duel impossible, Craig first explained that their combat should be like the slow swinging movements of the ancient samurai with their great curved swords, then discomfited them by demonstrating how effective this unorthodox manner of stage fighting could look. But Craig was not content with having them imitate what he could demonstrate. Once an actor himself, he was well aware that in performance it is all too easy to revert to old acting habits, whatever the director may have imposed in rehearsal. He provided them with five-foot doubleheaded axes, swords with "heavy weights" built into them, and spears "eight foot high and extra thick." With this massive armament, any clash was necessarily ponderous, all slashes sweeping, all movement stylized – and the same principles were carried over into other scenes. Where one of Ibsen's stage directions reads, "All rise; violent excitement," Craig substituted, "Up very slow. Move as one."[21]

This archetypal, even alien quality was reinforced by other elements of the production. As several reviewers remarked, the lighting, apart from obscuring the players' faces, was more natural (in illuminating the stage from above – by now the connection with Herkomer had been made). It also created the sense of "an age almost immeasurably remote from our own...unlike anything associated with ordinary life." The stage had been stripped of the conventional borders and "ceiling" battens or "flies," so that the eye reached out into the darkness of shadows or the apparent depths of sky in Craig's back cloth and gauze, instead of meeting any tangible enclosure, or was drawn upward by the vertical lines of curtain and falling light, which seemed to continue above the proscenium. This effect of limitless space gave the impression that the characters were "sunk in a gigantic shaft," and "utterly precludes any notion of realism" in the normal sense.

The result combined all the powers of suggestion achieved in the earlier Purcell Society productions so successfully that spectators literally filled in the blanks for themselves. For example, in the first act the darkness surrounding the sloping platform (the only actual scenery on stage) was described as "the sea, an inky pool, mist-hemmed, washing at its base." Paradoxically, this combination of natural and unnatural effects gave the impression of "a real unreality."[22] The light fell as in the everyday world – a contrast to the conventional stage illumination still as striking in 1903 as it had been in 1900 – yet its color was purely emotive: A sinister purple tone in act 1 created an "atmosphere of awe, of dread." Max Beerbohm, who saw the characters as inhuman monsters, described how "the strange, supernatural element" cast over every scene meant that "we shudder in unfathomable darkness, in immemorial frosts. The monsters here, as monsters, become positively real to us. We are positively afraid of them."[23]

The entry of Ornulf and his men on the rocky cliff in act 1 of *The Vikings*, with the dreamlike effect obtained by the gauze. Courtesy of UCLA.

These impressions were further reinforced by the music that Craig added to the play. As if for an opera, there was an overture, the themes from which were picked up in processional music for the entry to the banquet, in Ornulf's threnody for his dead sons, and in "storm music" for the last act – all composed by Martin Shaw in weird tones and phrases that were deliberately "unpleasing." Its discords and jarring notes were intended not only to illustrate the wild and barbaric tenth-century setting, but also to emphasize the elemental nature of the characters' emotions, emotions too powerful to find expression in tuneful or sophisticated orchestration. In addition, there was a prelude to each act, one being Wagner's thematically appropriate "Siegfried Idyll," which covered the scene changes and avoided the break in illusion that had presented such a problem in *Acis*.

Ibsen's treatment of the saga material was clearly an attempt to humanize legend, to give heroes individual faces. The characters have family ties, even occasional household concerns. However, any summary of the plot reveals a story of exaggerated violence and highly simplified motivations. The man who can slay a white bear that guards Hjordis is the man she will marry. Sigurd the Strong is in love with Hjordis, and kills the bear. But on learning of his weak half brother Gunnar's passion for Hjordis, in a spirit of Christ-like self-sacrifice, he pretends it was Gunnar who accomplished the heroic deed, and marries instead her sister Dagny. The play deals with the consequences of this act. Dagny, indignant at Hjordis, whose jealousy and discontent leads her to scorn Sigurd, reveals the truth about the bear's death. Too late, Hjordis acknowledges it is Sigurd she really loves and offers him the choice of fleeing or dying with her, so that they may live together or be united in Valhalla. When his Christian principles force him to reject both alternatives, she shoots him with her bow, then throws herself over the cliffs in despair, knowing that even in death they will be parted, he in heaven, she with her pagan gods. A subplot revolving about Käre the Peasant's feud with Gunnar leads to the death of Ornulf's seven sons and general ruin. Despite Craig's simplification of the dialogue to make it closer to colloquial speech – for instance, he substituted "you" for "thee," and "Father! She is your foster child!" for Dagny's "That meanest thou not; bethink thee, she is thy foster child!" – the whole emphasis of his production was on this *Götterdämmerung*.

In his view, the essence of Ibsen's drama was an allegorical combat, body versus soul, pagan versus Christian, rather than a human conflict, and he directed the actors to represent these qualities in their pure state: "Sigurd is little short of God. Gunnar is absolute man." Yet without involvement with the characters on a personal level, any sense of tragedy disappears. If they have no individual traits, then the ultimate loss of the lovers, parted even in death, arouses little pity. Similarly it would be hard to feel that it mattered whom Hjordis married if it doesn't affect her as an individual, but only has significance insofar as it follows or distorts patterns of fate. But Craig was clearly aiming at a more universal type of involvement on the level of archetypes. As in *Dido*, he substituted generalized, emotionally evocative scene titles for Ibsen's descriptions of specific places. "Helgeland, the seashore" and "A hall in Gunnar's house" became "Act I – The Rocks, Act II – The Feast, Act III – Light, Act IV – The Storm." To Beerbohm, "the extreme manner of fantasy" in the staging transformed "the barbarism of the North" into "something quite beyond the pale of human possibility," and another reviewer thought that Ellen Terry's positioning and gestures in the final confrontation with Sigurd made Hjordis seem "moulded on so heroic lines that she is rather a quality than a character." The masking effect of shadows, the integrating of the figures with a suggestively indistinct and mythical background, the ritualistic movement – all were designed to raise the action to this elemental but abstract plane. Every detail was intended to have symbolic resonance. One critic even described the music as "the accompanying wail of souls of those slain during the progress of the play."[24] The wood of Hjordis's bow was exaggeratedly curved into the form of a double serpent. Other weapons had twisted unsymmetrical blades or foot-long spikes that resembled gigantic fishhooks. Clubs looked like wooden dinosaur bones. Dagny's litter had a sinuous, almost organic shape, and doodled sketchnotes in Craig's promptbook clearly indicate that he was trying to create a symbolic association among the round Viking shields, the circular banqueting tables, and the truly universal image of the mythological snake eating its own tail – the Midgard serpent that encircled the world in Norse legend and the Eygptian emblem for eternity and immortality.

Perhaps no actors could be expected to play on this level, but unfortunately the conventional training of Craig's professional cast meant that their manner of characterization undermined his aims. What was needed was the style of acting that he suggested four years later in his essays entitled "On the Art of the Theatre," in which symbols drawn from the depths of the subconscious "without exhibiting the bare passions, would none the less tell us clearly about them." Instead of the "haphazard" or "incomplete" movements and gestures that imitate natural life, "a *noble artificiality*" would be created by selecting a single and clear-cut action for each moment of the play to give an effect "as solemn, as beautiful and as remote as ever" – words echoed by W. B. Yeats, who believed as strongly that the theater had to keep its distance from "a pushing world" if it were to become an art form.[25] What Craig actually got in *The Vikings* was basically naturalistic acting, which modulated into melodramatic posturing, and the customary display of the actors' personalities.

This was true even of Ellen Terry, although she was more in sympathy with his experimental approach than were the leading men. Her reading of the play as "a romantic drama" was rather different from Craig's mythic conception, and this carried through into her performance. When the play was first suggested she doubted that anyone would believe her in the part of Hjordis, and several critics remarked that she was "woefully miscast" – she of all people could hardly "be imagined as a fierce virago who kept chained bears in the house." However, many others applauded her performance, claiming that "rarely of late years has Miss Terry acted with more intensity" and reporting that "when Miss Terry fights death, not many dry eyes are to be found in the house."[26] Such conflicting opinions suggest that she played the role in a traditional way that delighted her faithful public from the Lyceum days, but one that was incompatible with the dramatic context that Craig had created. Indeed, during rehearsals he had commented that "the difficulties are many and formidable – they arise one and all, from stage traditions"; and after the production had folded (by the third week the box office no

Melodramatic acting in act 4 of *The Vikings*. (Note that the lighting created an impression of a mound so effectively that the artist has included it as a physical structure.) Courtesy of UCLA.

longer covered the expenses) he complained:

> I feel convinced that no *Vikings* can be done unless each character [*sic*: actor] will listen to the stage manager and hear what character he is to play. What the hell is the use of Act I – what's all the pother about on the rocks, the Rock and the Giants, the swords ten inches thick and blood flowing, wrestling of limb and

brain, if Hjordis is not the exact opposite of all this exterior might, what is the
storm of the play but the counterpart of the storm inside her heart, and what has
exterior storminess to do with her – absolutely NOTHING. "To side with the
wild sisters" and all that is the cry of her soul, not the instinct of her physique.
Soul is to her what physique is to everyone else in the play.[27]

Already here one can see the seed of Craig's ideal: a spiritual
theater, the expression of the soul as opposed to "the Art of the body,"
which led him to call for an Übermarionette in place of the actor. His
early productions can be seen not only as the source of his theories, but
also as practical demonstrations, at least in embryo, of that ideal Art of
the Theatre, which tends to be dismissed as unrealistic because formulating a philosophy for it took up so much of the rest of Craig's career that
he effectively withdrew from the stage. At the same time the conflicts
generated by *Bethlehem* and *The Vikings* help to explain his attempt "to
create works of art in the theatre without the use of the written play,
without the use of actors." Craig continued that sentence by reaffirming
"the necessity of daily work under the conditions which are today offered
us." But, in fact, after the production of *Much Ado About Nothing*, which
followed directly on *The Vikings*, he was responsible for directing only
two more plays – and even in his last production, *The Crown Pretenders*
(staged in Copenhagen in 1926), he found that the training of a completely
different generation of actors was just as inappropriate to his concepts of
staging. As more than one reviewer remarked, "The actors were playing
in the old realistic manner, and the better they played the more they
denied their relation to the set...In one scene, where the actors, almost
by chance, stylized their playing to meet the terms of the production, the
effect was magical."[28]

Whatever its reception by the general public, *The Vikings* was
recognized as the first production "to show that it is possible for a play
to be produced which may be judged by the same standard and enjoyed
to the same degree as poetry, painting and music." Yet this production
also marks the beginning of Craig's retreat from the theater. The contrast
between what he aimed at and what the actors would allow him to
achieve is already clear. He had his name listed no less than five times
on the program to emphasize "that a production, to be a real one, is the
work of one man and a company of technicians." But even late in the
rehearsals he was complaining that "all seems to me as unlike...what I
have always strived for in [my] work as can be," and admitted privately
to feeling "that I am trying to fill the position of artistic director on
sufferance . . . I do not feel responsible."[29]

Bethlehem and *The Vikings* had made Craig begin to see that
authors and the acting profession were obstacles in his march toward a

new theater, and *Much Ado* brought two other conditioning factors home to him in a particularly harsh and unmistakable way: the limitations imposed on creativity by commercial pressures and by the demands of an audience with preconceived ideas. Even in his early work these influences had been present. *Acis* had closed after a single week, though the run was intended to last for two weeks or longer, because, in Craig's words, "the Public could not be brought to see it." *Dido* had barely covered expenses, not even providing any form of salary for all the hours that Craig and Martin Shaw put into it. It did not come close to producing the capital for future productions even though it had received a generous subsidy in the sense that the amateur cast devoted their time free. If Craig had had to pay the seven principals and thirty-eight chorus members (even at the rate of £2 a week for the principals, which was the minimum he had received for major roles in 1896, and £1 a week for each of the chorus), and even if the rehearsal time could have been cut to a single month, it would have required a run of six-and-a-half weeks just to cover costs. In comparison, the 1896 Lyceum production of *Richard III*, with Irving in the title role and Craig as Edward IV, drew audiences for only four weeks and still made a profit.[30] There were no such hidden subsidies for *The Vikings*, and to keep the company solvent Craig was forced to rehearse *Much Ado* in a bare two weeks, limiting his designs to two very simple sets and using stock costumes.

This made it impossible for Craig to organize groupings in more than the broadest outline. In addition, Ellen Terry insisted on "the *old* play, and the *old* me in it" because it "would not be acceptable to the Public in a *different style* to the one they know." As Martin Shaw described it, the actors insisted on "scenery in the manner of Alma Tadema, costumes copied from Planché, conventional movements and positions – in short nothing which had not been done before." This was a fairly accurate picture of what was staged, apart from the church scene, where Craig was able to use the suggestive simplicity of draped curtains and shafts of colored light for a stained-glass effect. Here it seems likely that he saw the opportunity to give a clear definition of his stylistic reform by creating a contrast to the well-known and much-praised design for Ellen Terry's first performance in the role of Beatrice – an elaborate historical reconstruction, and one in which Godwin had a hand. Elsewhere the settings were extremely plain. A severe gray classical colonnade did duty for all, with a plain blue sky cloth behind for the garden and gray curtains drawn between the columns for indoor scenes. The only decorative props were the large circular floral wreaths for the masquerade, which Craig had used for the Harlequins of *The Masque of Love*. Even more significantly, his promptbook contains almost no directions to

Craig's design for the church scene of *Much Ado About Nothing* indicating the illusionistic simplicity of the setting. Courtesy of the Bibliothèque Nationale.

the actors apart from diagrams of the movements for two dances, indicating that the interpretation was left largely to the performers.

Craig's major contribution as a director seems to have been the by now characteristic insertion of almost continuous musical accompaniment – an overture, a minuet, two madrigals, a fanfare, a jig, and a Morris dance in the first two scenes of act 1, "music continually" in the third scene, and vocal pieces to cover scene changes. Two pieces for the church scene were taken straight from *Bethlehem*, and the inclusion of traditional folk songs and country dances relates directly to Craig's fascination with the masque form. This seemed to offer one possible way of unifying every aspect of a production under a single hand by making it possible for the director himself to create the "play" that he would then design and produce. But here, without sufficient time to drill the actors in the type of movement he required, the music alone was insufficient to control pacing and gesture. He may have wanted all (except Beatrice and Benedick) to be "stiff and restrained," as one prompt note suggests, but when *Much Ado* went on tour the cast obviously began to discard any formalization in favor of the stock characterizations and conventional movements that had proved successful in the past and that their audiences expected.

All long-running productions tend to develop new emphases by a sort of osmosis, sometimes changing focus completely through the interplay with the audience. Yet to Craig it was "Hell – I know of nothing more tormenting." What caused him anguish was being thought responsible for something he considered a travesty of his intentions. This attitude was to be reinforced by his experiences with Otto Brahm and Reinhardt, and led him to demand nothing less than his own theater. But there was also a sense in which financial success and applause were seen as suspect in themselves, which eventually caused Craig to reject any of the more usual yardsticks of theatrical success and even to cultivate "failure" as a guarantee of aesthetic integrity:

> Each time I see [*Much Ado*] a viler gaiety is added – speech is noisier and action floppier – thought infrequent, and taste unknown...You would get the full fervour of my feeling if you could hear Bach's Passion interpreted by the Gaiety Chorus under Raymondiana – And add to this, "contentment" on all the faces – contentment shrieking in their purses – They come off the stage and seriously take as the final verdict, the applause of a kind audience.[31]

From this point on, Craig began to think not merely of reforming the theater, but of a total revolution, one which would create an entirely new art form out of materials that owed nothing to the commercial theater. His conviction is well conveyed by the quotation he entered on the flyleaf of his promptbook for *Much Ado*: "Against stupidity the gods themselves contend in vain."

5

A PLAY OF IDEAS: PRINCIPLES, THEORY, AND AN ÜBERMARIONETTE

One criticism leveled at Craig is that his ideas were "a maze of suggestions...a mass of evasions and contradictions," a maze for which he was incapable of providing practical illustrations. Consequently, it is argued, he produced so few designs that he was forced to reprint the same ones in publication after publication.[1] In fact, repetition in his work is even more extensive than such critics have perhaps realized, though it exists for clearly different reasons than those that have been suggested. The same visual ideas can be traced from sketchbook to sketchbook, and there are constant echoes among designs for very different plays. But this is the result of a deliberate working method, rather than any inadequacy, and it indicates that Craig's theories were based on a selected number of key principles. As such, this repetition demonstrates the small value he placed on the uniqueness of a play's text. But as most of these principles derive directly from his productions between 1899 and 1903, and from the Lyceum theater, what it really brings out is his commitment to the practicable, and suggests as well that his "new theater" was not so much diametrically opposed to the old as a logical development from it.

For instance, Craig particularly admired one of Irving's scenes, the castle interior for the 1888 Lyceum *Macbeth* (see illustration on p. 21). Elements of that set reappear in Craig's designs throughout his career. A steeply rising staircase, broadened to fill the whole stage space, returned in "The Steps" (1906) and was duplicated as one of the components in the movable blocks of the Cranach *Hamlet* (1912–26). A column with steps curving up behind it recurred, progressively broadened and simplified, in a sketchbook for 1902, in a design for Lady Macbeth's sleepwalking scene in 1906, and in act 2 of the Moscow *Hamlet*, though there – as at the Lyceum – it was placed to one side of the stage instead of filling the entire center. The 1906 design was also published in *Towards a New Theatre* as well as in *Index to the Story of my Days*, and reused for one scene of Tyler's *Macbeth* in 1928. Another Lyceum scene, a rugged Scottish shoreline from *Ravenswood* in 1890, was also reflected in many different forms over the years. This image provided the inspiration for the rock structure of *The Vikings*, variations on which were used in *Macbeth* designs for both Beerbohm Tree and Tyler and in one sketch for *The Crown Pretenders*. In its best-known form, Craig's 1908 "Design for a stage scene," it showed Greek warriors fighting at the foot of a steeply raked cliff.[2] In each case the illusionistic, pictorial original was transformed into simple and massive shapes, neutral in tone and with a strong tendency toward abstraction. In each case, too, three-dimensional, architectural environments were substituted for two-dimensional scenes painted on back cloths. As Craig later said, "I avoided putting any place in my picture which could *not* be travelled into actually by the actors."[3]

In the same way, not only lighting techniques and "sky" effects, but even specific visual elements from *Acis* and *The Masque of Love* reappeared consistently. Craig used the prison grille again in his design for the first scene of *Caesar and Cleopatra* for Reinhardt, and the "tent" for one of the interior scenes of *The Pretenders*. He also considered reusing the enclosed circular table from *The Vikings* for the banquet in that production, and finally settled on a variation in which the main figures were seated facing outward on the external rim with the minor characters inside the circle. The flickering light of torches behind gauze, used in *The Masque* and *The Vikings*, was repeated here too and elaborated with three superimposed gauze screens:

> To show going away of torches... A perspective in movement. The men to stand still with torches. At X_1 cover with gauze 1: lower [torches] and incline to X_2: cover with 2nd gauze frame: sink and incline torches to X_3: cover with gauze 3, then slowly cover torches with open hands and close fists over them.

The original design of a broad enclosed space for the Shepherds in *Bethlehem*, with a low roof and arched windows above, recurred in the conspirator's scene of *Venice Preserved*. There it became a low arcade of columns (taken from Serlio's drawing of a "pilastre d'ordre toscan" that Craig had used for the colonnade background in *Much Ado*) with lintels just over the heads of the figures and with the high walls of a piazza in the background forming a second scene above. It was also echoed in a 1904 design for *The Merchant of Venice*, and formed the basis for a generalized "scheme of a scene the height of a full sized person. Very long and low – as in low bas-reliefs on tombs" with pillars at wide intervals supporting the "roof."[4] This led directly to some of the designs for the Cranach *Hamlet*. Even details of props and costumes were reused. The dresses of floating strips of tape in *Acis* reappeared on Hjordis and Dagny (see illustrations on pp. 102–3). An elaborate handheld censer from *Bethlehem* became a focal point in the setting for the church scene of *Much Ado*, and was suggested – together with a prince's costume from

Variations on *Acis and Galatea* and *The Vikings* in Craig's settings for the 1926 production of *The Pretenders*. Courtesy of Peter Fozzard.

the *Bethlehem* procession – for the Prince of Morocco's attendant in his *Merchant of Venice* designs for Ellen Terry (1908).

In fact, what Craig was working toward was a form of universalization: a multipurpose scene, which corresponded to his increasingly

Similarities in costume design: a dancer from *Acis and Galatea*. Courtesy of the Bibliothèque Nationale.

abstract concept of drama and which could be used for a variety of plays. One design – a high, narrow central archway in receding perspective, opening onto a platform with a cryptlike area beneath flanked on each side by stairways leading down to the lower stage – was titled both "Macbeth" and "Hamlet," and has strong similarities to his later models

Similarities in costume design: Dagny in *The Vikings*. Courtesy of the Bibliothèque Nationale.

for Bach's *St. Matthew Passion*. Patterns of movement were treated in the same way as well. A study of lines of soldiers marching down a ramp carrying spears and watched by a group looking out of an immense window, originally prepared for act 1 of *Much Ado*, became (with the window deleted and the soldiers given more prominence) "Henry V. Enter the Army." Finally Craig listed it, divorced from any specific play or situation, as a generalized "Design for a Movement."

A third source for Craig's key images was art and architecture.
He created his own iconography in scrapbooks of photographs and
reproductions clipped from art publications: Egyptian murals, Renaissance woodcuts, medieval palace facades, Japanese cherry blossoms.
Some provided inspiration for projects that were realized only on paper – for example, two sky-and seascapes by Ruskin, which Craig labeled
Peer Gynt. Others were the sources for some of Craig's major concepts.
Beneath a picture of the stairs leading down from the Vatican, Craig
noted, "steps, a fine theme" – one that was later realized as the studies
in mood and movement that he titled *The Steps*. Under a Gustav Doré
illustration of Dante and Vergil at the foot of a cliff he wrote, "What the
theatre misses!" – and indeed, he used it as the basis for a scene in
Hamlet. But even more significantly, the simplified and unified shape of
the background, the dramatically slanting light, the contrast in scale
between the towering masses and the tiny figures in this illustration,
were all to become dominant elements in the Scene that formed Craig's
final vision of a completely new art of the theater.

Still others of these pictures – such as Fra Angelico's *Dance of the
Angels* – formed the basis for patterns of movement in his productions,
or provided models for specific types of scene. For instance, a sketch of
the gateway to Agamemnon's tomb in Mykenae, pasted into an 1899
scrapbook, lies behind one of Craig's favorite scenic shapes: the great
square opening in a blank wall that rises the full height of the stage,
which was the main feature in act 3 of *The Vikings*, in one scene for *Venice
Preserved*, and in another for *Caesar and Cleopatra*, as well as in the settings
of *Electra* and *Rosmersholm* designed for Eleonora Duse. Similarly, childhood memories of "the Tall beds seen so often at Hampton Court," which
had provided the shape of Dido's canopied throne with its four slender
pillars, were repeated in exaggeratedly high four-poster beds for *Sword
or Song* (1903) and in Tyler's *Macbeth* a quarter of a century later. They
even provided the initial inspiration for Craig's ideal of renewing the
theater and influenced his demand for the use of "precious" materials:

> a room with a lofty bed haunts me … damask, silver, pale blue and crystal … the
> very first vision which led to an idea later on. The impossible, grand, motionless
> beds … [led to the ideal] of remaking the stage – to bring back its *apparent
> impossibility*. The drama was grand and perfect; great actors would come and go;
> but the stage itself was not fit to receive either – not like those beds. My idea was
> to make it fit for great plays and great acting.[5]

That 1928 New York version of *Macbeth*, Craig's last attempt to
compromise with the conventional theater, did considerable damage to
his reputation precisely because of this repetition, which appeared there

Multipurpose setting (for *Hamlet/Macbeth*) containing the basic elements that recur in Craig's designs – flights of steps, tiered stage levels, and the use of perspective to elongate such architectural features as archways. Courtesy of the Bibliothèque Nationale.

almost as self-parody. Craig had no hand in the way his ideas were to be realized on stage. He was convinced that Tyler did not understand them, and had little respect for the American theater. He had been disappointed in his hopes (based on unrealistic visions of American wealth) of financial support from the United States, and by the failure of Bel Geddes's plans for an international theater festival associated with the Chicago World Fair (which seemed to him to have been stolen from one of his own plans, and in which he overestimated the significance of his own proposed contribution). Financial necessity alone brought him to accept Tyler's commission, and he signed all the designs "C. P. B." for "Craig pot-boiler."

In 1908 he had used *Macbeth* to demonstrate how his principles of unity, proportion, and simplicity could bring out the emotional essence of a play, creating an inner, spiritual drama:

> How does it look, first of all to our mind's eye?
>
> I see a lofty and steep rock, and I see the moist cloud which envelops the head of this rock. That is to say, a place for fierce and warlike men to inhabit, a place for phantoms to nest in. Ultimately this moisture will destroy the rock; ultimately these spirits will destroy the men... Set them down on your paper; *the lines and their direction*, never mind the [reality of a] cliff...and remember that on a sheet of paper which is but two inches square, you can make a line which seems to tower miles in the air, and you can do the same on your stage for it is all a matter of proportion and nothing to do with actuality.
>
> What are the colours that Shakespeare has indicated for us? Do not first look at nature, but look in the play of the poet. Two; one for the rock, the man; one for the mist, the spirit... [use] only these two colours through your whole progress of designing your scene and your costumes, yet forget not that each colour contains many variations.[6]

But here, twenty years later, the effect was a potpourri of different elements borrowed from almost all of his previous productions. The Witches were given the grotesque bird masks and "root growth" on their legs (and Macbeth a "hedge-hog wig" for the banquet scene) from their sisters in *Dido*. The helmets and costumes came from *The Vikings*. The distorted expressionistic crosses, behind which the Witches danced beneath gaunt triangular gallows, were reminiscent of designs for Hofmannsthal's *White Fan*, which Craig had done in 1905. The pointed arch of the bridge with a stylized landscape of hills visible in the background beneath had originated as a design for *On Baile's Strand* in 1914 and was repeated from his production of *The Pretenders* two years earlier, as were the jagged windswept trees used for the heath scene. Craig's idea of lighting Macbeth's banquet with torches behind "a transparency which is kept in motion" was clearly drawn from his staging of previous banqueting scenes, though here there was one histrionic addition: Banquo's ghost appeared through the flames of the torches. When Macbeth bade his guests, "You know your own degrees; sit down," Craig's notes indicate an all-too-literal transcription of his ideas of symbolic geometry, with the "degrees" represented by four broad steps leading down from the rostrum on which Macbeth's table was placed. All these derivative elements were little more than unassimilated clichés, which Tyler's production did nothing to disguise.

Even more damaging – because it seemed to confirm the most common misinterpretation of Craig's work – was the emphasis on purely visual effects that were out of context and that detracted from the thrust of the play's action. To introduce a "Tall Bed," for example, Craig inserted a completely unnecessary scene before the sleepwalking sequence. Lady Macbeth is discovered in a canopied bed, "her body thrown about as though sleeping in disorder." Behind her the three witches appear as elongated blue fingers, moving silently. An anachronistic clock strikes midnight, "the far off sound of bagpipes is heard (marking time) and the scene fades – a pause. Curtains lowered – curtains raised..." Undramatic and statically pictorial, this invention demonstrates clearly (if unintentionally) that Craig's approach could neither be reduced to a series of staging techniques nor be applied independently of his vision of a radically different kind of theater. They were of no use to a director – even, in this case, to Craig himself – who interpreted a play from the conventional focus of plot, character, or even mood, instead of subordinating every element to a unifying symbolic idea. For once Craig's interpretation here was perfunctory. His note accompanying a sketch of Macbeth's severed head, a grotesque mask on the point of a spear, sums it up: "the end of the melodrama."[7]

Craig's past experience had already sufficiently demonstrated the need for a completely unified concept of theater. If his two early productions with Ellen Terry had convinced him that working with conventionally trained actors was impossible, his subsequent attempts to collaborate with other directors were – with the questionable exceptions of Stanislavski and Poulsen – disastrous. This became clear almost at the start of his career, as soon as his growing reputation as a director brought him invitations to work outside his own company. In 1904 Otto Brahm asked him to work on Hofmannsthal's version of *Venice Preserved* for the Lessing Theater in Berlin. Quite apart from language difficulties (which led Craig to believe that he was being employed as a director rather than simply as a designer, caused an almost total failure of communication between Brahm and himself, and meant that he was unable even to read the German adaptation he was supposedly interpreting), Brahm turned out to be completely unsympathetic to Craig's principles. Craig had been hired on reputation, sight unseen as it were. Brahm's reaction to Craig's designs revealed him to be precisely the sort of realist Craig's whole approach was designed to oppose. When Craig presented a starkly plain scene that had high unbroken curtains for walls and a fullheight portico on one side as the only opening, and that was bare of furnishings apart from two plain, square-shaped benches, Brahm demanded elaborate detail and doors with locks and handles. In response Craig complained that Brahm "does not know the first principles of the art [of the theater] – when lights have to imitate the hour of 5 p.m. and get down to 5.45 in an autumn evening, Brahm can absolutely wipe Tree off the face of the clock – when the Stranger enters in *The Lady from the Sea*, you can bet it is not a spirit entering but...an ordinary man – you can even tell what class ticket he has in his pocket." According to Craig, Brahm rejected as "impossible" anything he suggested. In reaction Craig made totally unrealistic demands: that the stage should be gutted (as the Imperial Theater had been for *The Vikings*) to create an effect of "endless sky"; that the Asphaleia System of hydraulic lifts to raise or tilt any section of the stage floor be installed; that the auditorium be rebuilt on the model of Bayreuth (as he had wanted for *Bethlehem*), with all the seats at the same level on an inclined floor. Ultimately only three of Craig's designs were used for the play's six different scenes, and almost no reviews gave much attention to the décor. Though one reviewer praised his "sombre night scene with its dead quietness" as "more powerful than anything else that I ever saw on a European stage," the consensus was that the general level of performance fell below the Lessing Theater's usual standard. Typical comments on the design were that they "did not suit the ensemble's style" and (unsurprisingly, as half the scenes were Craig's, half Brahm's resident designer's) that there was no unity of the acting style and the setting or of one scene and another.[8]

After this, Craig insisted on total control over any production he was involved in, and his refusal to compromise meant, in fact, withdrawing from the theater. Max Reinhardt's actors were perhaps the only troupe in Europe that offered the means of realizing his theatrical vision – and indeed had some of the qualities of his ideal Übermarionette – because Reinhardt had trained them to take direction "almost as if they were puppets, controlling every movement and gesture, the slightest change in intonation" and subordinating their personalities "to his own conception of the play." But it was precisely this degree of training that made it impossible for Reinhardt to transfer control to anyone else. So when Reinhardt asked him to design *Caesar and Cleopatra* and *The Tempest* in 1905, and *King Lear* and *The Oresteia* in 1908,

Craig's precondition that he alone "be master of the stage" was effectively a refusal. Similarly, when Jacques Rouché, the director of the Théâtre des Arts in Paris, invited Craig to produce any play he liked after seeing the Moscow *Hamlet,* Craig rejected the opportunity because "it's not a 'production' I want, but *a theatre.*"[9]

To some extent this attitude was justified. At Beerbohm Tree's request Craig designed a production of *Macbeth* despite his feeling that "even genius if it came there [Her Majesty's Theater] would never get on a step without a free hand" – and indeed Tree's traditionalist stage painter persuaded him that Craig's models and designs were impractical, so they were discarded and the models broken up. After Brahm (not unreasonably) refused to rebuild the Lessing Theater to accommodate Craig's ideas, Craig had responded "In short, change the art for the machine. Not while I'm alive!" This became his prime concern. When Scandiani offered him La Scala in Milan, he refused because he feared his ideas would become subordinated to the stage machinery, at that time (1921) the most advanced in Europe, though once he was finally persuaded to work with such machinery in *The Crown Pretenders* he was delighted by the technical possibilities. In Craig's view no compromise with the conventional theater was possible. Even though the Poulsens offered him "a free hand in every respect" with *The Pretenders,* he felt that "for all that I was only *assisting* in their production, not myself producing the piece." His first response to their invitation was, "Remember it is almost fifteen years since I did any work inside a theatre. The experience [with *Hamlet*] in Moscow decided me to wait until I should possess my own theatre."[10]

Already, in 1905, Craig believed he might achieve this. As he reported overconfidently to Martin Shaw, "Expect to receive wonderful news within 3 months. I may then have my own theatre and my own company. NOT ACTORS but a CREATURE of my own invention."[11] But when such hopes consistently failed to materialize, he was forced to find alternate means of defining his "Theatre of Tomorrow" – which rapidly became a new concept of drama itself – and as a result he published the first dialogue of "The Art of the Theatre." This dialogue, written in the space of a single week, recapitulated the principles that had developed out of his early productions, and pointed to the main areas that were to form his theory. There were three major points in his argument: The theater is a branch of art both equivalent to, and as unique in expression as poetry, music, and architecture. As such, it should have the same standards of aesthetic unity as the other arts. This could be achieved only if it were the work of one man; and a school should be founded to explore the principles of this art. As the London *Times* review of this booklet acknowledged, its "fundamental position" was "unassailable." But the details have led to considerable misunderstanding.

One of the most frequently quoted passages of this dialogue is usually taken as evidence that Craig was calling for the kind of synaesthesia associated with Wagner's *Gesamtkünstwerk*: "The Art of the Theatre is neither acting nor the play, it is not scene nor dance, but it consists of all the elements of which these things are composed... Action, words, line, colour, rhythm." Yet in his notes Craig specifically denied that combining the different arts of music, painting, and poetry, would in itself produce the kind of drama he wanted. In fact, the art that Craig was advocating is "total theater" in a rather different sense: one that singles out the different elements of drama in order to dispense with anything not specifically "theatrical." Craig draws a distinction between the "dramatic poet" and a "dramatist" who works "either in poetry or prose, but always in action: in poetic action which is dance, or in prose action which is gesture," and then dispenses with the playwright. The term "voice" replaces "words," and a "drama of silence," in which the actors express thought and emotion in movement alone, replaces the conventional "drama of speech."[12]

Revolutionary as this may have seemed, Craig's position is really an extension of Charles Lamb's well-known argument that plays such as *King Lear* should not be staged because no physical representation could ever approach their poetic vision. The implication in Lamb's argument is that the stage represents an inferior and imperfect art. For Craig, theater is the equal of literature, but a very different form of art that can reach its full potential only if it is no longer subordinated to the written word. The richer the verbal imagery of a play, and the more expressive its dialogue, the further the stage is forced into a simply illustrative function and the less it fulfills its true nature. Shakespeare and Shaw are useless to the theater, Craig claimed, because as literature their plays are complete in themselves. A third-rate script might serve as the basis for creating something close to a solely theatrical performance, like Irving's production of *The Bells*. But why incorporate a mediocre element, which can only diminish the imaginative significance of the whole? Do without the sort of dialogue created by a writer thinking in literary terms – which also means dispensing with the conventional characterization and plot contained in such dialogue – and theater might then become a "pure art" on its own terms.

To some extent, this conclusion can be traced back to the conflict between Craig and Housman. But it is also perhaps partly due to Craig's own lack of formal education: "I pick up a volume by Nietzsche. On one page alone are so many words the meaning of which I do not understand that the words are useless for me." However, this is extended into a general statement that anticipates the belief of an absurdist like Ionesco that language is a barrier to true communication, and reflects Craig's aim of reaching the broadest possible public on the most fundamental level. "Words are a bad means of communicating ideas – especially transcendent ideas – ideas which fly ... words should not be wasted – nor used except on rare occasions – for rare things are generally simple." In place of subtle psychological thought and complex poetic language, philosophy, sermons, and epigrams, the theater should present "visions" directly through "movement which is the very symbol of life."[13]

Even in the case of plays that he admired and considered suitable for his ideal theater, like those of W. B. Yeats, Craig criticized the use of words instead of symbolic gesture or movement to express emotional states. For example, in his copy of *On Baile's Strand*, where a woman declares, "No crying out, for there'll be need of cries / And knocking at the breast when it's all finished," Craig noted, "No need for this. She should suggest by anticipation which is stronger." Where the Fool describes "a great wave going to break," he crossed the lines out and substituted mime – "He makes a movement like rising wave: hands, arms and toes" – illustrated with a sketched figure rising sinuously to curl forward with his arms stretching down over his bent head. To illustrate the simplicity and suggestiveness that he looked for in dramatic action, Craig clipped from a history book an account of how Lady Holland announced the death of Fox to his friends simply by walking through the room with her apron thrown over her head. On it he noted, "Without words. No facial expression therefore no *personal* feeling. Action."[14]

If action was the prime element in Craig's theater, dance as "the poetry of movement" – one of his favorite phrases – was action's highest form. But he was not referring to traditional ballet, which he despised as artificial, elitist, and unnatural. "Dancing is not flying – we realize that man is not a bird. Dancing belongs very certainly to the good earth. Yet ... most trainers teach the pupils to hop, to float, to do everything to get into the air. I would teach them exactly the reverse." Equally, such modern forms as Dalcroze or Fokine's ballets for Diaghilev were rejected, despite approval of their technique and unified ensemble work, because gymnastics without what Craig considered a spiritual center seemed exotic or epileptic. For Craig, perfect movement created a mystical union with the universal rhythms of nature in such a way as to directly express the soul. By contrast, "the Russian Ballet [e.g., *Firebird* or *Scheherazade*] is essentially the Art which is created by the Body. Its perfection is physical. Its appeal is to our senses, not through them."[15]

Simplicity and rhythm in Isadora Duncan's dancing. The setting of a Greek amphitheater was chosen to illustrate the links between her dance and classical art. Courtesy of Lincoln Center, New York.

The person who was the model for this metaphysic of movement was Isadora Duncan. In contrast to other pioneers of modern theatrical dance, like Laban and Mary Wigman, she danced alone, without conventional costume or even the barest scenery. She never performed dance dramas, took on roles or strove to evoke archetypal associations. There were no leaps or pirouettes, only floating motions and gestures in a plain white or diaphanous robe – which Craig referred to as "rags," though she thought of them more poetically as cobwebs – against a gray curtain. Her favorite music was that of Chopin, lyrical rather than dramatic, but her dancing did not even require musical accompaniment. As Craig wrote to Martin Shaw, "Miss Duncan's *most* amazing dance is without music at all – and so wonderful are her rhythms that one does not miss the music...this dancing depends on nothing but herself." What system she had was derived from Dalcroze, whose school of movement was designed to awaken the performer to the emotional content of musical rhythms and to translate this into position and gesture. But, as she later admitted, her art was based on improvisation and her movements followed her fantasy. The keynotes were extreme simplicity and absolute naturalness, which came as a revelation to Craig in 1904 when he first saw her perform:

> ...a second prelude or étude – it was played through gently and came to an end – she had not moved at all. Then one step back or sideways, and the music began again as she went moving on before or after it. Only just moving – not pirouetting or doing any of those things which a Taglioni or a Fanny Essler would certainly have done. She was speaking her own language, not echoing any ballet master, and so she came to move as no one had ever seen anyone move before.[16]

Craig's passionate love affair with Isadora Duncan is one of the better-known parts of his life, and their letters – which span over twenty years and record a fascination with each other that borders on obsession in its extremes of ecstasy and agony, devotion and infidelity – clearly indicate her significance for Craig. The correspondence continued even after her death in 1927, in the form of his highly emotional annotations on almost every page of her posthumously published autobiography. He declared that her genius complemented his and considered her the only artist, apart from Appia, with whom he could have worked successfully.

Incongruously, because he was notoriously unable to handle even his own affairs competently, he became her business manager in 1906. He persuaded her to replace her single piano accompaniment with an orchestra, and brought in Martin Shaw as her conductor. He replaced her modest gray curtains, which were only five-and-a-half feet high and hung on rods from a row of short wooden pilasters to form an enclosed dancing area, with great blue drapes the height of the stage. She acted as his go-between with Duse and Reinhardt, and was responsible for persuading Stanislavski to employ him for the Moscow Art Theater. But, much more importantly, she was the catalyst that crystallized his artistic ideas. His early work with Martin Shaw led him to define movement and speech in terms of musical rhythm. Now Isadora Duncan's dancing brought him to see that "all written poetry and all music is based upon the laws which govern the poetry of *movement* . . . the beat of the feet upon the earth controls the musician and the poet."[17] The fact that some of her dances were performed without accompaniment convinced him that rhythm alone could form the basis of theatrical art. The arrangements of the curtains he devised for her, which derived from his designs for *Venice Preserved* and *Electra*, now struck him as appropriate for abstract movement, and when he came to work on Scene they provided one of the initial forms for its geometric shapes.

Isadora Duncan's ideas also shaped the philosophy that Craig's art eventually incorporated. What she was primarily concerned with has been called basic, even biological dance. One's first response to emotional or sensory stimuli is spontaneous movement, and her dancing was intended to reach and uncover the roots of that universal impulse. As she later described her aims when recalling her early experiments at the turn of the century, "For hours I would stand quite still, my two hands folded between my breasts, covering the solar plexus . . . I was seeking and finally discovered the central spring of all movement, the crater of motor power, the unity from which all diversities of movement are born, the mirror of vision for the creation of the dance – it was from this discovery that was born the theory on which I founded my school."[18]

Another aspect of this fundamentalist approach was the search for universal rhythms, in which form and movement would have the same unity as in nature. Isadora Duncan's earliest childhood inspiration for dancing came from the rhythm of ocean waves, and her aim in performance was to find artistic equivalents in which there was the same complete continuity among the human shape, the steps and gestures, the patterning of the dance as a whole, and the personality or emotion the dance expressed. She called this her "great and only principle . . . The waters, the winds, the plants, living creatures, the particles of matter itself obey this controlling rhythm of which the characteristic line is the wave." The result was an apparent naturalness and sincerity that struck observers as the opposite of "Art." Yet her biography shows that it took years of trial and practice to achieve this level of simplicity. As she outlined it, in terms that echoed Craig's demand for movement that would directly express the soul, her ultimate aim was to make the body "transparent...a medium for the mind and spirit." Her success in this reinforced his belief that a spiritual theater – as distinct from one that copied social realities – had no need of speech. "She said nothing. [Yet] she said everything that was worth hearing – and everything that everyone else but the poets had forgotten to say."[19] Soon afterward Craig was calling for "the abolition of the spoken word" because of its inevitable tendency to reduce drama to triviality; and in his copy of one of the early critical studies of his work, which quoted from "The Art of the Theatre" his decision to create the theater of the future "out of ACTION, SCENE, and VOICE," Craig noted in the margin that the word ACTION related specifically to Isadora Duncan.

These qualities of Isadora Duncan's dancing are all directly reflected in the essays and designs in which Craig defined his new art of the theater. Abstract action became its primary element, with the continuity of form and movement as its structural principle. Its aim and justification became the unmediated expression of a quasi-religious spirituality, one that rationally inclined nonbelievers might find difficult to appreciate. Its development became a process of elimination and simplification, removing even the human figure and creating a totally unified action by embodying movement in the scenery itself. By 1907 the form was set in a scenario entitled simply "Motion":

> The Beginning...the Birth...we are in Darkness...all is still...
>
> And from this Nothing shall emerge a spirit...Life...a perfect and balancing life...to be called Beauty... The Immortal Beauty of Change Eternal.
>
> A form simple and austere ascends with prolonged patience like the awakening of thought in a dream.
>
> Something seems to unfold, something to fold. Slowly...fold after fold loosens itself and clasps another till that which was void has become shapely. And now from East to West, one chain of life moves like a sea before us...
>
> Without Architecture we should have no Divine Place in which to praise. Without Music no Divine Voice with which to praise. Without Motion no Divine Act to perform.[20]

Except for the fact that there is no mention of a dancer, this could well be a description of the subjective effect of Isadora Duncan in performance. The pattern of unfolding action is much the same. Even the metaphors echo hers, which may explain something of their pretentious abstraction, although Craig was always prone to this kind of inflated symbolism.

A further influence on the way in which Craig's ideas developed was Isadora Duncan's fascination with Greek art. This was shared by the

avant-garde at the beginning of the century and reflected trends in philosophy and anthropology. The Cambridge School of Francis Cornford,
Jane Harrison, and Gilbert Murray had documented the origins of drama
in Greek religious ritual. Philosophers from Nietzsche to Ernst Cassirer
were asserting that "primitive" or mythical thought, which understood
experience in terms of prelogical images, was superior to the scientific
rationalism of contemporary Western civilization. Yeats called his work
"not drama but the ritual of a lost faith." When Reinhardt built his
"Theater of the Five Thousand," his aim was to recreate the sense of
community and Dionysian enthusiasm of the ancient Greek theater.
Eleonora Duse claimed, in a comment that Craig liked to quote as support
for his ideal of an Übermarionette, "To save the theatre, the [contempo-
rary] theatre must be destroyed, the actors and actresses must all die of
the plague. They...make art impossible. It is not drama that they play
but pieces for the theatre. We should return to the Greeks."[21] Similarly,
Isadora Duncan traced her style of dance back to an imagined classical
form, and believed the ancient open-air amphitheater provided ideal
conditions for her performances.

One of the earliest inspirations for Craig's notion of theatrical
reform had been a review article on the Comédie Française performance
of *Oedipus* and *Antigone* in 1894, and on an opera festival in 1895 at the
Roman theater in Orange.[22] This article had spoken enthusiastically
about the effect of using the severely simple facade of the 120-foot-high
rear wall as a permanent set, replacing the usual painted illusion of
temple or palace with the reality in stone. The "majestic" architectural
structure, which reduced operettas to triviality, was described as "suited
only to dramas inspired by the noblest of passions and dealing with the
noblest of themes." It served as a touchstone for the integrity of the
dramatic vision, and in contrast to the reviewer's expectations, the heroic
scale of the background "did not dwarf the human figures sustaining
serious parts." In tragedy or grand opera, "play and players alike were
upraised to a lofty plane of solemn stateliness by the stately reality of
those noble walls." As the article commented, the physical stature of the
performers would have been out of proportion even if they had worn
ten-foot-high stilts, yet the grandeur of the facade acted as an emotional
amplifier. In apparently instinctive reaction to their surroundings, the
actors' movements took on a ceremonial slowness, and their groupings
were given a natural balance and cohesion by the height of the scene.
Visual simplicity, in fact, was the keynote. The lack of any wings or
backstage area made it difficult to use furnishings or props, which in any
case would have been incongruous against the austere backdrop. As a
result, "the stage was full not of things but of people, and was wholly

alive. The eye was not distracted...but was entirely at the service of the mind in following the dramatic action." When Craig originally read the article, it had merely opened his eyes to new spatial possibilities for the stage. Now, after 1905, his aim became a return to the values of classical theater.

At the same time he had no desire to follow Godwin in reviving the external forms of the Greek stage. Similarly, he rejected Poel and the Elizabethan Stage Society's attempts to reproduce the performance conditions of the Globe for presenting Shakespeare's plays. Poel's stripping of the stage and his removal of illusionistic settings and nineteenth-century acting conventions, together with his use of curtains, in many ways paralleled Craig's work. But Craig believed that Shakespeare's stage was meaningless without its original Elizabethan audience, and he had never been concerned with historical accuracy. As the program for *Dido* had pointed out, he took "particular care to be entirely incorrect in all matters of detail." Although he increasingly immersed himself in the study of stage history, in itself such information was of incidental interest. Almost half the essays in *The Mask* were devoted to non-European and pre-nineteenth-century forms of theater. But they were truly relevant to Craig only as evidence to support his idea of a new theater, either by providing arguments to discredit theatrical developments since the Renaissance, or proving its viability by showing that other respected traditions contained the very qualities he was advocating. In his view any imitation of the past would be an "affectation," a "sham" that simply compounded the illusionism of the old Lyceum or the new naturalistic stage.

The painstakingly accurate Sam Wanamaker reconstruction of Shakespeare's Globe Theater – the 1990s fulfilment of Poel's aspirations in the 1890s – would have been anathema to Craig, reducing drama to a museum-piece and performances to a tourist attraction. Although he devoted a considerable portion of his career to interpreting Shakespeare's plays, Craig would also have rejected the function of the rebuilt Globe as a research tool, since his aim was always to bring out the "universal" vision in *Macbeth* or *Hamlet*. In contrast to exploring Shakespeare's original intentions (as the Globe is designed to do through recreating the physical context for his plays) each of Craig's Shakespearean productions was an expression of the modernist experience that used the full technical resources of today's stage, though the effect was abstract and anti-naturalistic. The two approaches are incompatible; and the line represented by the Globe is the only one most Shakespearean scholars would recognize as legitimate. However, Craig's approach is characteristic of specifically twentieth-century performance, being paralleled by Charles

Marowitz's *Collage Hamlet* (1964), Peter Brook's experimental treatment of *The Tempest* (1968) or Richard Schechner's New York *Makbeth* (1969). In a less radical way it also informs a production like Deborah Warner's 1995 *Richard II*, where casting a woman in the title role expresses contemporary sensibilities.

What Craig wished to revive was the essence of classical theater, not its archeology. For this even Shakespeare contained too many specific historical connotations, and Craig cast his gaze back to a more archetypal (and less immediately familiar) form: the tragedies of ancient Greece. On one level, the creative process of the Greek theater, in which Aeschylus had instructed the chorus in their dances as well as the protagonists in how they should deliver their lines, and in which the dramatist and director were the same person, was precisely what Craig aimed at in defining his ideal art as completely "the work of one man." But it was also the principles of an architectural, multipurpose setting (as distinct from specific or two-dimensional scenes), symbolic acting, simplicity, and perhaps above all the religious value of Greek drama that he wanted to restore. In addition, the origins of the theater provided an example for the most ambitious part of his undertaking. He was in danger of producing a stage form for which no plays had been written, and one that – given his intended "abolition of the spoken word" – would hardly attract a playwright. However, "in those days they built their theatres for their dramas, not their dramas in and for their theatres," and this encouraged him to attempt the single-handed creation of a drama that his new theater would express.[23]

After seeing *Acis and Galatea*, Yeats told Craig that he had rediscovered "an art which has lain hid under the roots of the Pyramids for ten thousand years, so solemn it is." Now, when formulating his theories, Craig repeated this almost word-for-word – but taking the metaphor literally. Instead of using "the great art which has lain buried under the fallen Temples of Greece and Asia" for the purpose of comparison, he made it a source for the qualities of what he called his "old new ideal."[24] As his phrase indicates, these essential principles were both generalized and romanticized. One of Craig's notebooks divided the whole history of European theater into six periods under three headings: "Acting or Action," "The Voice," and "Scene." The first period represented a purely notional idea of the archaic origins of drama, with marionettes only, instrumental music rather than vocalization, and no scene. Then, from the Greeks on, Craig traced what to him was a clear process of degeneration within each of the three elements. In the section on acting, Craig recounted how the chorus first appeared alone; then as set against one masked actor followed by a second (protagonist and antagonist), and after that against twelve actors and the half-masks of the *Commedia dell'Arte*. Finally the chorus was reduced to a single choral figure, or it disappeared altogether. Any form of mask vanished as well, and acting companies gradually grew from 20 to 100 people, with women added and all actors displaying individual personalities. In the section titled "Voice," Craig described a chorus of "sounds not dogma" (his term for the intellectual content in dialogue), which was followed by one or more voices distinguished from the chorus but "masked...and so not natural"; then, after the year 1600, by an expanding number of individual voices without any form of vocal chorus. In "Scene" he delineated the transformations of architecture from the Greeks to medieval church drama, then to imitation architecture (Palladio, Bibiena), and after that to "imitation artificial architecture" or realistic scenery.

This oversimplified and rather naive perspective reveals much more about Craig's own ideals than about stage history. His comments show that he looked on the process of renewing the theater as a progressive stripping away of accretions to return to the earliest and most fundamental forms. "I believe that the very *material* of the theatre needs simplifying... I do not wish to revert to an *old manner*, but I do not want to depart from a *noble tradition*. I wish to rebuild on old truths." These truths he defined as the superiority of art (which hints at a future and spiritual state) over life (which represents the physically present, and hints at nothing beyond itself). "I wish to remove *the Word* with its *Dogma* but to leave *Sound*, or the voiced beauty of the soul. I wish to remove *the Actor* with his *Personality* but to leave *the Chorus of masked figures*. I wish to remove *the Pictorial Scene* but to leave in its place *the Archetictonic [sic] Scene*."[25]

Although ancient Greece was his primary inspiration, Craig also found the same "universal principles" in other theatrical forms, from Indian and Cambodian dance to Javanese puppet plays and Nō drama. He had the opportunity to see a Nō performance in 1900 when a Japanese troupe visited London. Although some critics referred to Japanese qualities in Craig's work, there was no discernable Japanese influence on his early productions because the stylized acting was too alien to be immediately useful. As one reviewer complained, "The [Japanese] players...all have the appearance to a Western eye of grotesque mechanical toys. None of their movements resemble ours, their faces seem bizarre masks, and their voices have the peculiar metallic timbre of the gramophone. The question whether they are expressing joy or sorrow, fear or exaltation, is for the audience often the merest guesswork." Now, a decade later in 1910, the "Nō dances" as Craig called them – a description that clearly reflected his own concept of drama – provided a parallel that could help to define his ideas by offering "supreme examples of brevity and fine tradition."[26]

In fact it was precisely those elements of the Nō that the public had found incomprehensible in 1900 that Craig wanted for his Übermarionette; and the qualities he singled out were the apparent absence of violent passion in the Nō; its highly conventionalized symbolism, in which every gesture held clear significance; its distance from everyday life, or its "unnaturalness"; and its simplicity and spiritual suggestion.

One element that Greek theater shared with the Nō was the mask. Those that Craig had experimented with in his early productions were grotesque only, but now he saw the mask as the symbol of the human face. As such it came to be the symbol of his new theater itself, and gave the journal in which he published most of his theoretical essays its title. On one level, it paralleled his simplified, universalized scenery in embodying a relatively small number of archetypes that could be reused in a multiplicity of situations. On another, masks effectively ruled out individual emotion and the egoism that made ordinary actors unsuitable material for Craig's concept of art. Simplicity and intensity replaced variety, so that "instead of six hundred, but six expressions shall appear on the face."[27] Unlike *Commedia dell'Arte* masks, these would represent psychological states or moral qualities such as fear or pity, pride or sensuality, rather than social types.

This corresponded to Craig's aim of creating a drama of spiritual essences. The mask was to be restored to the stage specifically as "the visible expression of the mind...the only right medium of portraying the expressions of the soul as shown through the expressions of the face." Again, however, Craig's intention was to design new forms that would be simultaneously universal and contemporary, not historical. Indeed, his ultimate hope was to train actors to achieve an equivalent effect of depersonalized emotion by muscular tension alone. In a note that prefigures one of the characteristic avant-garde acting techniques, he called Irving "a prophet foretelling secrets of the future of the actor's art by that mask with which he veiled the weaknesses of his face...to impart the secret agonies of his soul...pointing with almost motionless gesture to the path leading to the great art of gesture...trained to an expressionless stone nobility."[28] In using Irving as an example of the physical control that Craig believed indispensable for capturing poetic vision as much as for its expressive qualities, the true relationship of the living actor to his notorious Übermarionette is summed up.

Like many innovators, Craig habitually overstated his ideas in order to distinguish them clearly from orthodox thought and to gain attention. Unfortunately, all too often the impact of such a tactic is at the expense of intelligibility, and few of Craig's ideas have been more misunderstood than the Übermarionette. His argument was against the "actor," but not against the human performer per se. He rejected the conventional approach to acting, together with those trained in it who were unable to rise above its vices. In his view, the major of these vices was the display of personality and emotions, which formed the main attraction of the existing theater but which put the body at the mercy of psychological forces under imperfect control at best. It meant that actors wanted always to be sympathetic or central instead of subordinate to the dramatic requirements of the piece. To produce a degree of emotional unity in which all the gestures, as a whole, would form a clear and distinct intellectual image – one, moreover, that would not vary from performance to performance – the actor had to have total physical control, which precluded personal vanity.

Instead of outlining a system of training that might achieve this, Craig chose to challenge the acting profession by calling such control an "impossible state of perfection," and went further to set up an absolute distinction between art and life. "Art arrives only by design," whereas the use of human figures as a medium for expression can only (in the present state of the theater) create accidental effects. Similarly, actors draw attention to themselves as people, whereas "the highest art is that which conceals the craft and forgets the craftsman." As general aesthetic principles such statements are unexceptional. But for the stage to be judged by the same criteria as sculpture or music demands a level of abstraction that rules out what is normally thought of as "dramatic," particularly when these criteria are drawn from symbolist art. Craig quoted Blake and Pater to support his contention that art should not deal with physical actuality, or "flesh and blood life," but with its opposite, the world of visionary imagination that he characterized as "solemn... beautiful and ... remote."[29] And as an apparently logical corollary, he proposed replacing the human being on the stage with inanimate figures or puppets.

There is, of course, a basic contradiction in using inanimate objects to express "a living spirit." But if we examine the qualities Craig attributes to puppets it becomes clear that his real aim was not quite so radical. What he specifically refers to are the puppet's "noble artificiality" in portraying abstract emotional states rather than in projecting live emotions; its symbolic character, which presents human nature in generalized or generic, rather than individual terms; and its subordination to the aesthetic requirements of the drama. Yet the one thing that cannot be achieved with puppets is the flowing rhythms of natural movement, which Craig was simultaneously proclaiming as the basis of his new art form. It is arguable that the puppet was only pushed forward through an association of ideas from "A Note on Masks" in the very first number of

The stylization and externalization of moral qualities: mask from *Dido and Aeneas.*
Courtesy of the British Library.

The Mask. There Craig had quoted a comment by Anatole France that
attributed precisely these qualities to M. Signoret's puppet theater:
"These marionettes resemble Egyptian hieroglyphs, that is to say something mysterious and pure, and, when they perform a play by Shakespeare or Aristophanes, I seem to see the poet's vision as if unfolded by
sacred figures on the high walls of a temple."

     In fact Craig was really arguing for "a new form of acting,
consisting for the main part of symbolical gesture. Today they *impersonate . . . tomorrow they must represent.*" As he commented in a letter to
Martin Shaw, his rejection of actors was a provisional expedient, "until
a breed can be grown which are like the rest of my thought, *hard,
clearcut, passionless.*"[30] This remained an unrealized ideal and, in the
absence of such Übermarionettes, he experimented with eightfoot-
high articulated wooden figures. He also planned productions of
Maeterlinck's early plays, subtitled "Drames pour Marionettes" though
written for ordinary performance. These appealed to him because the

The stylization and externalization of moral qualities: mask from *The Masque of Love*. Courtesy of the Bibliothèque Nationale.

dream action required actors to model themselves on "the slow and deliberate gesture of all Puppets – each has to move as a somnambulist." But despite his claim that the puppet stage possessed "every element necessary to a *creative* and a *fine art*," with perhaps one exception his own puppet dramas were no more than parody plays: an outlet for his frustration rather than material for a new dramatic form. His real aim was to create a Western equivalent to the highly trained actors of the Nō drama, which in his view exemplified the same intrinsic qualities as the theater of ancient Greece:

> The Japanese [dance drama] with its strict ritual, its noble conservatism which still preserves traditional postures without change or modification, its obedience

to a fine tradition, its perfect control of its material – that is, the human body –
approaches more nearly to the stately and splendid ceremonies of the past, of
which, among us, some trace yet lingers in the symbolic gestures of the priests
celebrating mass, and thus it partakes more nearly of the nature of an art.[31]

Craig looked on himself as a rediscoverer rather than an originator. His aim was to return the theater to its primal state, though without copying the original (and therefore alien) forms of expression; and the two elements that all the oldest traditions of theater shared were religious content and a high degree of stylization. This aim anticipates the attempts by directors like Brook and Grotowski to create a "theater of ritual" in the 1960s. But for Craig's contemporaries, a return to the religious origins of drama meant an updated mystery play or a play that incorporated direct echoes of the Mass, like Housman's *Bethlehem* and Edmond Harancourt's *La Passion* (performed on Good Friday, 1890). However, although Craig claimed to be "respectful" toward all manifestations of religion, he rejected Christianity along with conventional notions of spirituality that he characterized pungently as "white wings, upturned eyes, mutterings and mumblings devoid of humanity, and a general appearance of the sickly." Instead he proclaimed himself "a Pagan," and his "sacred theatre" was intended to express a vaguely defined pantheistic humanism. The actual forms of religious service or medieval drama were therefore of as little direct use to him as were the specific symbols and gestures of Japanese or Javanese drama. Still, at the same time the Church provided the basis for his concept of an "exquisite and precious" theater, in which the materials out of which the costumes (or in Craig's terms, vestments) and scenery were made would be as real as the devotion experienced, and in which the "noble symbols were popular without being understood."[32] Church architecture, too, became the model for one of his final scenic ideals.

In short, as Craig later emphasized, scenery in itself was of secondary importance to him. The common view that his main contribution was as a designer distorts the true focus of his art. Scenic reforms alone could be little more than decorative and superficial. To be effective they had to be accompanied by a new style of acting, and neither would have any internal coherence without a radically different concept of drama itself. As he correctly perceived, all the elements of theater – dramatic action and dialogue, the actor, scenery and lighting, audience expectations, even the architecture of the auditorium – were interdependent. Meaningful change could be achieved only by stripping away all accumulated conventions in order to redefine the whole basis of drama. By a natural association of ideas, reinforced by some of the intellectual and artistic trends of the time, this process took Craig back to the origins of drama and led him to search for equivalents in Eastern traditions. Although the direction Craig's work took is to some extent dated by its symbolist principles, his path was to be well trodden by the avant-garde after Antonin Artaud, and can be summed up by his demand that "instead of the artist of the theatre, let us in future speak of the *Ritualist*."[33]

6

TOWARD A NEW THEATER: MASQUES, SCREENS, AND A *HAMLET*

Craig's view that piecemeal reforms could never change the essential nature of the theater or reverse the long-standing trend toward realism may have been correct. But the comprehensive nature of his alternative was equally self-defeating. Its scope was overambitious for one man, however gifted, and it was hardly surprising that the principles he formulated were never fully translated into practice. As a result they lacked the definition that comes only from tangible demonstration and, despite his descriptive references to parallels in other dramatic traditions, his theories seem curiously abstract. Even his stage productions and the designs that established his influence hardly provide examples, because he dismissed them as compromises with the kind of theater they were originally intended to replace. Commenting on his famous production of *Hamlet* in 1912, for example, he described it as "old work. I have passed it all, gone into places where I have really seen something – a glimpse of something wonderful." Similarly, he warned the reader of *Towards A New Theatre* that the drawings, which appeared to illustrate his vision, in fact bore little relationship to his ideal: "All that I have put in the book now lies behind me."[1] As he repeated in both his notebooks and his published work, his theater existed only in the imagination. Although he believed he was moving toward it, he never claimed actually to have reached it.

From this perspective his effective influence could be only on the level of general inspiration. He offered an ideal rather than provided a new theatrical form. Even his demand that every aspect of a performance express the vision of a single person, if theater were to qualify as an art, called for something equivalent to the Renaissance ideal of a universal man. This "Artist of the Theatre" had not only to design the scenery, costumes, and lighting, and to direct every gesture of the actors (which would require a certain degree of acting skill) but he also had to be a playwright, constructing the drama performed by the actors and writing the dialogue spoken by them; a musician, composing whatever music accompanied the performance; and even an architect, capable of re-designing a theater. A measure of Craig's achievement is how closely he came to realizing this ideal. He started his career as an actor, then taught himself to draw. He studied theater architecture, collected information on every aspect of theatrical history, and built scale models of experimental stages. He also began to create his own plays.

Given Craig's rejection of the spoken word and of the kind of meaning ordinary dialogue could convey, these were scenarios rather than fully developed plays. In opposing the staging of Shakespeare, he argued that what distinguished Shakespeare's art was the poetry of ideas, which operated on a purely mental level; that acting out his words destroyed the coherence of this imagery because a spectator's mind was distracted by the appeal to his senses. Conversely, the only way such poetry could be captured in a performance was to substitute a totally visual representation, cutting all the words so that no appeal to the intellect would detract from the perception of physical images.

This was Craig's aim, a form of drama created solely from the physical elements of theatrical presentation. Figures were to be shown engaged in symbolic action and set in emotionally evocative contexts. Although he presented this as a revolutionary reversal of conventional assumptions about drama, it was really an extension of Irving's claim that "the theatre is bigger than the playwright, that its destiny is a higher one than that of the mouthpiece for an author's theses, and finally that plays are made for the theatre and not theatre for plays." The danger in dispensing with the imaginative values of the playwright is that drama becomes reduced to spectacle. As a mere show, it arouses aesthetic appreciation at the expense of the emotional involvement that can make a performance a communal act. To avoid this, Craig turned to a traditional form of drama with strong communal associations. Shakespeare had been a magnificent (yet untheatrical, in Craig's view) aberration. But Elizabethan drama provided other, very different models: "The Masques – the Pageants – these were light and beautiful examples of the Art of the Theatre."[2]

The masques of Ben Jonson and Inigo Jones had been celebrations of the Jacobean court: allegorical glorifications of the virtues attributed to the king, which were portrayed by the courtiers or by the royal family itself. As such the masques were ceremonial and their presentation was highly stylized. The figures were symbolic personifications with no individualizing traits. Plot situations were reduced to the triumph of good over evil, and the characteristic action was a dance or a tableau. Craig had already used some of these structural elements in his early productions – the masque/antimasque antiphony in *Dido and Aeneas*, and allegorical figures and dances in *The Masque of love*. However, instead of imitating the sixteenth-century form, he found what seemed to be a continuing, live tradition in which to work.

One aspect of nineteenth-century romanticism had been the rediscovery of folk art, from ballads to country festivals and Morris dancing.

This was linked with the Gothic Revival, which seemed to offer moral values that might redeem Victorian materialism, and found expression as much in William Morris's artisan community and in Herkomer's art school with its theatrical performances as in Godwin's architecture. It provided much of Craig's early inspiration, and in one sense his art was an extension of this neomedievalism. The reawakened interest in mystery plays, which had brought Craig "valuable and valued instruction in theatrical craft" in the form of Theodore Child's article titled "A Christmas Mystery in the Fifteenth Century," was part of this movement. So was the founding of the Purcell Society itself. And when he defined "Ceremony" as integral to his theater of the future, among the examples he listed "The Lord Mayor's Show" as "belonging to civil rites."[3]

The kind of thing he had in mind was *Beauty's Awakening: A Masque of Winter and of Spring*. When it was performed by the Art Workers Guild at the London Guildhall in 1899, Craig found the execution inadequate – "so many designers...and far too few theatre craftsmen." But the imaginative qualities aimed at by the Art Workers corresponded in general terms to some of his later principles: in particular, their rejection of "realism and illusion" in favor of "an allegory of the beautiful," which led to formalized patterning – "design, then, instead of illusion" – and to an emphasis on purely "Poetic and Ethic aims, Beauty of Design and Ornament." The setting, a single central archway flanked by an arcade of columns, is echoed in many of his designs, though characteristically he elongated the arch and simplified the architectural shapes that the Art Workers had embellished with elaborate Gothic ornamentation. The pageant itself, carefully distinguished from a play by its creators, also contained thematic similarities to Craig's own masques in its mix of traditional symbols and contemporary social comment, even if its focus was rather different.

Fayremonde, representing "the Spirit of all things beautiful," is cast into an enchanted sleep by a witch with the self-explanatory name of Malebodea. Trueheart (the London County Council perhaps, in the flattering shape of a knight in shining armor with a shield bearing the city crest) searches for her, accompanied by Hope and Fortitude. He battles against "the Demons attendant upon London...Bogus: who is both ancient and modern. Cupiditas: whom we all have in our hearts tho' we fain would deny it. Jerrybuiltas or Jerry: whom we have cherished so long and understood so well. Ignoramus: first cousin to Philistinus"; and when these sordidly modern demons rally, "the music tells first of their reluctance, then of their resolution, and when at last they are of one mind they unite in a grotesque and fantastic dance around the witch."

Fayremonde's dreaming is presented in pageants entitled "The Seven Lamps of Architecture" and "The Fair Cities of the World." Labour, Invention, and (in a rather direct appeal to captains of industry in the audience) Commerce awaken her, and the masque ends with a tableau of triumph. Even without dialogue, the visual symbolism, reinforced by descriptive theme music and broadly expressive acting, was almost too accessible. Indeed, the Art Workers declared, "what meaning there is in the Allegory that underlies our action is not far to seek."[4] But part of the value of this model for Craig was precisely that it demonstrated the possibility of communicating on a nonverbal yet popular level.

A second type of civil "ceremony," which seemed popular in a rather more conventional sense, was the harvest festival. While looking for material to incorporate in *Bethlehem*, Craig came across a description of "some country people celebrating their harvest home" near Windsor in 1598: "Their last load of corn they crown with flowers, having besides an image richly dressed, by which they would perhaps signify Ceres; this they keep moving about, while men and women, men and maidservants, riding through the streets in the cart, shout as loud as they can till they arrive at the barn." Immediately Craig set about constructing his first original masque, *The Harvest Home*, taking pains to emphasize its traditional and antique nature by claiming that he had found the details in a scholarly study of *Ancient Mysteries* (a book that deals solely with mystery plays, and contains no reference whatsoever to secular festivals). In fact, comparable festivities could still be found at that time, in a consciously preserved, rather artificial form, on some of the larger country estates.[5] This simple procession was elaborated into a minidrama based on a sequence of well-known folk songs. After the harvesters, singing, "Hail to our harvest home, this day of all the year/We reapers make good cheer" reach the barn, followed by children singing an "ABC song – Fool, Fool came to School," bells are heard and a group of Morris dancers come on. The applause at the end of their "capering" is counterpointed by the song of a "sad lover" which fades away into the distance outside. The ceremonial passing around of the garlanded straw dolly is followed by "Hobby Horses with an exact presentment of the dance which took the town and country-side by storm in the time of the Merry Monarch." Then, archetypal folk song figures are introduced. A shepherdess and a shepherd sing a kissing-duet,

> and the Miller [of Dee] is called. He is slow. Business with musicians. Children with paper mills...2 gunshots heard outside – they rush out and drag in Poacher – 2 dogs. 2 sons – He is made to sing [Lincolnshire] Poacher's song. Then gun dance, "can you not hit it." Final note he takes aim at audience, everyone shrieks and rushes forward to Poacher, all laugh.

This drama is punctuated by madrigals and by traditional favorites like "Go no more a' roving" and "St. George for England," and the festivities end with children dancing around a miniature maypole, and with all joining in "The King's Jig, the strains of which are heard far away in the distance as the merry makers retire to their homes."[6] Craig intended to perform this at harvest-time on country estates, and published a prospectus in 1903 advertizing it. But the potential cost of transporting thirty to forty performers, plus musicians, long distances for single performances lasting only three-quarters of an hour ("or longer, if desired") made the scheme impractical.

This was the closest Craig came to recreating an actual traditional ceremony, and there is something artificial in the idea of presenting a highly colored version of dancers and songs for the entertainment of the very people who should have been in reality performing them themselves. After this, with the exception of his plans for a festival production of *The St. Matthew Passion*, Craig restricted his concepts to the stage, where "noble artificiality" was in keeping. The intention of exactly reproducing folk dances was also an aberration for Craig. He later criticized Cecil Sharp and his troupe of Morris dancers for doing precisely that. In his view, Sharp's performers put themselves in a formal straitjacket by heeding their desire for historical authenticity instead of improvising rhythmic movement to express their inner natures. "They dress up, bells and white suits and bows. They have a look in the glass – 'Am I quite tidy?' Then with a determined air they go to their self-inflicted doom, conscious to the last."[7] But some of the *Harvest Home* material found its way into the production of *Much Ado*, which was almost transformed into a masque itself by the number of songs and dances Craig and Martin Shaw introduced. The (for Craig) unusually light and comic tone also persisted initially in association with this dramatic form, and later that year he proposed doing an "Alhambra Masque [the Alhambra being a popular variety theater] under a *nom de ballet*" to get away from the aesthetic preconceptions established by tragedies such as *Dido* and *Acis* and the almost unremitting gloom of *The Vikings*.

At the same time Craig began experimenting with more serious themes, as evidenced by *The Masque of Hunger*, *The Masque of Lunatics*, *The Masque of London*, and *The Dance of Death*. These were developed, together with brief outlines of other scenarios jotted down in one of his notebooks ("Theatre. Shows and Motions, 1905–1909" – a "motion" being the traditional English term for a puppet play), as subjects "for the best pupils of the school to attempt to improvise on," or for Craig himself to "bring onto my stage." They therefore have central importance, though they were little more than rough notes; and they indicate a degree of social criticism that is usually completely overlooked in Craig's work. For instance, London was presented as a grimy commercial hell, akin to T. S. Eliot's "unreal city" in *The Wasteland*, where dead souls are tormented by being forced into degradingly materialistic trades or menial occupations. This vision was set against an idealized world of philosophy and poetry – a great hall flooded with light – the inhabitants of which cannot believe that such spiritual misery could exist.

The most fully realized of these scenarios was *The Masque of Hunger*, which went through several versions, and for which Craig designed scenes and movements in considerable detail. He called it a "mimo-drama," and its essence was contained in the figure of a man in a hideous mask of grief, whose amplified breathing expresses over-whelming emotion.

> From his right arm hangs a little, dead boy, which he stretches out to the audience. He shows this figure to all, moving it from left to right and from right to left, and all the time the sound of restrained bellowing is heard. His move-ments are slow and deliberate...from every side, and beneath him, come the many echoes of his solitary cry, and these echoes take new shapes, resolving into the words "Pain – Pain – and Sorrow – "

Then a black rain begins to fall and hides the figure from sight. Originally that single image was the whole drama, but Craig elaborated the action and distanced it by adding an on-stage audience and turning it into a play within a play. The general statement about human misery was transformed into a comment on social inequality by providing a contras-ting image. A brightly lit palace and Louis XV headdresses filled the stage, so that the beggar now appeared in the more ordinary darkness of material deprivation, rather than in the bleak night of the soul. This made the political point more specific, but at the expense of emotional imme-diacy. A prelude was added, which emphasized the theatricality of the performance. Figures in eighteenth-century costumes are revealed "preparing the room for a masquerade, arranging the chairs for the [on stage] spectators... Two others take up their positions in the centre of the stage and begin to act at acting (all of this in dumb show)." The rest seat themselves with the affected airs of aristocrats, and one "swishes back a curtain from a small circular window letting in a flood of moonlight, like a lime" that falls on the figures of the "actors." As these "spectators" applaud, "the king's waltz tune" is heard in the distance, and their sudden nervous activity makes the audience realize that what they have taken for great lords are only servants aping their masters. But when the true court enters, their mannerisms are more, not less exaggerated, and the servants' parody turns out to be more human than the grotesque

Archetypal figures and the mime-within-a-mime of *The Masque of Hunger*. Courtesy of the Bibliothèque Nationale.

reality of the rich. The king is "a kind of money king," bloated with overeating, and he is wheeled in "like a large frog" on a plushly cushioned

> invalid's throne...those who propelled him were the chief gentlemen of the Court. Their progress was made in this manner: first four steps, and then everyone nearly fainted with fatigue – a fanning – a smelling of salts during a pause, silence, and a tiny, squeaky voice from the depths of the cushions calling for relief. Then another bold effort – four steps forward and another pause with the same play repeated.

The masked figure, holding out the shrunken body of a starved child, then provides the entertainment for these decadent courtiers, while the servants peer at them from the corners.

Such multiplying levels of theatricality and illusion are highly imaginative, and point forward to Pirandello and Genet. But their appeal is mainly intellectual, and to regain anything approaching the emotional power of the original simple image in isolation, Craig had to use visual

Rhetorical gesture and choreographed groupings in the final scene of *The Masque of Hunger*. Courtesy of UCLA.

overkill. In the final scene he envisaged upward of sixty or seventy people on stage, massed choral groupings and swirling, rhetorically dramatic movements. Crowds of starving beggars were to invade the palace, forming a dark wall of figures along the proscenium and enclosing the brightly lit courtiers, who are huddled together in a diminishing perspective at the rear. Out of wails and sobs a somber chant arises: "Shall we show you how the peasant carries home his dead."[8] On one side a human pyramid strains upward toward a funeral pyre. On the other, ragged figures thrust out accusing arms in a gesture modeled on Fuseli's painting of the Weird Sisters from *Macbeth*. But in place of Fuseli's three pointing figures, Craig had fifteen.

Craig, like many of the socially aware but politically naive avantgarde artists of his time – Ezra Pound, the futurist Marinetti, the German expressionists Bronnen and Johst – was led by his anti-establishment feelings toward the fascist camp. His frustration with the society that declined to support his work persuaded him to offer his art to Mussolini, whom Craig admired perhaps more for his theatrical personality than for his politics. His journals became filled with anti-Jewish comments: His exaggerated ideas about the wealth of the Jewish community and his inability to persuade them to support his theatrical schemes made them the focus for his resentment. Perhaps more out of opportunism than commitment, he proposed his plans for an annual performance of Bach's *St. Matthew Passion* as a festival celebrating the principles of fascism. And even after Mussolini's patronage failed to materialize, he still felt enough sympathy for the movement to carry a message from Goebbels to Erwin Piscator, offering him a theatrical position under the Nazis, when he visited Russia in 1935.

At the same time he always realized that the essential qualities of his art were aesthetic, and came to believe that its proper function was the positive evocation of spiritual values rather than negative social criticism. But he reasoned that this was not an apolitical withdrawal, as such values in themselves were implicitly revolutionary, being anti-materialistic. As a result, his plans for "Shows and Motions" following *The Masque of Hunger* became more visionary. The political themes were transposed to a symbolic plane, as in "notes for a performance on the death of Socrates," in which an evil social establishment was to be presented as a wall of masked faces, picked out by lights from a background of darkness – a technique that anticipated the most striking visual effect in Reinhardt's expressionistic production of *A Dream Play* in 1921. In fact the scenes of this mimodrama are explicitly labeled "visions," and the action embodies archetypal images designed to draw on the subconscious. Socrates "has only one action and his face (a glass mask) glows ever brighter and brighter... The jailers lay hands on him – but only seize phantoms – on each side of him has appeared [the figures of] his NAME and his DEAD BODY... He looks like Dionysius."[9]

Similarly, in the masque of *Psyche*, which he also called a "Project for Ballet, " the swirling groups of pointing figures from *Hunger* were internalized rather than social symbols. They represented the "doubts and fears" of the heroine, who herself stood for an element of the subconscious. In his notes on seventeenth-century French theater Craig had admired the daring vision capable of conceiving *"une gloire"* on the stage, and the themes of his later notes for masques become increasingly religious, even including one titled *World Creation*, which asserted that "in the beginning... the Spirit of God moved upon the face of the waters – Consider – First the movement comes before all else. It was the beginning, it must be *our* beginning."[10]

When Craig looked back on his progress from the perspective of 1905, the year of his first major essay outlining the principles of his theater, he rejected even his Purcell productions on the grounds that "we may have 'interpreted' better – but we *created* not a jot," and listed his masques as the "first attempts" at creating his new art form. However, these masques were basically extensions of conventional theater and still relied on the ordinary resources of the stage. They also retained plot and motivation, however minimal, and characters, however symbolic. In essence, they simply translated the spoken word into a visual language that was its equivalent rather than an alternative. Craig's true aim was far more radical. *"If you can find in nature a new material, one which has never yet been used by man to give form to his thoughts, then you can say you are on the high road towards creating a new art."*[11]

This was a tall order. But if it meant anything, it at least meant that drama created out of conventional elements would be of as little use as the work of playwrights like Shakespeare and Shaw. The new theater had to have "pieces of its own art" to perform. Inspired by Isadora Duncan, Craig saw the artists of his future theater as "ministers to the supreme force – movement," which could act as direct revelation of the spiritual instead of obliquely representing it through the shapes of the physical world. "The Art of the Theater [by which Craig always meant **his** new art form, as distinct from all other types of theater] has sprung from action – movement – dance."[12] Every element had to embody this, and Craig's masques should be seen as pointers in that direction, with their affinity to ballet and their capacity for development toward such a symbolic abstraction as *World Creation*.

Working tentatively toward this, Craig had begun to make designs that he listed as "A Movement Design for Theatre" and "A Study in Scene and Movement," rather than designs for existing plays. Then he started to construct imaginary dramas around them. In these, the movement of figures and light replaced plot. There was no dramatic action in the usual sense, but rather a developing progression of emotional states. If in his view the theater had to "strive towards the condition of music," this was the spatial equivalent of a symphony or – perhaps more accurately – a tone poem. As examples he created four designs simply titled *The Steps*, each representing a "mood." Experiments with the opportunities for movement provided by steps had long occupied him, from the series of broad platforms that made up the original stage for *Dido and Aeneas* to the sharply sloping rock construct of *The Vikings*. One of the scenes for *Psyche* was little more than a complex structure of staircases, with two on each side leading up to a central platform in a pyramidal shape, and two further sets running diagonally down from their midpoint to join in a central flight of steps at the bottom. Sixteen out of thirty-eight designs in *Towards A New Theatre* included steps in one form or another, and in one the stairway was designated as a "neutral spot." Now, in 1905, this neutrality became a central dramatic focus, to be filled with subtly evocative changes in significance. "Among all dreams that the architect has laid upon the earth, I know of no more lovely things than his flights of steps...I have often thought how one could give life (not a voice) to these places, using them to a dramatic end... And so I began with a drama called *The Steps.*"[13]

Each of the four "acts" or "moods" had the same setting: a long, broad flight of steps that filled the whole stage between two high walls. But different colors and angles of light, harmonizing with the expressive movement and positioning of human figures, were designed to create sharp changes in emotional effect. The brightness of morning was set against the shadows of evening, groups of children against single actors, leaping dances against solemn, flowing gestures, to create visual rhythms of counterpoint and parallels. These rhythms were intended to make such a powerful impression that the scene itself would appear to echo them. For example, in the second mood, Craig showed "many girls and boys jumping about like fireflies" on the level above the steps, while on the flat space below "in the foreground, and furthest from them, I have made the earth respond to their movements. The earth is made to dance." By contrast, in the fourth mood people are largely immobile or absent, and it is objects in the scene that provide the main movement. The time, night, corresponds to the emotional state represented by the only visible figure, sorrow. He moves briefly "hither and thither upon this highway of the world" from the shadowed to the moonlit wall, against which he leans, near the bottom of the steps, and remains motionless with his head sunk on his breast.

> Then things commence to stir; at first ever so slowly, then with increasing rapidity. Up above him you see the crest of a fountain rising like the rising moon when it is heavy in autumn. It rises and rises, now and then in a great throe, but more often regularly. Then a second fountain appears. Together they pour out their natures in silence. When these streams have risen to their full height, the last movement commences. Upon the ground is outlined in warm light the carved shapes of two large windows and in the centre of one of these is the shadow of a man and a woman. The figure on the steps raises his head. The drama is finished.[14]

The two fountains, occupying the same space where the children danced in the second mood, provide a visual equivalent to the joy the children derive from the world of nature, though the reference to autumn translates youthful innocence into stately maturity. The light cast from the windows echoes the configuration of the fountains, in the same way that the floor "danced" in response to the children's movements. An audience is clearly expected to go through the sequence of feeling presented by the stage, from world-weary sorrow and isolation to hope

The Steps, fourth mood: the use of visual parallels and counterpoint to evoke mood.

and the promise of fulfillment. Yet the expression of these emotional states is left abstract, so that each spectator can define them in terms of his or her personal experience. In short, the type of "revelation" contained in this art of movement relates to the audience. Each spectator is led to discover his inner nature, and to perceive his/her existence as an integral part of the cyclical patterns of nature.

  The key element here, the "new material" out of which a new art form might be created, was the moving scene. Its origins were in Craig's use of plain drapes to form stark architectural shapes, suggestive rather than representational, for act 4 of *Venice Preserved*. As he commented with reference to that design, "When I began looking into the idea [of employing curtains in place of scenery], I saw almost infinite possibilities in it, and...developed the idea until it began to grow into a serious study." By 1907 he was creating a type of setting that would be more flexible than drapes, and that was capable of being moved invisibly to create continually changing shapes; one that could be used "to translate what we call *Movement*" independently of actors or dancers: his screens.[15] Even though these were announced as a revolutionary new principle, designed for a purely abstract form of stage presentation, they were never in fact intended to be self-sufficient. They provided a context for actors, not a replacement for them, and the way Craig pushed their adoption for poetic plays indicates that he hoped their use would revolutionize the theater from within. In fact, while highly imaginative, his screens were hardly radical. Indeed also they remained to some extent interchangeable with drapes; Craig's deployment of the screens in the first act of his Moscow *Hamlet* was modeled on a design for curtains made six years earlier (see illustration on p. 154).

The earliest sketches show screens arranged in asymmetrical geometric shapes in order to divide the stage into distinct and differently lit acting areas. As preliminary working drawings, these were devoid of human figures, and it has been generally assumed that they represent the move toward pure abstraction that Craig apparently was calling for in his essays. But when he began to develop the principles for their use on a model stage, he always included actors in the form of cardboard or wooden miniatures. When photos were taken of the model without these figures, Craig inked them in. Their function may have been (as his son and collaborator Edward suggests) simply to give an idea of scale to those model scenes. Yet these two-dimensional cutouts were identical with his famous "Black Figures," and these show a wide variety of clearly defined characters and dramatic poses. (The folds of costumes and details of features were carved in light relief, and Craig found they could be used exactly like woodcuts to make prints.) The earlier Black Figures – for "a Greek drama" – represent idealized and generalized actor-figures. Later ones show actors portraying symbolic archetypes, such as "Fear" and "Lust," whereas the series for *Hamlet* is individualized. They range from heroic stylization to the grotesque, with one (the Second Grave Digger) recalling strongly the Shepherds in *Bethlehem*. These were actually used as models by the cast of the Moscow *Hamlet*. Even in the photographs recording configurations of screens that were not designed for any particular play, the clearly dramatic groupings of many of these figures and the use of sometimes ten or more in a single scene indicate the intended relationship between the screens and conventional theater.

As early as 1896, Craig's notebooks show an interest in techniques such as the use of gauzes to create scenes that could be changed during the action. Now his screens provided a medium that could create

> a sense of harmony and a sense of variety at the same time. We may be said to have recovered one of the Unities of the Greek Drama ... We pass from one scene to another without a break of any kind, and when the change has come we are not conscious of any disharmony between the new scene and that which is past.[16]

Craig saw the screens as the appropriate scenic material for his ideal religious theater because they presented the world of the poetic imagination, and the first arrangements that he made on his model stage were for a drama that he called "The Poetic Dreamer." There is a popular notion of fantasy as flimsy and floating. Craig's screens, with angles and mass brought out by the shadows from strong sidelighting, by contrast, seemed to give the visions of poetry a sharply-cut reality. Equally, their simplicity provided a ground for the spectators' imagination to work on, as distinct from the ornate scenery ordinarily used for fantasy settings, which presented someone else's imaginings for their admiration. Indeed, to Craig one of the selling points of his screens was their economy. Not only were their initial construction costs low, but also exactly the same screens could be reused for play after play – although Craig later limited their suitability to performances of the kind of tragedy that omits "the trivialities" of daily life and concentrates on "large happenings."[17]

These screens that allowed "1000 shapes" to be created out of a single "scene" were of canvas stretched over wooden frames and were

Flexible architectural shapes to create the world of the poetic imagination on stage. The model with ten two-dimensional wooden figures shows a simple, architectural use of screens. Courtesy of HRC.

painted in monochrome white or light yellow. (In Moscow Craig also experimented with wood and metal coverings.) They were of varying widths but of uniform height, self-supporting, double-hinged, and mounted on retractable castors to provide maximum flexibility. In themselves, they were an extension of the "flats" out of which interior scenes are ordinarily built on the stage. But although the screens' novelty lay more in the concept of how they were to be used than in the objects themselves, Craig managed to patent them as "Improvements in Stage Scenery," and his application is worth quoting as a comprehensive description of his aims:

> In the representation of such plays [poetic drama] the producer has hitherto been obliged to choose between the alternatives of either employing scenery formed and painted so as to produce the illusion of the actual scene intended by the playwright, or using plain curtains as a background. Many persons have come to the conclusion that the latter method has certain aesthetic advantages and it has the material advantage of cheapness and easy transport.
>
> The object of my invention is to produce a device which shall present the aesthetic advantages of the plain curtain but shall further be capable of a multitude of effects which although not intended to produce an illusion shall nevertheless assist the imagination of the spectator by suggestion.
>
> My device is further intended to combine the artistic variety and mechanical advantages of painted scenery with the portable nature of the curtain...
>
> The screens may be used as background and in addition...may be arranged as to project into the foreground at various angles of perspective so as to suggest various physical conditions, such as, for example, the corner of a street, or the interior of a building; by this means suggestion, not representation, is relied upon and nevertheless variety is obtainable.[18]

The specifications provided illustrations of how those arrangements might work in practice. Diagrams 1 and 2 show the interior of a room that could be changed in the course of a performance to suggest the walls and receding perspectives of a street or town square (in diagrams 5 and 6) by shifting only two screens.

Craig hoped originally that this invention would be picked up by other directors, who would create new arrangements and discover for themselves, through mastering its potential for mobility, that abstract movement was the essence of drama. The only principle he suggested at first was that "the aim of the Arranger is to place his screens in such a position that by moving the minimum number of leaves he may produce the desired amount of variety."[19] With this in mind he presented Yeats with a set of screens for the Irish National Theater in 1909.

Yeats experimented with them for almost a year, and was so excited by the possibilities for creating moods from expressive light and

Fig.1.

Fig.2.

Fig. 5.

Fig. 6.

The patent specifications for Craig's screens (January, 1910), illustrating the simple changes needed to transform an interior into an exterior.

shade that he completely rewrote *Deirdre* to take advantage of them. In composing a play, once he had created an outline of the action, he worked out the context for each scene on a set of model screens, then wrote the dialogue around it. In 1911 the Abbey Theater staged three plays with Craig's ivory-colored screens. But for the most successful of these productions, *The Hour Glass*, Yeats turned to Craig for the screen arrangements of each scene. The results were a striking departure from Yeats's earlier practice:

> Up till the present year we always played it in front of an olive green curtain, and dressed the Wise Man and his Pupils in various shades of purple (with a little green here and there) and because in all these decorative schemes, which are based on colour, one needs, I think, a third colour subordinate to the other two, we dressed the Fool in red-brown... Last winter, however, we revived the play with costumes taken chiefly from the designs by Mr. G. Craig, and with screens he has shown us how to make and use... with effects that depend but little on colour, and greatly upon delicate changes of tone.[20]

The reception was favorable, although some of the praise was hardly what Craig wanted. One review praised the "more or less *static* scene as a [harmonious] medium for the presentment of such poetic dramas," and another referred to the limelight from the auditorium as "throwing a *glaring* yellow light on the screen." Yeats was pleased with the elegant simplicity of the screens and the delicacy of natural lighting achieved with them (in contrast to having effects of highlight and shadow painted on the scenery, as had been the Abbey practice up to then). But quite apart from that, he was enthusiastic because with the screens "one enters into a world of decorative effect which gives the actor a renewed importance. There is less to compete against him, for there is less detail, though there is more beauty." After seeing these productions, Jack Yeats wrote to Craig that "all the play writers ought to have model theaters with your screens and they should fold them about until they suggest a play to them" – as he said he now did himself. He commented, however, that he had seen only interiors on the Abbey stage and could not imagine the screens suggesting any outdoor landscape, except street scenes, successfully.[21] Perhaps it was this that prompted Craig to add "extra pieces" to the screens in the form of doorways, windows, and (for *On Baile's Strand* in 1914) pictorial screens with windswept trees or rocky cliffs outlined on them.

At a public demonstration with his miniature screens in 1911, Craig created contrasting scenes for Hofmannsthal's *Electra*, a Molière comedy, a winding Italian street, and an Egyptian temple. Reports stressed how effective this simple instrument was: "One obtained vistas of colonnades and pillars, dim recesses lost in the distance or suddenly made visible by the play of electric light. The illusion was very complete." Craig received requests for his screens from two English theaters. He let Yeats, as an artist who shared his aims, experiment with them to discover new effects, but in practice Craig was not prepared to allow others the same freedom. He insisted that plans for the layout of the screens had to be obtained from him for each play, not just the first, and that "nothing be altered or added."[22]

In the same way, when he presented Ellen Terry with a set of eighteen-foot-high screens with which to perform *The Merchant of Venice*, he drew outlines of all the positions for each screen and light as well as giving her a demonstration of the intended effects on his model stage. These designs are complex, with sinuous curving shapes across the stage in one scene, necessitating a large number of thin screens, receding perspectives, and straight walls for the next. Here, as in his public demonstration, the screens were used as the equivalent of conventional scenery; but the scene changes were too major for their movements to be

Craig's stage layout of the screens for act 2 of *The Merchant of Venice*, 1911. In scene 3 (Shakespeare's scenes 3, 4, 5, and 6), the hidden steps lead up to an "extra piece" – a six-foot-high rostrum used for Jessica's balcony – and the false thirteen-foot-high inner proscenium is required to mask the tops of the screens. Courtesy of UCLA.

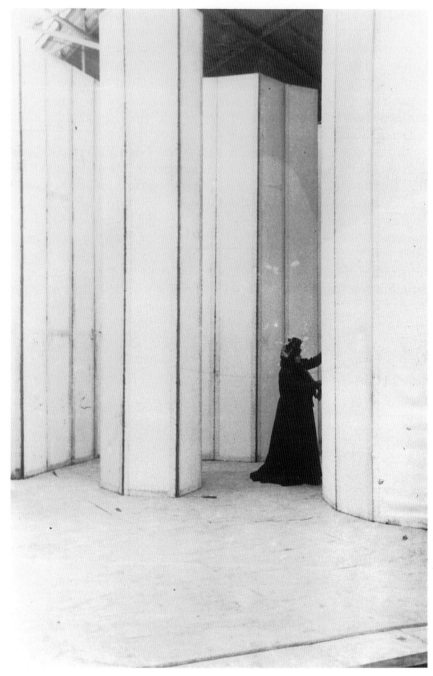

Ellen Terry, with screens arranged for act 3 of *The Merchant of Venice*, 1911. Courtesy of Edward Craig.

made in view of the audience, apparently autonomously, without the stage hands appearing and without a break in the action. Perhaps for this reason Ellen Terry never used them. The only full test of their potential was Craig's own *Hamlet* production in Moscow.

Of all Shakespeare's plays, *Hamlet* was Craig's most constant preoccupation. The Prince of Denmark had been one of his first leading roles as an actor, and when he played it in London in 1896 he wore Irving's costume from the Lyceum production of ten years before. As the last piece he personally directed, with the isolated exception of *The Pretenders* sixteen years later, it therefore spans the whole of his work on the stage – as distinct from the ideal theater of his imagination – and continued to be a frequent reference point in his writing. Despite his call for "the abolition of the spoken word," and his conviction that tragedy in particular demanded the silence of naked action removed from the verbalizing that brought in everyday concerns, *Hamlet* remained in his view a play for dialogue – precisely because, to him, Hamlet's tragedy lies in the fact that he talks instead of acts. The remarkable consistency of his interpretation of the play indicates the underlying coherence of his work. Indeed, his 1912 production harked back to Irving's own reading of the character: "The eye should be wild, not vacant, and the glances piercing...his melancholy rises with striking and noble images, to an astounding pitch of sublimity. The tone and manner should have a correspondent weight or majesty."[23]

By 1907 Stanislavski was moving beyond the naturalistic "crickets and mosquitoes" of his Chekhov productions in search of a deeper kind of realism that would reflect "the life of the human spirit." But his experiments with symbolist drama – Knut Hamsun's *The Drama of Life*, Leonid Andreyev's *The Life of Man*, and Maeterlinck's *The Bluebird* – had been unsuccessful. The acting techniques he had developed for internalizing emotion and translating unexpressed thoughts into physical action were useless for plays that had abstract figures and no subtext. In *The Life of Man*, Stanislavski discovered some effectively illusionistic stage tricks, such as a black velvet background (allegedly taken from Beardsley's art) against which characters and props could be made to materialize or disappear like visions. But these were simply external, and Maeterlinck had complained that the mystical level of his *Bluebird* fantasy was totally missing. So, prompted by Isadora Duncan (who was as horrified by the black velvet as Craig himself was to be on seeing *The Life of Man* when he arrived at Moscow in 1908), and impressed by the first copy of *The Mask*, Stanislavski invited Craig to direct *Hamlet* for the Art Theater.

This was undoubtedly the most carefully prepared of all Craig's productions. Because of its postponement when Stanislavski fell seriously ill, Craig had three years to think it through, even though publication of *The Mask* took up much of his time. On his visits to Moscow he discussed each scene and the psychology of the characters in detail with Stanislavski, and in Italy he worked out every movement with his screens on a model stage constructed to the dimensions of the Moscow Art Theater (MAT) and fitted with eight rows of electric lights that duplicated its lighting system. He then demonstrated these to Stanislavski and to his aide Suler (Sulerzhitski), who rehearsed the actors.

Craig complained that working at such a distance forced him to create settings, to design costumes, and to dictate the *mise-en-scène* separately, instead of doing all three "things together and on the stage of the theatre, so that they should be one piece...so that that one piece should have one impulse behind it." Yet when he outlined an ideal method of directing, it followed his practice here, though with one significant addition: direct involvement of the actors in the creative process. After roughing in the dramatic situations in very broad terms, the scenes were to be constructed in miniature and the positions of each actor plotted with cutout figures. The "director or inventor in chief" then runs through the whole performance on the model stage for the actors, who now "elaborate the pattern" in discussion, and "such suggestions as seem to strengthen the action" are written down. At this point only is the production transferred to the full-size stage, and the actors work through the play with every improvisation carefully noted by stenographers. A second run-through on his model stage follows, incorporating the impro-visations and including "each actor speaking for his special figure." Further rehearsals then "finish everything *up to a point.*" Up to a point only, because (as Craig wrote, his concept of an Übermarionette notwith-standing) even during the public performances the actors should be free to improvise, and the director's task is simply "to cut out all which is unnecessary." Indeed, after the preliminary rehearsals in Moscow, Craig reported, "I was never so clear as at present as to what I want... In *Hamlet* I am nearer my *Masque of Love* than *Vikings.*"[24]

Although the final shape of the production fell in some ways far short of what he had imagined, Craig's interpretation was true to his concept of an interior, spiritual form of drama. His basic idea of the play as a conflict between two mutually destructive elements – Hamlet as spirit versus all that surrounds him as matter – exactly corresponded to his analysis of *Macbeth* in the first copy of *The Mask*. So did his use of a very limited range of symbolic colors to indicate the relative amounts of these two elements in each character, and to unify all the figures into a mass that would harmonize with the scene. When Stanislavski complained that the costumes were "shabby, uninteresting, quite the

Craig's design for the court scene, with Hamlet reclining downstage and the screens arranged in a flat wall across the rear.

opposite of exquisite," he discovered that Craig indeed intended the costumes to "sink into the scene and be lost, so that for once the actors' faces and voices will tell the tale without interruption."[25] All were in shades of somber gray and beige (apart from Gertrude and Claudius, whose regal robes were gold – and Ophelia, for whom Stanislavski substituted white in deference to the romantic preconceptions of his public) with specks of scarlet or green highlighting textures, and lines of gold on folds.

The best example was in Craig's staging of the court scene of act 1. Gertrude and Claudius were set on a gold-backed throne high above the courtiers, whose heads appeared to protrude through slits in a single vast golden cloak that swirled down from their shoulders to hump over the seated or crouched figures massed below. (In fact the unity was illusory. An actress playing one of the courtiers has described how the effect was achieved: For this scene, all the people on stage, dressed entirely in gold, "were arranged on wooden platforms so as to represent symbolically the feudal ladder... The actors were distributed on various planes, their mantles flowed out and gave the impression of a monolithic golden pyramid.") Limes turned the neutral color of the straight wall of screens behind into a dull yellow, and a diagonal shaft of light fell on the throne "like molten gold." In front, alone and in a band of deep shadow, Hamlet reclined "fallen, as it were, into a dream." A light black tulle curtain, or gauze, was stretched directly behind him and cut him off sharply from these gold-draped figures, giving them a misty effect. On Claudius's line, "Come away," this gauze was slowly loosened so that, although the figures remained in place, their outlines were gradually blotted out as if they receded from Hamlet's thoughts rather than moved off the stage. As Craig explained to Stanislavski, "In this golden court, this world of show, there must not be various individualities as there would in a realistic play. No, here everything melts into a single mass." This was so impressive that the scene received an ovation (something unheard of at the MAT). One reviewer enthusiastically described the blurring of the outlines as the fog rolling in, but this effect was not simply decorative. Rather, it illustrated one of Craig's main principles: "In a poetic play the figures – faces – costumes – and all should be so much one that they actually resemble each other. *Unity is necessary...* All the parts of the play should so adhere one to the other that they make up the play."[26]

This was one of the few scenes that remained exactly as Craig envisaged it, perhaps because his concept was remarkably close to ideas that Stanislavski had already developed before Craig first arrived in Moscow.[27] It was also the kernel from which Craig's interpretation grew. It incorporated elements from some of his first ideas for *Hamlet*: The positioning of Hamlet in shadow downstage, set sharply apart from the well-lit court at the rear, had appeared in a sketch as early as 1901. The double throne and voluminous cloak came from a sketch of 1905 for the play scene, and the grouping and the gauze dividing Hamlet from the court were already set in the design of 1906, in which Craig first noted the type of curtain arrangement that developed into his screens. Here he had also envisaged a multiplying group of kings and queens ranged down each side of the scene, and on another sketch, showing a king seated on a throne with a similar zigzag arrangement of wall downstage right, Craig noted that "his thoughts [are] unfolded on the screens by his conscience, a figure who appears first." Both these ideas were discarded, although they survived in a modified form well into rehearsals for the "To be or not to be" scene. Suler recorded that "at the end of the soliloquy Hamlet stands behind the tulle with an enormous shadow in back of him. On the side screens shadows are continually moving around him and with him, flickering like black fumes"; Craig's sketch of the scene shows these shadows as elongated figures echoing and multiplying Hamlet's posture.[28] But the dreamlike symbolism carried through in more general terms, as did the single plain set that varied in shape from scene to scene, and these became the central concepts of Craig's production.

The golden court scene, representing "the note of tyranny and grandeur," was specifically Hamlet's dream, which the audience sees through his eyes. The whole play was conceived as a monodrama, and at one point Craig wanted Hamlet, in whose mind this vision was played out, on stage throughout every scene: "He can be in the distance, lying, sitting, in front of the people acting, at the side, behind, but the spectator ought never to lose sight of him." Similarly, to bring out the spiritual pole of the play, he envisaged introducing openly symbolic figures to external-ize Hamlet's thoughts: Madness, Murder – and in particular, Death, a female shape who would appear at Hamlet's side during his "To be or not to be" monologue and remain there in all the following scenes, as inseparable from him as his shadow.

Death in fact became one of the keynotes of Craig's interpretation of the play. The performance opened with the Ghost. Against high gray screens, suggesting castle ramparts rising out of shadows that masked the gaps of entrances between each set of screens, the phantom appeared to emerge out of the walls. Far from the regal apparition of Shakespeare's text, this supernatural figure represented the physical horror of death in an image drawn from medieval iconography with what Stanislavski called "ultra-realism": a corpse devoured by worms and wrapped in a decaying shroud that hobbled its legs, the tatters of which suggested shreds of flesh hanging from whitened bones. By contrast, a second death figure, female instead of male, was to be associated with ecstatic music. This figure was Hamlet's alter ego, invisible to him but enticing him onward. She embodied death in the sense that Craig referred to it in his essays: the world of the imagination, directly reflecting the life of the spirit and completely divorced from the physical world. "She must be beautiful, glowing, and during his reverie she leans towards him and lays her head on his shoulder." Stanislavski persuaded Craig to adopt a more conventional presentation of the play, for he was afraid that the Russian public would simply reject his ideas in toto if they were shown in such a radical form. Hamlet's Daemon appeared in the Cranach *Hamlet*, an edition published by Kessler in 1929 and lavishly illustrated by Craig with woodcuts – both Black Figures and compositions of movable blocks representing the screen arrangements. Craig began working on this edition immediately after the production, and considered it his definitive interpretation of the play. But even in Moscow, the psycho-logical approach was kept. As Hamlet's vision, the court was "the grotesque caricature of a vile kind of royalty," and Claudius spoke "as if

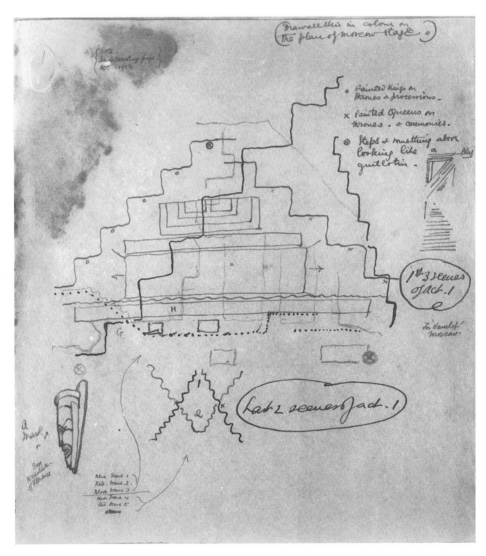

Craig's 1906 stage layout for act 1 of *Hamlet*, with the wavy lines indicating the drapes that the screens replaced. (The references to Moscow date from at least two years later.) Courtesy of UCLA.

he were an automaton; his jaws snap on the words, he grunts them out ferociously."[29]

Despite Stanislavski's caution, Craig not only cut out all the stage directions (with more justice than in *the Vikings* or *Bethlehem* because, as he had pointed out in "The Art of the Theatre," these were generally later additions to Shakespeare's text, representing conventionally accepted interpretations), but also altered the emphasis of long passages considerably and introduced additional scenes. On one level, he saw the play in terms of "A Masque of Theatre," one that reflected his own artistic aims. "In *Hamlet* all that is living in the theatre is struggling with these dead customs that want to crush the theatre." He enlarged the role of the Actors, together with their dumb show of "The Murder of Gonzago." He added a scene in which they donned costumes and makeup, tuned musical instruments, and warmed up with vocal exercises and gestures. Most observers felt that this interpolated backstage activity crystallized the theatricality of the whole production, and the Actors' performance became the climax of the play. Their faces were sharply illuminated by hand-held lights stretched out immediately in front of them on the ends of long staffs. Above the sleeping king's couch was a cutout moon strung on a rope between two poles (with the grouping corresponding exactly to the print in the Cranach *Hamlet*). Their gestures were stylized and exaggerated. The emotions expressed by the Actor declaiming his set speech on Priam's death were echoed by the movements of a choral group, and the dumb show was accompanied by an on-stage orchestra who interpreted the music they played with their bodies. The Actors were also intended to wear larger than life-size masks, but Stanislavski reduced these to elaborately formalized wigs and beards.

Craig had wanted this quality of overt performance to carry through the whole production, with stagehands in special costumes coming onto the stage at the beginning of each scene to set the lights and arrange the scenery. He even suggested that everything "be conveyed without words, by the movements of the actors illustrated by music," so giving the whole play the status of the dumb show. When this was rejected out of hand, he urged that there be a small orchestra on stage throughout, the music of which would key the tone for the actors' delivery and impose uniformity. True to his "system," Stanislavski opposed this on the grounds that any "music" must come from the actors' personal emotions, not from externally regulated intonation. But Craig insisted that Shakespeare, unlike Chekhov, contained no feelings to be found between the lines because everything was directly expressed in the dialogue, and he persuaded Stanislavski to try a rhetorical style of acting, "hard and cold – conventional in its movements and in its sounds." For Craig, artifice – if it were based on the play element of theatricality and not on pretentiousness – was the key to reforming drama. By reducing live human expressiveness to two dimensional stylization it might be possible to move beyond everyday appearances to the spiritual world of the imagination. So, he claimed, "if we were to conventionalize each movement and sound we should create, as it were,

The Actors' scenes as worked out with Black Figures on Craig's model stage, and their translation into production: Actors making-up; the use of hand-held lamps to illuminate their performance; the orchestral accompaniment; the dumb show murder of Gonzago; B. M. Alfonin in the dumb show. Courtesy of Edward Craig and HRC.

an impression of something *flat*... To conventionalize life's movements and sounds is to create a new kind of life, and in my opinion that is the whole reason for the existence of the artist."[30]

In Craig's view one way of achieving this was through the type of acting he admired in Irving, who swept on and off the stage, struck attitudes, glared, gasped, whispered with bated breath, and chanted his words. However, where actors were resistant to this method, the effect could also be created through the way each scene was treated – by selecting only the most significant images and following his principle that a director's task was to cut out all but essential actions. This became Craig's aim here: "No movement unless necessary. Thin out all ... until none but the six or ten *main movements* in the scene are left." The same process of simplification was to be applied to the dialogue. For instance, Craig believed that only the first and last sentences of Hamlet's speech, "Seems, madam? nay it is; I know not 'seems,'" were needed. "These four lines express an important thought and must be spoken accordingly. All the rest of the monologue must be pronounced more as music, so that the thought becomes so much lost in the sounds that the audience simply *does not follow* the thought." The same kind of musical tirade, a bravura style that Craig admired in Italian acting, was to be used for the ... whole of Act 1, scene 3 (Ophelia being forced to deny Hamlet's love by her departing brother, then by her father). When Stanislavski objected that "in order to play a scene at such a quick tempo the actors would have to move about as little as possible ... Don't forget that the most difficult thing for an actor is to stand still in the middle of an empty stage," Craig replied, "Yes, yes, I know that. But can't you really see Ophelia in this scene, crying and grimacing, but without any deep feeling, standing motionless in one place with hardly any movement?"[31]

What Craig never seemed to realize was that these stylized approaches were all too open to misinterpretation, both by the actors and by the audience. Being derived from widely known and accepted conventions, they could hardly help but evoke the same range of pre-conceptions and responses. Of course there are intrinsic problems with this degree of stylization. As Bernard Shaw had already discovered, using melodramatic formulas, even when inverted, meant that audiences tended to read his plays as straight melodrama instead of as an attack on it. Faced with an unusual, non-naturalistic mode of presentation, Craig's spectators were all too likely to see it in terms of whatever (outdated) artificial conventions they were familiar with – such as the rhetorical exaggeration of "Court Theater" acting, or the clichéed emotional high-tening of melodrama – overlooking the actual qualities of Craig's vision. Above all, "flat" characterization could easily be misinterpreted as stock figures. Actors too were likely to fall back on such standard techniques when called to express themselves in a radically new way: particularly in this case, where the MAT actors were committed to the naturalistic understatement required by Chekhov's plays, and a language barrier forced Craig to direct the production through intermediaries who had little understanding of his aims. And indeed this confusion was echoed in the Moscow reviews of *Hamlet*.

There may have been inherent flaws in Craig's theory of stylized acting – and it is certainly true that not one of his productions measured up to what he imagined – but in fact the *Hamlet* performance could hardly be called a fair test of Craig's ideas. Stanislavski's actors felt that Craig was making impossible demands. Hamlet was to enter in one scene as if swept in by a gale, then bend forward to touch the ground with outstretched arms, twisting his torso in movements that were simultaneously sharp, musical, and plastic, and end by stretching upward with his spine arched backward to the audience. When Ophelia swooned she was to hurl herself headlong down a steep flight of stairs. Kachalov, as Hamlet, was low-key and almost scholarly – anything but the physical actor Craig required. Alisa Koonen, who played Ophelia, complained that Craig's directions were unrealizable and that "no actress could do it."

In the court scene – in which the actors did try to achieve the effect Craig designed – the courtiers, whose costumes weighed as much as thirty-five pounds, had to remain absolutely still for so long that some of the actresses lost consciousness. But the real problem was that the cast was never given a clear picture of Craig's concept. Partly because of the language difficulties, Craig never rehearsed the actors himself, and there were complaints from the performers that he showed no interest in them. He isolated himself with his model theater, and worked entirely through intermediaries – Stanislavski and Suler – who were used to a very different style of acting.

However, Stanislavski had been well into preliminary rehearsals before any discussions with Craig about characterization or blocking, so that from the start Craig was working against preconceived ideas. Long breaks in the production process, together with cast changes, compounded the difficulties. In addition, by 1911 Stanislavski was using rehearsals to test his developing system of realistic acting. Craig wanted three quite distinct tones in the presentation: realism for the scenes of comic relief, heightened realism verging on caricature for the tragic action, and abstraction for Hamlet. Stanislavski provided Kachalov with subtexts for each of Hamlet's scenes, ignoring Craig's earlier insistence that in Shakespeare every emotion is directly expressed, and wrote asking Craig's permission to present the characters more subtly and less "naively." The result can be illustrated by the interpretation of Polonius. Craig conceived of him as a toad, and he was made to look like one. His head, with its straggling white hair and heavy-lidded eyes, was topped with a skull cap covered with wart-like diamonds and squares. But the characterization of Polonius was understated and naturalistic.

In any case it was unrealistic to hope to establish a radically unconventional acting style in a single production. Indeed, Stanislavski had originally offered Craig an ongoing contract for several productions, with at least two in the first year, as he realized that "only constant training can bring forth the results desired" from the actors. Inevitably all that could be achieved was a compromise. This was underlined in a

From stylization to melodrama: N. O. Massalitinov as Claudius, O. L. Knipper as Gertrude, V. I. Kachalov as Hamlet. Courtesy of UCLA.

public statement by Suler: "Our theatre, having learnt from Craig, is trying to bring to fruition everything *that it considers feasible.*" But unfortunately, as at least one reviewer noted, compromise destroyed the integrity of Craig's vision and conflicted with the effect of the screens.

> A conventionalized staging requires conventionalized acting: the Art Theater did
> not understand this...life-like movements, life-like gestures should have been
> indicated by conventionalized gestures, like those we see in old Byzantine
> icons...monochrome denuded walls, even the very stone graveyard with square
> pillars would not have seemed strange and out of place if we had seen in them
> life as "conventionalized" in substance, with conventionalized gestures and
> vocal intonations.[32]

In fact it is surprising that so much of Craig's symbolic interpretation came across, and this can only be seen as evidence for the powerful imaginative effect of the screens. They clearly imposed a unity of tone and a degree of abstraction that were sufficient in themselves to color any naturalistic acting, and Jacques Rouché, the director of the Théâter des Arts in Paris, believed he had seen a work that was completely original in the stylization and simplification of both scenery and character.

Whether the conventionalized acting Craig envisaged could ever have worked remains an open question. Stanislavski reported that the actors had been forced to revert to his naturalistic method of presentation because, in attempting to speak the verse Craig's way, they "fell back upon declamation, a dead seesaw rhythm." Craig responded that they had lacked the commitment that alone could give formalization imaginative substance. "You did weakly what I would have had you do powerfully. You fell back instead of advancing...because you had sworn *never to be theatrical*, and that is the sole thing to be." At the same time, he was at least equally responsible, having effectively boycotted rehearsals ("For why see too often what cannot be corrected?"). There is a great deal of unintended irony in such diary entries as: "Wolkonsky also spoke of my production of *Hamlet* – he had seen 3 acts rehearsed yesterday. This is more than I have seen!!...it is hard to remain patient and silent while my imaginings are being messed about."[33]

As Craig spoke neither Russian nor French, and Stanislavski no English, there were problems of communication at all points in the production. It is doubtful whether either understood the other's interpretation of the play, and the transcript of their discussions gives the impression of two parallel monologues that never meet, with one of Stanislavski's constant remarks being, "that is another play." Stanislavski thought Craig believed that art could be created only out of "dead material" and that he "dreamed of a theatre without men and women, without actors. He wanted to supplant them with marionettes." This was a good example of how Craig's way of exaggerating to challenge preconceived ideas actually worked against him. All Craig later claimed to have meant was that the dead material of the existing theater and realistic acting had to be removed, and – far from wanting puppets completely subordinated to the will of a director-artist – Craig complained about the lack of initiative shown by the *Hamlet* cast.

Although... he clung to his ideal of an Übermarionette as an actor who was totally in control of his emotions and his means of expressing them, Craig commented that "after two years of this Moscow Art Theatre I find in it a man who has an even worse opinion of the Actor than I have – Stanislavski. He uses them as one uses needle and threads – It is... quite inhuman." If he had in fact wanted to reduce the status of the actor, as readers of his essays popularly supposed, this was his first real opportunity. Instead he reaffirmed the necessity for improvisation, even if with the reasonable proviso that it always correspond to and reinforce the director's underlying concept.

Similarly, Stanislavski, misled by a reference in one of Craig's letters, thought Craig wanted Hamlet portrayed as a Christ figure. Actually, Craig had tried to describe a visionary like Shelley or Blake, and in fact projected himself into the play. As Craig was later to comment, "I have so much more to add about *Hamlet* under the title of 'Hamlet and my very self.'"[34] In preparing the production he had come to identify with Hamlet, and saw the Ghost as his own father and Ophelia as all the numerous women who had disappointed him.

It is hard to see how this suggestion could have been effectively put across on the stage. At the same time it clearly relates to Craig's concept of the play as a monodrama, and to a great extent the originality of his interpretation was due to its autobiographical nature. But even when Craig's readings were specific, Stanislavski tended to revert to conventional images. The worst example was the characterization of Ophelia. Craig had insisted that all of Polonius's family were "despicable people... It is only when she begins to go mad that she gradually grows into a more sympathetic figure." When asked why such an idealistic person as Hamlet would fall in love with "an insignificant little creature," the answer was that "he was in love with his own imagination, with an imaginary woman." However, by the time of the performance the accepted sentimental view of a meek Ophelia – so gentle that rejection of her love kills her, so noble that she is still able to bless the man who destroys her – had replaced this psychologically perceptive (and autobiographical) interpretation, and Ophelia was presented as "a girl with a pure soul."[35]

The same watering down of Craig's ideas affected even the screens, though this was the element of the production most directly under his control, and one that reviews singled out for praise:

> Mr. Craig has the singular power of carrying the spiritual significance of words and dramatic situations beyond the actor to the scene in which he moves. By the

Ground plan and elevation for *Hamlet*, act 1, scene 3 (Laertes' departure), showing one of the "extra pieces" – the ship painted on a special screen.

simplest of means he is able in some mysterious way to evoke almost any sensation of time or space, the scenes even in themselves suggesting variations of human emotion... A completely realized success of his theories.[36]

As the evidence of Craig's models shows, there was to be a different arrangement of screens for each of the twenty scenes in the play. They could radically alter the size and shape of the acting area, changing from a flat wall across the very rear of the stage for the court scene to a claustrophobic enclosure with corners jutting forward almost to the proscenium for Polonius's study. The shape could also provide a spatial representation of a character's state of mind, as in act 3, scene 3, in which concave leading into convex curving walls echoed the indecision of Hamlet's "Now might I do it, pat..." Or, by moving some screens while leaving others in the same position from one scene to another, they could give a sense of progressive development, as in act 4. Here the continual transformations provided a vision of subtly shifting relationships, at least in Craig's vision. (In the actual production, the first three scenes of act 4 were all cut, as indeed was the King's prayer scene, omitted at the final dress rehearsal to prevent the production from running overtime.)

Model for *Hamlet*, act 2, scene 1 (Polonius's study).

Model for *Hamlet*, act 3, scene 3 ("Now might I do it, pat"). The double Black Figure represents Hamlet with his Daemon. Courtesy of Edward Craig.

A straight line of a wall with one large rectangle jutting forward, set diagonally across the stage to form an exterior for the opening scene, became an enclosed corner by swinging the further end forward onto the other diagonal, while the rectangle shrank into a square, self-standing column. This column formed the central pillar in a row of five placed

The continuing relationships created by shifting the screens in *Hamlet*, act 4, scenes 1, 2, 3, 5 and 6. Courtesy of Edward Craig.

straight across the middle of the stage for the council hall of scene 3; a row that was then reduced to four, ranged around a massive circular column in the center area behind as a fortress like tent for Fortinbras. The line straightened again for scene 6 to form a battlemented wall and lower court, with the pillars being joined by screens that linked the first with the second and the third with the fourth at the rear corners, and extended the front edges of the first and fourth out to the sides, while steep narrow steps filled the center space. Finally, in the very last scene of the play, the two center pillars were moved forward and apart, the staircase was replaced by broad low steps, and the background was filled with an arrangement that suggested perspectives of receding columns, half temple altar, half palace entrance – though Stanislavski reversed this, significantly increasing its dramatic effectiveness. He filled the central archway with two rows of massed spears that moved back and forth to suggest the approach of Fortinbras's army, so that instead of a perspective into a distant interior, the interior with the bodies of Hamlet and the others became the foreground.

Oddly, Craig's use of screens has come to be generally considered an error in judgment, either because it is thought that they were suited only to portray abstract movement (which meant that using them as settings for specific actions reduced them to a merely illustrative function), or because it is believed that they were too much at odds with the existing theater technology to provide the scenic fluidity required for such a play as *Hamlet*.[37] It is certainly true that Craig had to dispense with the thinly opaque roof over the acting area that had been intended to complete the visual impression. It is also true that the complexity of the varying shapes meant that the movement of the screens could never have been achieved invisibly, or without any break in the action, as Craig's patent specification suggests should have been the case. However, most of the critics who consider the screens impractical point as evidence to the passage in Stanislavski's *My Life in Art*, which describes how the screens fell over the actors like dominoes on the first night. Yet Craig himself repeatedly protested that this never happened at any performance, and demanded that Stanislavski delete the passage from future editions. Even though the description is still there, Stanislavski privately acknowledged that this did not in fact happen during a scene, nor on the first night, but in rehearsal during one of the changes. Eventually, in a letter to Craig, he enclosed a "sworn statement" from the stagehands testifying that the incident was due to their error rather than to any inherent instability in the screens themselves.[38]

The screens constructed by the MAT carpenters do not seem to have followed Craig's patent designs, and being ten feet higher than the sets presented to Yeats or Ellen Terry, may well have been less stable. But the fact that they had collapsed at all, even in rehearsal, meant that the screens were braced and weighted down for the performance, which negated a major part of their value. Any repetition of the accident would of course have been disastrous. But if the risk had been taken, and if Craig's suggestion of specially costumed stagehands had been adopted, there would have been no need for the curtain that covered each change – something on which Stanislavski indeed had always insisted – nor for the long pause that actually occurred between each scene. When there were completely different arrangements of screens in two successive scenes and the change could not be accomplished without breaking the flow, Craig had envisaged music to preserve continuity of mood, as at the end of the opening scene:

> Only the glimmer of a glow remains as at the beginning of the scene, that is, in the same place where the Ghost had appeared.
> When the glow dies out, a bell is heard.
> The chime changes to a rumble – the pealing of wedding bells.
> The rumble increases and the notes of a cracked bell grow prominent. They are mingled with the sounds of a funeral march, growing ever more distant.

Elsewhere the screens could have been shifted openly during exits and entrances as an integral part of the performance, and with the scenes shortened by speeding up the actors' delivery in the many extended passages that Craig considered less than essential, the effect would have been near the almost continual movement that he envisaged. "No break in the play. The scenes shall grow one out of the other and will be like the dance of the seven veils."[39]

In many ways, the screens seem to be the right instrument for creating the shapes of places "never seen before except in the mind's eye" that Craig considered the only appropriate setting for poetic drama. Even his symbolic interpretation of Hamlet, though highly idiosyncratic and limiting on one level, has fascinating potential, as his analysis of the opening shows:

> A sweep of dark sky is indicated with one solitary star; it is a cold night, nothing stirs. Suddenly a bell tolls the hour. A man, hidden until now in the shadow, is seen to rise slowly, and remains listening. Then he paces restlessly to and fro, the place filling him with a certain dread. His march continues. He passes in front of us; now he is engulfed in some huge unfathomable shadow, from which he presently emerges into the grey light. He seems like some ghost; he resembles that which he fears to meet.[40]

As even Suler allowed, however one might rate Craig's instruction to the actors, the poetic quality of his concepts and their translation into

The model for the final scene of *Hamlet*, later used by Craig as a generalized example of how screens might be "employed for a large stage scene" in any play.

an evocative composition were striking. At the same time he was undoubtedly difficult to work with. Apart from his exasperating financial demands, he quarreled with Stanislavski, abducted and seduced Stanislavski's secretary (by his own admission) when Isadora Duncan flirted with Stanislavski over dinner, and antagonized Suler by refusing to allow his name to appear on the program because Suler had questioned some of his decisions.

Such displays of temperament may have been due to Craig's own dissatisfaction with the rehearsal process. However, the production had attracted unprecedented worldwide attention and the foreign reviews were almost uniformly enthusiastic. The Moscow Art Theater's visit to Berlin in 1905 had first established its reputation outside Russia, but it was these reviews that really put the theater on the cultural map for western Europe. They were also partly responsible for Craig at last finding a patron to finance his school. The Russian reviews, however, were highly critical. The more conservative papers attacked the whole interpretation. Those who were impressed by the symbolic concept and the screens damned the acting and made Stanislavski all too aware of the "tremendous distance there is between the scenic dream of an artist...and its realization on the stage." Stanislavski himself attributed the gap to the unsatisfactory nature of "all the existing scenic means." But Craig put it down to working through intermediaries, who prevented him from improvising his ideas and imposed a *"pause* between the

The final scene as presented on the Moscow Art Theater stage, with the central screens removed and the massed spears of Fortinbras's army visible. Courtesy of the Novosti Press Agency.

thought and the act," which "spoils all my work."[41] This immediacy, which would allow a director literally to play on the stage like a musical instrument, was one of the qualities he believed could be realized in Scene – the three-dimensional alternative to the screens that he had prefigured in 1907 with the series of etchings titled "Motion."

During the years of preparation for *Hamlet* he had also visualized other ways of extending the kind of flexibility offered by the screens. He had formulated a distinction between "Two Theatres: A. The theater of space. 1) proportion 2) relationships developing imagination – B. The theatre of speech. When the figure *fills* the space till it dominates the scene [then] its voice can be heard." This pronouncement was accompanied by three small sketches: the first with a large figure filling almost the complete frame, and a tiny tower behind it in the distance to illustrate the dominant single actor; the second with the same figure reduced to minuteness in a huge frame (represented as the same size on paper), and with the tower now a monolithic shape that fills almost the whole height of the opening, showing that when the scene dominates "the figure is not heard"; and a third of the same proportions but with a unified group of actors, in which "the tower still dominates, but the figures must now be heard – as mass."[42] As a rationale for using choral movement to balance the human figure against architectural sets in a way that would really take

Design for the opening of *Macbeth*: musical and visual correspondences.

advantage of the visual potential of the stage, this too contains an essential element of Scene. The shape and position of the tower also strongly resemble a design for the very beginning moments of *Macbeth*, before the witches enter. This design of stony ledges rising to a single, square-sided column of rock with diagonal shafts of light striking one side provides a good example of the symbolic evocation Craig wanted from his semi-abstract scenes: "The straight pillar was to give the spectators the same feeling as Beethoven gives his hearers in the opening of his Symphony Eroica." In addition to illustrating the qualities of a "theater of space," the contrast between the relative sizes of figure and frame in the first sketch and their sizes in the other two sketches relates to the idea of a totally flexible stage that Craig outlined in describing the use of his screens: "With the scene goes a special [adjustable] proscenium, every shape being thus obtained."[43] He had intended to incorporate this into the *Hamlet* production – where, for instance, the stage opening in the grave scene would have been half-height to give the impression of a crypt – but technical limitations allowed him to construct only a simple false proscenium. This gave the stage opening proportions similar to the panoramic proscenium of *Dido and Aeneas*, but represented no advance. Neither height nor width could be changed during performance. However, Craig did return to the idea in the Cranach edition of *Hamlet* (which was specifically intended to "make good" what had been missing in the Moscow production). For this he invented a method of creating prints with the use of interchangeable blocks, which not only provided a continual stream of new arrangements, following each other without pause as he had intended the screens to do, but also simultaneously altered the shape of the frame to give a different scale to the actors. As another variation, in one model he had constructed a circular inner proscenium, through which a scene of ramparts, towers, and steps could be seen. A note on his frequently reproduced photograph of this model reads, "Good . . . but not for *Hamlet*," and it provided one of the inspirations for his *St. Matthew Passion*.

As a result of these new interests, Craig came to feel increasingly that the *Hamlet* production diverged from his aims. It could not be altered to incorporate the next stage in the development of his ideas, and even before the performance he came to feel that it was "wasting my time. I seek to know. I do *not* seek a position or success – and this work in Moscow is old work. I have passed it all." As he admitted, he had caught only a glimpse of the final form that his concept might take. But significantly, upon rereading this passage in 1956, he related it specifically to Peter Brook. Even though Brook was still working pictorially at that time, what Craig's new position brings to mind is Brook's research into the roots of drama, which returned the stage to an "empty space." Now, as his work on *Hamlet* came to an end, Craig declared that his aim was "to study the theatre. I do not want to waste time producing plays . . . I want to leave behind me the seeds of the art – for it does not yet exist, and such seeds are not to be discovered in a moment."[44]

7

THE THEATER OF THE FUTURE:
SCENE, PUPPETS, AND A RELIGIOUS FESTIVAL

As Craig had noted in 1909, his ideal theater, which would "strive towards the condition of music," existed "only in the imagination." Its final form was never realized on the stage, and indeed – as had happened with the Moscow *Hamlet* – it effectively distracted Craig from practical work. But from 1906 on, an increasing number of jottings and scenarios in his notebooks, designs and models, and interviews and articles, culminating with the text of *Scene* in 1922, allow a fairly complete reconstruction of his visonary art form. The way these ideas are expressed is fragmentary, and their final shape evolved only gradually. So there are many contradictory elements, some of which were never fully resolved. On one hand, the thrust is away from actors to puppets and finally to abstract movement. On the other, Craig stresses the value of his concept as a context for human figures. Similarly, he claimed that his "invention" was not a mechanism, yet he realized that it would require all the resources of complex machinery; he spoke of outdoor performances lit by the sun, because the sun had become an important thematic symbol, when all his descriptions and designs presuppose artificial lighting and a roofed-in theater.

Critics have used such contradictions as arguments for dismissing Craig's vision. But these ideas have an inner consistency, and in light of this almost all of his innovations and theories – the screens, *The Steps*, the Übermarionette – which otherwise seem eclectic, are clearly integral parts of a whole. At the same time, even though he claimed that his designs were only a poor substitute for actual performance on the stage and that he would have preferred "to work directly with the material which the theatre offers," those designs still represent a move toward abstraction and away from actual performance. In developing what he called interchangeably Scene and "A Vision," his approach was indeed visionary rather than practical, and this is the point at which anyone devoted to live theater is forced to question the validity of his ideas.

As he later noted when commenting that he could not have done another production with Stanislavski, "Had he asked me to develop some experiments with him and *not before the public* it would have been quite another matter... the further I went [in developing theories] the more I disliked the intrusion of the public."[1] Indeed, by the end of the First World War, Craig had developed a persecution complex. International events deprived him of funds for his work, closed the school he had finally established, made publication of *The Mask* impossible, and even caused his model theaters to be dismantled or broken up when his center in the Arena Goldoni was requisitioned by the Italian army. What made it worse was that at the same time he saw others, like Reinhardt, developing stage techniques that he looked on as his own. As a result he deliberately altered his records of the experiments he carried out on his large model stage (Model A) for fear that his ideas would be stolen, and when he published *Scene* he left his description vague, omitting any technical details.

When Craig came to analyze classical and early medieval drama, which offered very different artistic values to the modern theater he rejected, he decided that their common distinguishing factor was architecture. Whether amphitheater or church, the space in which a play was performed itself provided the setting – a permanent and "genuine" place, in contrast to a mock representation of somewhere else, "scene" rather than scenery. "A work of architecture. Unalterable except for trifling pieces here and there – except for the everlasting change which passed from morn till morn across its face as the sun and moon passed."

This architectural quality was what he wished to reproduce, but in a modern form and not as in, say, Godwin's production of *Helena in Troas*, which attempted to reconstruct an actual Greek stage, and which therefore only reintroduced illusionistic scenery in a different way. To achieve a single architectural scene that could be used to suggest many different types of location, Craig separated the strictly structural elements of buildings from the ornamental, and reduced these to "the essential parts" that were common to all, whether temple, palace, or peasant's hut, classical, Eastern, or modern European. What he was left with were "flat floor – flat walls – flat roof."[2] Variations in ground plans together with the use of light and a single detail – a certain style of door, a grilled window – would then be sufficient for an audience to visualize any particular setting from impressionistic suggestions.

All this could be, and indeed was, achieved by Craig's screens, with their "extra pieces" and the translucent ceiling he had envisaged using in conjunction with them. It was also, in fact, nothing new. As a technique of representation, this refined conventional practice rather than changed it. It was still essentially mimetic in intention. In a draft for an unpublished article Craig even referred to the nineteenth-century "eidophusikon" as a precursor of the mobile stage that he came to call "Scene." This was an almost cinematographic form of spectacular realism, reproducing the sights and sounds of shipwrecks or cities in flames without the use of actors, and replacing plot with the development of an event. However, in relation to the kind of poetic drama Craig had in mind, realism was inappropriate. As he commented: "How ridiculous and how unreal!"[3] In contrast, what Craig had in mind was the representation of the heroic, which abstraction alone conjured up. The link with the eidophusikon was in the way the scenery itself had been transformed into an active dramatic agent. This was the true principle of Scene, although Craig continued to refer to it as an instrument that could be used for staging conventional plays with localized settings.

The quality that had made scenery dramatic in the eidophusikon was movement, and Craig put this together with his reduction of architecture to its essential elements. So when he began to work out the basis of Scene, his definition was "that it shall be of solid form, of three dimensions, and moveable." The inspiration for the actual shape that this idea eventually took came from two sources, Serlio's *Architettura* and Manfred Semper's *Handbuch der Architektur*. Craig had acquired a copy of Serlio's work in 1903 to aid him in designing settings for the hurried *Much Ado* production. Although initially he used it simply to borrow the correct shape of sixteenth-century columns and arches, he found that the geometrical diagrams "held me in 1904 or whenever it was, and today [1946] as I sit here the same book again holds me... I look at it and endless thoughts are born within a few moments." Then, a year later in Berlin, he came across Semper's illustration of the Asphaleia System. Together these provided him with what he referred to as his "instrument," a term coined when he exhibited the first etchings illustrating "The Art of Revelation" as "studies for fifteen separate motions or moods of movement... translated through an instrument."[4]

In one volume of *Architettura* Serlio deals explicitly with the theater, and Craig translated his description of the differences among tragic, comic, and pastoral scenes on the Renaissance stage for the opening number of *The Mask*. Yet the vital inspiration came from the other volume of Serlio's work, which has no theatrical reference at all. The two specific diagrams that provided Craig with the idea for Scene illustrated general principles of architectural perspective. They showed a ground plan, divided into squares, with the elevation of walls corresponding to those squares. Craig immediately transposed the plan into a stage floor, cut into different sections, each of which could be raised or lowered to create deep wells, open spaces, steps, platforms, or partitions. A logical extension was "a roof composed of the same shapes as the floor. Suspended cubes, each cube exactly covering (and meeting when lowered) each square on the floor."

The diagrams from Serlio's *Architettura* that inspired Scene, with Craig's annotations. Courtesy of the Bibliothèque Nationale.

What Craig believed he had discovered was a scene so mobile that it was capable of "scientific movement" in any direction or tempo, and uniquely responsive to the control of an Artist of the Theater: "Each section of this floor can rise and fall at will by mechanical means; each section of this roof can descend or ascend, echoing as it were the movement of the floor; each side can as it were fold and unfold at all parts and can be moved at will, and this movement of the entire stage can be so governed by time as to produce rhythm."[5] He also believed that this mechanism could be developed to the point at which a director (himself) could work it from a console at the rear of the auditorium during a performance, so responding directly to the emotional moods of the audience.

For Craig the primary advantage of this total mobility was its expressiveness. As noted on the flyleaf of the thesaurus that Ellen Terry gave him when he first began to try to formulate his ideas in writing, "Expression is the Deed of the Artist." In reviewing all the techniques of theatrical presentation from the Greeks to the nineteenth century, his primary criterion for picking out the right elements for his ideal stage was "whether or no they are capable of expression. That and little else." But there was also another motive behind this selection. The way he reduced all the varied architectural forms to universal essentials was one aspect of this. Craig's stated aim was to simplify "the possibilities of Drama." The rationale for this was that such a simplification made possible a stronger and more immediate appeal to the imagination, but there was a secondary effect that he never explicitly admitted. It was only through such reduction that the theater could become a medium a single man could control. Whatever the appropriateness to the modern spirit, which Craig defined as "the spirit of incessant *change*," there was also a practical value for a director in a theatrical form in which movement and expressiveness would be limited to architectural shapes and the play of light.

Craig's frustration with the gap between an idea and its execution was one of the main reasons for his rejection of the conventional theater. The Moscow *Hamlet* was simply an extreme example of something he had already complained about in *The Vikings* production. "I do not feel responsible, and one scene or another, one colour or another, one emotion, movement or intention or another seems to me a matter of indifference if it cannot be changed and altered...by a momentary idea." What he wanted was an instrument with which to translate "volcanic improvisation" directly into stage action. That meant eliminating all the accidental elements of performance, the main one being the actor, who either imposed his own interpretation or could present a director's inspiration only in a fixed form established long since in rehearsals, even when his conventional training did not distort the director's intentions. Craig believed he had found such an instrument in Scene, in which the human voice and figure could be replaced by "Light – shadow – motion through impersonal mediums – and silence."[6]

Craig's concept of a melodramatically exaggerated and emphatic form of acting, though derived from Irving and Duse, anticipated the ecstatic style of German expressionists in the 1920s, who used rhetorical gestures, glowing eyes, and facial masking to transmit emotional states directly from an actor's subconscious to the audience. The mobile scene had the same intention on a larger and more abstract scale. It would allow the director, as the artist creating a theatrical piece, to communicate a series of "moods" directly and subliminally through the symphonic movement of shapes and light. The musical analogy is one that Craig himself drew. He described the ceaselessly changing movement of three-dimensional shapes as equivalent to the orchestration of sounds in music, and his earliest jottings on the pages of Serlio compared the intended effect of Scene to that of *The St. Matthew Passion*.

> Remember how imperceptibly [the Oratorio] opens – how it proceeds – advancing in its severe order – its superb rigidity without haste or delay – lawfully – how it relies on its compact and simple *form* to move us – how like a tree it rears itself upwards... It is so that this Oratorio catches me – and it is some such progression that I wanted to put before you in my "movement"...

As in Bach's music, the progression and counterpoint that created structural forms would evoke specific emotions without explanatory words or even the presence of an actor. Craig's aims had changed radically. "The desire to *impersonate* this or that character vanished, and in its place appeared the larger and far more satisfying impulse *to represent the idea*... to endow with soul some lifeless material."[7]

The Theater of the Soul (the title of a book by Eduard Schuré) was almost a catchphrase of the period. For Schuré and most others, it referred to conventional drama with a spiritual message, or acting techniques intended to explore and express the psyche. By contrast, Craig considered that there was no point in defining such a theater in terms of content, as it was the form that determined what the meaning would be. Therefore, "*the method of its delivery* [not the message] should be the main consideration. The soul will not speak through the body... Those who get nearer to the true translation of the soul's message are those who use the most divine materials." Interpreting Shakespeare, he had focused on the conflict between the spirit and the body or material world that imprisons it. Now he believed he had discovered a theatrical form that could deal with such a subject without the surface disguise of everyday life. Alongside one of his designs for *Lear*, which showed a man in a blizzard, he commented:

> If we should have no snowstorm visualized, but only the man making his symbolical gestures which would suggest to us a man fighting against the elements... this would be better... Following that line of argument in its logical sequence, then, would it not be still more near to art if we had no man, but only movements of some intangible material which could suggest the movements which the soul of man makes battling against the soul of nature?[8]

However, the use of the word "intangible" is a giveaway. Craig never developed a mechanism flexible enough for the instrument he imagined.

Hydraulics were one potential solution. These had already become a regular part of stage equipment by the 1880s. At Mackaye's Madison Square Theater in New York, for example, the whole stage was a gigantic lift shaft, with two platforms, one above the other, to allow settings to be changed while a scene was being played. When the lower of the two stages was the acting area, the other was out of sight in the flies, and when it was brought down, the lower one was in the basement. Even more to the point was the Asphaleia System. This system, in use at theaters in Budapest, Prague, and Vienna around the turn of the century, made it possible to raise sections of the stage floor to form platforms of various heights, and their surfaces could even be tilted or rotated.

But the hydraulic lifts by which this was achieved were too cumbersome for the type of movement Craig had in mind. They could be installed only beneath a limited number of sections in the stage, their tempo of operation could not be varied, and they did not include the retractable walls, filling the space between a raised section and the floor, that formed the essence of Craig's visual concept. By the 1920s, the available technology was even more sophisticated, but the nearest Craig came to realizing his ideas was a simplified working model constructed in 1923 by his son, who has commented that

> EGC never had a mind that could comprehend the working of even the simplest machine, so of course he had no theories as to how the mechanism for moving *Scene* would work. In early days he was sitting at the bottom of a lift shaft in which the lift moved up and down on a great shaft housed in the basement and was propelled by some hydraulic system. He took it for granted that he could mass hundreds of those shafts together and get the effect that he wanted. The little model that I made with "simple pulleys" was just to show what effects could be achieved when they were properly lighted from different angles. It was not a model to prove that it could work mechanically. I only used 25 cubes and a painted background, but it was very effective.[9]

On this miniature scale, counterweights and pulleys enabled Craig to set the wooden cubes in motion by remote control. Here he could have demonstrated the abstract play of movement that he had outlined on the flyleaf of Serlio's *Architettura*. From an initial state of nothingness, where "the floor seems to be an absence – the roof a void," one column rises in the center as "a single atom." Behind it another rises: "always a double birth, repeating and repeating." As other columns rose, the first sank again. "Now to right and left one chain of life moves like a sea... Slow shapes... continue to arise in endless numbers," folding and unfolding "until there stand before us vast columns of shapes, all single yet all united – none resting." This metamorphosis ended when an aesthetically complete form was achieved and the artist-director's vision reached its definitive expression, then "all is still."

The Asphaleia System, from Semper's *Handbuch der Architektur*.

Clearly, the subject matter of this kinetic experience was to be artistic creation itself. So the theme would always be the same, although the arrangements of light and perspective changed in each performance as each movement gave a new inspiration that was to be translated instantaneously into three-dimensional forms. The stage space was envisaged as a mindscape, a neutral ground on which the imaginations of the artist and the spectator might meet. As Craig put it, "Some spirit seems to work there in the space, as in a gentle mind," and the abstraction was designed to activate the same creative impulse, not simply passive appreciation, in a spectator. The first column rising out of the emptiness, for instance, was intended to be "like the awakening of a thought in a dream."

But without mechanical aptitude, this ideal instrument could never be developed. Instead Craig was forced to compromise. His first sketch shows screens being used in conjunction with cubes. Later notes describe them disguised as cubes, with leaves the same width as the sides of the cubes and in graduated heights, from fifteen feet to five, to give a sharply diminishing perspective. This was clearly not a viable solution. The mixture of horizontally folding screens and vertically moving columns would have been cumbersome, and the false perspective would have made it impossible to use any kind of figures. In any case, the element of fake architecture or scenic illusion inherent in it was precisely what Craig intended to abolish.

But on other levels the various compromises with which he experimented in order to find workable ways of realizing his ideas had more potential than any conceivable use of the purely abstract form he had in mind. For instance, because a scene flexible enough to provide continuously varying visual effects was beyond his reach, he was unable to dispense with human figures. Instead, he suggested ways of limiting the individuality of the actor: using masks to communicate emotion on a more precisely controllable and generalized level than facial expressions, or massing actors into large groups in which emotion would be expressed through the choreographed movement of the whole.

At first glance Craig's ideas for using this mechanized Scene seem vague and imprecise. Its actual performance qualities are described only in very general terms, and this makes them difficult to evaluate. But he also considered replacing human actors with puppets. Whatever the practical disadvantages in terms of a totally mobile stage, puppets were closely associated in Craig's mind with Scene. He wrote extensively on their use, and his ideas concerning them can be extrapolated to give concrete examples of the type of performance he intended.

The actor's disadvantage, in Craig's view, was that the human figure pointed inevitably toward realism on the stage, and caused audiences to confuse actuality with art. It also focused attention on personality, as opposed to vision, distracting the audience from the aesthetic pattern of the whole to particularities. The premise behind this argument is that theater should have the same characteristics and be approached with the same expectations as one of the fine arts – something that could never be achieved while human individuals themselves formed the artistic medium. At its simplest, as Craig put it in a review of a book on Marie Taglioni, "we write about an artist's *work*, but we write about the performer's person." By contrast, as "a model of man in motion," puppets represented actions in a highly stylized way that evoked a poetic vision, instead of holding "the mirror DOWN to nature." There was never any intention of disguising the artificiality of marionettes. Indeed, Craig emphasized this quality. The more a puppet's movements resembled a person's, the closer it came to giving an impression of something else – to being a surface illusion, rather than to catching *"the spirit of the thing."*[10]

In this Craig was at one with the symbolists, who had turned to marionettes as a means of abstraction and generalization. When

Craig's earliest design for Scene, incorporating screens together with the moving cubes. Courtesy of the Bibliothèque Nationale.

Lugné-Poë founded his Théâtre de l'Oeuvre, he first intended it to be a puppet theater. Jarry's *Ubu* trilogy had originally been written for puppets, and Maeterlinck called his early plays "Drames pour Marionettes." For the symbolists, puppets automatically presented a hieratic image of life. They stood in the same relationship to human individuals as a national flag does to a nation. Their physical limitations reduced any dramatic action to its essentials. As artificial objects they stood for an artist's vision instead of presenting it in a fully realized form, so that the spectator had to complete the images in his own mind.

This meant that any vision gained direct imaginative relevance because each spectator filled in the details from his or her own experience. For instance, Jarry's "ABSTRACT theatre," in which puppets or puppet like figures replaced the conventional actors' psychological and individualized self-portraits with "the effigy of the CHARACTER," was intended to confront the public "like the exaggerating mirror in the stories of Madame Leprince de Beaumont, in which the depraved saw themselves with dragons' bodies, or bulls' horns, or whatever correspond to their particular vice." Alternatively, for Maeterlinck, this imaginative immediacy was intended to carry the spectator beyond individuality altogether onto an archetypal level of purely poetic experience.

But in both cases the value of using puppets was essentially the same. "Impersonal puppets, beings of wood and cardboard, possess a pure and mysterious life. Their aspect of truth catches us unawares, disquiets. Their elemental gestures contain the complete expression of human feelings."[11] And, even though actors, not puppets, were used for Maeterlinck's plays as well as for the first performances of *Ubu Roi* at the Théâtre de l'Oeuvre, both types of work required the actors to take on marionettelike qualities. Maeterlinck's somnambulistic action could be represented only in slow movements and deliberate gestures. Jarry's simplistic clichés and *grand guignol* slapstick ruled out psychological subtleties; his actors wore masks and (according to Yeats's description) hopped around the stage like wooden frogs.

Craig wrote puppet plays of both types. *The Drama of Fools*, a satiric and at points Jarryesque collection of minidramas, attacked society. It was an outlet for his frustration after the closing of his school and the dismantling of the model stages on which he had been working out his Art of the Theater. Others – in particular, one titled *The Scene*, written in 1914 – provide a commentary on his ideas. In *The Scene* two puppets discuss the nature of theatrical performance. One believes he has "a soul" that makes him the equal of the "God" who created him, and claims he is "absolutely self-dependent." This is demonstrably false because he has strings attached to his limbs, strings that he has to ask the other puppet to move when he wishes to change position. From his viewpoint, however, these strings connect him directly with God, and "the reason why I had to ask your help to get down just now is that God has become helpless lately." In fact he represents the human actor in the modern agnostic age, the being whose egoism has broken "the old divine unity" and whose "body refuses to be an instrument." He strikes Shakespearean poses, fills his voice with shades of personal emotion, and sees performance in terms of the stock roles of the nineteenth-century acting company. By contrast, the other puppet is fully aware of his artificial status as a man-made object and has "no 'soul' so far as I know, for I do not know what it is." But, when the first puppet typecasts him as "a Juvenile Lead," he replies, "I am a God ... I am an Image – the Image of a God – I am therefore a God to those who believe in me." The setting of this minidrama is the movable geometrical cubes of Scene, and in a prologue the second puppet demonstrates (to a musical accompaniment that underscores their rhythmic nature) "all the movements which a marionette is capable of. These exclude all movements which are called useful or realistic."[12]

The primary quality Craig was searching for, though it is not present in the rather simplistic verbal discussion of this script, was symbolic suggestion. His jottings made in 1922 for an unpublished book referred to the Chinese theater as an example of his ideal. There everything was left to the spectator's imagination; a bare stick could become a blossoming almond tree. His aim was to create a contemporary European equivalent of this highly conventionalized Eastern theater, though he never explored the degree to which symbolic communication is dependent on fixed and widely accepted forms. Puppet drama, like classical ballet, has its own established conventions. But Craig's concepts were all designed for the ordinary theater, even if they were worked out by scaling them down to model stages. So puppets gave way to other types of figures.

One idea was to use two-dimensional human silhouettes, which would hold "a characteristic pose ... for an entire act" (an extension perhaps of the *schemata* or fixed attitudes taken up by classical Greek actors at moments of emotional intensity). The movement was reserved for the mobile cubes of the Scene. Another idea, as inanimate figures could be of any size, was to use stature as an indicator of each silhouetted character's moral status or significance in the drama. Lesser figures – or those who existed in the world of physical action, as distinct from those who represented spiritual states – could be made one-third the size of major figures. However, in Craig's words, the essence of this art "is to be all Movement" and its chief characteristic was to be a seamless flowing of ceaselessly changing shapes, so neither puppets nor immobile silhouettes were really appropriate.

A third idea, using puppets and actors simultaneously, had been suggested by Craig for one point in the Moscow *Hamlet*. It provides a good illustration of the imaginative symbolic use of inanimate figures that he was envisaging. For Polonius's interrogation of Hamlet in act 2, Craig wanted a marionette representing the Prince to move slowly toward Polonius (waiting on a shallow forestage) down a brightly lighted central corridor designed to give a zigzag perspective of immense depth and distance. As the marionette approached, it would appear to grow larger, because scaled-up versions of the figure, book in hand, were to be substituted as it moved briefly out of sight at the end of each turn in the corridor. When it reached a gigantic size, Polonius hurries to meet it, and a strong spotlight on the now empty forestage allows the actor to take the place of his effigy and switch positions with Polonius unobserved by the audience. At the same time the flat screens on either side of the corridor move inward so that the forestage now appears to be a continuation of the passageway. The lights go up on the corridor again to show a mirror image of Polonius scurrying forward out of the depths toward Hamlet, seen in silhouette on the now darkened forestage and reading a book with his back to the audience. As they meet the dialogue begins. This staging was rejected, not without some justice, as being too complex to carry out.

An early model showing silhouetted Black Figures ("2 Roman actors and 3 others") against the background of Scene. Courtesy of Arnold Rood.

In fact, despite their symbolic value, puppets were not really an appropriate means to Craig's end. If "figure and scene must both move harmoniously together – mingling their values," in practice this could be achieved effectively only by using human actors.[13] Indeed, as Edward Craig has pointed out in rebutting the notion that this ideal stage was no more than a retreat from the theater into abstraction, of the nineteen etchings published in *Scene* only two show geometric shapes without human figures.

In this series of etchings, people pursue others through passage-ways formed by the columns, walk pensively through arcades, descend despairingly into the depths, stretch out their arms to the light that streams between high towers, or fill the stage floor in front of a single monolith. But these are not conventional actors. Their movements are dramatic, but never declamatory. There is no indication that these figures speak. They are more like dancers than actors, and in three of the designs the actions they perform are recognizable dances. In Craig's view, "all nature is silent when it acts and speech cannot take the place of action...let acts speak for themselves." Words appealed to reason and could communicate only limited meanings. Movement was a universal language, allowing such variety of interpretation that contact with the spectator would never be disrupted by disagreement with what was

Black Figures, with the difference in size standing for relative symbolic significance. The smaller figures represent Hamlet and Laertes fencing. The first of the larger figures represents Hamlet with his Daemon, and the others are general figures for a Roman drama. Courtesy of HRC.

expressed. It was "simple for all to understand feelingly." Like the Japanese puppets that Craig considered particularly effective because "they use their full force of silence," a purely visual stream of images would have the strongest symbolic impact, communicating on the pre-verbal, subconscious level of the mind.

If dialogue were used, it would be separated from the action. The words would be recited or sung by an offstage chorus as an accompaniment to the movements of silent figures, as Craig had done with Cupid's part in *The Masque of Love* and in his experiments with silhouettes, where he had also followed the example of Japanese puppet theater. Or the actor himself might make sharp divisions among the various modes of expression, as in one of Craig's scenarios. "Harlequin enters – he moves and when he has reached the *end* of his movement he pauses – *body fixed*. Harlequin speaks – when he has finished he makes a pause – then he makes some clear and illuminating *action* [gesture] – he rests again – no sound, no movement – then the music picks up the thread of the pattern."[14]

One of the confusing aspects of the etchings published in *The Scene*, which was taken as evidence for the impracticality of Craig's ideas, is that the actors appear to change radically in size. In some designs the figures are dwarfed by columns that tower like skyscrapers. In others they fill the frame and their heads rise above their architectural background. However, these shifts in proportion make perfect sense in the context of the adjustable proscenium that Craig had intended to supply with his patent screens, though (like Scene itself) he never worked out a mechanism for putting his idea into practice.

The concept of an adjustable proscenium was not new in itself. Like the lighting techniques in Craig's early productions, it came from Herkomer, who had proposed a system of counterweights and screws to change the size of the opening from scene to scene in aid of dramatic realism (see the illustration on p. 34). But in Craig's ideal theater the proscenium was to be the most flexible part of the stage: expanding for massed crowd scenes or to put a figure into a diminishing perspective; contracting until a spread-eagled man could touch all four corners (as in Leonardo da Vinci's figure studies) to focus on the single actor alone for a soliloquy such as "To be or not to be..." Like the lens of a movie camera, a panorama could be changed to a close-up without breaking the action. This versatility was to be carried through to the whole structure of the stage. Craig envisaged a stage floor that could be sunk until it was five feet below the line of sight from the front row of the stalls, so that the whole audience could look down over low walls set up all over the stage floor in place of conventional background scenery and see a bird's-eye view of separate actions going on simultaneously in different rooms, as in medieval paintings. He also anticipated the concept of "environmental theater," experimented with by the American Performance Group in the sixties, suggesting that a theater be constructed in which the spectators would move around the actors to choose their own perspectives on the action.

Even if modern technology could have been used to construct such a flexible stage, the cost would have been prohibitive, and the desired effects could hardly be achieved in the conventional theater. In the last scene for his 1926 production of *The Crown Pretenders*, Craig designed a perspective that receded to what looked like massive gates. But even if the impression of a line towering miles high could be achieved on a piece of paper only two inches square (his often-quoted example), the human figure was not responsive to such treatment. The Danish actors struggling to get through the gates looked ridiculous. Similarly in 1928 he had to content himself with a revolve in the *Macbeth* designs he did for Tyler, though this fell far short of the flexibility he wanted:

> a turntable stage is only a nuisance...what is needed is a stage which can move all ways – tip forward – back – sides *during the scene* – raise this X, lower that group or figure... For example we all need to see Macbeth exactly as placed here at moment [in the Banquet scene, stretched over the table, prostrate with shock] and, to this end, these tables – "degrees" – platforms [in the foreground] should be able to tip up gradually – Macbeth raised – the table to slant a bit – Lady Macbeth to be higher (as here), the front lines of guests lowered... This moving stage would be of assistance to the spectators *who cannot move around* – and to the actors – and so to the whole play.[15]

However, Craig had a more ambitious goal in mind for his Scene than providing a background for conventional dramatic plays. The most successful visual element of *The Pretenders* production was Craig's use of light – particularly his projections, which gave a free impression of tall airy columns for the cathedral scene and of a spiraling snowstorm against which the ghost of Bishop Nicholas appeared. Indeed, light had such significance for Craig, both as a symbol, as a means of evoking emotional moods, and as a technique for painting a scene, that his theater deserves to be called "The Theater of Light."

Adolph Appia is the name that springs to mind when we think of light used as a living medium to bring moving actors into emotional harmony with the stage space and to express "the inner nature of all experience." In many ways Appia shared Craig's principles. He too proposed that poetic drama be the work of a single artist – the director – who controlled the interaction of light, movement, and music, forming a synthesis of the different theatrical elements to create "a supreme union of all art." Like Craig, his aim was to find a modern equivalent for the classical Greek theater, in which drama was the event, the act itself, not spectacle. He had followed Craig, independently, in abolishing footlights, in using light and shadow instead of paint to give plastic form and color to scenery, and in replacing the realistic representation of the material world with an atmospheric suggestion of spiritual states. His concept of using light as "a means of externalizing...most of the colours and forms that painting freezes on the canvas and of distributing them dynamically in space" is almost an exact transcription of one of Craig's principles. So too is his vision of simplifying the stage picture while introducing sophisticated electrical equipment, which could be regulated in precise detail, so that "the actor no longer walks *in front* of painted lights and shadows; he is immersed in an atmosphere *that is destined for him* ... We no longer seek to give the illusion of *a forest* but that of *a man* in the atmosphere of a forest."[16] Craig considered Appia to be the only theater artist with whom he could have collaborated, but believed that Appia had not gone far enough.

The human actor remained the primary means of expression in Appia's concept. Craig (perhaps overstating his position in response) insisted when they met to discuss their theatrical ideas that "the true and sole *material* for the Art of the Theatre" was "LIGHT – and through light, movement." The neutral pale gray of Scene was to be given shifting emotional tones by the changing colors of light, and the primary reason for moving the cubes was so that they could "receive the play of light."[17] But light also had a significant thematic value for Craig. God's first command in Genesis was "Let there be light." The sun had traditionally been seen as the element that fostered biological life. If on one level the subject of his theatrical art was to be artistic creation itself, on a wider level this could be seen as mirroring the creation of the universe.

In its first draft, the text of *The Scene* referred to light in quasi-religious terms. It compared the abstract movement of the cubes to the ever-changing dynamic of nature, and defined "the essential of Drama" as "Acts of God." Such phrases were omitted from the final version, perhaps because Craig felt that any touch of mysticism would only confirm the view that his ideas were impractical. However, from about 1909 on, his notebooks are filled with metaphysical scenarios that are clearly intended for performance on his mobile scene. Although these are little more than rough jottings – none were developed – their thematic consistency clearly indicates the nature of Craig's vision.

The Art of the Theater that he called for was not concerned simply with technical reforms. As he had announced in 1907, "A new religion will be found contained in it. That religion will preach no more, but it will reveal...it will unveil thought to our eyes, silently – by movements – in visions."[18] At the same time, these visions were to be abstract and evocative, rather than the definitive images of painting or sculpture. What they expressed was a generalized religious sense, not a theology. Craig had rejected the sentimental clichés of conventional belief when confronted with the tinsel angels and Marian pieties of Housman's *Bethlehem*. What he saw as inherent to his new forms of dramatic presentation was not a Christian message, but a pantheistic nature worship. As the sun, from Craig's perception of natural phenomena, seemed to be the source of movement as well as of light, and was one of the traditional symbols for divinity, it became the Creator, the Lawgiver, God.

The sun's rays were a rather obvious metaphor for revelation, and Craig called his scenarios *Illuminations*. They range from the representation of a single day to a *Ceremony of the 365 Days and Nights*, and were intended to have the same effect as natural manifestations of change and movement, which can appear significant and dramatic without containing any explicable message. As an art in its own right, rather than as mimetic illustration, movement would have the same quality as music, which Craig defined as "sense without meaning."

This might have been an accurate description of those *Illuminations* that represent nothing beyond the procession of hours or seasons. "The Sun is a symbolic representation of life...by [its] rhythm time becomes beautiful... A cause and effect it may have, meaning it has none. Why then do 'artists' today struggle so hard to give a meaning to everything?" But the more developed these jottings and sketches become, the further they move away from this ideal. When *The Creation* is organized into seven "days," opening "with the light, which faint at first as though travelling from afar, sets everything in motion" until "last of all a man walks into the midst," then it clearly contains conventional and extrinsic meaning. Later *Illuminations* even conflate theatrical performance and religious worship, moving toward a mythology of art in which the devotional object becomes Craig's new theater itself, as in one titled *Through Night to Light*. Here the scene becomes an imagined amphitheater in which "thousands of men and women draw together in the dark." These are Craig's followers, "waiting in *The New Theatre*" for the "consciousness of God" that the performance is to bring:

> The sun has shot one ray of its immortality upon the very centre of the circle...
> It plays upon a large crystal basin in which the coldest water lies motionless...
> The force of the Ray becomes terrific. Suddenly a cry goes up – "the water is all

gone" – a great conflagration... The Force of God is seen, is felt. A hundred men in white [enter] bearing a silver sphere upon their shoulders...300 voices are chanting praise to God... Fountains spring up, white birds are loosed and raise themselves in air...voices rise higher and higher. This is the first ceremony in praise of the God of all things – the creator of life and motion – the symbol of our art.[19]

The elevated poetic prose of these *Illuminations* may be a measure of their importance to their author, but the iconography is crude and the pretentious amalgam of symbolic action and religious service is unconvincing. However, the focus of these scenarios is central to Craig's art. The intention behind his theatrical reforms is summed up in a letter from Isadora Duncan after the tragic death of her children, a letter that draws together many of the thoughts that he returns to again and again in his notebooks. "You are creating the only world that is worth living in – *the imagination* – ...releasing poor souls from the inferno of *reality* and *matter* [you] lift them up out of 'life' into the *only life*, up where the spirit can fly – freed from this abominable bad dream of matter."[20]

Craig's rejection of naturalistic drama, his symbolist approach, his attempts to replace stage illusion with the atmospheric suggestiveness of light and the actor with a moving scene – all are aspects of this metaphysical aim. Their common factor is a move toward abstraction, which expresses an etherealization of the physical, a desire to dissolve matter into spirit and create a mystical dream of reality. In Craig's terms, it is "to get something entirely opposed to life as we see it," which he called "Death" (as being the opposite to material existence, like the female double for Hamlet).[21] But even he must have been aware that no symbolic action he could imagine would have the evocative force of Christian imagery. So he turned to *The St. Matthew Passion* as the logical extension of Scene, and dedicated the etchings illustrating *Scene* "to Old Bach."

Martin Shaw had introduced Craig to the oratorio as early as 1899. It was one of the works on his first list of planned productions in 1900, and by 1901 he was already creating designs for it with great flights of steps and shafts of light as the visual equivalents of majestic chords of music. This blending of Wagnerian concepts of synaesthesia (in which all the different arts would be united) with symbolist "correspondences," (in which visual impressions and sounds were seen as equivalents) was to become an integral part of Scene. The movement of light and three-dimensional shapes was specifically intended to elevate drama to "the condition of music" (to borrow Walter Pater's words, as Craig did), though the translation from one medium to another was more literal than this suggests. Craig in fact believed that the "laws of movement" and the "laws of music" were interchangeable, as he intended them to be in the *Macbeth* design, in which shape (the single pillar) and light (strong diagonals) were designed to reproduce in visual terms the emotions evoked by the opening chords of a symphony[22] (see the illustration on p. 172).

In fact the relationship between Scene and *The St. Mathew Passion* is explicit in one notebook, where designs for both appear on facing pages. The first sketch is inscribed, "To veil the weakness in *Human Character* and *illumine* the *Heroic*." It shows a "Hero and 6 spirits": the former standing on an upper stage with groups of figures fading on either side into the light streaming between the columns of Scene, the latter ranged on a forestage below. The second is labeled "The Hero...to reveal to the spectator the deity of man" and shows a similar arrangement of figures. But now the Scene is framed by the great arches that form the main feature of the later *St. Matthew Passion* model (a note gives the scale: "170 feet to top of arch from stage") and lines of steps zigzag from one edge to the other, linking the lower and upper acting areas.[23]

Already, in his polemic entitled "The Actor and the Über-marionette," Craig had demanded acting that could represent the heroic, or reveal "the god" in man, by (again quoting Pater) "stripping away the involuntary and restless tremors of the flesh." His notebooks relate this to Scene, which is presented as the appropriate context for actors as heroes – in contrast to the "mean scene," which imitates human surroundings and drags even great actors like Irving down to its level. Scene was a space that could be dominated only by an actor *"masked* from the head to foot by sheer calculation (as in Greece before Aeschylus)...compelling his audience to enter into another state of being – something we call heavenly."[24] This was translated into a more conventionally religious context when Craig came across a twelfth-century church at Giornico in 1910 during one of the breaks in the *Hamlet* production. What caught his attention were the proportions of the high arches over the nave, and the unique positioning of the altar on a bridge curving over a triple archway leading down to the crypt. He immediately saw this as the natural setting for any religious drama, because it gave a perfect symbolic representation of the traditional spiritual universe. "No other church or stage," he wrote enthusiastically, "had such a bridged path from earth to heaven nor so open an inferno. The most beautiful, the most mystic – most human – theatre I have ever seen."[25]

Craig pasted two photographs of this church into his daybook for 1910. On one of them he painted white figures representing actors, and in a letter to Ellen Terry, he cited E. K. Chambers and J. A. Symonds to support the contention that the Mass was the original as well as the

A photo of the church at Giornico that inspired the model for *The St. Matthew Passion*, with Craig's annotations. Courtesy of HRC.

purest form of drama, using a thumbnail sketch of a *Quem quaeritis* performance in Giornico as an illustration. By 1914 he had constructed a twelve-foot-high model stage, specifically for *The St. Matthew Passion,* in which the main features of Giornico were reproduced. The crypt, set back from a forestage on a low platform, was now divided into acting areas of different widths and was visually cut off from the space above, which corresponded to the chancel, although narrow interior stairs united the two. The bridge now led up to vast flights of steps climbing to an upper platform with only the sky behind, a curving cyclorama to "liberate the senses" framed by the great arch.

All of Craig's major concepts were brought together in this model. It had the potential for the evocative, three-dimensional movement that he had explored in *The Steps.* It had a similar monolithic quality and allowed the same possibilities for the play of light as Scene, though the shapes were now fixed. In addition, its structure now had clear symbolic resonance, and as a universal setting for an archetypal drama the flexibility offered by the screens (the only one of Craig's concepts that was unrepresented) was unnecessary. It also had the permanent, architectural quality of the classical stage, which he had wanted to reproduce. It is worth noting that the essential elements – an upper area reached by steps over a colonnade, with a high central arch above – also appear in various combinations in the plates illustrating Roman and sixteenth-century theaters in *Scene,* as well as (together with a forestage dais labeled "pulpito") in Serlio's ground plan of the Marcellus Theater. Beside this Craig had noted: "I would develop this spot for modern theatre to new purposes."[26]

Craig never pulled his ideas for *The St. Matthew Passion* together into a formal *mise-en-scène.* Inevitably his sketches treat the different moments of the oratorio in isolation and in no particular order. But there is sufficient consistency – even though the notes, designs, and photographs of the model cover more than a decade – to give a fairly complete picture of his intentions. The figure of St. Matthew would stand on a central pillar immediately above the center of the bridge. As the Evangelist, he would start to tell the story. On the platforms on either side above the bridge would be the solo singers, attired in gray costumes that merged their figures with the architecture.[27] The scenes of spiritual crisis and "the celestial" action were to take place above the bridge: The Agony in the Garden on the topmost platform, Christ carrying his cross up the endless steps on his road to Golgotha. The other, more human scenes from Christ's Passion, such as the Last Supper, were to take place on the chancel level. "The more terrestrial parts" – Judas's betrayal and the plotting of the high priests – were to be "in the lower portion of the

The model for *The St. Matthew Passion* (twelve feet high), with Black Figures indicating a scale of over 300 feet from the top of the outer arch to the floor of the lower stage. Photograph: Helen Craig.

scene," the crypt, formed by a row of permanent openings of different sizes and designed to have the same effect as a contracting or expanding proscenium.

The principle in using this lower area – in sharp contrast to the overarching expanse of sky (and spiritual freedom) above – was that the space should correspond to the number of actors, each scene "seeming

Scene design for *The St. Matthew Passion*, showing the different use of various levels and the Evangelist on the central pillar. Courtesy of the Bibliothèque Nationale.

crammed to overflowing." The lights would rise on the smallest cell to reveal a single disciple, enclosed by a frame that exactly fitted his standing figure. They would then dim away and rise in the largest area to show Pilate gathered with the high priests. The same highly symbolic contrasts mark other elements of the scenario: a lurid red light might be used for Judas, pastel colours for Mary and her group.

The chorus stands or reclines on the steps, moving or rising only at climactic moments, as in the aria describing the Crucifixion, in which the soprano's ecstatic vision –

> See ye, see the Saviour's outstretched Hands!
> He would draw us to Himself.
> Come!

– catches up the chorus, which responds three times with the cry of
"Where?" Apart from these few moments, Craig wanted the complete
separation of various elements of communication that he had proposed
for the use of puppets or for the way figures might interact with the
moving columns of Scene. The orchestra was to be invisible and, following something Craig claimed Monteverdi had once done in the seventeenth century, was distributed around the auditorium as well as behind
the grilles at the rear of each opening in the crypt, so that the source of
the music could not be located and sound would totally envelop the
audience like an atmosphere. The singers would tell the story and give
the words of the protagonists, but without gestures or facial expressions.
The actions would be performed and the protagonists embodied by silent
and masked figures, whose mimed gestures were precisely regulated by
the tempo of the music.

   In outlining a proposal for the production of *The St. Matthew Passion*
in Rome, Craig specified that "in addition to the *solo singers*...there will
be: a full-sized *chorus*, the performers of a *sacred dance*...[and] a large
number of *figuranti*," though Christ was to be "the sole Heroic figure."
The sacred dance was to be a grotesque dance of death, similar perhaps
to the witches' suggestively sinister antimasque in *Dido*, though very
slow. It was to be performed by tap dancers in the interval between the
two parts of the oratorio and "danced to the tap of drums. No music...the thud of the bones of the heels of the dancers – the snap of their
jaws – blithe laughter in small bursts...the world of the grave."[28] In
contrast to this, the spiritual focus of the action was to be translated into
purely symbolic terms, with the ceremony of the Mass taking the place
of the Crucifixion, and the singer's description of the elevation of Christ
to the cross being represented by the elevation of the Host. Similarly, the
closing moments were modeled on a benediction Craig had witnessed in
Fiesole, where the candles in the church were extinguished one by one as
the service progressed. One after another each area of the stage was to be
darkened during the long final chorus, while the sky slowly changed
from light blue to deep purple.

   From the first Craig had seen *The St. Matthew Passion* as a festival
drama, equivalent to the ancient Greek theater; an idea that had been
confirmed by a concert performance he attended in 1906. It took place

Variations of scenic effect created by lighting on the model for *The St. Matthew Passion* (Helen Craig). Photograph: Helen Craig.

before what Craig described as an immense audience at the Kristal Palatz in Amsterdam, and convinced him that any type of chamber performance was wrong. The scope of the work demanded an audience of "several thousand people, not richer or poorer than others," and it could not be effectively produced on a small scale, for a self-selecting elite, as *Dido* and *The Masque of Love* had been. He had envisaged it initially as being performed in the ruins of some ancient amphitheater, and later tentatively proposed the open-air theatre at Marly le Roi, a semicircular raised-earth stage backed by a wall and trees, as a suitable location when he visited it in 1912. Alternatively, he considered using any large-enough building, and inspected the Panthéon and the Palace of Versailles during a stay in Paris. But because Bach's subject was the Passion, obviously it could "be best performed at Easter and in a church – some church no longer used, but large enough, which could be kept specially for this Easter performance year by year."[29] As his scenic ideas developed it became clear that they could not be realized by converting any existing building. By 1914 he was envisioning a mammoth theater, specially erected for performances of the oratorio, in which the structure of the stage would form a permanent set. His scale model deliberately preserved the architectural atmosphere of a church.

There was nothing inherently impossible in these plans. One aspect of the symbolist movement had been a religious revival. There was at least one French precedent, an updated mystery play that had been given annual performances during Holy Week in the 1890s, and the traditional passion play at Oberammergau was becoming a regular and increasingly popular festival. On the other hand there was the example of Max Reinhardt, who in 1919 built himself his Grosses Schauspielhaus, the "Theatre of the Five Thousand" which was intended to provide the same focus for the whole community as did the theater in classical Greece. One of Reinhardt's most spectacular successes had been a sacred drama, Vollmoeller's *Miracle*, and although his sentimentalized and overblown illusionistic spectacle was the reverse of what Craig had in mind – the dramatic representation of *The St. Matthew Passion* was to be "nothing like one of those Reinhardt performances, with everyone shouting and waving their arms in the air and people catching hold of a man and dragging him away and putting him on a cross" – the general effect at which Reinhardt aimed was the same as Craig's. As Reinhardt's associate Arthur Kahane described it, "Under the influence of these mighty spaces, these big, severe lines...the petty and unimportant – elements that are not eternal in us – cease to have effect. [Such a] theater can only express the great eternal elemental passions and the problems of humanity. In it spectators cease to be mere spectators; they become people; their emotions are simple and primitive, but great and powerful, as becomes the eternal human race."[30]

The possibility of staging *The St. Matthew Passion* continued to occupy Craig for the rest of his active life. When he received carte blanche from New York to produce any play by Shakespeare or Maeterlinck, he cabled back, "Have finished with all talk-plays – will do Bach's Passion if you wish." When Poulsen approached him in 1926, he made no attempt to disguise the fact that his interests were almost exclusively focused on musical drama, and although he did agree to design Ibsen's *The Crown Pretenders*, he cautioned that "my mind likes to concern itself very little with historical tragedy." When the opportunity for meeting Mussolini arose, it was sponsorship for *The St. Matthew Passion* for which he hoped, and he drew up a "proposal for the production in Roma... Easter 1936 and annual thereafter." The Italian government was to construct a stage that followed his model and an auditorium that was to hold from eight thousand to over ten thousand spectators.

The artistic goals of the proposed performances were equally ambitious and summed up the symbolic, spiritual, and universal qualities that Craig had been moving toward in all his work from 1907 on. "The aim of the work will be to make an impression which will penetrate and endure... the dramatic will be pushed to the furthest limit possible"; what would be created in performance out of Bach's material was "the one supreme dramatic work of art which can be understood by everybody, of every land and language, of every belief."[31] However, despite the rather overly ingenuous identification of the penetrating and enduring spiritual impression with "the spirit of Fascismo," and despite references to involving "volunteer fascisti" in the performance as the silent *figuranti* who were to mime the action, this proposal came to nothing.

The St. Matthew Passion has a special place in Craig's life. It was the one work that continued to occupy him through all the different stages of his development. Yet it was the only major project that remained almost unknown until the model was reconstructed by Edward Craig for a centenary exhibition in 1972. Even details of Scene had been published, though the etchings and description gave only the most general outline of his concept. But Bach remained in his notebooks. It is significant that such a focal work was not, in a conventionally recognizable sense, dramatic. Being an oratorio, it has voices, but no action to perform; a symbolic story, but no plot; a scene – one that unites the imagined biblical context with the performance itself as part of a religious service – but no scenery; dialogue, but no conversation. As such, it could provide the model for a new form of theater, which would preserve the continuity of the dramatic tradition while making it possible to discard all the mimetic elements that were embodied in conventional plays and staging. In 1909 Craig had made a list of the theatrical elements that his Art of the Theater would discard, in descending order of importance, indicating at the side what each was to be replaced by:

> The Human face and form – Masks...
> The Play   – Ceremony
> The Spoken word   – Song

Finally man himself would disappear, and what remained would be "light – shadow – motion through impersonal mediums – and silence."[32] This last step clearly related to Scene in its most abstract and extreme form, which went too far even for Craig himself, as the consistent inclusion of figures in his designs indicate. But the plans for *The St. Matthew Passion* give a good example of how masks and song might be used to create a drama of ceremony.

It is also characteristic, however, that Craig's production never developed beyond notes, designs, and a model. What Craig was really offering, perhaps, was an aesthetic for using the new resources of machinery and lighting now available to the stage. Yet, as his reluctance to authorize others to use his screens indicates, he came to realize that imitation of his work would achieve little. This was something that the debacle of the Broadway *Macbeth* also all too graphically demonstrated. In a sense, then, his challenge was more effective without tangible examples to which to point on stage. At the same time, any artist who aims to revolutionize his medium without working in it is in a highly questionable position, and perhaps the only viable avenue for Craig to achieve general reform in the theater would have been through educating the next generation of "theater artists" in his school.

8

FINAL BOW: A SCHOOL AND THE PRINTED WORD

The need for a school had been clear to Craig from the start. Working with amateurs in rented halls where he could design his own stages had given him the freedom to follow his ideas, but had at the same time prevented him from realizing them fully because, as he later said, of "the limits of the money at my disposal – i.e. next to nothing – and the untrained material."[1] The apparent solution was to move into the professional theater. Yet he rapidly found that this imposed even more frustrating restrictions. When he wanted to transfer *The Masque of Love* to the Coronet Theater in 1903, its manager rejected any idea of constructing a lighting bridge immediately behind the proscenium, and refused permission to remove the footlights, to place lights on the side walls of the auditorium, or even to alter the dimensions of the stage picture by constructing a false top for the proscenium. When Craig first directed a cast of experienced actors in *The Vikings*, later the same year, he discovered that the expertise they had acquired in conventional productions worked against everything he was trying to achieve. With *Much Ado* he found that they also reverted to their old habits almost as soon as the rehearsal period was over, effectively sabotaging his conception. Not surprisingly, as soon as he came up against the inertia of established stage practices, Craig began calling for "a School for the Art of the Theatre."

In 1903 Craig announced that he was opening a school, and found suitable studios in London. Not altogether surprisingly, as his claim to attention at the time was based solely on six rather esoteric productions, two of which had received very mixed reviews, and on a prospectus that referred only to "a school of my *belief*" – a belief as yet nowhere articulated – this attracted neither financial patrons nor potential students. But this very lack of response convinced him that nothing else would serve his aims. Barely a month later he noted that "the school scheme...seems more necessary and inevitable every day: not because I am not producing play after play, but because it will soon be impossible for me to produce [even] a scene of a play without the school."[2]

In 1905, after the fiasco of his collaboration with Brahm, Craig again went searching for support for a school, this time in Germany, and believed he had found backing from Hugo von Hofmannsthal for a small independent theater with his own company. That plan also came to nothing, but it shaped his concept of what a school should be: a work-shop for developing his own theories and translating them into prac-tice, rather than a conservatory for teaching different performance skills. Thus "students" would be apprentices instead of pupils, and he outlined the form their training would take in his "First Dialogue on the Art of the Theatre," written in the same year. Sketching in his own experience, this described a potential director as someone who had gained stage experi-ence as an actor and who had moved on to explore how the different elements of theater might be used. Once "he had understood the right use of actors, scene, costume, lighting and dance [the level Craig himself had achieved], and by means of these had mastered the crafts of inter-pretation, he would then gradually acquire the mastery of action, line, color, rhythm and words."

Even in the "Second Dialogue" of 1911, which draws up what seems to be a more conventional program for a school, the true focus is still on developing Craig's Art of the Theater. This proposed five years of study, to include voice and movement training for actors and training in design for scene painters and lighting technicians. But it is this training itself, and not a trained group of artists and craftsmen, that is defined as "the results of their labours." At the top of the list of the school's aims stand "(1) A practical demonstration of the best method to be employed for building and directing a national theatre as an ideal theatre, and in a manner hitherto deemed impossible. (2) The improvement...of the me-chanical appliances of the modern stage." The proposed school is indeed identified as "a college of experiment in which to study... *voice, scene* and *action.*" But voice is abstracted into sound, scene translated as light, action transformed into motion. The envisaged curriculum is in fact a process of experimentation leading through "the better knowledge" of these three fundamental elements to "the invention of better instruments through which the purer beauty of both sound and light may be passed." The end product was to be written or filmed records of these experiments "of incalculable value – not only to us in our future efforts, but to those who shall resume the search when we may be forced to abandon it."[3]

This workshop concept was pathbreaking, and points directly forward fifty years to the Center for Theater Research of Peter Brook, and to the Theater Laboratories of Grotowski and others. It foreshadows them particularly in Craig's desire to discover the preverbal fundamen-tals of communication, to return to the roots of drama, and to refine "the material of the theatre in *words, scene, movement* to the minimum." His ex-periments would strip away the traditional accretions of mimetic staging, simplifying the means of theatrical expression, and then evolving a uni-versal "vocabulary of human motion" and vowel sounds. As he outlined the program in 1911 in a proposal that Stanislavski fund a school in Florence for the Moscow Art Theater, it would build from experiments to determine first the expressive range of the human body alone, and then the potential for communication in relationships between single figures and groups, until after three years "the whole *principle* governing action" and "the *principles* of improvisation or spontaneous acting" could be demonstrated.[4]

Again, nothing came of this, though Craig claimed that Stanislavski took over this approach in developing his "method" (conveniently over-looking its basis in psychology rather than in physical movement). Meanwhile a group of Craig's supporters in England, including the critic Haldane MacFall, W. B. Yeats, and Ezra Pound, had formed a committee "to promote the Art of the Theatre as interpreted by Gordon Craig" through arranging a drama festival for him to be held at some future date in the Crystal Palace. This never got beyond initial discussions because the whole concept revolved around productions by Craig himself. Still resenting what he had come to think of as the philistinism of the British theatrical establishment, Craig refused to produce any play in London. So the committee transformed itself into "a Society for founding a School for the Art of the Theatre," with the aim of raising £25,000 through a program of lectures, exhibitions of Craig's designs, and demonstrations with Craig's model stages.[5] Meetings were held almost weekly from September 19, 1912, to June 3, 1913, when the society resolved to limit its activities to publicity for the school, as it had failed to raise sufficient money even to cover its expenses. That the school was founded at all was due to the generosity of Lord Howard de Walden, who independently provided £5,000 in 1913 and promised a further £2,500 for each of the next two years.

Four years earlier, Craig had noted that many different kinds of schools would be needed to reform the theater, ranging from the practical and technical to the theoretical and experimental. The advertisement he published in 1912 clearly opted for the second category. "It will not be an institution for 'teaching' any art, nor for learning the crafts of acting, of decorating, or of lighting." Instead, "a body of earnest workers...will strive by means of experiment and research to rediscover and recreate those magic and elemental principles of beauty, simplicity and grace... revealing the means of doing what is left undone by the modern theatre...and create in the course of time a solid basis upon which the workers of the future will be able to build a vital and supreme Art."[6]

Now a group of fifteen students joined Craig at the Arena Goldoni, the small neoclassical stage on the outskirts of Florence where Craig had already established the publishing offices of *The Mask*.

A pamphlet was issued reaffirming Craig's artistic principles in the context of the new school. Previous theatrical reforms, it argued, had been limited to externals – changes from thrust stage to proscenium, improvements in the machinery of illusion, new methods of lighting. By contrast, here "the essence" of theater would be renewed. Freed from constraints of commercialism or public performance, ancient traditions could be revived in new forms. As a miniature copy of a Roman amphitheater, the Arena Goldoni became the architectural symbol for what Craig called the theater of the future: "a place no less sacred in its character, no less uplifting in its influence on the national life, than were the great temples of an earlier day – those temples in which were celebrated the stately and splendid exhilarating ceremonies in praise of the Creation."[7]

Although gymnastics, fencing, dancing, mimodrama, improvisation, and voice training were listed in the curriculum, the only things actually studied seem to have been the use of Craig's screens, the potential of Herkomer's lighting techniques, the effectiveness of different types of masks, the possibilities offered by marionettes, and all aspects of theater history. (One of the adjuncts to the school was to be a theatrical museum, and it was from this that Craig's own magnificent collection grew.) Unfortunately the position of the pupils was ambiguous. They were intended to be co-workers, and "at the same time students of Mr. Craig's methods."[8] In practice this meant that they functioned as unpaid technical assistants. Also, Craig printed a set of rules for the students, which showed an almost paranoid fear of his ideas being stolen – even though the very reason for the school was to spread those ideas. Students had to undertake "not to join any other School of a similar nature," and not "to send anyone outside the School any photograph or drawing of anything concerning the School or the work being done there." Even the rules themselves were "not to be shown, nor in any way made known, to any person outside the School."[9]

The result, as Craig noted parenthetically in the margin of his own copy of the rules, was that some students found themselves unable to work under such conditions. No criticism of the school was allowed, and "the first group...all proved unable to stick to their guns. When hard work or some self-sacrifice was needed they fled." Whether the school would ever have produced results in the form of public demonstrations or performances is an open question. In 1909 Craig had asked himself, "What then will you do in your arena?" and had answered, "I *may* give ceremonies – processions – movements...slight things." In 1911 he was playing with the notion that the school should "produce ONLY *Hamlet*," but in such a way that the production "will be able to be visited many

times without the audience being able to say 'we have seen it before' ... "
Elsewhere, contrasting the three years and £ 13,000 needed for staging the
Moscow *Hamlet* with his current enterprise, he envisaged that "five years
after the school is founded" the simplified systems of costume, scene,
movement, and vocal expression to be developed would enable his group
"to produce dramas of our own souls in a material form within 48 hours
and at a cost of £ 20."[10] However, the First World War intervened, the
Arena Goldoni was requisitioned by the Italian army, and funds from
Lord Howard de Walden were cut off. The school was officially dis-
banded and the model stages, the most tangible products of its single
year of operation and the visible exposition of Craig's ideas, were
dismantled – though not in fact broken up, as Craig later claimed, perhaps as a way of justifying the effective end of his career in the theater.

There was a series of abortive efforts to relaunch the school. In
1915 and 1919 Craig held exhibitions of his model stages, screens, and
marionettes in Rome to raise money for the school, and published yet
another prospectus. After the war Jacques Rouché, whose *L'Art théâtrale
moderne* had been referred to by Craig as one of the books "which best
explain the idea for which the school stands," offered him a stage in Paris.
But Craig was still more interested in exploring the principles of theater
than in mounting productions. In 1935 there was talk of establishing a
workshop for Craig in Moscow. All came to nothing.

But throughout this period of social upheaval and thwarted personal plans, Craig continued to publish *The Mask*, which had become
perhaps the most influential theater journal in all of the intense and exciting years of the first quarter of the century. From the opening issue in
1908, which set the tone with Craig's contentious polemic. "The Actor
and the Über-Marionette," it appeared first monthly and then as a
quarterly until 1929. Interrupted only by war, though continually threat-
ened by bankruptcy, which sometimes meant that several issues were
compressed into one, it became Craig's mouthpiece, his soapbox, even his
stage. It contained theoretical essays on movement, scene design, and
the social function of drama; historical articles on all the great theatrical
traditions and periods from ancient Greek tragedy to Bunraku puppets,
from the Japanese Nō to the *Commedia dell' Arte*; and critical appreciations
of all the main figures in the "new movement" – Diaghilev, Duse, and
Isadora Duncan, Maeterlinck, Meyerhold, and Max Reinhardt. It
documented what was happening in the major European theater centers;
translated and reprinted source material on Renaissance theater construction, sixteenth-century masques, and eighteenth-century costume design;
and reviewed theater books and exhibitions. Its range was encyclopedic,
but its perspective was single and consistent. Each subject was treated in

such a way as to show the superiority of stylization over realism, of aesthetic simplicity over conventional artificiality. Every argument was designed to contribute to the vision of a new theater, defining its relationship to tradition by attacking pedantic revivals of dead forms, like the Elizabethan Stage Society, and clarifying its principles by comparing classical ballet, the Ballets Russes, and the free forms of modern dance.

From the beginning, *The Mask* was conceived as an instrument for creating a radical shift in accepted ideas about theater. Its aim was to revolutionize, not simply to inform, and free copies of the first issue were sent to all the leading directors in Europe. Having come to the conclusion that any work he produced in the existing conditions would be distorted by commercialism, undermined by the star system, or compromised by the resistance to innovation he had experienced in his dealings with theater managements, and that, given the transience of performance, any stage demonstrations of his new Art of the Theater would be soon forgotten, Craig turned to a long-term program. He was the first of the twentieth-century directors to realize that publications had the potential for creating wider and more fundamental reforms than productions. Example might condition the expectations of the general public – the artistic consumer – in the one city where a reformer's theater was based. Ideas expressed in print could reach other directors, who might have little chance of seeing any pathbreaking productions – thus influencing the artistic producer and creating a chain reaction in many different centers.

As Craig put it, "One arena does not make an Art of the Theatre . . . it needs 100 or 1000 people to make it visible to the many." His hope in issuing *The Mask* was "that through that publication I might in time come to change the whole theatre – not plays alone, but playing, sceneries, construction of theatres – the whole thing."[11] However, in Craig's mind *The Mask* was never meant to be completely self-sufficient. It was to be complemented by his school, which was intended to "give form and substance to all that *The Mask* for six years has been saying, actualizing that for which *The Mask* has prepared the way. Thus Practice and Theory, Theory and Practice act and react, and each confirms and strengthens the other."[12] In the end, *The Mask* had to stand on its own, but it was theory in a highly dramatic (if carefully disguised) form.

Out of the twenty regular contributors, seventeen were really Craig himself, which was why the focus was so consistent. John Balance, Charles Borrow, Allen Carric, Edward Edwardovitch, Florian M. Florian, Adolf Fuerst, Franz Hoffer, Jan van Holt, Jan Klassen, Louis Madrid, George Norman, Oliver, Guilio Pirro, Schmerz, C. Ticketts, Felix Urban, and the editor, John Semar, were all pseudonyms. Each had a distinct personality, espoused a different perspective, or symbolized a particular quality in Craig's ideal theater. The name Semar came from the fat little black Javanese marionette with a white face. The significance of Balance, the most direct proponent of Craig's ideas, was spelled out in the first issue: "The king (to the artist) is ... the delicately worked handle without which the scales could not exist, and upon which the eye of the measurer must be fixed. Therefore I have taken these scales as the device of our new art, for our art is based upon the idea of perfect balance, the result of movement." These figures corresponded, quarreled, formed alliances against each other, and resolved their disputes – always, of course, in such a way as to promote the ideals of the "new movement," particularly as those ideas were embodied in the work of Gordon Craig. They lent theory a sense of dramatic vitality, giving Craig's demands greater force by making them seem firmly rooted all over Europe, as well as allowing an apparently objective description of his concepts. As Craig wrote to Ellen Terry, "*The Mask* is an idea – a play – in it come characters, each of whom wears a mask ... the writer becomes impersonal in assuming his mask just as an actor becomes impersonal."[13]

Whatever the direct influence of *The Mask* (and the Moscow *Hamlet* was at least one tangible effect), it certainly helped to create a climate open to new ideas and critical of conventional practices. Craig's early productions had impressed artists as different as Yeats and Granville-Barker, who invited Craig to join first the Maeterlinck Society, then the English Stage Society. Barker later commented that "as with all idealists, Mr. Craig's influence has been mainly destructive ... *Bethlehem* destroyed for me once and for all any illusion I may have had as to the necessity of surrounding every performance of a play with the stuffy, fussy, thickly bedaubed canvas which we are accustomed to call stage scenery ... he opened my eyes to the possibilities of real beauty and dignity in stage decoration."[14] Reinhardt sent assistants to England to report on *The Vikings*, had copies made of Craig's designs when they were exhibited in Berlin, and invited Craig to direct productions of *King Lear* and the *Oresteia*. The Moscow *Hamlet* had a lasting influence on Meyerhold and Vaktangov, and made a great impression on Rouché as well. But Craig's writings spread his ideas everywhere.

Diaghilev, Lugné-Poë, André Gide, Appia, and Copeau, who stated that he was following Craig (among others) in founding the Vieux Colombier, were all drawn by *The Mask* to visit him in Florence. Jean-Louis Barrault called *On the Art of the Theatre* his "catechism ... the true artist's guide to the theatre" which he "was never without," and claimed that Craig was "the perfect artist of the theatre." Strindberg reportedly found "golden words" in Craig's writings.[15] But the influence of his books and journals can best be indicated by the number of invitations he received from people who had never seen his work on stage. Cochran, the impresario responsible for the famous production of *The Miracle*, approached him in 1913; Scandiani, the manager of La Scala, in 1921. In 1922 Ernest Dare invited him "to form a company on new lines" at the Bijou Theater in London, and the American Stage Company proposed an association. There were the Poulsens in Copenhagen and Tyler in New York, and in 1932 the Habima company asked him to direct for them in Jerusalem. In 1935 Amaglobeli, the director of the State Academic Little Theater in Moscow, invited him to mount a production, and Ormerod Greenwood offered the Group Theater as a nucleus for a theater company of Craig's own. Even after the Second World War there was a continuing stream of visiting playwrights, directors, and critics – among them Sean O'Casey, Julian Beck, Peter Brook, and Kenneth Tynan – all drawn by the vision preserved in his essays.

However, *The Mask* was also partly responsible for the fact that Craig never fulfilled his promise as a director. The constant need for new articles and fresh material made incessant demands on his time and diverted his energies from the stage, even during the Moscow *Hamlet*. Yet in a sense, as an ongoing collection of short essays covering the whole range of theater, it was the perfect vehicle for a man with so many diverse enthusiasms that he was seldom able to concentrate on any one thing sufficiently to complete it. Between 1906 and 1907, for instance, he was simultaneously working on designs for *Rosmersholm* and *Hamlet*; rewriting and choreographing the *Masque of Hunger*; working out the principle of his screens and making the first miniature sets for the model theater he constructed; experimenting with the concept of Scene and doing the first drawings to illustrate the kind of effects that might be achieved with such a radically new stage form; making the first of his series of Black Figures; preparing material and doing the woodcuts that were published in the first issues of *The Mask*; overseeing the construction of his costumes and sets for *Electra*; negotiating with Duse about sequels to the *Rosmersholm* production; and attempting to act as Isadora Duncan's business agent.

Hardly surprisingly, given this level of activity on so many fronts, Craig's career is a list of unfinished projects. *The St. Matthew Passion* remained a half-formed work of brilliant but disconnected insights and effects. No mechanism was ever developed for Scene, so the images of unceasing movement stayed frozen in a series of designs and etchings never to be realized in the theater. Even some of the technical problems involved in using the screens were never solved. The flexible proscenium, and the new relationships he imagined between stage and auditorium, were never translated into architectural plans, let alone bricks and mortar. None of the masques that he worked on after *The Masque of Love* reached the stage, and in his eyes not one of the productions he directed fully represented his ideas, despite critical acclaim. He later dismissed not only *Macbeth* and *Rosmersholm*, over which he had had little control, but also *The Vikings, Hamlet,* and *The Crown Pretenders* with the terse comment, "nothing of this to my satisfaction."[16]

Yet to some extent this was the inevitable price for such a global vision of theatrical reform. Toward the end of his career, Craig regretted having "very wantonly spent too much time throwing challenges to the old theatre" in his designs and writings, "instead of getting hold of one playhouse and steadily establishing proof upon proof of the excellence of our ideas and plans."[17] Even so, paradoxically, Craig's ideas have had a wide and lasting impact precisely because they were never given a finished, concrete expression. Some of the elements of his Art of the Theater would have dated badly. Others – in particular, the quasi-religious material around which his later theatrical forms became centered – would have seemed unacceptably pretentious or too far removed from contemporary consciousness. Those that were ahead of their time, such as Scene, could now be put into practice relatively easily with advances in technology. But even so Scene could at best provide one possibility of staging, and would be suited to only a limited range of dramatic material. At worst it might seem an idiosyncratic curiosity. Certainly that has been the fate of Terence Gray's "Dance Drama" – a direct 1930's copy of Craig's ideas, that amalgamated the concept of Scene with semitransparent screens set up in the shape of movable hollow pillars, with the rather cheaply spectacular addition of back lighting in all imaginable hues within these pillars. In either case, the elements of Craig's new theater would hardly act as the challenge to total theatrical reform that can be seen as the real value of Craig's work.

To some extent, too, projects remained incomplete and productions never measured up to his ideas because every achievement formed the basis for a fresh departure. Craig's theories were in a state of continuous development. One characteristic of modern drama seems to be that new forms supersede each theatrical reform as soon as that reform becomes established enough to react against. If Craig's ideas have survived, it is perhaps because they never became fixed in an identifiable style of production. The proposed title for one of the books that he planned, but never wrote, is characteristic: *The New Movement – and the Newer One.* It was in his notes for this book that Craig singled out the Chinese theater as an ideal, because in it everything was left to the spectator's imagination – a bare stick could become a blossoming tree. The same could be said of his own work.

9

CURTAIN CALL: CRAIG'S VISION AND CONTEMPORARY THEATER

The need for Craig's reforms is still evident, in some ways perhaps more so than even in 1900. Many of the devices Craig's sketches call for, which were unavailable to him at the time, are now standard stage equipment. The sophisticated lighting effects, which he evolved in his early productions and continued to explore throughout his life, have become routine. However, at least in the commercial theater this modern technology continues to be used to portray a nineteenth-century mindset. Naturalistic stage pictures are still the norm on Broadway or in the West end, and the lavishly illusionist spectacles of the Musical in the 1990s is a striking example. The fall of a city and escape by helicopter, or magical journeys through underground waterways and a crashing chandelier would have fitted perfectly into the old Lyceum repertoire – indeed the nineteenth-century theatrical approach is explicit in many of these Musicals, with *Miss Saigon* being based on Puccini's *Madame Butterfly*, or Andrew Lloyd-Webber transcribing a play from the 1880s for *Phantom of the Opera*. Leaving aside the architectural and monumental specifics of Craig's mechanized stage, his call for a completely new style of theater remains a challenge to find appropriate uses for an artistic medium that has been transformed by the fallout of progress.

At the same time, Craig's influence can be traced in many different aspects of twentieth-century theater. One aspect, generally overlooked, is his role as the first to collect theater artifacts and ephemera on a coherent basis, as well as preserving all his own designs, scenarios, plans and records. As such Craig counts as the father of all the theater archives that now form an integral part of museums and research libraries: indeed his own collection (designated a "national treasure" by the French government to prevent Craig selling it abroad[1]) formed the basis of the theater history department in the Bibliothèque Nationale. In addition, his writing method – using pieces from his collection as inspiration and documentary material for his wide-ranging articles in *The Mask* – is a prototype for modern theater scholarship. As already noted, he was also the first practitioner to publish extensive theoretical essays explaining and promoting, even substituting for his stage work; and the sheer scale of his publications is impressive: nine books (one of which,

On the Art of the Theater, appeared in two different editions) outlining his developing ideas about staging, two studies of Irving and Ellen Terry, plus an autobiography; five books and portfolios of designs; and three separate quarterly journals – written almost singlehandedly, as well as edited and even printed by Craig – one of which, *The Mask*, appeared for almost 21 years and ran into 15 volumes. Many of these were widely read by other directors and designers, particularly *On the Art of the Theater*, and although the indirect nature of this kind of influence makes it hard to document, the way so many theatrical innovators from the early 1920s on followed the same path indicates something of Craig's effectiveness. The dadaists and the surrealists published manifesto after manifesto. In Russia Meyerhold published essays outlining his "biomechanics," and Stanislavski detailed his acting method and artistic life. In Germany Erwin Piscator wrote extensively on the principles behind his "political theater," while Brecht accompanied his plays with a whole series of articles outlining his theories of "epic" drama. In France Copeau published several major pieces on "renovating the drama," while even Antonin Artaud who rejected verbal communication as one of his prime theatrical principles, laid out his revolutionary vision of performance in a volume of essays (which, just as for Craig, took the place of stage productions). And the list continues, with Barrault who founded his own journal in the 1950s, and with Peter Brook and Jerzy Grotowski in the Sixties, Richard Schechner in the Seventies, or Eugenio Barba in the Eighties. However different their various prescriptions for theatrical renewal, all were following Craig's lead – not only in resorting to print to spread their ideas, but in their radical rejection of traditional theater and the visionary extremism of what they were proposing as a replacement.

His indirect influence on stage practice has been equally widespread, yet he was so much a part of his own time that it is almost impossible to pick out his contribution from the general current. Appia's essays on rhythmic space and active lighting, which directly paralleled Craig's ideas, were published just one year before Craig's early productions, although it was not until 1912 (the same year as Craig's Moscow *Hamlet*) that Appia had an opportunity of testing his concept in performance. The same rejection of late nineteenth-century stagecraft, with its illusionistic spectacle and fake naturalistic detail, surfaced everywhere – Strindberg and the expressionists, Maeterlinck and the symbolists, Appia's designs for Wagner, the "dance dramas" of Dalcroze and Laban in Germany or Yeats's "plays for dancers," the French surrealists – and while Craig's writings certainly paved the way, his prescription was one among many. In much the same way, Craig's stagings between 1900 and

1903 were an integral part of the movement that spread studio or "Art Theaters" across Europe. These formed a focus for theatrical experiment in the first decade of the century; and though Craig's was by no means the only or even the first example, he was certainly one of the more significant catalysts. The impression *Dido* or *Acis* had made on Yeats provided part of the inspiration for Lady Gregory's Irish Players, whose 1911 visit to New York together with the publication of Craig's *Towards a New Theater* in 1913 were key factors in the development of the "Little Theater" movement in America.

Another example is the masks that became a common element of experimental performance in the 1920s. Even if there were many other sources for the use of masks, Craig – who had adopted the Mask as the emblem of his Art of the Theater and as the name of his "Illustrated Journal" – was directly responsible for this trend. Masks became central to the work of Jacques Copeau, whose Vieux-Columbier was the most prestigious of the Art Theaters, not only in performance, but as tool for training actors, as a source for improvising dramatic scenarios, and as the basis for reconstituting the Commedia dell'Arte. And Copeau, who visited Craig's school at the Arena Goldoni in 1915, had derived major elements of his approach from *On the Art of the Theater* in addition to *The Mask* (in which Craig had published articles on the Commedia as well as urging its revival).[2] Similarly, when Eugene O'Neill joined the Province-town Players – which, partly through this association, became the most significant of America's Little Theaters – he began to use masks, even though his earlier sea-plays and his mature drama were both intensely naturalistic. Although in these experiments O'Neill was mainly influenced by the expressionists, his "Memorandum on Masks" echoes Craig almost word for word. The search for "a new form of drama" depended on "the idea of mask as a symbol of inner reality" – "a drama of souls, and the adventures of 'free wills,' with the masks that govern them and constitute their fates" – enabling audiences "to hear the sublime poetry as the innate expression of the spirit of the drama itself, instead of listening to it as a realistic recitation...by familiar actors." Indeed, O'Neill added to Craig's argument against acting as a display of individual personality, and claimed the mask as "more subtly, imaginatively, suggestively dramatic than any actor's face can ever be" giving "the opportunity for a totally new kind of acting... After all, masks did not extinguish the Greek actor, nor have they kept the acting of the East from being an art."[3]

Craig had no specific disciples, certainly no direct imitators. Even Copeau's stylistic development was far removed from Craig's vision, though his interest in religious festival drama during the 1930s is a direct

echo of Craig's *St. Matthew Passion* project. Indeed Copeau's 1935 production of *Savonarola* in Florence (where Savaronola had actually been
burned at the stake in 1498) reproduced key elements of Craig's plans: an
architectural setting – the facades and statues of the Piazza della Signoria –
with multiple staging on tiered levels, sacred music and massed choirs,
a cast of hundreds, and seating for 4,000 spectators. Yet however tenuous
his impact on his own contemporaries, Craig's principles are still current.
His ideas pervade avant-garde experiments of the 1970s and Eighties,
even if his whole ideal of theater as an "Art" was denied by the style of
their performances, while the work of the leading contemporary post-
modernist is an exact equivalent of Craig's vision.

Given the breadth of Craig's interests, and the way he pursued
tangents that frequently contradicted his main ideas, it is hardly surprising if his minor speculations anticipated a large number of other later
innovations that were quite independent from his work, from Jessner's
use of endless flights of steps for his expressionist productions in the
early 1920s to Schechner's "environmental" theater in the 1970s. However, the line is clear in the avant-garde in the 1970s. Barrault, who
acknowledged Craig's influence, supported Peter Brook's Center for
Theater Research (which in many ways corresponds to Craig's only
partly realized hopes for his theater school); and Brook was a catalyst for
much of the experimental work over the last quarter-century.

It was initially Artaud's essays that caused Brook to turn from
commercial and classical productions to explore fundamental questions
such as, "What is a theatre? What is a play? What is an actor? What is a
spectator? What is the relation between them all?" Yet these were
precisely the same issues that had formed the basis for Craig's explora-
tions 60 years before, and the answers that Brook arrived at recapitulated
the essential elements of Craig's vision in a changed form. Brook's concept
of the stage as "an empty space" can be seen as a logical extension of
Craig's aim in clearing the theater of all its accumulated conventions, and
Brook returned to the origins of performance in an even more extreme
way, setting out "to explore what the conditions were through which the
theatre could speak directly...without the help and hindrance of shared
cultural signs and tokens". This meant (as with Craig: see pp. 206–7 above)
the substitution of sounds for verbal language, the search for universal
gesture in ritual, the replacement of individualized characterization with
archetypal figures. It also led to vast, quasi-religious performances of
creation-myths (on one level reminiscent of Craig's scenarios like "Motion"
or "Through Night to Light" – see pp. 117 & 192 above): *Orghast*, produced at Persepolis in 1971, or *The Mahabharata*, 1985. Indeed in its original
setting – inside a stone-quarry near Avignon, where the rock cliffs formed

the backdrop – and in the precisely controlled movements, rigidly stylized gestures and simplified symbolic expression of its performers, *The
Mahabharata* fulfilled many of Craig's demands. At the same time, the
orgastic, primitivistic quality typical of Brook's work through this period
gives it a completely different tone, and his privileging of the actor is in
sharp contrast to Craig's ideal of the Übermarionette: Brook's search for
the "roots" of theater having led to

> work based on the fact that some of the deepest aspects of human experience
> can reveal themselves through the sounds and movements of the human body
> in a way that strikes an identical chord in any observer, whatever his cultural
> and racial conditioning. And therefore one can work without roots, because the
> body, as such, becomes a working source.[4]

In some ways even Samuel Beckett's later plays correspond to
Craig's principles. Their abstraction and simplification echo his attempt
"to refine the material of the theatre in *words, scene, movement* to the
minimum."[5] In a piece like *Breath* there are no words, just a single
(repeated) cry. In *Not I* only a disembodied mouth is clearly visible,
speaking to a motionless figure in the shadows, while in *Rockabye* the only
movement is an almost imperceptible oscillation of a single woman in a
rocking-chair. There is in fact a distant link to Craig through Yeats, whom
Beckett admired, although Beckett's theatrical approach is the expression
of (specifically existentialist) philosophical tenets that have no counterpart in Craig's thought. However, the theatrical artist whose work is
closest to Craig's, perhaps because he also shares a career as a designer
and visual artist, is Robert Wilson.

Wilson's theater is strikingly pictorial, gaining purity of line
through a rigorous simplification of the stage action. This continually
approaches stasis, yet paradoxically the spectator's awareness of movement and its significance is heightened by slow-motion or isolating each
component of a move. Gesture is restricted for precision and clarity,
actors objectified and depersonalized, language reduced to patterns of
sound. Dramatic sequences are segmented, interleaved, repeated, creating arbitrary structures where the aesthetic patterning replaces conventional meaning. Figures and objects become abstracted to symbols. At the
same time, although the overall impression is austere, even naive,
Wilson's stage effects require the full use of all the technical resources
available to the contemporary theater; and the key elements in his
productions is light. Lighting is used not only to evoke the passage of
time or give physical reality to non-representational and symbolic settings, but to conjure up psychological states and communicate emotion.

The effect is consciously symphonic. In all this, even if he arrived there by a different route, Wilson exactly duplicates Craig's "Art of the Theater." The active use of light and abstract movement were the primary elements of Craig's vision, which also depended on technology subsumed in art. For both, performance is analogous to music and open symbolism replaces naturalistic representation, while the primary impact is visual. Indeed their working-method is directly comparable. Where Craig created designs out of which he evolved scenarios, Wilson sketches sequences of "story boards" illustrating each point in the dramatic action, and bases his production on these drawings.

Wilson's starting point was the use of performance as therapy for autism, which he points to as an increasingly common psychological response to the pressures of contemporary life, and this underlies the treatment of language in his texts where variations in the aural shape of words is used for "graphic" expression. The resulting audio-visual collage of apparently disconnected images deconstructs conventional representations of reality: a deconstructionism that makes Wilson's approach specifically contemporary in sharp contrast to the harmonious aesthetics of Craig's ideal. However his development has taken in much the same dramatic material as Craig: Shakespeare (Heiner Müller's version of *Hamlet* in 1986, *King Lear*, 1990), the Greek classics (*Alcestis*, 1986) and even opera (*Madame Butterfly*, 1994). Many of his productions have been based on myth, echoing Craig's search for the origins of theater, although Wilson combines ancient Greek sources with American junk-culture images (contemporary mythic material) in a post-modern collage. Wilson parallels Craig in defining his work as a drama of "interior image;" and it also contains quasi-religious overtones, as well as tending to the monumental. Apocalyptic themes continually resurface, as in his 1972 *KA MOUNTAIN AND GUARDenia Terrace* which took 268 hours to perform over seven days and covered a whole mountain top, ending on the summit with the burning of a cut-out of the Manhattan skyline and its replacement by an image of the Lamb of God. Similarly the final episode of the central section in *The CIVIL warS* (a 20 hour multi-lingual, multi-media epic costing an estimated $2.5m and originally intended for performance at the 1984 Olympics) is a documentary film of skyscrapers being demolished with explosives while the cast face the audience with fixed smiles. Wilson's collaborator Heiner Müller described *The CIVIL warS* as "theater of resurrection:" a title that could equally be applied to Craig's later scenarios or his *St. Matthew Passion* project.[6]

It is particularly in the style of acting Wilson demands that his theater most obviously fulfils Craig's ideals. While seldom using actual

masks, his actors' facial expression is frequently set in mask-like immobility – blankly neutral or grotesquely distorted – and he rehearses his
actors in extreme physical control, each gesture minimal and rigidly precise. In his 1986 staging of Müller's *Quartet* one of the actors hung
head-down from a rope, revolving slowly with one arm outstretched at
an exact angle, through a whole scene; during her long aria of betrayed
hope in *Madame Butterfly* the soprano was enclosed in a narrow cylinder
of light and required to project her voice up inside it. At times his actors
are no less sculptural than Craig's "Black Figures," as with an Angel in
Alcestis poised immobile while her stiffly folded cloak furled itself (drawn
by an almost invisible wire) wing-like around her body.[7] Wilson has
effectively realized Craig's ideal of an Übermarionette.

Craig's concepts, at the core of the most fully developed post-
modernist form of theater, are still relevant. They may no longer be
identified with his name – indeed the way his ideas are being realized on
the stage by an artist such as Robert Wilson goes far beyond what Craig,
with the limited stage machinery available to him, had been capable of
imagining. Yet the fact that the same principles are being developed
independently demonstrates the continuing importance of Craig's work.

10

PROGRAMME NOTES: CRAIG ON THEATER

This selection of Craig's writings is not intended to represent the whole range of his ideas, but to illuminate key elements in his "Art of the Theater". It is also compiled from works that are less accessible, out of print or unpublished, although some of the most significant passages are included from Craig's major theoretical work, *On the Art of the Theater*. (Where passages have been cut within extracts, this is indicated by asterisks.)

Prologue – Craig and Nineteenth Century Melodrama

Irving at the Lyceum (1930) from *Henry Irving*

I HAVE said that I cannot describe Irving's performance in *The Bells*: but though I cannot describe it (and the whole play was merely a series of variations on one theme – Irving), I will try and put down a few notes of little moments remembered.

At his entrance, the applause was so instantaneous that it became part and parcel of the play – without it, or had it been at all lacking in warmth, one could have grown hypercritical, and delivered oneself of some wise words regarding the evil tendency of applause in a playhouse.

* * *

This applause was no false note, whereas silence would have been utterly false... for though Irving endured and did not accept the applause, he deliberately called it out of the spectators. It was necessary *to them* – not to him: it was something they had to to experience, or to be rid of, or rather, released from, before they could exactly take in what he was going to give them.

So then, the applause came down like thunder, as Irving appeared in the door-way with the ordinary cry: "It is I." Now no one has ever been known to hear these words distinctly – they resolved themselves into a single exclamation – the door flung open – the figure is in the room, God knows how – with arms extended, face alight, and this single ejaculation: "'t's I."

In those days – as in the noble days of the Greek Drama – as in those of the Nō Drama of Japan – an important entrance was to be preceded by suspense, and then to come as a surprise, or like a chapter-heading of some grand old romance: it thrilled, and was intended to thrill.

Do you remember these chapter-headings: *The Shoulder of Athos, The Baldric of Porthos,* and *The Handkerchief of Aramis; A Mousetrap in the Seventeenth Century; On the Utility of Stove Pipes:* they come from a book I need not name – and, *How to get rid of Dormice; The Cemetery of the Château d'If:* do you remember the excitement? Well then – we had reached this state of excitement, of expectancy, of watching, by the time the storm of applause greeted a spectacular entrance on to the stage in these older days.

I can only speak of Irving's entrances, but I believe that with Edmund Kean an entrance was also something to experience.

The *manner of coming on* made it extraordinary with great actors – it was this manner of timing the appearance – measuring its speed and direction – which created a rhythm that was irresistible.

An exit was important too – very important: but the going off of an actor was nothing comparable with the prime importance of his coming on.

To prepare for this entrance in *The Bells,* the entire first fifteen minutes of the play conspired.

The talk all hovered around the thought of the man who was coming, and about other things somehow connected with him.

The storm raging outside the house, the sudden blowing open of a window in the next room, which smashed a whole trayful of crockery and glass as it swung open – the looking at the clock which told of the overdue traveller – the slow, quiet talk which mumbled on – and above all, the queer "hurry music," as it is called, which was astonishingly dramatic: all these things led up to the first point to be made, and made with decision: "Here is the man!" And now watch what he will do – better still, how he will do it – best of all, watch his face and figure, and follow what it is these are hinting at.

Irving once on, the shout of applause going up, he lowers his arms, he lowers his head, he relaxes his force all over, seems to turn it off to an almost dead calm, while the applause rolls on and up. Twice, maybe three times, he, as it were, shifts one foot (his right, I think it was), and by this slight and meaningless gesture a limit is being reckoned to the applause which goes on and on – no other motion except that the foot, in shifting, sends a slight vibration, also without significance, through the whole person before us – and then as the applause dies away, at the first sign of it dying, the actor clips it off by a sudden gesture of awakening from his long and patiently-endured ordeal – flings cap and whip to right and left, and begins to shed his coat, his muffler, as his wife and daughter run to help him off with them.

The story of *The Bells* is this: A man, not by habit or by instinct a murderer, murders a Polish Jew for his money. He needs money – his child is crying in its cradle for food, and by chance this Jew stops at his hut in a storm, and the man sees him undo a belt which, as it clanks on the table, emits the sound of untold riches. This tempts him, he resolves on the deed, and when the Jew, refreshed by his punch and comforted by the warmth, goes on his way through the snow-storm, the man, taking a short cut across the fields, arrives at a cross-road and, hacking him down with an axe, takes the belt full of gold, drags the body to a limekiln, burns it and, now become rich, relieves the want of his household and thereafter lives a blameless life – finally becoming Burgomaster of his village.

But wherever he goes – whoever speaks to him – whatever he sees or hears, even as he stands speaking to someone about ordinary things, there comes to his ears the far-off sound of the sledge-bells of the Polish Jew. Haunted by this, he lives his life in sorrow which increases and increases until one night, dreaming that he is in the dock and being convicted and sentenced to death, he wakes only to die, believing that he is being hanged.

The thing Irving set out to do was to show us the sorrow which slowly and remorselessly beat him down. As, no matter who the human being may be, and what his crime, the sorrow which he suffers must appeal to our hearts, so Irving set out to wring our hearts, not to give us a clever exhibition of antics such as a murderer would be likely to go through. He does not appeal to any silly sentimentality in you – he merely states the case by showing you that quite obviously here is a strong human being who, through a moment of weakness, falls into error and becomes for two hours a criminal – does what he knows he is doing – acts deliberately – but (and here is Irving) acts automatically, as though impelled by an immense force, against which no resistance is possible.

To return to the moment after the first entrance – the process of getting rid of his coat and brushing off the snow as he stands on the mat by the door being over, he works his way down to a chair in the centre (Irving was always in the centre – he had no inferiority complex) and there, taking off his boots, he begins to put on and buckle his shoes.

* * *

It was, in every gesture, every half move, in the play of his shoulders, legs, head and arms, mesmeric in the highest degree – slowly we were drawn to watch every inch of his work as we are drawn to read and linger on every syllable of a strangely fine writer.

It was the perfection of craftsmanship.

While he is taking off the boots and pulling on the shoes, the men at the table, who are smoking and drinking lazily, are telling in drawling tones that just before he came in, they were saying that they did not remember a night like this since what was called the Polish Jew's winter.

By the time the speaker had got this slowly out – and it was dragged purposely – Irving was buckling his second shoe, seated, and leaning over it, with his two long hands stretched down over the buckles. We suddenly saw these fingers stop their work; the crown of the head suddenly seemed to glitter and become frozen – and then, at the pace of the slowest and most terrified snail, the two hands, still motionless and dead, were seen to be coming up the side of the leg ... the whole torso of the man, also seeming frozen, was gradually, and by an almost imperceptible movement, seen to be drawing up and back, as it would straighten a little, and to lean a little against the back of the chair on which he was seated.

Once in that position – motionless – eyes fixed ahead of him and fixed on us all – there he sat for the space of ten to twelve seconds, which, I can assure you, seemed to us all like a lifetime, and then said – and said in a voice deep and overwhelmingly beautiful: "Oh, you were talking of that – were you?" And as the last syllable was uttered, there came, afar off, the regular throbbing sound of sledge-bells.

* * *

And the next step of his dance began.

He moves his head slowly from us – the eyes still somehow with us – and moves it to the right – taking as long as a long journey *to discover a truth takes.* He looks to the faces on the right – nothing: slowly the head revolves back again, down, and along the tunnels of thought and sorrow, and at the end the face and eyes are bent upon those to the left of him ... utter stillness ... nothing there either – everyone is concerned with his or her little doings – smoking or knitting or unravelling wool or scraping a plate slowly and silently – a long pause, endless, breaking our hearts, comes down over everything, and on and on go these bells. Puzzled, motionless ... he glides up to a standing position: never has anyone seen another rising figure which slid slowly up like that: with one arm slightly raised, with sensitive hand speaking of far-off apprehended sounds, he asks, in the voice of some woman who is frightened, yet does not wish to frighten those with her: "Don't you ... don't you hear the sound of sledge-bells on the road?" "Sledge-bells?" grumbles the smoking man; "Sledge-bells?" pipes his companion; "Sledge-bells?" says the wife – all of them seemingly too sleepy and comfortable to apprehend anything ... see anything ... or understand ... and, as they grumble a negative, suddenly he staggers, and shivers from his toes to his neck; his jaws begin to chatter; the hair on his forehead, falling over a little, writhes as though it were a nest of little snakes. Everyone is on his feet at once, to help: "Caught a chill"..."Let's get him to bed"...and *one* of the moments of the immense and touching dance closes – only one – and the next one begins, and the next after – figure after figure of exquisite pattern and purpose is unfolded, and then closed, and ever a new one unfolded in its wake. As we watched this figure, we felt as silent and as still as when we hear of things too sad to realize; and when it was over and we might move, we knew that this was the finest point that the craft of acting could reach.[1]

Scene Changes – Tradition and Craig's Vision

Foreword II (1919) from *Towards A New Theater*

ONCE upon a time, stage scenery was architecture. A little later it became imitation architecture; still later it became imitation artificial architecture. Then it lost its head, went quite mad, and has been in a lunatic asylum ever since. Some day, when my school comes into being, we will issue a book dealing with the historical facts of this case. I shall see to it that my scenic work receives justice – (I fear that very little of it will ever see salvation) – but here and now is not the time nor the place to pull it too much to pieces. I could do that probably more thoroughly than any of my critics do. My remarks apply to the designs (with eight exceptions) in this book. These thirty-two drawings represent work done between 1900 and 1910. That work is now part of my past, and although I can look back at it with interest, I have no very great sentimental affection for my work of yesterday just because it is mine. That it is not so entirely without sense or without taste doesn't in my opinion excuse the fact that it is not quite right as stage scenery. It will not bear comparison with the noblest scenery when the conditions of the stage were noblest. At the noblest period that we know of, there was little talk of "simplicity," and less talk of illusion, and the scene *painter* was utterly unknown. In those days they built their theaters for their dramas, not their dramas for and in their theaters. They played in the day-time, and with the sun streaming upon the actors and audience alike, and didn't indulge in what is called "lighting effects."[2] They didn't waste an enormous amount of time trying to get some false colour that would look true by artificial light. Neither did they paint their faces with magenta and yellow ochre so as to look as if they had just come from the country.

But they didn't abstain from doing these things to be more natural, but only so as to be truer.

* * *

When Drama went indoors, it died; and when Drama went indoors, its scenery went indoors too. You must have the sun on you to live, and Drama and Architecture must have the sun on them to live. Of course you may say that "hanging on" is "living," but it is practically being dead–alive. Drama was able to be out of doors and in the sun because, instead of being a nightly amusement, it was a rare festival. People have always spoken about it as being a religious festival, but perhaps it is a mistake nowadays to underline this, because the word "religious" to us means one thing and in the old days it meant another thing. How best to describe what it was in the old days? Probably if you were to stand in St. Mark's Square – or even in Trafalgar Square, for the matter of that – on a sunny day, and see a couple of hundred pigeons wheeling round the square, flapping their wings, enjoying themselves in their own god-like way, you would get the nearest idea to what a Greek festival was like. And have you ever noticed that the people in the square passed on and took no notice of such an event? No; you will find that even the dullest man in the street will stay and watch the performance. Just such a performance is being played in front of my window as I write. Over fifty or sixty people have stopped to watch it, and that without a single advertisement having been put up. There are many people who will tell you that the Greek drama attracted because of its display of human passions, because of its beautiful girls dancing (such people always imagine that beautiful girls danced in the Greek dramas), or because of some subtle intellectual force which held the audience in its grip, and so forth. But it was nothing of the kind. It was simply that the Greeks had captured many of the secrets of nature from the birds, from the trees, from the clouds, and were not afraid to put such simple secrets to a religious use. And the chief secret which they caught was a small part of the secret of movement. It was the movement of the chorus which moved the onlookers. It was the movement of the sun upon the architecture which moved the audience.

A later-day critic, speaking of a performance given in some open-air theater in Italy, where the architecture was the only scenery employed, tells of the emotion created by the passage of the sun during the drama. He was unable to describe it exactly, and I think that very few people could do so either, and then only in a poem. But he spoke of how time seemed actually to be in motion. The movement was felt, but felt through seeing.[3]

After the Greek came the Christian theater – that is to say, the Christian Church. The theme of their drama, if no more tragic than that of the Greeks, was perhaps gloomier. For scenery, architecture again was used, and we may see what kind of stage they had by looking at photographs and drawings of the choirs and sanctuaries of all the early Christian churches. We see stages rising one above the other, the windows placed at certain angles to illumine the stages, the entrances so arranged that movements of single figures or groups are made significant. We see the seats for the musicians, we see the very places on which the chief performers (for we may call them performers) stood, in which direction they faced, and even what they did. All this is recorded. The drama they played is known as the Mass.[4] The main difference between this theater and the theater of the Greeks is that it was closed in, although daylight, and sunlight in particular, was still employed.

The people flocked to these religious theaters as bees to a hive. Not a word that was spoken could they understand, for all was in Latin, and yet they flocked. Could you guess why they went there? It cost them nothing but what they chose to give. Perhaps that was the reason. Anyway, do not let that worry us; let us keep to the scenery.

Against the architectural background were placed decorations of gold and jewels, silks, velvets, and other precious materials. I wonder if the people would have preferred these things if they had been made out of paste-board and tinsel? I wonder if the same excitement and reverence could have been awakened before a Cross of papier-mâché?

What made this wonderful theater a failure after a few hundred years? Nothing but the exhibition of limbs in a circus. That was too much for the people. They couldn't resist it. One understands it, but one doesn't understand the nature of the rulers who were so mad as to put that before a not very grown-up Europe. As well might one take one's children to see "Scheherazade" as call the children of a nation away from so beautiful a drama as the Mass to see a lot of boys and girls dancing nude in a circus. For the people in Europe at that time were just as innocent as our children are. You may say that it was time that they should grow up; but look how they have grown up. You will say that I am not quite exact, and that there is as much stupidity in children as there is divinity in them. I agree with you. But if there is an equal amount of both – and I think that this is true – why make a point of encouraging the stupidity? You will say that the religious theater had grown dull, and that the other thing was a relief. So like Europe, that "relief"; the whole of modern deterioration seems to be based on that word "relief." In the old days, when a champion prize-fighter was getting the worst of it, and was at his last gasp, there was no talk of relief. I believe that one of the methods employed was to seize hold of a bradawl and plunge it into him. Now it is all relief. However, let us get back to the scenery, if you please.

After the Greek and Christian theaters had gone under, the first false theater came into existence. The poets wrote elaborate and tedious dramas, and the scenery used for them was a kind of imitation architectural background. Palaces and even streets were fashioned or painted on cloths, and for a time the audience put up with it. These plays were performed in actual palaces, and as the people could not get a glimpse of them, they thought they would create a theater of their own, and at the same time they set out to give the aristocracy a treat. Then the great Commedia dell'Arte arose.

As a background they took the houses and palaces of a street, not painted palaces, nor painted houses, but the real houses out in the street. Architecture again. Open air again. Sun again. And this theater survived for about three hundred years. It gave birth to Shakespeare and to Molière, and the Shakespeare theater is about the last theater that flourished in the open air.

What numbers of books have been written about this Shakespearean theater, as if it were an original idea, as if it were the first of its kind, as if never before had the open theater been "given a chance," as if it were the beau ideal of that kind of thing. As a matter of fact, the Shakespearean theater was the very last and the weakest breath of the open-air theater. We should avoid anything like a return to the Shakespearean theater, because it was built on the mere leavings of a former magnificence. I suppose there are thousands of books and articles written about this Shakespearean stage. How many books are there about the Commedia dell'Arte and its stage, about the Christian theater and its stage, or about the Greek theater and its stage? I have seen a few, but hardly any of them are adequate. As a background to his plays, Shakespeare had a nice little wooden cosy corner of a stage erected in a bear-pit, but his plays really belong to a much more magnificent open-air theater than that. The poor wooden "O" which he regretted so much is made into a very pompous "O" to-day, and if we are to do Shakespeare justice on his own lines, we shall build him a theater very different from that of the Globe, if also very different from that of Drury Lane.

After the Shakespeare stage passed away, the daylight was shut out for ever. Oil lamps, gas lamps, electric lamps, were turned on, and the scenery, instead of being architectural, became – pictorial scenery. You cannot call it picture, for picture is that which is concerned only with two dimensions, and were you to ask Leonardo da Vinci or Cezanne, I think that they would agree with me that scenery is not *picture*. Yet every day we get people speaking of scenery as if it were picture, and even painters have the temerity to enter the theater and put on to the stage the result of their studies as painters. They are all descendants of Bibiena, and I hope they are proud of him. Nothing pleases them so much as the artifice of the modern theater, and they "use" the stage, at the same time having a contempt for its tricks. I suppose that they like this so much because they know nothing about the beauty of the ancient theater. I can only think of this as their excuse, but it brings us no nearer to a noble stage – it brings us no nearer to noble scenery. Many of my own scenes, of which there are forty in this book, in my opinion bring us very little nearer.

When I began working, there was no school for theatrical art, there was no one to tell me these things that I have told you; and it is only now, after many years' working, that I have seen the direction in which we are all going. And now I do not point back to the Greeks, I do not point back to the Christian Church, nor to any noble theater that we have possessed, nor tell you to reconstruct these. I care not a scrap about the past, but only about the future; but what the finest in the past teaches us is exactly the same as the finest in the future, and to reach this old new ideal – perhaps even to surpass it in time – I go towards a new Theater.

"The Actor" (1930) from *Henry Irving*

Irving was the nearest thing ever known to what I have called the Übermarionette.

Now an Übermarionette is all sorts of things at which I have hinted in books and drawings which I have made since 1907. I only hope that I have not wearied anybody with the notion of an actor who should be all that a marionette is and much more – and that I do not weary you now. But there is a point that I never touched on. It is a human point, and it is related to Irving, for from Irving the whole notion receives corroboration.

* * *

In dancing his rôle, Irving went to the extreme limits possible to an actor of the nineteenth century, of preserving the last tingle of the mighty Greek tradition. He was not ill informed about that tradition, but he held and expressed a few ill-considered opinions about it. He wrote rather freezingly about "tragedy on stilts," and the artificiality of Greek theater work. Yet of all the actors of the nineteenth century, he instinctively expressed in his work his devotion to the Greek idea – for in his bones he felt its ancient fires revive.

He danced, he did not merely walk – he sang, he by no means merely spoke. He was essentially artificial in distinction to being merely natural.

* * *

Irving did as many other great actors of England have done – he took Shakespeare as his guide and master. Little, but successful actors prefer to take up with the latest thing – not so Irving. And Shakespeare helped him, for in Shakespeare is a great, a curious rhythm, and it was this he captured. In what an audacious manner does Shakespeare break the staid laws which the steadier poets preserve as they would preserve their lives! How he risks all, and with all the ease of an adventurer. When in that mood, he cannot slip – and all his errors, great or small, serve but to make him who he is – Shakespeare, and not, positively not, one of the Elizabethans. Is Irving not to do this too, if he can? Indeed he does it – he did it, and became Irving, not merely a Victorian. Endless seemed the labour to achieve this – no school to help. So Irving trained himself, and began to prance and turn and glide and sing, and – it began to go all right.

* * *

Irving had caught the most difficult Shakespearean rhythm, and was suiting the action to the word.

Every now and again the words were natural, but as a rule they were more than natural – they were highly artificial. And thus it came about that Irving positively designed (as M. Fokine has designed) dances which fitted perfectly to the speeches given him by Shakespeare.

When he came to melodrama, to *The Bells, the Lyons Mail,* or *Louis XI,* he realized that a good deal more dance would be needed to hold up these pieces – and then it was that, putting out all his skill, he wiped the floor with the rôle and danced it like the devil. When it was Shakespeare he was dealing with, he had merely to wipe the beautiful glass window-panes. His movements were all measured. He was forever counting – one, two, three – pause – one, two – a step, another, a halt, a faintest turn, another step, a word. (Call it a beat, a foot, a step, all is one – I like to use the word "step.") That constituted one of his dances. Or seated on a chair, at a table – raising a glass, drinking – and then lowering his hand and glass – one, two, three, four – suspense – a slight step with his eyes – five – then a patter of steps – two slow syllables – another step – two more syllables – and a second passage in his dance was done. And so right through the piece – whatever it might be – there was no chance movement; he left no loose ends. All was sharp cut at beginning and end, and all joined by an immensely subtle rhythm – the Shakespearean rhythm – discerned by Brodribb when wondering how to do it, and not a soul to tell him how.

From the first to the last moment that Irving stood on the stage, each moment was significant...every sound, each movement, was

intentional – clear-cut, measured dance: nothing real – all massively artificial – yet all flashing with the light and the pulse of nature. A fine style.

His movements being measured, rhythmic, planned, it may be too obvious
to state that the action of his face was part of all this, and was measured
too: yet it may not have occurred to one or two of my readers that this
control of feature till immobility was achieved, constituted a mask.

Some actors paint away one face and make themselves another
face; they even build up these faces – one for every new part: but then
these actors have little to say with the face. It stands to reason that if you
have much to say with the face, the sooner it becomes a mask, the quicker
you'll be able to speak with it. For a mask never fidgets; it endures, and at
the slightest touch it becomes expressive, it lights up and speaks.

Irving was all for these slight, significant touches. Anything spraw-
ling was simply not Irving. With him all had to be delicate, economical
work – all done in sharp-cut lines, no bungling – no rough-and-tumble.

Spontaneity he valued, but seldom indulged in: what he did, he
did by design. He did not respect that artlessness which fails to reveal
art. He was not merely fond of his art – his art of acting was his religion.
To be playful and go-as-you-please about it – to be spontaneous, unless
by the grace of God – was to him a sign of idiocy.

There seems to have been a day when, after witnessing what is
called "an inspired performance of genius," "full of feeling," he took
himself aside and said: "My boy, listen to me. In the next twenty or thirty
years, you may be called upon to perform some eight thousand times,
and as you may possibly not feel inspired each time you perform, you
may, during the course of a very stren-u-ous rôle, not feel inspired for
more than – er – let us say – um – ten minutes per act. I think, therefore,
you will do well to remember that by taking great pains you can, shall
we say – um – *design* a part, a rôle, so carefully that, inspired or not,
you'll be demmed interesting. The less 'feeling' the better. See what I
mean, my boy?"

And so it was that each syllable and each pause, each step and
each look, was as nearly perfectly designed and of a piece with the whole
as could possibly be.

I believe that this is what the great actors of Japan did – designed
their parts – and I believe they still do it.

Unlike the Japanese actors, Irving was not athletic. He could on
occasion bound across the stage, when it was imperative, but he did not
seek for opportunities to display the agility that was in his wiry frame;
Harlequin had done that for so many years, and done it to perfection. No,
the really agile portion of his body was his face – his mask.[5]

The faces of some actors are podgy and loquacious, saying an infinite deal of nothing: his was clean-cut, expressionless till he let it speak, and when it spoke it said one thing at a time, clearly.

"But was he natural?" is always being asked. Indeed he was – natural like lightning – but not natural like the ape. Some there are who will for ever think that to be commonplace is to be natural. They find it very natural in an actor to drift on and off the stage, to tactfully avoid saying or doing anything that might astonish anyone in the audience – to look and act as much like a cypher as possible – slightly sleepy about the eyes – toll-loll. To these, then, it must appear that if an actor is expressive he is unnatural – if he astonishes, he is positively eccentric – if he is dramatic, a scandal.

Irving was astonishing us always – he was terrible in tragedy: not terrifying as a sudden thunder-clap, but as when the whole of nature seems to suffer and to become more still and more and more quiet, so did Irving do. There is a flash – something is struck – something terrible has happened, without rumblings or crash. These come afterwards; then the clouds conspire and, like a crowd of actors, create a fearful noise – but the tragedy, the terrible thing, has happened. The force which struck and blinded us, has withdrawn, and is once again veiled within its secret temple. Irving in tragedy was not like the storm which splutters out, but like one which gathers and then strikes, once. Once aware of this, we were awake.

AGAIN, Irving was natural, yet highly artificial. He was natural in that he did not remind one of either an ape or a god, but of a man. He was artificial, as certain plants seem artificial – we don't call them artificial flowers, for they are actually alive and growing. And Irving was artificial as these – as an orchid – as a cactus – exotic and stately, forbidding, and so curiously composed as to be what we may call architectural – attractive as are all shapely things.

Every moment was formed.

* * *

IT was brought against Irving that he could not speak our English tongue.

He would say *"Gud"* for *"God"*; *"Cut thrut dug"* for *"Cut throat dog"* (Shylock); *"Tack the rup frum mey nek"* for *"Take the rope from my neck"* (Mathias in *The Bells*); *"Ritz"* for *"Rich"* (Mathias); this word *rich*, spoken as *ritz – ritz – ritz – ritz*, he repeated, as some will remember, during the scene of dreaming, where he imagines he is in a field and awaiting the coming of the Polish Jew, and hears the bells of his sledge afar off, coming nearer and nearer. The effect of the *ritz* instead of *rich* was this: instead of the sound reminding us of an old housewife shooing the fowls away from the kitchen door, we were horribly thrilled, as at the ominous sound of the serpent about to strike, and we were aware that a duet between the regular throb of the bells and this voice was being sung. At the end of a long sustained series of these sounds, he sprang – he struck down the imaginary Jew – and fell in a heap on top of him. Again, when, in the same dream, he spoke the line: *"How the dogs howl at Daniel's farm – how they how-ow-owl-l-l-l,"* it had to be admitted that we never said it like that – I must confess that it can be only once said so, and by one man only, and in this very scene. But how it stirred the imagination, this one word.

A Rising Action – Craig on Design

"The Steps I" (1919) from *Towards A New Theater*

I THINK it is Maeterlinck who pointed out to us that drama is not only that part of life which is concerned with the good and bad feelings of individuals, and that there is much drama in life without the assistance of murder, jealousy, and the other first passions. He then leads us up to a fountain or into a wood, or brings a stream upon us, makes a cock crow, and shows us how dramatic these things are. Of course, Shakespeare showed us all that a few centuries earlier, but there is much good and no harm in having repeated it. Still I think that he might have told us that there are two kinds of drama, and that they are very sharply divided. These two I would call the Drama of Speech and the Drama of silence, and I think that his trees, his fountains, his streams, and the rest come under the heading of the Drama of Silence – that is to say, dramas where speech becomes paltry and inadequate. Very well, then, if we pursue this thought further, we find that there are many things other than works of Nature which enter into this Drama of Silence, and a very grand note in this Drama is struck by that noblest of all men's work, Architecture. There is something so human and so poignant to me in a great city at a time of the night when there are no people about and no sounds. It is dreadfully sad until you walk till six o'clock in the morning. Then it is very exciting. And among all the dreams that the architect has laid upon the earth, I know of no more lovely things than his flights of steps leading up and leading down, and of this feeling about architecture in my art I have often thought how one could give life (not a voice) to these places, using them to a dramatic end. When this desire came to me I was continually designing dramas wherein the place was architectural and lent itself to my desire. And so I began with a drama called "The Steps."

* * *

In each design, I show the same place, but the people who are cradled in it belong to each of its different moods.

"Venice Preserved" (1919) from *Towards A New Theater*

WE ARE BUILDING THEATERS SIXTY OR SEVENTY YEARS BEHIND THE TIMES, AND IT IS NOT THE SHIPS THAT ARE GOING TO LOSE THE BATTLE WHEN THE DAY COMES, IT WILL BE THE THEATERS AND THOSE OTHER ANTIQUATED INSTITUTIONS.

Worse than that. We are not even building old theaters. The other day I was in a garden city which is supposed to be, experimentally, rather ahead of the times. No one was to be found who would build a theater for the young fellows who were working to create a theater there, and who have been working to create a theater there for a couple of years. If this had been a German garden city – and I believe Germans are beginning to build them – one of the first things which they would have put down as necessary, as essential to the life of the place, would have been a theater, designed by one of the most go-ahead young architects, in which a different play would be performed every night – classical as well as modern plays – in which probably one thousand people could be seated, in which the most advanced of our dramatic writers, stage managers, scene painters, and the rest, would be given full opportunity to go ahead. And the extraordinary thing is that no one in England will believe it when an Englishman brings news from Germany of the great activity of the German theater.

I suppose hardly any of you have read Otway's "Venice Preserved," but, as you can imagine, it is laid in Venice – a Venice built by Otway, who perhaps knew very little about it, and cared less, but who followed the fashion of the time, and employed Venice as a background for his drama of passion. Hugo Von Hoffmansthal of Vienna had adapted more or less freely Otway's masterpiece for a German theater director, and I was asked in 1904 to go over to Berlin and design the scenes and costumes for the tragedy and to superintend the production. I did this as well as I could under the conditions, and as an indication of the circumstances, I will give you an example of what I mean. I showed this picture, for the last scene but one, to the director, who formerly had been a literary critic, and who had only studied the theater for a few years, and then not as an artist, but as a "literary gent." He looked at it with some suspicion. He then looked at me with more suspicion, and asked me where was the door. I said, "But there is no door." I said, "There is a way in and a way out." He said, "Yes, but I see no door handle nor lock. You cannot have a door without a handle." But again I repeated "There is no door. There is a way in and a way out." This very nearly sent him into a rage, but he changed and became quite calm again and pleased when I informed him that it was copied exactly line for line from an old Italian manuscript. I leave the reader to guess whether I had copied it or to. You see the trouble is, and always will be, that certain theatrical men in high places have no imagination. I did not want this nice old gentleman to imagine a door, but I wanted him through his imagination to see that no door was necessary, and I only succeeded when I assured him that it was a replica of an actuality.

"On Scene and Movement" (1907) from *On the Art of the Theater*

Let me tell you at the commencement that it is the large and sweeping impression produced by means of scene and the movement of the figures, which is undoubtedly the most valuable means at your disposal. I say this only after very many doubts and after much experience; and you must always bear in mind that it is from my experience that I speak, and that the best I can do is but to offer you that experience. Although you know that I have parted company with the popular belief that the *written* play is of any deep and lasting value to the Art of the Theater, we are not going so far as to dispense with it here. We are to accept it that the play still retains some value for us, and we are not going to waste that; our aim is to increase it. Therefore it is, as I say, the production of general and broad effects appealing to the eye which will add a value to that which has already been made valuable by the great poet.

First and foremost comes the *scene*. It is idle to talk about the distraction of scenery, because the question here is not how to create some distracting scenery, but rather how to create a place which harmonizes with the thoughts of the poet.

Come now, we take *Macbeth*. We know the play well. In what kind of place is that play laid? How does it look, first of all to our mind's eye, secondly to our eye?

I see two things. I see a lofty and steep rock, and I see the moist cloud which envelops the head of this rock. That is to say, a place for fierce and warlike men to inhabit, a place for phantoms to nest in. Ultimately this moisture will destroy the rock; ultimately these spirits will destroy the men. Now then, you are quick in your question as to what actually to create for the eye. I answer as swiftly – place there a rock! Let it mount up high. Swiftly I tell you, convey the idea of a mist which hugs the head of this rock. Now, have I departed at all for one eighth of an inch from the vision which I saw in the mind's eye?

But you ask me what form this rock shall take and what colour? What are the lines which are the lofty lines, and which are to be seen in any lofty cliff ? Go to them, glance but a moment at them; now quickly set them down on your paper; *the lines and their direction*, never mind the cliff. Do not be afraid to let them go high; they cannot go high enough; and remember that on a sheet of paper which is but two inches square you can make a line which seems to tower miles in the air, and you can do the same on your stage, for it is all a matter of proportion and nothing to do with actuality.

You ask about the colours? What are the colours that Shakespeare has indicated for us? Do not first look at Nature, but look in the play of the poet. Two; one for the rock, the man; one for the mist, the spirit. Now, quickly, take and accept this statement from me. Touch not a single other colour, but only these two colours through your whole progress of designing your scene and your costumes, yet forget not that each colour contains many variations. If you are timid for a moment and mistrust yourself or what I tell, when the scene is finished you will not see with your eye the effect you have seen with your mind's eye, when looking at the picture which Shakespeare has indicated.

It is this lack of courage, lack of faith in the value which lies in limitation and in proportion which is the undoing of all the good ideas which are born in the minds of the scene designers. They wish to make twenty statements at once. They wish to tell us not only of the lofty crag and the mist which clings to it; they wish to tell you of the moss of the Highlands and of the particular rain which descends in the month of August. They cannot resist showing that they know the form of the ferns of Scotland, and that their archæological research has been thorough in all matters relating to the castles of Glamis and Cawdor. And so in their attempt to tell us these many facts, they tell us nothing; all is confusion:

> "Most sacrilegious murder hath broke ope
> The Lord's anointed temple, and stole thence
> The life o' the building."

So, do as I tell you. Practise with the pencil on paper both on a small scale and on a large scale; practise with colour on canvas; so that you may see for yourself that what I say to you is true – and, if you are an Englishman, make haste: for if you do not others who read this in other countries will find in it technical truths and will outstrip you before you are aware of it. But the rock and its cloud of mist is not all that you have to consider. You have to consider that at the base of this rock swarm the clans of strange earthly forces, and that in the mist hover the spirits innumerable; to speak more technically, you have to think of the sixty or seventy actors whose movements have to be made at the base of the scene, and of the other figures which obviously may not be suspended on wires, and yet must be seen to be clearly separate from the human and more material beings.

It is obvious then that some curious sense of a dividing line must be created somewhere upon the stage so that the beholder, even if he look but with his corporal eye, shall be convinced that the two things are separate things. I will tell you how to do this. Line and proportion having suggested the material rock-like substance, tone and colour (one colour) will have given the ethereal to the mist-like vacuum. Now then, you bring this tone and colour downwards until it reaches nearly to the level of the floor; but you must be careful to bring this colour and this tone down in some place which is removed from the material rock-like substance.

You ask me to explain technically what I mean. Let your rock possess but half the width of the stage, let it be the side of a cliff round which many paths twist, and let these paths mingle in one flat space taking up half or perhaps three quarters of the stage. You have room enough there for all your men and women. Now then, open your stage and all other parts. Let there be a void below as well as above, and in this void let your mist fall and fade; and from that bring the figures which you have fashioned and which are to stand for the spirits. I know you are yet not quite comfortable in your mind about this rock and this mist; I know that you have got in the back of your head the recollection that a little later on in the play come several "interiors" as they are called. But, bless your heart, don't bother about that! Call to mind that the interior of a castle is made from the stuff which is taken from the quarries. Is it not precisely the same colour to begin with? and do not the blows of the axes which hew out the great stones give a texture to each stone which resembles the texture given it by natural means, as rain, lightning, frost? So you will not have to change your mind or change your impression as you proceed. You will have but to give variations of the same theme, the rock – the brown; the mist – the grey; and by these means you will, wonder of wonders, actually have preserved unity. Your success will depend upon your capacity to make variations upon these two themes; but remember never to let go of the main theme of the play when searching for variations in the scene.

By means of your scene you will be able to mould the movements of the actors, and you must be able to increase the impression of your numbers without actually adding another man to your forty or fifty. You must not, therefore, waste a single man, nor place him in such a position that an inch of him is lost. Therefore the place on which he walks must be the most carefully studied parts of the whole scene. But in telling you not to waste an inch of him I do not therefore mean to convey that you must *show* every inch of him. It is needless to say more on this point. By means of suggestion you may bring on the stage a sense of all things – the rain, the sun, the wind, the snow, the hail, the intense heat – but you will never bring them there by attempting to wrestle and close with Nature, in order so that you may seize some of her treasure and lay it before the eyes of the multitude. By means of suggestion in movement you may translate all the passions and the thoughts of vast numbers of people, or by means of the same you can assist your actor to convey the thoughts and the emotions of the particular character he impersonates. Actuality, accuracy of detail, is useless upon the stage.

* * *

I let my scenes grow out of not merely the play, but from broad sweeps of thought which the play has conjured up in me, or even other plays by the same author have conjured up. For instance, the relation of *Hamlet* to *Macbeth* is quite close, and the one play may influence the other.

* * *

We are concerned with the heart of this thing, and with loving and understanding it. Therefore approach it from all sides, surround it, and do not let yourself be attracted away by the idea of scene as an end in itself, of costume as an end in itself, or of stage management or any of these things, and never lose hold of your determination to win through to the secret – the secret which lies in the creation of another beauty, and then all will be well.

In preparing a play, while your mind is thinking of scene, let it instantly leap round and consider the acting, movement and voice. Decide nothing yet, instantly leap back to another thought about another part of this unit. Consider the movement robbed of all scene, all costume, merely as movement. Somehow mix the movement of the person with the movement which you see in your mind's eye in the scene. Now pour all your colour upon this. Now wash away all the colour. Now begin over again. Consider only the words. Wind them in and out of some vast and impossible picture, and now make that picture possible through the words. Do you see at all what I mean? Look at the thing from every standpoint and through every medium, and do not hasten to begin your work until one medium *force* you to commence. You can far sooner trust other influences to move your will and even your hand than you can trust your own little human brain. This may not be the methodical teachings of the school. The results they achieve are on record, and the record is nothing to boast about. Hard, matter-of-fact, mechanical teaching may be very good for a class, but it is not much good for the individual; and when I come to teach a class I shall not teach them so much by words as by practical demonstration.

By the way, I may tell you one or two things that you will find good not to do. For instance, do not trouble about the costume books. When in a great difficulty refer to one in order to see how little it will help you out of your difficulty, but your best plan is never to let yourself become complicated with these things. Remain clear and fresh. If you study how to draw a figure, how to put on it a jacket, coverings for the legs, covering for the head, and try to vary these coverings in all kinds of interesting, amusing, or beautiful ways, you will get much further than if you feast your eyes and confound your brain with Racinet, Planchet, Hottenroth and the others. The coloured costumes are the worst, and you must take great care with these and be utterly independent when you come to think about what you have been looking at. Doubt and mistrust them thoroughly.

* * *

Keep continually designing such imaginative costumes. For example, make a barbaric costume; and a barbaric costume for a sly man which has nothing about it which can be said to be historical and yet is both sly and barbaric. Now make another design for another barbaric costume, for a man who is bold and tender. Now make a third for one who is ugly and vindictive. It will be an exercise. You will probably make blunders at first, for it is no easy thing to do, but I promise you if you persevere long enough you will be able to do it. Then go further; attempt to design the clothing for a divine figure and for a demonic figure: these of course will be studies in individual costumes, but the main strength of this branch of the work lies in the costume as mass. It is the mistake of all theatrical producers that they consider the costumes of the mass individually.

It is the same when they come to consider movements, the movements of masses on the stage. You must be careful not to follow the custom. We often hear it said that each member of the Meiningen Company composing the great crowd in *Julius Caesar* was acting a special part of his own. This may be very exciting as a curiosity, and attractive to a rather foolish audience, who would naturally say: "Oh, how interesting to go and look at one particular man in a corner who is acting a little part of his own! How wonderful! It is exactly like life!" And if that is the standard and if that is our aim, well and good.

But we know that it is not. Masses must be treated as masses, as Rembrandt treats a mass, as Bach and Beethoven treat a mass, and detail has nothing to do with the mass. Detail is very well in itself and in its place. You do not make an impression of mass by crowding a quantity of details together. Detail is made to form mass only by those people who love the elaborate, and it is a much easier thing to crowd a quantity of details together than it is to create a mass which shall possess beauty and interest. On the stage they instantly turn to the natural when they wish to create this elaborate structure. A hundred men to compose a crowd, or, let us say, all Rome, as in *Julius Caesar*; a hundred men, and each is told to act his little part. Each acts himself, giving vent to his own cries; each a different cry, though many of them copy the most effective ones, so that by the end of the first twenty nights they are all giving out the same cry. And each of them has his own action, which after the first twenty nights is exchanged for the most effective and popular action; and by this means a fairly decent crowd of men with waving arms and shouting voices may be composed, and may give some people the impression of a vast crowd. To others it gives the impression of a crush at a railway station.

Avoid all this sort of thing. Avoid the so-called "naturalistic" in movement as well as in scene and costume. The naturalistic stepped in on the Stage because the artificial had grown finicking, insipid; but do not forget that there is such a thing as *noble* artificiality.

* * *

This tendency towards the natural has nothing to do with art, and is abhorrent when it shows in art, even as artificiality is abhorrent when we meet it in everyday life. We must understand that the two things are divided, and we must keep each thing in its place; we cannot expect to rid ourselves in a moment of this tendency to be "natural"; to make "natural" scenes, and speak in a "natural" voice, but we can fight against it best by studying the other arts.

Therefore we have to put the idea of natural or unnatural action out of our heads altogether, and in place of it we have to consider *necessary or unnecessary action*. The necessary action at a certain moment may be said to be the natural action for that moment; and if that is what is meant by "natural," well and good. In so far as it is right it is natural, but we must not get into our heads that every haphazard natural action is right. In fact, there is hardly any action which is right, there is hardly any which is natural. Action is a way of spoiling something, says Rimbaud.

And to train a company of actors to show upon the stage the actions which are seen in every drawing-room, club, public-house or garret must seem to every one nothing less than tomfoolery. That companies are so trained is well known, but it remains almost incredible in its childishness. Just as I told you to invent costume which was significant, so must you invent a series of significant actions, still keeping in mind the great division which exists between action in the mass and action in the individual, and remembering that no action is better than little action.

I have told you to make designs for three costumes of a barbaric period, each particularized by some special character. Give action to these figures which you have made. Create for them significant actions, limiting yourself to those three texts that I have given you, the sly, the bold tenderness, the ugly and vindictive. Make studies for these, carry your little book or pieces of paper with you and continually be inventing with your pencil little hints of forms and faces stamped with these three impressions; and when you have collected dozens of them select the most beautiful.

And now for a word on this. I particularly did not say the most "effective," although I used the word "beautiful" as the artists use it, not as those of the stage use it.

I cannot be expected to explain to you all that the artist means by the word beautiful; but to him it is something which has the most balance about it, the *justest* thing, that which rings a complete and perfect bell note. Not the pretty, not the smooth, not the superb always, and not always the rich, seldom the "effective" as we know it in the Theater, although at times that, too, is the beautiful. But Beauty is so vast a thing, and contains nearly all other things – contains even ugliness, which sometimes ceases to be what is held as ugliness, and contains harsh things, but never *incomplete* things.

Once let the meaning of this word *Beauty* begin to be thoroughly felt once more in the Theater, and we may say that the awakening day of the Theater is near.

Problem Drama – The Director and the Art of the Theater

The First Dialogue (1905) from *On the Art of the Theater*

STAGE-DIRECTOR
You have now been over the theater with me, and have seen its general construction, together with the stage, the machinery for manipulating the scenes, the apparatus for lighting, and the hundred other things, and have also heard what I have had to say of the theater as a machine; let us rest here in the auditorium, and talk a while of the theater and of its art. Tell me, do you know what is the Art of the Theater?

PLAYGOER
To me it seems that Acting is the Art of the Theater.

STAGE-DIRECTOR
Is a part, then, equal to a whole?

PLAYGOER

No, of course not. Do you, then, mean that the play is the Art of the Theater?

STAGE-DIRECTOR

A play is a work of literature, is it not? Tell me, then, how one art can possibly be another?

PLAYGOER

Well, then, if you tell me that the Art of the Theater is neither the acting nor the play, then I must come to the conclusion that it is the scenery and the dancing. Yet I cannot think you will tell me this is so.

STAGE-DIRECTOR

No; the Art of the Theater is neither acting nor the play, it is not scene nor dance, but it consists of all the elements of which these things are composed: action, which is the very spirit of acting; words, which are the body of the play; line and colour, which are the very heart of the scene; rhythm, which is the very essence of dance.

PLAYGOER

Action, words, line, colour, rhythm! And which of these is all-important to the art?

STAGE-DIRECTOR

One is no more important than the other, no more than one colour is more important to a painter than another, or one note more important than another to a musician. In one respect, perhaps, action is the most valuable part. Action bears the same relation to the Art of the Theater as drawing does to painting, and melody does to music. The Art of the Theater has sprung from action – movement – dance.

PLAYGOER

I always was led to suppose that it had sprung from speech, and that the poet was the father of the theater.

STAGE-DIRECTOR

This is the common belief, but consider it for a moment. The poet's imagination finds voice in words, beautifully chosen; he then either recites or sings these words to us, and all is done. That poetry, sung or recited, is for our ears, and, through them, for our imagination. It will not help the matter if the poet shall add gesture to his recitation or to his song; in fact, it will spoil all.

PLAYGOER

Yes, that is clear to me. I quite understand that the addition of gesture to a perfect lyric poem can but produce an inharmonious result. But would you apply the same argument to dramatic poetry?

STAGE-DIRECTOR

Certainly I would. Remember I speak of a dramatic poem, not of a drama. The two things are separate things. A dramatic poem is to be read. A drama is not to be read, but to be seen upon the stage. Therefore gesture is a necessity to a drama, and it is useless to a dramatic poem. It is absurd to talk of these two things, gesture and poetry, as having anything to do with one another. And now, just as you must not confound the dramatic poem with the drama, neither must you confound the dramatic poet with the dramatist. The first writes for the reader, or listener, the second writes for the audience of a theater. Do you know who was the father of the dramatist?

PLAYGOER

No, I do not know, but I suppose he was the dramatic poet.

STAGE-DIRECTOR

You are wrong. The father of the dramatist was the dancer. And now tell me from what material the dramatist made his first piece?

PLAYGOER

I suppose he used words in the same way as the lyric poet.

STAGE-DIRECTOR

Again you are wrong, and that is what every one else supposes who has not learnt the nature of dramatic art. No; the dramatist made his first piece by using action, words, line, colour, and rhythm, and making his appeal to our eyes and ears by a dexterous use of these five factors.

PLAYGOER

And what is the difference between this work of the first dramatists and that of the modern dramatists?

STAGE-DIRECTOR

The first dramatists were children of the theater. The modern dramatists are not. The first dramatist understood what the modern dramatist does not yet understand. He knew that when he and his fellows appeared in front of them the audience would be more eager to *see* what he would do than to *hear* what he might *say*. He knew that the eye is more swiftly and powerfully appealed to than any other sense; that it is without question the keenest sense of the body of man. The first thing which he encountered on appearing before them was many pairs of eyes, eager and hungry. Even the men and women sitting so far from him that they would not always be able to hear what he might say, seemed quite close to him by reason of the piercing keenness of their questioning eyes. To these, and all, he spoke either in poetry or prose, but always in action: in poetic action which is dance, or in prose action which is gesture.

PLAYGOER

I am very interested, go on, go on.

STAGE-DIRECTOR

No – rather let us pull up and examine our ground. I have said that the first dramatist was the dancer's son, that is to say, the child of the theater, not the child of the poet. And I have just said that the modern dramatic poet is the child of the poet, and knows only how to reach the ears of his listeners, nothing else. And yet in spite of this does not the modern audience still go to the theater as of old to see things, and not hear things?

* * *

They are there with their thousand pairs of eyes, just the same as of old. And this is all the more extraordinary because the playwrights and the plays have altered. No longer is a play a balance of actions, words, dance, and scene, but it is either all words or all scene. Shakespeare's plays, for instance, are a very different thing to the less modern miracle and mystery plays, which were made entirely for the theater. *Hamlet* has not the nature of a stage representation. *Hamlet* and the other plays of Shakespeare have so vast and so complete a form when read, that they can but lose heavily when presented to us after having undergone stage treatment. That they were acted in Shakespeare's day proves nothing. I will tell you, on the other hand, what at that period was made for the theater – the Masques – the Pageants – these were light and beautiful examples of the Art of the Theater. Had the plays been made to be seen, we should find them incomplete when we read them. Now, no one will say that they find *Hamlet* dull or incomplete when they read it, yet there are many who will feel sorry after witnessing a performance of the play, saying, "No, that is not Shakespeare's *Hamlet*." When no further addition can be made so as to better a work of art, it can be spoken of as "finished" – it is complete. *Hamlet* was finished – was complete – when Shakespeare wrote the last word of his blank verse, and for us to add to it by gesture, scene, costume, or dance, is to hint that it is incomplete and needs these additions.

PLAYGOER
Then do you mean to say *Hamlet* should never be performed?

STAGE-DIRECTOR
To what purpose would it be if I replied "Yes"? *Hamlet* will go on being performed for some time yet, and the duty of the interpreters is to put their best work at its service. But, as I have said, the theater must not forever rely upon having a play to perform, but must in time perform pieces of its own art.

PLAYGOER
And a piece for the theater, is that, then, incomplete when printed in a book or recited?

STAGE-DIRECTOR
Yes – and incomplete anywhere except on the boards of a theater. It must needs be unsatisfying, artless, when read or merely heard, because it is incomplete without its action, its colour, its line and its rhythm in movement and in scene.

* * *

PLAYGOER
But I have seen some few plays which seemed to satisfy me.

STAGE-DIRECTOR
If you have been entirely satisfied by something obviously mediocre, may it not be that you were searching for something less than mediocre, and you found that which was just a little better than you expected? Some people go to the theater, nowadays, expecting to be bored. This is natural, for they have been taught to look for tiresome things.

* * *

If you were for once to see an actual piece of theatrical art, you would never again tolerate what is to-day being thrust upon you in place of theatrical art. The reason why you are not given a work of art on the stage is not because the public does not want it, not because there are not excellent craftsmen in the theater who could prepare it for you, but because the theater lacks the artist – the artist of the theater, mind you, not the painter, poet, musician. The many excellent craftsmen whom I have mentioned are, all of them, more or less helpless to change the situation. They are forced to supply what the managers of the theater demand, but they do so most willingly. The advent of the artist in the theater world will change all this. He will slowly but surely gather around him these better craftsmen of whom I speak, and together they will give new life to the art of the theater.

PLAYGOER

But for the others?

STAGE-DIRECTOR

The others? The modern theater is full of these others, these untrained and untalented craftsmen. But I will say one thing for them. I believe they are unconscious of their inability. It is not ignorance on their part, it is innocence. Yet if these same men once realized that they were craftsmen, and would train as such – I do not speak only of the stage-carpenters, electricians, wigmakers, costumiers, scene-painters, and actors (indeed, these are in many ways the best and most willing craftsmen) – I speak chiefly of the stage-director. If the stage-director was to technically train himself for his task of interpreting the plays of the dramatist – in time, and by a gradual development he would again recover the ground lost to the theater, and finally would restore the Art of the Theater to its home by means of his own creative genius.

PLAYGOER

Then you place the stage-director before the actors?

STAGE-DIRECTOR

Yes; the relation of the stage-director to the actor is precisely the same as that of the conductor to his orchestra, or of the publisher to his printer.

PLAYGOER

And you consider that the stage-director is a craftsman and not an artist?

STAGE-DIRECTOR

When he interprets the plays of the dramatist by means of his actors, his scene-painters, and his other craftsmen, then he is a craftsman – a master craftsman; when he will have mastered the uses of actions, words, line, colour, and rhythm, then he may become an artist. Then we shall no longer need the assistance of the playwright – for our art will then be self-reliant.

PLAYGOER

Is your belief in a Renaissance of the art based on your belief in the Renaissance of the stage director?

STAGE-DIRECTOR

Yes, certainly, most certainly. Did you for an instant think that I have a contempt for the stage-director? Rather have I a contempt for any man who fails in the whole duty of the stage-director.

PLAYGOER

What are his duties?

STAGE-DIRECTOR

What is his craft? I will tell you. His work as interpreter of the play of the dramatist is something like this: he takes the copy of the play from the hands of the dramatist and promises faithfully to interpret it as indicated in the text (remember I am speaking only of the very best of stage-directors). He then reads the play, and during the first reading the entire colour, tone, movement, and rhythm that the work must assume comes clearly before him. As for the stage directions, descriptions of the scenes, etc., with which the author may interlard his copy, these are not to be considered by him, for if he is master of his craft he can learn nothing from them.

* * *

PLAYGOER

Then is all the stage direction of the world's plays worthless?

STAGE-DIRECTOR

Not to the reader, but to the stage-director, and to the actor – yes.

PLAYGOER

But Shakespeare –

STAGE-DIRECTOR

Shakespeare seldom directs the stage-manager. Go through *Hamlet*, *Romeo and Juliet*, *King Lear*, *Othello*, any of the masterpieces, and except in some of the historical plays which contain descriptions of possessions, etc., what do you find? How are the scenes described in *Hamlet*?

PLAYGOER

My copy shows a clear description. It has "Act I., scene i. Elsinore. A platform before the Castle."

STAGE-DIRECTOR

You are looking at a late edition with additions by a certain Mr. Malone, but Shakespeare wrote nothing of the kind. His words are "Actus primus. Scæna prima."...

* * *

PLAYGOER

I see now. Evidently Shakespeare relied upon the intelligence of the stage-men to complete their scene from his indication.... But is this the same in regard to the actions? Does not Shakespeare place some descriptions through *Hamlet*, such as "Hamlet leaps into Ophelia's grave," "Laertes grapples with him," and later, "The attendants part them, and they come out of the grave"?

STAGE-DIRECTOR

No, not one word. All the stage directions, from the first to the last, are the tame inventions of sundry editors, Mr. Malone, Mr. Capell, Theobald and others, and they have committed an indiscretion in tampering with the play, for which we, the men of the theater, have to suffer.

PLAYGOER

How is that?

STAGE-DIRECTOR

Why, supposing any of us reading Shakespeare shall see in our mind's eye some other combination of movements contrary to the "instructions" of these gentlemen, and suppose we represent our ideas on the stage, we are instantly taken to task by some knowing one, who accuses us of altering the directions of Shakespeare – nay more, of altering his very intentions.

PLAYGOER

But do not the "knowing ones," as you call them, know that Shakespeare wrote no stage directions?

STAGE-DIRECTOR

One can only guess that to be the case, to judge from their indiscreet criticisms. Anyhow, what I wanted to show you was that our greatest modern poet realized that to add stage directions was first of all unnecessary, and secondly, tasteless. We can therefore be sure that

Shakespeare at any rate realized what was the work of the theater craftsman – the stage-manager, and that it was part of the stage-manager's task to invent the scenes in which the play was to be set.

PLAYGOER

Yes, and you were telling me what each part consisted of.

STAGE-DIRECTOR

Quite so. And now that we have disposed of the error that the author's directions are of any use, we can continue to speak of the way the stage-manager sets to work to interpret faithfully the play of the dramatist. I have said that he swears to follow the text faithfully, and that his first work is to read the play through and get the great impression; and in reading, as I have said, begins to see the whole colour, rhythm, action of the thing. He then puts the play aside for some time, and in his mind's eye mixes his palette (to use a painter's expression) with the colours which the impression of the play has called up. Therefore, on sitting down a second time to read through the play, he is surrounded by an atmosphere which he proposes to test. At the end of the second reading he will find that his more definite impressions have received clear and unmistakable corroboration, and that some of his impressions which were less positive have disappeared. He will then make a note of these. It is possible that he will even now commence to suggest, in line and colour, some of the scenes and ideas which are filling his head, but this is more likely to be delayed until he has re-read the play at least a dozen times.

PLAYGOER

But I thought the stage-manager always left that part of the play – the scene designing – to the scene painter?

STAGE-DIRECTOR

So he does, generally. First blunder of the modern theater.

PLAYGOER

How is it a blunder?

STAGE-DIRECTOR

This way: *A* has written a play which *B* promises to interpret faithfully. In so delicate a matter as the interpretation of so elusive a thing as the spirit of a play, which, do you think, will be the surest way to preserve the unity of that spirit? Will it be best if *B* does all the work by himself? or will it do to give the work into the hands of *C, D,* and *E,* each of whom see or think differently to *B* or *A?*

PLAYGOER

Of course the former would be best. But is it possible for one man to do the work of three men?

STAGE-DIRECTOR

That is the only way the work can be done, if unity, the one thing vital to a work of art, is to be obtained.

PLAYGOER

So, then, the stage-manager does not call in a scene painter and ask him to design a scene, but he designs one himself?

STAGE-DIRECTOR

Certainly. And remember he does not merely sit down and draw a pretty or historically accurate design, with enough doors and windows in picturesque places, but he first of all chooses certain colours which seem to him to be in harmony with the spirit of the play, rejecting other colours as out of tune. He then weaves into a pattern certain objects – an arch, a fountain, a balcony, a bed – using the chosen object as the centre of his design. Then he adds to this all the objects which are mentioned in the play, and which are mentioned in the play, and which are necessary to be seen. To these he adds, one by one, each character which appears in the play, and gradually each movement of each character, and each costume. He is as likely as not to make several mistakes in his pattern. If so, he must, as it were, unpick the design, and rectify the blunder even if he has to go right back to the beginning and start the pattern all over again – or he may even have to begin a new pattern. At any rate, slowly, harmoniously, must the whole design develop, so that the eye of the beholder shall be satisfied. While this pattern for the eye is being devised, the designer is being guided as much by the sound of the verse or prose as by the sense or spirit. And shortly all is prepared, and the actual work can be commenced.

PLAYGOER

What actual work? It seems to me that the stage-manager has already been doing a good deal of what may be called actual work.

STAGE-DIRECTOR

Well, perhaps; but the difficulties have but commenced. By the actual work I mean the work which needs skilled labour, such as the actual painting of the huge spaces of canvas for the scenes, and the actual making of the costumes.

PLAYGOER

You are not going to tell me that the stage-manager actually paints his own scenes and cuts his own costumes, and sews them together?

STAGE-DIRECTOR

No, I will not say that he does so in every case and for every play, but he must have done so at one time or another during his apprentice-ship, or must have closely studied all the technical points of these complicated crafts. Then will he be able to guide the skilled craftsmen in their different departments. And when the actual making of the scenes and costumes has commenced, the parts are distributed to the different actors, who learn the words before a single rehearsal takes place. (This, as you may guess, is not the custom, but it is what should be seen to by a stage-director such as I describe.) Meantime, the scenes and costumes are almost ready. I will not tell you the amount of interesting but laborious work it entails to prepare the play up to this point. But even when once the scenes are placed upon the stage, and the costumes upon the actors, the difficulty of the work is still great.

PLAYGOER

The stage-director's work is not finished then?

STAGE-DIRECTOR

Finished! What do you mean?

PLAYGOER

Well, I thought now that the scenes and costumes were all seen to, the actors and actresses would do the rest.

STAGE-DIRECTOR

No, the stage-manager's most interesting work is now beginning. His scene is set and his characters are clothed. He has, in short, a kind of dream picture in front of him. He clears the stage of all but the one, two, or more characters who are to commence the play, and he begins the scheme of lighting these figures and the scene.

PLAYGOER

What, is not this branch left to the discretion of the master electrician and his men?[6]

STAGE-DIRECTOR

The doing of it is left to them, but the manner of doing it is the business of the stage-manager. Being, as I have said, a man of some intelligence and training, he has devised a special way of lighting his scene for this play, just as he has devised a special way of painting the scene and costuming the figures. If the word "harmony" held no significance for him, he would of course leave to it the first comer.

PLAYGOER

Then do you actually mean that he has made so close a study of nature that he can direct his electricians how to make it appear as if the sun were shining at such and such an altitude, or as if the moonlight were flooding the interior of the room with such and such an intensity?

STAGE-DIRECTOR

No, I should not like to suggest that, because the reproduction of nature's lights is not what my stage-manager ever attempts. Neither should he attempt such an impossibility. Not to *reproduce* nature, but to suggest some of her most beautiful and most living ways – that is what my stage-manager shall attempt. The other thing proclaims an overbearing assumption of omnipotence. A stage-manager may well aim to be an artist, but it ill becomes him to attempt celestial honours. This attitude he can avoid by never trying to imprison or copy nature, for nature will be neither imprisoned nor allow any man to copy her with any success.

PLAYGOER

Then in what way does he set to work? What guides him in his task of lighting the scene and costumes which we are speaking about?

STAGE-DIRECTOR

What guides him? Why, the scene and the costumes, and the verse and the prose, and the sense of the play. All these things, as I told you, have now been brought into harmony, the one with the other – all goes smoothly – what simpler, then, that it should so continue, and that the manager should be the only one to know how to preserve this harmony which he has commenced to create?

PLAYGOER

Will you tell me some more about the actual way of lighting the scene and the actors?

* * *

A friend of mine – an actor – once told me that if there were no footlights all the faces of the actors would look dirty.

STAGE-DIRECTOR

That was the remark of a man who did not understand that in place of the footlights another method of lighting the faces and figures could be adopted. It is this simple kind of thing which never occurs to those people who will not devote a little time to even a slight study of the other branches of the craft.

PLAYGOER

Do not the actors study the other crafts of the theater?

STAGE-DIRECTOR

As a rule – no, and in some ways it is opposed to the very life of an actor. If an actor of intelligence were to devote much time to the study of all the branches of the theatrical art he would gradually cease to act, and would end by becoming a stage-manager – so absorbing is the whole art in comparison with the single craft of acting.

PLAYGOER

My friend the actor also added that if the footlights were removed the audience would not be able to see the expression of his face.

STAGE-DIRECTOR

Had Henry Irving or Elenora Duse said so, the remark would have had some meaning. The ordinary actor's face is either violently expressive or violently inexpressive, that it would be a blessing if the theaters were not only without footlights but without any lights at all.

* * *

But let us return to a more serious and a more interesting topic than this lack of expression and this footlight matter. We had passed in review the different tasks of the stage-manager – scene, costume, lighting – and we had come to the most interesting part, that of the manipulation of the figures in all their movements and speeches. You expressed astonishment that the acting – that is to say, the speaking and actions of the actors – was not left to the actors to arrange for themselves. But consider for an instant the nature of this work. Would you have that which has already grown into a certain unified pattern, suddenly spoiled by the addition of something accidental?

PLAYGOER

How do you mean? I understand what you suggest, but will you not show me more exactly how the actor can spoil the pattern?

STAGE-DIRECTOR

Unconsciously spoil it, mind you! I do not for an instant mean that it is his wish to be out of harmony with his surroundings, but he does so through innocence. Some actors have the right instincts in this matter, and some have none whatever. But even those whose instincts are most keen cannot remain in the pattern, cannot be harmonious, without following the directions of the stage-manager.

PLAYGOER

Then you do not even permit the leading actor and actress to move and act as their instincts and reason dictate?

STAGE-DIRECTOR

No, rather must they be the very first to follow the direction of the stage-manager, so often do they become the very centre of the pattern – the very heart of the emotional design.

PLAYGOER

And is that understood and appreciated by them?

STAGE-DIRECTOR

Yes, but only when they realize and appreciate at the same time that the play, and the right and just interpretation of the play, is the all-important thing in the modern theater. Let me illustrate this point to you. The play to be presented is *Romeo and Juliet*. We have studied the play, prepared scene and costume, lighted both, and now our rehearsals for the actors commence. The first movement of the great crowd of unruly citizens of Verona, fighting, swearing, killing each other, appals us. It horrifies us that in this white little city of roses and song and love there should dwell this amazing and detestable hate which is ready to burst out at the very church doors, or in the middle of the May festival, or under the windows of the house of a newly born girl. Quickly following on this picture, and even while we remember the ugliness which larded both faces of Capulet and Montague, there comes strolling down the road the son of Montague, our Romeo, who is soon to be lover and the loved of his Juliet. Therefore, whoever is chosen to move and speak as Romeo must move and speak as part and parcel of the design – this design which I have already pointed out to you as having a definite form. He must move across our sight in a certain way, passing to a certain point, in a certain light, his head at a certain angle, his eyes, his feet, his whole body in tune with the play, and not (as is often the case) in tune with his own thoughts only, and these out of harmony with the play. For his thoughts (beautiful as they may chance to be) may not match the spirit or the pattern which has been so carefully prepared by the director.

PLAYGOER

Would you have the stage-manager control the movements of whoever might be impersonating the character of Romeo, even if he were a fine actor?

STAGE-DIRECTOR

Most certainly; and the finer the actor the finer his intelligence and taste, and therefore the more easily controlled. In fact, I am speaking in particular of a theater wherein all the actors are men of refinement and the manager a man of peculiar accomplishments.

PLAYGOER

But are you not asking these intelligent actors almost to become puppets?

STAGE-DIRECTOR

A sensitive question! which one would expect from an actor who felt uncertain about his powers. A puppet is at present only a doll, delightful enough for a puppet show. But for a theater we need more than a doll. Yet that is the feeling which some actors have about their relationship with the stage-manager. They feel they are having their strings pulled, and resent it, and show they feel hurt – insulted.

PLAYGOER

I can understand that.

STAGE-DIRECTOR

And cannot you also understand that they should be willing to be controlled? Consider for a moment the relationship of the men on a ship, and you will understand what I consider to be the relationship of men in a theater. Who are the workers on a ship?

PLAYGOER

A ship? Why, there is the captain, the commander, the first, second and third lieutenants, the navigation officer, and so on, and the crew.

STAGE-DIRECTOR

Well, and what is it that guides the ship?

PLAYGOER

The rudder?

STAGE-DIRECTOR

Yes, and what else?

PLAYGOER

The steersman who holds the wheel of the rudder.

STAGE-DIRECTOR

And who else?

PLAYGOER

The man who controls the steersman.

STAGE-DIRECTOR

And who is that?

PLAYGOER

The navigation officer.

STAGE-DIRECTOR

And who controls the navigation officer?

PLAYGOER

The captain.

STAGE-DIRECTOR

And are any orders which do not come from the captain, or by his authority, obeyed?

PLAYGOER

No, they should not be.

* * *

STAGE-DIRECTOR

And is that not called discipline?

PLAYGOER

Yes.

STAGE-DIRECTOR
And discipline – what is that the result of?

PLAYGOER
The proper and willing subjection to rules and principles.

STAGE-DIRECTOR
And the first of those principles is obedience, is it not?

PLAYGOER
It is.

STAGE-DIRECTOR
Very well, then. It will not be difficult for you to understand that a theater in which so many hundred persons are engaged at work is in many respects like a ship, and demands like management. And it will not be difficult for you to see how the slightest sign of disobedience would be disastrous. Mutiny has been well anticipated in the navy, but not in the theater. The navy has taken care to define, in clear and unmistakable voice, that the captain of the vessel is the king, and a despotic ruler into the bargain. Mutiny on a ship is dealt with by a court-martial, and is put down by very severe punishment, by imprisonment, or by dismissal from the service.

PLAYGOER
But you are not going to suggest such a possibility for the theater?

STAGE-DIRECTOR
The theater, unlike the ship, is not made for purposes of war, and so for some unaccountable reason discipline is not held to be of such vital importance, whereas it is of as much importance as in any branch of service. But what I wish to show you is that until discipline is understood in a theater to be willing and reliant obedience to the manager or captain no supreme achievement can be accomplished.

PLAYGOER
But are not the actors, scene-men, and the rest all willing workers?

STAGE-DIRECTOR
Why, my dear friend, there never were such glorious natured people as these men and women of the theater. They are enthusiastically

willing, but sometimes their judgment is at fault, and they become as willing to be unruly as to be obedient, and as willing to lower the standard as to raise it. As for nailing the flag to the mast – this is seldom dreamed of – for *compromise* and the vicious doctrine of compromise with the enemy is preached by the officers of the theatrical navy. Our enemies are vulgar display, the lower public opinion, and ignorance. To these our "officers" wish us to knuckle under. What the theater people have not yet quite comprehended is *the value of a high standard and the value of a director who abides by it.*

PLAYGOER

And that director, why should he not be an actor or a scene-painter?

STAGE-DIRECTOR

Do you pick your leader from the ranks, exalt him to be captain, and then let him handle the guns and the ropes? No; the director of a theater must be a man apart from any of the crafts. He must be a man who knows but no longer handles the ropes.

PLAYGOER

But I believe it is a fact that many well-known leaders in the theaters have been actors and stage-managers at the same time?

STAGE-DIRECTOR

Yes, that is so. But you will not find it easy to assure me that no mutiny was heard of under their rule. Right away from all this question of positions there is the question of the art, the work. If an actor assumes the management of the stage, and if he is a better actor than his fellows, a natural instinct will lead him to make himself the centre of everything. He will feel that unless he does so the work will appear thin and unsatisfying. He will pay less heed to the play than he will to his own part, and he will, in fact, gradually cease to look upon the work as a whole. And this is not good for the work. This is not the way a work of art is to be produced in the theater.

PLAYGOER

But might it not be possible to find a great actor who would be so great an artist that as manager he would never do as you say, but who would always handle himself as actor, just the same as he handles the rest of the material?

STAGE-DIRECTOR

All things are possible, but, firstly, it is against the nature of an actor to do as you suggest; secondly, it is against the nature of the stage-manager to perform; and thirdly, it is against all nature that a man can be in two places at once. Now, the place of the actor is on the stage, in a certain position, ready by means of his brains to give suggestions of certain emotions, surrounded by certain scenes and people; and it is the place of the stage-manager to be in front of this, that he may view it as a whole. So that you see even if we found our perfect actor who was our perfect stage-manager, he could not be in two places at the same time. Of course we have sometimes seen the conductor of a small orchestra playing the part of the first violin, but not from choice, and not to a satisfactory issue; neither is it the practice in large orchestras.

PLAYGOER

I understand, then, that you would allow no one to rule on the stage except the stage-manager?

STAGE-DIRECTOR

The nature of the work permits nothing else.

PLAYGOER

Not even the playwright?

STAGE-DIRECTOR

Only when the playwright has practised and studied the crafts of acting, scene-painting, costume, lighting, and dance, not otherwise. But playwrights, who have not been cradled in the theater, generally know little of these crafts. Goethe, whose love for the theater remained ever fresh and beautiful, was in many ways one of the greatest of stage-directors. But, when he linked himself to the Weimar theater, he forgot to do what the great musician who followed him remembered. Goethe permitted an authority in the theater higher than himself, that is to say, the owner of the theater. Wagner was careful to possess himself of his theater, and become a sort of feudal baron in his castle.

PLAYGOER

Was Goethe's failure as a theater director due to this fact?

STAGE-DIRECTOR

Obviously, for had Goethe held the keys of the doors that impudent little poodle would never have got as far as its dressing-room;

the leading lady would never have made the theater and herself immortally ridiculous; and Weimar would have been saved the tradition of having perpetrated the most shocking blunder which ever occurred inside a theater.

PLAYGOER

The traditions of most theaters certainly do not seem to show that the artist is held in much respect on the stage.

STAGE-DIRECTOR

Well, it would be easy to say a number of hard things about the theater and its ignorance of art. But one does not hit a thing which is down, unless, perhaps, with the hope that the shock may cause it to leap to its feet again. And our Western theater is very much down. The East still boasts a theater. Ours here in the West is on its last legs. But I look for a Renaissance.

PLAYGOER

How will that come?

STAGE-DIRECTOR

Through the advent of a man who shall contain in him all the qualities which go to make up a master of the theater and through the reform of the theater as an instrument. When that is accomplished, when the theater has become a masterpiece of mechanism, when it has invented a technique, it will without any effort develop a *creative art* of its own. But the whole question of the development of the craft into a self-reliant and creative art would take too long to go thoroughly into at present. There are already some theater men at work on the building of the theaters; some are reforming the acting, some the scenery. And all of this must be of some small value. But the very first thing to be realized is that little or no result can come from the reforming of a single craft of the theater without at the same time, in the same theater, reforming all the other crafts. *The whole renaissance of the Art of the Theater depends upon the extent that this is realized*. The Art of the Theater, as I have already told you, is divided up into so many crafts: acting, scene, costume, lighting, carpentering, singing, dancing, etc., that it must be realized at the commencement that ENTIRE, not PART reform is needed; and it must be realized that *one* part, one craft, has a *direct* bearing upon each of the other crafts in the theater, and that no result can come from fitful, uneven reform, but only from a systematic progression. Therefore, the reform of the Art of the Theater is possible to those men alone who have studied and practised all the crafts of the theater.

PLAYGOER

That is to say, your ideal stage-manager.

STAGE-DIRECTOR

Yes. You will remember that at the commencement of our conversation I told you my belief in the Renaissance of the Art of the Theater was based in my belief in the Renaissance of the stage-director, and that when he had understood the right use of actors, scene, costume, lighting, and dance, and by means of these bad mastered the crafts of interpretation, he would then gradually acquire the mastery of action, line, colour, rhythm, and words, this last strength developing out of all the rest... Then I said the Art of the Theater would have won back its rights, and its work would stand self-reliant as a creative art, and no longer as an interpretative craft.

PLAYGOER

Yes, and at the time I did not quite understand what you meant, and though I can now understand your drift, I do not quite in my mind's eye see the stage without its poet.

STAGE-DIRECTOR

What? Shall anything be lacking when the poet shall no longer write for the theater?

PLAYGOER

The play will be lacking.

STAGE-DIRECTOR

Are you sure of that?

PLAYGOER

Well, the play will certainly not exist if the poet or playwright is not there to write it.

STAGE-DIRECTOR

There will not be any play in the sense in which you use the word.

PLAYGOER

.But you propose to present something to the audience, and I presume before you are able to present them with that something you must have it in your possession.

STAGE-DIRECTOR

Certainly; you could not have made a surer remark. Where you are at fault is to take for granted, as if it were a law for the Medes and Persians, that that *something* must be made of words.

PLAYGOER

Well, what is this something which is not words, but for presentation to the audience?

STAGE-DIRECTOR

First tell me, is not an idea something?

PLAYGOER

Yes, but it lacks form.

STAGE-DIRECTOR

Well, but is it not permissible to give an idea whatever form the artist chooses?

PLAYGOER

Yes.

STAGE-DIRECTOR

And is it an unpardonable crime for the theatrical artist to use some different material to the poet's?

PLAYGOER

No.

STAGE-DIRECTOR

Then we are permitted to attempt to give form to an idea in whatever material we can find or invent, provided it is not a material which should be put to a better use?

PLAYGOER

Yes.

STAGE-DIRECTOR

Very good; follow what I have to say for the next few minutes, and then go home and think about it for a while. Since you have granted all I asked you to permit, I am now going to tell you out of what material an artist of the theater of the future will create his masterpieces. Out of ACTION, SCENE and VOICE. Is it not very simple?

And when I say *action*, I mean both gesture and dancing, the prose and poetry of action.

When I say *scene*, I mean all which comes before the eye, such as the lighting, costume, as well as the scenery.

When I say *voice*, I mean the spoken word or the word which is sung, in contradiction to the word which is read, for the word written to be spoken and the word written to be read are two entirely different things.

And now, though I have but repeated what I told you at the beginning of our conversation, I am delighted to see that you no longer look so puzzled.

BERLIN: 1905.

A Play of Ideas – Calling for New Symbolism

"A Note on Masks" (1909) from *The Theater Advancing*

ALMOST all the things which were held as essential in the Theater of the ancients have so degenerated to the ludicrous that it is impossible to speak of them without evoking laughter – laughter in the common people, and a particular kind of bored drawl in many of the cultured. It seems to me that I shall never forget trying to explain to a certain Doctor T – that a piece of work which a friend of mine had just invented for the theater was to be given without the use of words. He would not allow (I remember his gravity) that a serious subject should be treated on the stage without words. And when I explained in what way my friend had resolved to do this, how strange was the tone in which Doctor T – shot out the one word, "Ah, Pantomime!"

Dancing, Pantomime, Marionnettes, Masks; these things so vital to the ancients, all essential parts of their respected Art of the Theater at one time or another, have now been turned into a jest.

Dancing – a straight toe like an icicle, strapped in like a "Bambino" in an overpink tight; something on the top of it like a powder-puff, and the whole thing set whirling at an enormous rate like a teetotum; it is the modern public dancer – or when it be not this, it is in every case, and I make no exception, merely a parody of the magic of Isadora Duncan.

Or two persons like bears hugging one another, and slowly and heavily as bears growling their way round a room, plod, wriggle, plod, bump; bump, kick; this is the modern private dancer. And it is permitted.

These things being permitted and being so obviously ridiculous (even for a ridiculous age), and being labelled as the dance, it stands to reason that when the word "Dance" is mentioned seriously, one of these two ridiculous pictures is conjured up by the listener. Indeed, people are even prevailed upon to smile on reading in the Bible that King David danced among the women before the Ark. They picture to themselves a fancy King David attired either as a powder puff or as a fox, trotting, whirling, or lumbering around on a dusty road – probably up-hill. Why, the thing is inconceivable! It is of no use for Royal Academicians to draw pictures of the famous Artist-King as sedately advancing with a harp in his hands like a courtier of the time of Louis XIV. Here again the thing is become inconceivable because sad and ridiculous; and as the imagination of man, owing to industrialism, is not very brilliant, it stands to reason that people give up the idea of serious and beautiful dancing as having really existed in daily life, and fall back into the modern distortion.

The case is even worse with Pantomime. At best the world conceives of pantomime to be what the French actors are so good at, and at the worst they think it is Clown and Pantaloon. French actors are charming and delightful; Clown and Pantaloon are entrancing; but these are undoubtedly not the best exponents of the Art of Pantomime.

So if you point to the case of Buddha teaching symbolic gesture or "Pantomime" to his pupils, the world will instantly think of Harlequinade or "L'Enfant Prodigue," and dressing Buddha (in their mind's eye) in coloured, diamond-patterned tights, or the loose white costume of Pierrot, will giggle as they try to be serious about it all.

The Marionnette, too; speak of him in good society, even in learned society, and there will be an awkward moment or two. It seems that he has become one of those things that one must not mention; like the novels of Dumas, he is only for boys and girls; and if you remind any one that he figured in the Feast of Bacchus when the Egyptians celebrated those rites, people will instantly think of a poor doll tied to a stick, and resembling nothing so much as Aunt Sally.

* * *

Dancing, Pantomime and the Marionnette, three essentials of the old Dramatic Art, have been allowed to go to seed, and people wonder why the Dramatic Art of to-day is so indifferent in quality, and the professors explain it by talking much about the Dramatic Characterization, Logic of Construction, Three Unities, and so forth, and quote from Brunetière, Edmund Burke, and other wise men who study the moon by looking at it in deep wells.

And then the Mask, that paramount means of dramatic expression, without which acting was bound to degenerate!

Used by the savages when making war at a time when war was looked upon as an art; used by the ancients in their ceremonies when faces were held to be too weak, too slight, an element; used by those artists of the theater, Aeschylus, Sophocles and Euripides; found essential to their highest drama by the Japanese masters of the ninth and four-teenth centuries; rejected later on in the eighteenth century by the European actors, and relegated by them to the toy-shop and the fancy-dress ball, the Mask has sunk to the level of the Dance, of Pantomime and of the Marionnette. From being a work of art carved in wood or ivory, and sometimes ornamented with precious metals or precious stones, and later made in leather, it has frittered itself away to a piece of paper, badly painted or covered with black satin.

I shall not here deal historically with the Mask, for it is my particular wish not to divert the reader from the point at issue, which is the importance of the Mask to the life of the Theater of *to-day* and of *tomorrow*. It is as important now as it was of old, and is in no way to be included among the things we have to put aside as old-fashioned – must in no way be looked upon merely as a curiosity, for its existence is vital to the Art of the Theater.

The historical study of this question will only assist those who already perceive the value and importance of reviving in the Theater the famous and beautiful vitality of its earlier days. To those who know nothing of this value the historical study of the Mask is useless, for, like the dealer in antiques, they will but collect material for the sake of col-lecting, and any old thing, provided it be of good craftsmanship and excessively rare, will attract them.

I have spoken and written in praise of the Mask over and over again. I see the gain to the Theater which is attached to this thing. What I tell is not new; it is what all artists know.

Human facial expression is for the most part worthless, and the study of my Art tells me that it is better, provided it is not dull, that instead of six hundred expressions, but six expressions shall appear upon the face of the performer. Let us take an example:

The judge sits in judgement upon the prisoner, and he shall display but two expressions, each of which is in just proportion with the other. He has two masks, and on each mask is one main *statement*, these statements being tempered by *reflections* – the hopes and fears of not merely the judge, but of Justice and Injustice.

Drama which is not trivial, takes us *beyond reality* and yet asks a human face, the realest of things, to express all that. It is unfair.

It is this sense of being beyond reality which permeates all great art. We see it in the little clumsily painted pictures of those periods when the true *Beyond* was of more importance than a right perspective, when the perspective of thought and feeling held first place. We see it in the marvellous little Etruscan figures of but an inch high – one faces me as I write – a tiny little piece of bronze, charged with an overwhelming spirit, but which would be refused at the Royal Academies of to-day because, alas! its hand is as big as its head, and the toes of the foot are not defined; because it does not wriggle itself into a pose, but is poised with firm conviction – conviction, a thing detested by committees, and hence refused admission to the Academies which are governed by committees.

Masks carry conviction when he who creates them is an artist, for the artist limits the statements which he places upon these masks. The face of the actor carries no such conviction; it is over-full of fleeting expression – frail, restless disturbed and disturbing. It once would have seemed doubtful to me whether the actor would ever have the courage to cover his face with a mask again, having once put it aside, for it was doubtful whether he would see that it would serve as any gain. But now the time gives it proof, for the cinematograph favours the Art of the Theater in that it reduces the number of theaters year by year.

The Mask will return to the Theater; of that I grow ever more and more assured; and there is no very great obstacle in the way, although there is some slight danger attached to a misconception of its revival and a mishandling of its powers.

First of all it is not the Greek mask which has to be resuscitated; rather is it the world's mask which is going to be created. There is something very depressing in the idea of groping eastwards among ruins for the remains of past centuries. It is a great trade to-day, but not for the purposes of the Theater. They dig for the marbles and the bronzes and the statuettes; they unearth tombs; they rummage even for crinolines of 1860; they admire these things.

The Theater may admire the old Greek masks, and those of Japan and India, of Africa and America, but it must not dig in the ground for them; it must not collect then to copy them; it must not waste what power it has as a creator in attending to its fads; it must not play the antiquary.

That such a danger as this exists and needs guarding against is most evident. Some time ago, we do not know how far back (the collector knows), the world became tired of creating and took unto itself the rage for the old-fashioned.

This craze for the antique has become a general habit, and the more antique the more the craze. Old furniture, houses packed with old furniture; old books, tapestries, all sorts of seedy metal work, even down to coins – though here the one true collector, the millionaire, is careful to keep as modern as he can. And this love of the antique is growing, so that to-day it is positively eating into the very people themselves, and they are becoming as antique as that which they collect, with this difference, that the old stuff has still some life in it and they have none.

This love of the antique has come into the Theater now and then; it entered into England with William Poel and his Elizabethan Stage Society. Those who know Mr. Poel know him to be a man of distinction, cultivated, and an authority upon the stage of the sixteenth century. But what is that for the purpose of the living Theater? All of us feel that those connected with the stage should be distinguished and culti- vated, and authorities on all questions pertaining to the stage; but they should possess that only as a basis, and on that basis they should build anew and not merely exhibit the basis itself, saying "Lo, the ruins of the sixteenth century! Tickets sixpence; plan of excavations, twopence extra."

There have been others besides Mr. Poel. There have been the revivalists of the so-called Greek Theater – a dreadful thing entirely in Greek. Those, too, who reproduced almost a facsimile of the Mediaeval Theater: a group in Russia did this.

It would be a sad thing, therefore (as all resuscitation in art is so worthless), if masks, sham-Greek in idea and modern in their quality, should be brought into the Theater, appealing only to the curious by creating a subject for small talk. No! the Mask must only return to the stage to restore expression – the visible expression of the mind – and must be a creation, not a copy.

There is a second danger – the danger of the innovator. As Art must not be antique, neither can it be up-to-date. I think it is Whistler who points out that Art has no period whatever. It has only vitality or affectation, and under "affectation" come both the imitation of the antique and the up-to-date, what is to-day well called "the latest thing."

The vitality of an art depends upon its artists and their willing- ness to work under the laws which have ruled their art from the commencement. Not laws put down by committees to suit a period, but the commandments unspoken and uninscribed – that nice Law of Bal- ance which is the heart of perfect Beauty, and from which springs Freedom, that Freedom which we hope and believe is the soul of Truth. To move incessantly towards this Truth is the aim of artists, and those of the Theater must not lag behind.

As has been said many times before, this will be nothing new. I have said it is what the men of the Theater began thousands of years ago; it is what the men of the Theater relinquished a few hundred years ago as beyond their strength. When we shall resume this we shall not be merely repeating; it will be no echo of a past century; the spirited reticence and passionate desire which led men to use the Mask in past ages should be the same now that it ever was, and should never die. It is such an inspiration as this that we should turn to and in which we should trust. Therefore let no one attempt to put this thing on one side into the antique shop, or on to the other as an eccentric explosion of Futurism.

FLORENCE, 1909.

"From Representation to Revelation" (1907) from
On the Art of the Theater

In the beginning with you it was Impersonation; you passed on to Representation, and now you advance into Revelation. When impersonating and representing you made use of those materials which had always been made use of; that is to say, the human figure as exemplified in the actor, speech as exemplified in the poet through the actor, the visible world as shown by means of Scene. You now will reveal by means of movement the invisible things, those seen through the eye and not with the eye, by the wonderful and divine power of Movement.

There is a thing which man has not yet learned to master, a thing which man dreamed not was waiting for him to approach with love; it was invisible and yet ever present with him. Superb in its attraction and swift to retreat, a thing waiting but for the approach of the right men, prepared to soar with them through all the circles beyond the earth – it is Movement.

* * *

From sound has been drawn that wonder of wonders called Music. Music, one could speak of it as St. Paul speaks of love. It is all love, it is all that he says true love should be. It suffereth all things, and is kind; is not puffed up, doth not behave itself unseemly; believeth all things, hopeth all things – how infinitely noble.

And as like one sphere to another, so is Movement like to Music. I like to remember that all things spring from movement, even music; and I like to think that it is to be our supreme honour to be the ministers to the supreme force – movement. For you see where the theater (even the poor distracted and desolate theater) is connected with this service. The theaters of all lands, east and west, have developed (if a degenerate development) from movement, the movement of the human form. We know so much, for it is on record: and before the human being assumed the grave responsibility of using his own person as an instrument through which this beauty should pass, there was another and a wiser race, who used other instruments.

In the earliest days the dancer was a priest or a priestess, and not a gloomy one by any means; too soon to degenerate into something more like the acrobat, and finally to achieve the distinction of the ballet-dancer. By association with the minstrel, the actor appeared. I do not hold, that with the renaissance of the dance comes the renaissance of the ancient art of the Theater, for I do not hold that the ideal dancer is the perfect instrument for the expression of all that is most perfect in movement. The ideal dancer, male or female, is able by the strength or grace of the body to express much of the strength and grace which is in human nature, but it cannot express all, nor a thousandth part of that all. For the same truth applies to the dancer and to all those who use their own person as instrument. Alas! the human body refuses to be an instrument, even to the mind which lodges in that body. The sons of Los rebelled and still rebel against their father. The old divine unity, the divine square, the peerless circle of our nature has been ruthlessly broken by our moods, and no longer can instinct design the square or draw the circle on the grey wall before it. But with a significant gesture we thrill our souls once more to advance without our bodies upon a new road and win it all back again. This is a truth which is not open to argument, and a truth which does not lessen the beauty which exhales from the dearest singer or the dearest dancer of all times.

To me there is ever something more seemly in man when he invents an instrument which is outside his person, and through that instrument translates his message. I have a greater admiration for the organ, for the flute and for the lute than I have for the human voice when used as instrument. I have a greater feeling of admiration and fitness when I see a machine which is made to fly than when I see a man attaching to himself the wings of a bird. For a man through his person can conquer but little things, but through his mind he can conceive and invent that which shall conquer all things.

I believe not at all in the personal magic of man, but only in his impersonal magic. It seems to me that we should not forget that we belong to a period after the Fall and not before it. I can at least extract a certain hint from the old story. And though it may be only a story, I feel that it is just the very story for the artist. In that great period previous to this event we can see in our mind's eye the person of man in so perfect a state that merely to wish to fly was to fly, merely to desire that which we call the impossible was to achieve it. We seem to see man flying into the air or diving into the depths and taking no harm therefrom. We see no foolish clothes, we are aware of no hunger and thirst. But now that we are conscious that this "square deific" has been broken in upon, we must realize that no longer is man to advance and proclaim that his person is the perfect and fitting medium for the expression of the perfect thought.

So we have to banish from our mind all thought of the use of a human form as the instrument which we are to use to translate what we call *Movement*.

* * *

I wish to leave all open and to make no definite rules as to how and by what means these movements are to be shown. This alone let me tell you. I have thought of and begun to make my instrument, and through this instrument I intend soon to venture in my quest of beauty. How do I know whether I can achieve that or not? Therefore how can I tell you definitely what are the first rules which you have to learn? Alone and unaided I can reach no final results. It will need the force of the whole race to discover all the beauties which are in this great source, this new race of artists to which you belong. When I have constructed my instrument, and permitted it to make its first assay, I look to others to make like instruments. Slowly, and from the principles which rule all these instruments some better instrument will be made.

I am guided in the making of mine by only the very first and simplest thoughts which I am able to see in movement. The subtleties and the complicated beauties contained in movement as it is seen in Nature, these I dare not consider; I do not think I shall ever be able to hope to approach these. Yet that does not discourage me from attempting some of the plainest, barest and simplest movements; I mean those which seem to me the simplest, those which I seem to understand. And after I have given activity to those I suppose I shall be permitted to continue to give activity to the like of them; but I am entirely conscious that they contain but the simplest of rhythms, the great movements will not yet be captured, no, not for thousands of years. But when they come, great health comes with them, for we shall be nearer balance than we have ever been before.

I think that movement can be divided into two distinct parts, the movement of two and four which is the square, the movement of one and three which is the circle. There is ever that which is masculine in the square and ever that which is feminine in the circle. And it seems to me that before the female spirit gives herself up, and with the male goes in quest of this vast treasure, perfect movement will not be discovered; at least, I like to suppose all this.

And I like to suppose that this art which shall spring from movement will be the first and final belief of the world; and I like to dream that for the first time in the world men and women will achieve this thing together. How fresh, how beautiful it would be! And as this is a new beginning it lies before men and before women of the next centuries as a vast possibility. In men and women there is a far greater sense of movement than of music.

* * *

I believe in the time when we shall be able to create works of art in th Theater without the use of the written play, without the use of actors; *but* I believe also in the necessity of daily work under the conditions which are to-day offered us.

The word TO-DAY is good, and the word TOMORROW is good, and the words THE FUTURE are divine – but the word which links all these words is more perfect than all; it is that balancing word AND.

FLORENCE, 1907.

Towards a New Theater – Craig on his Screens

"A thousand Scenes in One Scene" (1923) from *Scene*

Never would I hold that a painter or a writer can be true dramatist – using their powers over design and over words – and these alone. Never have I held so. Always have I been misrepresented as holding these views.

I have heard even one great play-writer publicly saying that I am a painter...and that my scenes are all I am thinking of.

I have made scenes – this is because I see a need, – and possess a talent, for making the place or scene in which drama has to move.

But I have been actor – and I am primarily that: I am able to write a little. I consider no time lost which is spent towards qualifying as a master (though maybe only a little master) of the theater – and thus, maybe, of drama. So much as apology for my shortcomings.

And here we will go on to consider what are the duties of a Master of the Drama and Theater.

They are today, to recognise that the theater as work-place – its stage, scene, actors, and other assistants, is an unwieldy, untidy, and unpractical affair at best, and (I think) to set to work first to simplify it, and then re-elaborate it, and both with the utmost caution.

To simplify an affair of this kind time is necessary. It cannot be done in a month – nor in ten months; maybe not even in ten years.

And to simplify it you must first come to know it so well that as you eliminate you do not reject an essential part of the machine. To simplify the stage has been the work I have devoted myself to for the last twenty-five years.

I think I have done what I set out to do.

Whether there remains time for me to do what further I had in view remains to be seen.

Now, what I simplified was not merely bits of scenery, and lighting effects, rags of costume and incidental music.

I simplified the possibilities of drama.

No scene that I worked at was worked at for its own sake. I thought solely of the movement of the drama...of the actors...of the dramatic moments...those long, slow movements and those 'flashes of lightning' (Coleridge). I saw as I progressed that things can, and therefore should, play their parts as well as people: that they combine with the actor and plead for the actor to use them, as the chairs in Molière's plays testify. Not merely are they three or four dead chairs which he placed on the centre of the stage. Yet writers call on us to regard the emptiness of his stage – merely three chairs, they say. Are they mad, these men? Don't they know how Molière made these chairs act – how they are *alive*, and working in combination with the actors?

The chairs and tables in modern plays of which the great Italian actress complains are dead, – there may be six more or sixteen more, or six less; all is as it was...dead scene...a curse to actors and acting.

A so-called 'real' room is what we present on a stage today,...real and yet quite dead – expressionless – unable to act.

Molière's chairs, tables properties of all kinds, were few; he had learned from Italy that they had to be few to be heard – and each of them had to speak at the right moment.

Shakespeare's properties could speak too – although Cromwell and his puritans tore out their tongues and almost dehumanised the whole Shakespearian drama for us.

The tradition once lost, it has never quite recovered its original force.

So, then, to create a simplified stage is the first duty of a master of the drama.

Not by rejecting electricity because of its defects: not by returning to tallow candles: not by returning to masks: by *avoidance* of nothing, by *returning* to nothing – but by this process...

By reviewing all the theatrical things known of or once known of as serviceable to the stage,...testing them in private, and rejecting those which seem hollow and useless, and retaining all those which stand the test.

What test? – the test whether or no they are capable of expression. That and little else. We must ask ourselves –

Does a wax candle serve us to express the rising sun? – If yes, then use it. Does it not serve? – then reject it. But test it first – pooh-pooh nothing till you've tested it. Does a mask serve us to express such and such a human emotion? If it does, use it; – if not, away with it. Does chanting serve any purpose? – if so, what purpose? – is it of value? – then retain chanting: if none, away with it. Does this or that system of gesture serve? – preserve it – or be done with it. Can actors be taught? – to what extent? Which form of stage is the right one for such and such a play – which next best, which least good. Choose the best. Does it not exist? Then build one. Whatever the answers, abide by them. These and a hundred other notions – hopes – fears – have all to be tested to simplify that machine known as the theater. This will prove very expensive you may fancy. Fancy is not to be relied on, fact is more sure and fact shows us that to avoid testing everything is the most expensive method of all.

* * *

The scene stands by itself – and is monotone. All the colour used is produced by light, and I use a very great deal of colour now and again, – such colour as no palette ever can produce. I think I may say that I have not seen colour so rich used in any scene on any stage but this...

Now for a word on this word "simplified":...let me explain what I mean by it.

The world once used reed pens – then quill pens – and then steel pens. These they dipped into bottles of ink: many times would a man dip his pen into the ink before he could write a page of his letter.

Someone then invented the fountain pen. A man can write his whole letter without dipping his pen once into any bottle.

The world then invented the typewriting machine.

I would liken my scene to the fountain pen and not to the typewriting machine.

It is not a piece of mechanism; it is a simple device, shaped like screens – angular – plain.

Why is it shaped as it is? – why plain, flat screens or walls?

I will tell you. You must suppose me to be doing in front of you rapidly what it took me many years to do slowly. Suppose me, then, searching to find the essential form of the habitation of man, so as to afterwards making a stage habitation for the stage man.

I make rapidly two hundred and fifty models of his various habitations all over the earth. I make two as used by him 5000 B.C., three 2000 B.C., five 500 B.C., ten 100 B.C., twenty 100 A.D., thirty 1000 A.D., sixty 1500 A.D, fifty 1700 A.D., and seventy 1900 A.D

I put them up in a line: – I study them.

I intend to reject every piece of each habitation which I do not find in all the others.

Why?

In order to discover which pieces every man since the year one has found essential.

Why?

So as to make *one* scene.

Why?

Because this scene-making is something of an art and not a toy factory.

I do not want the litter of the nursery in my theater.

I do not want to waste yearly thousands of pounds on the usual bric-à-brac found in the modern theater.

Because it is a waste of money – wood – canvas, and I do not want to waste the spectator's powers and temper as spectator and the artist's powers as artist. The artist is to speak to spectators through scene, he is not to display a large doll's house for them.

Having rejected in the two hundred and fifty models any piece which cannot be found in every other piece, I find I am then left with the essential parts which form the habitation of man. The walls remain:

The floor.

The ceiling ... nothing else.

And how are these shaped?

Are there pillars on them, near them? – do parts protrude – the roof, for example? – some cornice – some skirting? Are there doors, windows, kerbs, and so forth? No. Because I found no such things in all the models. I found that the only things in every habitation of man were flat floor – flat walls – flat roof.

The flat roof is the only part of the human habitation which began at once to vary.

So now you see how it is that my screens, my SCENE, is composed as it is of plain flat walls. I wished to reduce scene to its essentials and I found it reduced itself. I have but done as ordered.

I *then added mobility to it.*

Why?

First because it seemed to demand it. Secondly because it continued to demand it. It demanded it on behalf of the actor. This mobility allows him to move in a differently shaped scene each night for as long as he wishes. Suppose he does not feel at home in this shape, he can change it and rechange it. It is like a hundred pairs of gloves – he can soon find a pair to fit and please him.

Being a device and not an actual habitation, it seemed to ask that I should so make it that it could *seem* now to be the inside and now the outside of any habitation ever known in the world – mud hut or temple, – Palais de Versailles or Mr Harrod's shop.

And can it be these four places?

It can *seem* like all four ... it can seem like four hundred other places. It has a quite clear resemblance to four hundred different places.

I do not mean to say that I shall always show you the wallpaper that is in Mr Harrod's office ... or always the gilding in Versailles Palace – or always the marble in the temple or the mud in the hut ... But I will give you the form of the four places, the light belonging to each – and three or four details – here a door added – here a grille and here an alcove which, when you see them, shall somehow bring up to your mind the conviction that you see what I intend you to see.

* * *

What does the device do? you ask.

How does it act?

It does this: it turns in part or whole to receive the play of light.

I would sum up the whole matter in these words.

– Then it is all a matter of the light?

Let us not be in too great a hurry with our 'all a matter of' – I am afraid I cannot say that it is *all* a matter of any *one* thing.

Simplicity and elaboration are not arrived at by any quicker process than that by which a perfect runner or a perfect swimmer achieves the simplification and elaboration necessary to outstrip the others ... and with the runner and swimmer it is not all a matter of this or that ... it is a matter of attending to a hundred things all the time.

Let us go on. In creating a scene for a drama which is worth hearing and worth seeing, we have never to forget what the spectators require.

One of the first of their demands is that they shall be able to see and hear the actor as he performs before us, especially his face (or mask) – and his hands and person.

Therefore any theory which attempts to state the uses of light in relation to scene without stating the use of light to the acting is value – less.

Here then are a few general facts which it is useful to remember.

1. You can see a face – a hand – a vase – a statue better when it is backed by a flat plain non-coloured surface than when backed by something on which a coloured pattern or some other object is painted or carved.

2. The shadow of a thing (face, hand, or statue) is visible to the eye without difficulty or distraction, and is visible at the same time as is the thing itself.

3. When the face, hand, or statue is removed, a plain screen is a dull thing to look at – the eye tires.

4. The eye cannot look at two objects at the same time. When we listen to a speaker, be it in a room or in a hall or in a theater, we look at one thing only – his face.

5. In a theater our eyes follow the speaker; therefore when two are speaking it is usual and it is best for these two to be as near one another as possible.

6. It is essential they shall be in sympathy in their work. Any division in this and we shall at once feel the division and see neither of the actors – our thoughts will wander to the scenery.

7. The screen against which an actor is best seen is a white one – for it can be shaded to any tone of grey, blackened by shade; coloured any colour, and that without changing the colour of the actor's face, hands or figure.

8. There is no need at all for any actor's face to be cast into shadow and the expression lost until it loses distinction of expression...then, indeed, it seems best to blot it out.

9. There was never any need of scenery to take an overdue prominence until the day when the actor lost his power of expression, his power to act, and until he began to resent the right uses of scene and light.

10. The use of light to the actor is that it will aid him and collaborate with him if he will show it consideration. For light can be used in many dramatic ways – it is for the actor to come to know at least fifty or eighty of these ways. At present he acknowledges about six.

11. The use of light to the actor is only to be studied by the actor if he will observe the way light plays its subtle part in real life. If he will observe he will soon come to realise that stage lighting can be his best friend in his work. As an aid to his observation the treatise by Leonardo da Vinci on light can help an actor sufficiently advanced in his studies.

Having stated some of the uses of light to the actor, I can now proceed to state the relation of light to this scene.

The scene turns to receive the play of light.

These two, scene and light, are, as I have said, like two dancers or two singers who are in perfect accord.

The scene supplies the simplest form made up of right angles and flat walls and the light runs in and out and all over them.

The scene is not merely put up (though it stands on its own feet by the way) on the stage without thought of *how* it be placed and some light turned on without considering *what* light – whence it comes – and what it sets out to do.

In the *placing* of the scene, and in the *turning* to receive the light, and in the *placing* and *directing* of the light lie the little difficulties.

Again, the relation of light to this scene is akin to that of the bow to the violin, or of the pen to the paper.

For the light *travels* over the scene – it does not ever stay in one fixed place,... travelling it produces the music. During the whole course of the drama the light either caresses or cuts, – it floods or it trickles down, – it is never quite still though often enough its movement is not to be detected until an Act has come to an end, when, should we have any power of observation left (and drama should cure us of any furtive desire to observe), we find our light has changed entirely.

Scene and light then move.

I may have any number of pieces in my scene and I may have any number of lamps...

The text is read at the pace at which it will be delivered, and at each appointed cue a single or a double leaf of my screen moves – at the same time one of my lamps will begin to play its light at a given strength and from a given position and in a given direction.

At each cue another leaf or other leaves turn – advance – recede – fold up or unfold – imperceptibly, or maybe on some occasions markedly, while at the same time other lamps will begin to functions move their position, change their strengths, alter their direction.

My screens can pass from and to any spot on the stage floor and nothing obstructs their passage.

My light can pass from and to any position in the air or on the stage and so play upon any spot I require.

* * *

I can colour my screens or the actor's form to a great extent in the same degree and with the same strength and quality as a painter uses on his canvas. I employ only light... he employs his paints.

I am limited by my medium as he is by his, and both of us have to obey our particular tools and materials. – He cannot do anything beyond paint on a flat surface in colours – I can do no more than project my light on to my screens and figures.

But whereas he had his materials and tools discovered for him and a method of long-standing taught him, I have had to find out my materials and tools, and I have been obliged to invent a method for using them.

Therefore, if I have not yet reached as perfect a method of using these things as he has, and if I cannot reach it before I am obliged to give up the work, others to whom I shall leave my plans and experiments must continue on after I have done and discover better ways if they can.

* * *

THE 'SCENE' AND THE POETIC DRAMA

The highest form of modern theatrical art is the performance of the poetic drama. It neither reaches the altitudes of the old religious drama nor falls to the splendid depths of the musical comedy, but is something betwixt and between, and it is considerably nearer to the higher than the lower.

Thus everyone must acknowledge that there is much of the modern musical comedy and melodrama in Shakespeare, but that there is more spiritual drama. Shakespeare even condescends to the touch of the music hall and is at home in it, but from it he is continually rising to touch those heights called by some...the impossible.

It is for this poetical drama that the scene which is the subject of this article was created.

Since making it its creator has felt that it will be of service not only to the theater, but also to the dramatic poet; and hopes that both to the stage and to the poet it will prove of great practical use,...using the word 'practical' in its fullest signification.

Description of the Scene   The scene is made up usually of four, six, eight, ten or twelve screens, and, although sometimes of more than twelve, seldom of less than four. Each part or leaf of a screen is alike in every particular except breadth, and these parts together form a screen, composed of two, four, six, eight or ten leaves. These leaves fold either way and are monochrome in tint.

The height of all these screens is alike.

These screens are self-supporting and are made either of a wooden frame covered with canvas, or of solid wood.

With screens of narrow dimensions curved forms are produced, for larger rectangular spaces broader leaved screens are used, and for varied and broken forms all sizes are employed.

Sometimes a flat roof is used with these screens, at other times the space above the top line is shown.

The scene being monochrome, the minimum of light is required to illuminate it, as there is much reflection from each leaf. Ordinary battens that are used in the theater, and also daylight, can be used for its illumination.

The screens can be so arranged that by moving three leaves a great change in effect is produced.

The art of using this scene to the best advantage is a delicate one and acquired only with practice. The aim of the arranger is to place his screens in such a position that, by moving the minimum number of leaves, he may produce the desired amount of variety. Where the maximum amount of variety is required the change is less easy to accomplish, for, in art as well as in nature, sudden contrasts cause more trouble because, as a rule, undesirable.

Sometimes certain additions may be made to this scene, such as a flight of steps, a window, a bridge, a balcony, and of course the necessary furniture, though great care and reserve must be exercised in making these additions so as to avoid the ridiculous.

Artistic Values   This scene is a living thing.

In the hands of an artist it is capable of all varieties of expression, even as a living voice and a living face are capable of every expression. The scene remains always the same, while incessantly changing.

Some may ask how such a thing can possibly be, and one can only ask such questioners to study the human face.

Every human face is shaped more or less the same, and is made up of two eyes, a brow, a nose, a mouth, a chin and so forth; move any one of these parts ever so little, and we note a different expression.

This scene resembles the human face.

It is obvious that the advantage of such a scene will be best understood and felt by those who see it; but its uses can at any rate be recorded to some advantage.

Through its use we obtain a sense of harmony and a sense of variety at the same time. We may be said to have recovered one of the unities of the Greek drama without losing any of the variety of the Shakespearean drama.

We pass from one scene to another without a break of any kind, and when the change has come we are not conscious of any disharmony between it and that which is past.

I have said of this scene that it is a living thing, that it is capable of expression and I must here warn you, from personal experience in its use, that it is so living that, unless treated as a living thing, it is quite likely not to respond to the will of the manipulator or arranger.

Accidental effects can be obtained which are beautiful even as a beautiful accidental effect can be produced on a piano, but no one without knowing this scene intimately, that is to say, without having studied it more than carefully, can produce harmony from its planes. It even refuses to obey the artist entirely when the artist is not in the right mood; and its inventor has worked with a set of screens for a day or two searching for an especial form for a screen in *Hamlet* and been totally unable to bring out any expression from its flatness; yet in the process of overcoming the difficulty perhaps a more perfect harmony has been ultimately produced.

The results obtained have found favour with all the poets, a few of the actors, all the stage managers and some of the directors of theatres to whom they have been shown, and the scene has also won the approval of the stage hands, whose praise the inventor values. To all of these he declares himself beholden for many suggestions which have improved the instrument.

Advantages to Actor and Stage Manager   Now one of the advantages of this invention is that, should the actor feel after a few nights that he could play the scenes better in a different arrangement, and have a clear idea as to his wishes and how to obtain them, he can test his ideas in the morning on the model and make his changes that same evening.

If after a month or so he wishes to change again, either because he thinks something can be improved by giving himself more liberty as actor, or for any other reason, he can again make any change which seems to him desirable. In fact the scene is as much for the actor as it is for the stage manager or the poet.

If the actor feels that he cannot play his part in a certain scene he has only to go to the stage manager, and together, with the model on the table, they can work out a new arrangement.

The advantages which the use of this model offers to the stage manager are exceptional.

The Model Stage and Scene   To begin with, the model with which he works is always ready to his hand. He keeps it in his study and is thus able continually to test ideas which come into his head as to the poetic drama which he has to produce. He has not to wait for the scene painter to bring him a model which, if he does not like, he has to have changed and rechanged; but he has at his disposal a model scene which he can be always changing and arranging, and from which he can derive ideas for the movement of his figures.

Possessing the model, he is not saddled with a cumbersome and elaborate 'model stage' of the usual pattern; he need not fear to touch the thing lest it fall to pieces, or the strings and wires get tangled. He has a workman-like model to use…no litter, no strings, no paper; no longer a toy but clean and solid wood.

He is often at a loss how to fashion scenes for these old plays which have held the boards for so long. In his study he fancies a passage here, a long wall somewhere there, pillars here; but he is unable to put these down on paper, and if he could do so it would still be unsatisfactory. He could not see the thing, he could not measure his distances, he could not tell whether there is enough space for a man to come on there, whether there will be room enough on the stage for this passage to go back in that direction, and in his helplessness he is obliged to tell the scene painter to make the design. But with the scene which is here offered him, and with this small model stage all this preliminary work will be made many times easier. He can do it himself.

He is producing *Richard III* for instance. He wants a vast throne-room for the one scene and he wants to follow it up by a small cell. He can place his screens upon his model stage, and turn them this way and that until he has got his throne room. He can then mark the results down upon the ground-plan drawn to scale with which the inventor provides him.

After he has done this he can move one or two leaves of the screen so as to bring all the screens to form a smaller, prison-like place.

At the first attempt he will not have much success. He will then probably begin by forming the smaller scene first and he will try if it is not possible to work backwards, passing from the second to the first scene, from the smaller to the larger instead of from the larger to the smaller. He may probably find that this makes his task easier.

But he who finds the greatest difficulty at the outset in arranging scenes from these screens is more likely than another to produce ultimately more important results if he persevere; but one should avoid if possible the feeling that there is something very difficult about the manipulation of the scene.

Some say that this is the poet's scene. To a certain extent in its first state it is more his scene than anyone else's, for it represents the world perhaps better than any other scene has done…that particular world created by the poets, the world of imagination. The poets themselves have said so.

But let not the casual reader think that this indicates something flimsy and floating. Nothing of the kind. It is something sharp-cut, something vivid and definite, as firm in its outline as it is flexible in its movement, and this, I believe, is what the poets have always held such a world to be.

Finally, in connection with this scene the inventor has planned several additional inventions by means of which doors, windows, cornices, staircases, trees, hills, clouds, stars, sun, moon and all can be placed before the audience, and that without calling in a single extra man to assist the usual staff.

Practical Values of this 'Scene' It saves the manager's time, for after he has once mastered its simple mechanism he is able in a short time to produce arrangements with his model which shall give the effect he requires. It also saves him the time which would otherwise be spent in discussing plans and models with the scene painters, carpenters and workmen.

The fact that the scene is self-supporting saves the time which is usually wasted in hanging scenery and in finding spare places for the accommodation of the different cloths, cut-cloths, built-out pieces, etc.

It saves the manipulator's time as, the screens being easy to move from one position to another, one full set can change to another full set in less than thirty seconds.

The maximum wait between the acts need not exceed seven minutes at most, and it can even be less if desired. Eighteen men can strike the largest set and leave the stage empty in twenty seconds. A smaller change can be effected in four to ten seconds by fewer men. It is greatly owing to the fact of each screen being self-supporting that this becomes possible. It also saves time in all that concerns the lighting.

Time is wasted in rehearsing the lights because such rehearsal in so many instances means guessing which light is best; here it is saved because the simplest light is the best; that is to say, the light of the battens. The inventor tells us that, whereas in former experiments he usually did away with the battens, he has found they work perfectly easily with this scene. It has been continually demonstrated, in fact, that no other light is so good.

Another saving of time in regard to the lighting is that the manager can calculate with more precision than formerly the necessary strength of his limes.

We come then to the advantages in the matter of storage.

It is a great saving of time here also to be able to store this scene in the theater itself, for as a rule much time is wasted in sending to the warehouse for the heavy scenery of the popular drama, and on the continent even more time is lost in this labour than in England owing to the nightly changes. But in any theater where the programme is changed a great saving of time is effected through the use of this scene.

* * *

There is also the initial saving in expenditure in the purchase of scenery, since instead of a complete set for each play one set may be used for all. In fact this scene may from all points of view be described as '*Multum in parvo*'.

On the ground of its practicality patents have been obtained in Europe, including Germany, and in America, and, after having experimented with the full sized models which have been made in Moscow and in London, it has been found that it answers all expectations and fulfils every requirement of the popular drama.

In fact it has proved economical both artistically and commercially, and the European managers before whom it has been tested confirm this estimate of its value.

It will be of interest here to quote the two following extracts from *The Times* (London), the former written after a 'demonstration' of the use of the scene by its inventor, at his studio in London in 1911; the latter an extract from the account sent by *The Times'* special correspondent in Moscow, after the first production of *Hamlet* with the screen scenery, at the Arts Theater in that city. The *Hamlet* production has since then been already given over one hundred and fifty times in the same theater.

September, 23, 1911.

The device is extremely simply. It consists of folding screens, which will stand of themselves without being fastened either to the stage or to ropes, rollers, or beams in the 'flies'. The screens can be made of any size required. They may be 30ft. high or only 8ft.; they may have three folds or a dozen, and each fold may be 1ft. wide or 6ft. Three men in three minutes could move or remove a whole scene and, folded flat, each screen would take up very little space. The obvious advantages are the ease and quickness with which these things can be handled and the simplicity of the manipulation. To change a scene would no longer be to roll up or roll down great canvases, to screw and unscrew bolts, to adjust and fasten ropes, to remove entirely an elaborate built-up set, and put another in its place. A complete change of scene can be obtained merely by rearranging a few screens. And when it is necessary (as in the case of touring companies) to take away the complete scenery of a play, the carpenters, instead of working all night and losing some very important piece of the outfit, could transport the folded screens to the van at a reasonable hour. Moreover, that terror of Monday morning in provincial theaters...the 'scene-plot'...is reduced to a simple plan of the stage marked out in squares with the positions of the screens shown by letters or figures, and a quarter of an hour's work ought to make the whole set of changes clear to the stage-hands.

Ease and quickness of manipulation are matters that interest the public no less than the stage-manager and scene-shifters. On the playing of Shakespeare, for instance, such a device would have wide and deep effects. But the question most likely to occur to the public first of all is what kind of scenery these screens provide. Not, of course, the scenery of detail and archaeology, the scenery of crowded fact and 'realisation of a period'. But an hour's experimenting with Mr

Craig's model stage revealed a very wide variety of suggestions, moods, settings, properly so called, for drama. The model screens exhibited were all in monochrome, which was practically the 'self-colour' of the material of which the models were made; but indoor and outdoor scenes alike were made each in a few seconds and in two or three movements, and the purport of each was unmistakable. Quite extraordinary effects of space and spirit were obtained; and in this the lighting played a very important part. For one advantage of these screens is that the light can be directed from almost any point, and a change of light makes a change of mood, or even of place. Mr Craig's own desire appears to be to dispense as far as possible with any colouring on the screens themselves, partly because each screen can thus take on a much wider range of characters, so to speak, than if it were coloured. Most of the colouring would be obtained by means of coloured lights; and there would be no danger that a scene painted for one light would be robbed of its effect by being seen later under another light...an error too often made with scenery as we know it. Further definition...in a forest scene, for instance...can be obtained by means of an ingenious device for casting shadows; and 'properties'...chairs, tables, and the like...can be as easily used with these screens as with the curtains of the Elizabethans or with the built-up sets of the modern stage...

A street scene that would have done equally well for London, Florence, or Baghdad was made with three screens in three seconds; and there seems to be no reason why, with a sparing use of colour and pattern, a modern drawing-room should not be as clearly suggested as a castle or a magic island. A proscenium that can be easily enlarged or reduced forms a subsidiary part of the scheme; and sloping stages could, if necessary, be made flat for the reception of the screens.

It is claimed that the new scenery is cheap, easily and quickly provided, simply and quickly worked, and adaptable to practically all needs. It is certainly of wonderful effect in the suggestion of place and mood; and experiment with the models only whets the appetite to see a stage equipped with the new scenery on the full scale.

Moscow, January 9, 1912.

Every scene in the *Hamlet* has for its foundation an arrangement of screens which rise to the full height of the proscenium, and consist of plain panels devoid of any decoration. Only two colours are used...a neutral cream shade and gold. A complete change of scene is created simply by the rearrangement of these screens, whose values lie, of course, not so much in themselves as in their formation and the lighting.

Mr Craig has the singular power of carrying the spiritual significance of words and dramatic situations beyond the actor to the scene in which he moves. By the simplest of means he is able, in some mysterious way, to evoke almost any sensations of time or space, the scenes even in themselves suggesting variations of human emotion.

Take, for example, the Queen's chamber in the Castle of Elsinore. Like all the other scenes, it is simply an arrangement of the screens already mentioned. There is nothing which definitely represents a castle, still less the locality or period; and yet no one would hesitate as to its significance...and why? Because it is the spiritual symbol of such a room. A symbol, moreover, whose form is wholly dependent upon the action which it surrounds; every line, every space of light and shadow going directly to heighten and amplify the significance of that action, and becoming thereby something more than its mere setting . . . a vital and component part no longer separable from the whole. Whatever Mr Craig has done he has obviously done it not only with the touch of an artist, but also with all the care and reverence of a true lover of Shakespeare.

To judge from his work he is not so much a revolutionary as a reformer. Far from being an enemy to theatrical tradition, he seems to realise better than any one how much valuable material for his art lies buried in that limbo of things forgotten. He has gone back over a field whose fertility so many have ignored, and drawn from it all that is best and most useful to him.

The Theater of the Future – Craig and the Performer

"The Actor and the Übermarionette" (1907)
from *On the Art of the Theater*

"TO SAVE THE THEATRE, THE THEATRE MUST BE DESTROYED, THE ACTORS AND ACTRESSES MUST ALL DIE OF THE PLAGUE. . . . THEY MAKE ART IMPOSSIBLE." – ELEONORA DUSE: *Studies in Seven Arts*, ARTHUR SYMONS. (CONSTABLE, 1900.)

ACTING is not an art. It is therefore incorrect to speak of the actor as an artist. For accident is an enemy of the artist. Art is the exact antithesis of pandemonium, and pandemonium is created by the tumbling together of many accidents. Art arrives only by design. Therefore in order to make any work of art it is clear we may only work in those materials with which we can calculate. Man is not one of these materials.

The whole nature of man tends towards freedom; he therefore carries the proof in his own person that as *material* for the Theater he is useless. In the modern theater, owing to the use of the bodies of men and women *as their material*, all which is presented there is of an accidental nature. The actions of the actor's body, the expression of his face, the sounds of his voice, all are at the mercy of the winds of his emotions: these winds, which must blow for ever round the artist, moving without unbalancing him. But with the actor, emotion *possesses* him; it seizes upon his limbs, moving them whither it will. He is at its beck and call, he moves as one in a frantic dream or as one distraught, swaying here and there; his head, his arms, his feet, if not utterly beyond control, are so weak to stand against the torrent of his passions, that they are ready to play him false at any moment. It is useless for him to attempt to reason with himself. Hamlet's calm directions (the dreamer's, not the logician's directions, by the way) are thrown to the winds. His limbs refuse, and refuse again to obey his mind the instant emotion warms, while the mind is all the time creating the heat which shall set these emotions afire. As with his movement, so is it with the expression of his face. The mind struggling and succeeding for a moment, in moving the eyes, or the muscles of the face whither it will; the mind bringing the face for a few moments into thorough subjection, is suddenly swept aside by the emotion which has grown hot through the action of the mind. Instantly, like lightning, and before the mind has time to cry out and protest, the hot passion has mastered the actor's expression. It shifts and changes, sways and turns, it is chased by emotion from the actor's forehead between his eyes and down to his mouth; now he is entirely at the mercy of emotion, and crying out to it: "Do with me what you will!" His expression runs a mad riot hither and thither, and lo! "Nothing is coming of nothing." It is the same with his voice as it is with his movements. Emotion cracks the voice of the actor. It sways his voice to join in the conspiracy against his mind. Emotion works upon the voice of the actor, and he produces the impression of discordant emotion. It is of no avail to say that emotion is the spirit of the gods, and is precisely what the artist aims to produce; first of all this is not true, and even if it were quite true, every stray emotion, every casual feeling, cannot be of value. Therefore the mind of the actor, we see, is less powerful than his emotion, for emotion is able to win over the mind to assist in the destruction of that which the mind would produce; and as the mind becomes the slave of the emotion it follows that accident upon accident must be continually occurring. So then, we have arrived at this point: that emotion is the cause which first of all creates, and secondly destroys. Art, as we have said, can admit of no accidents. That, then, which the actor gives us, is not a work of art; it is a series of accidental confessions.

* * *

Therefore the body of man, is by *nature* utterly useless as a material for an art. I am fully aware of the sweeping character of this statement; and as it concerns men and women who are alive, and who as a class are ever to be loved, more must be said lest I give unintentional offence. I know perfectly well that what I have said here is not yet going to create an exodus of all the actors from all the theaters in the world, driving them into sad monasteries where they will laugh out the rest of their lives, with the Art of the Theater as the main topic for amusing conversation. As I have written elsewhere, the Theater will continue its growth and actors will continue for some years to hinder its development. But I see a loop-hole by which in time the actors can escape from the bondage they are in. They must create for themselves a new form of acting, consisting for the main part of symbolical gesture. To-day they *impersonate* and interpret; to-morrow they must *represent* and interpret; and the third day they must create. By this means style may return. To-day the actor impersonates a certain being. He cries to the audience: "Watch me; I am now pretending to be so and so, and I am now pretending to do so and so;" and then he proceeds to *imitate* as exactly as possible, that which he has announced he will *indicate*. For instance, he is Romeo. He tells the audience that he is in love, and he proceeds to show it, by kissing Juliet. This, it is claimed, is a work of art: it is claimed for this that it is an intelligent way of suggesting thought. Why – why, that is just as if a painter were to draw upon the wall a picture of an animal with long ears and then write under it "This is a donkey."

* * *

There is a stage expression of the actor "getting under the skin of the part." A better one would be getting *"out* of the skin of the part altogether." "What, then," cries the red-blooded and flashing actor, "is there to be no flesh and blood in this same art of the theater of yours? No life?" It depends what you call life, signor, when you use the word in relation with the idea of art. The painter means something rather different to actuality when he speaks of life in his art, and the other artists generally mean something essentially spiritual; it is only the actor, the ventriloquist, or the animal-stuffer who, when they speak of putting life into their work, mean some actual and lifelike reproduction, something blatant in its appeal, that it is for this reason I say that it would be better if the actor should get out of the skin of the part altogether. If there is any actor who is reading this, is there not some way by which I can make him realize the preposterous absurdity of this delusion of his, this belief that he should aim to make an actual copy, a reproduction? I am going to suppose that such an actor is here with me as I talk; and I invite a musician and a painter to join us. Let them speak.

* * *

I who represent an art distinct from all these, shall remain silent.

"Tell us," asks the painter, "is it true that before you can act a part properly you must feel the emotions of the character you are representing?" "Oh well, yes and no; it depends what you mean," answers the actor. "We have first to be able to feel and sympathize and also criticize the emotions of a character; we look at it from a distance before we close with it: we gather as much as we can from the text and we call to mind all the emotions suitable for this character to exhibit. After having many times rearranged and selected those emotions which we consider of importance we then practise to reproduce them before the audience; and in order to do so we must feel as little as is necessary; in fact the less we feel, the firmer will our hold be upon our facial and bodily expression." With a gesture of genial impatience, the artist rises to his feet and paces to and fro. He had expected his friend to say that it had nothing whatever to do with emotions, and that he could control his face, features, voice and all, just as if his body were an instrument. The musician sinks down deeper into his chair. "But has there never been an actor," asks the artist, "who has so trained his body from head to foot that it would answer to the workings of his mind without permitting the emotions even so much as to awaken? Surely there must have been one actor, say one out of ten millions, who has done this?" "No," says the actor emphatically, "never, never; there never has been an actor who reached such a state of mechanical perfection that his body was *absolutely* the slave of his mind. Edmund Kean of England, Salvini of Italy, Rachel, Eleonora Duse, I call them all to mind and I repeat there never was an actor or actress such as you describe." The artist here asks: "Then you admit that it would be a state of perfection?" "Why, of course! But it is impossible; will always be impossible," cries the actor; and he rises – almost with a sense of relief. "That is as much as to say, there never was a perfect actor, there has never been an actor who has not spoiled his performance once, twice, ten times, sometimes a hundred times, during the evening? There never has been a piece of acting which could be called even almost perfect, and there never will be?" For answer the actor asks quickly: "But has there been ever a painting, or a piece of architecture, or a piece of music which may be called perfect?" "Undoubtedly," they reply. "The laws which control our arts make such a thing possible." "A picture, for instance," continues the artist, "may consist of four lines, or four hundred lines, placed in certain positions; it may be as simple as possible, but it is possible to make it perfect. That is to say, I can first choose that which is to make the lines; I can choose that on which I am to place the lines: I can consider this as long as I like; I can alter it; then in a state which is both free from excitement, haste, trouble, nervousness – in fact, in any state I choose (and of course I prepare, wait, and select that also) – I can put these lines together – so – now they are in their place. Having my material, nothing except my own will can move or alter these; and, as I have said, my own will is entirely under my control. The line can be straight or it can wave; it can be round if I choose, and there is no fear that when I wish to make a straight line I shall make a curved one, or that when I wish to make a curved there will be square parts about it. And when it is ready – finished – it undergoes no change but that which Time, who finally destroys it, wills." "That is rather an extraordinary thing," replies the actor; "I wish it were possible in my work." "Yes," replies the artist, "*it is a very extraordinary thing*," and it is that which I hold makes the difference between an intelligent statement and a casual or haphazard statement. The most intelligent statement, that is a work of art. The haphazard statement, that is a work of chance. When the intelligent statement reaches its highest possible form it becomes a work of fine art. And therefore I have always held, though I may be mistaken, that your work has not the nature of an art. That is to say (and you have said it yourself) each statement that you make in your work is subject to every conceivable change which emotion chooses to bring about. That which you conceive in your mind, your body is not permitted by Nature to complete. In fact, your body, gaining the better of your intelligence, has in many instances on the stage driven out the intelligence altogether. Some actors seem to say: "What value lies in having beautiful ideas? To what end shall my mind conceive a fine idea, a fine thought, for my body, which is so entirely beyond my control, to spoil? I will throw my mind overboard, let my body pull me and the play through;" and there seems to me to be some wisdom in the standpoint of such an actor. He does not dilly-dally between the two things which are contending in him, the one against the other. He is not a bit afraid of the result. He goes at it like a man, sometimes a trifle too like a centaur; he flings away all science, all caution, all reason, and the result is good spirits in the audience, and for that they pay willingly. But we are here talking about other things than excellent spirits, and though we applaud the actor who exhibits such a personality as this, I feel that we must not forget that we are applauding his personality, *he* it is we applaud, not what he is doing or how he is doing it; nothing to do with art at all, absolutely nothing to do with art, with calculation, or design." "You're a nice friendly creature," laughs the actor gaily, "telling me my art's no art!

* * *

You take away our finest dream, and you give us nothing in its place." "No, no, that's not for me to give you. That's for you to find. Surely there must be laws at the roots of the Art of the Theatre, just as there are laws at the roots of all true arts, which if found and mastered would bring you all you desire?" "Yes, the search would bring the actors to a wall." "Leap it, then!" "Too high!" "Scale it, then!" "How do we know where it would lead?" "Why, up and over." "Yes, but that's talking wildly, talking in the air." "Well, that's the direction you fellows have to go; fly in the air, live in the air. Something will follow when some of you begin to. I suppose," continues he, "you will get at the root of the matter in time, and then what a splendid future opens before you! In fact, I envy you. I am not sure I do not wish that photography had been discovered before painting, so that we of this generation might have had the intense joy of advancing, showing that photography was pretty well in its way, but there was something better!" "Do you hold that our work is on a level with photography?" "No, indeed, it is not half as exact. It is less of an art even than photography.

* * *

If you can find in Nature a new material, one which has never yet been used by man to give form to his thoughts, then you can say that you are on the high road towards creating a new art. For you have found that by which you can create it. It then only remains for you to begin. The Theatre, as I see it, has yet to find that material." And thus their conversation ends.

For my part I am with the artist's last statement. My pleasure shall not be to compete with the strenuous photographer, and I shall ever aim to get something entirely opposed to life as we see it. This flesh-and-blood life, lovely as it is to us all, is for me not a thing made to search into, or to give out again to the world, even conventionalized. I think that my aim shall rather be to catch some far-off glimpse of that spirit which we call Death – to recall beautiful things from the imaginary world; they say they are cold, these dead things, I do not know – they often seem warmer and more living than that which parades as life. Shades – spirits seem to me to be more beautiful, and filled with more vitality than men and women; cities of men and women packed with pettiness, creatures inhuman, secret, coldest cold, hardest humanity. For, looking too long upon life, may one not find all this to be not the beautiful, nor the mysterious, nor the tragic, but the dull, the melodramatic, and the silly: the conspiracy against vitality – against both red heat and white heat? And from such things which lack the sun of life it is not possible to draw inspiration. But from that mysterious, joyous, and superbly complete life which is called Death – that life of shadow and of unknown shapes, where all cannot be blackness and fog as is supposed, but vivid colour, vivid light, sharp-cut form; and which one finds peopled with strange, fierce and solemn figures, pretty figures and calm figures, and those figures impelled to some wondrous harmony of movement – all this is something more than a mere matter of fact. From this idea of death, which seems a kind of spring, a blossoming – from this land and from this idea can come so vast an inspiration, that with unhesitating exultation I leap forward to it; and behold, in an instant, I find my arms full of flowers. I advance but a pace or two and again plenty is around me. I pass at ease on a sea of beauty, I sail whither the winds take me – *there*, there is no danger. So much for my own personal wish; but the entire Theater of the world is not represented in me, nor in a hundred artists or actors, but in something far different. Therefore what my personal aim may be is of very little importance. Yet the aim of the Theatre as a whole is to restore its art, and it should commence by banishing from the

Theater this idea of impersonation, this idea of reproducing Nature; for, while impersonation is in the Theater, the Theater can never become free. The performers should train under the influence of an earlier teaching (if the very earliest and finest principles are too stern to commence with), and they will have to avoid that frantic desire to put *life* into their work; for three thousand times against one time it means the bringing of excessive gesture, swift mimicry, speech which bellows and scene which dazzles, on to the stage, in the wild and vain belief that by such means vitality can be conjured there. And in a few instances, to prove the rule, all this partially succeeds. It succeeds partially with the bubbling person-alities of the Stage. With them it is a case of sheer triumph *in spite* of the rules, in the very teeth of the rules, and we who look on throw our hats into the air, cheer, and cheer again. *We have to*; we don't want to consider or to question; we go with the tide through admiration and suggestion. That we are hypnotized our taste cares not a rap: we are delighted to be so moved, and we literally jump for joy. The great personality has triumphed both over us and the art. But personalities such as these are extremely rare, and if we wish to see a personality assert itself in the Theater and entirely triumph as an actor we must at the same time be quite indifferent about the play and the other actors, about beauty and art.

* * *

The modern theater-manager thinks the stage should have its plays gorgeously decorated. He will say that no pains should be spared to bring every assistance towards cheating the audience into a sense of reality. He will never cease telling us how important all these decorations are. He urges all this for several reasons, and the following reason is not the least: He scents a grave danger in simple and good work; he sees that there is a body of people who are opposed to these lavish decorations; he knows that there has been a distinct movement in Europe against this display, it having been claimed that the great plays gained when represented in front of the plainest background. This movement can be proved to be a powerful one – it has spread from Krakau to Moscow, from Paris to Rome, from London to Berlin and Vienna. The managers see this danger ahead of them; they see that if once people came to realize this fact, if once the audience tasted of the delight which a sceneless play brings, they would then go further and desire the play which was presented without actors; and finally they would go on and on and on until *they*, and not the managers, had positively reformed the art.

Napoleon is reported to have said: "In life there is much that is unworthy which in art should be omitted; much of doubt and vacillation;

and all should disappear in the representation of the hero. *We should see him as a statue in which the weakness and the tremors of the flesh are no longer perceptible."* And not only Napoleon, but Ben Jonson, Lessing, Edmund Scherer, Hans Christian Andersen, Lamb, Goethe, George Sand, Coleridge, Anatole France, Ruskin, Pater,[7] and I suppose all the intelligent men and women of Europe – one does not speak of Asia, for even the unintelligent in Asia fail to comprehend photographs while understanding art as a simple and clear manifestation – have protested against this *reproduction* of Nature, and with it photographic and weak actuality. They have protested against all this, and the theatrical managers have argued against them energetically, and so we look for the truth to emerge in due time. It is a reasonable conclusion. Do away with the real tree, do away with the reality of delivery, do away with the reality of action, and you tend towards the doing away with the actor. This is what must come to pass in time, and I like to see the managers supporting the idea already. Do away with the actor, and you do away with the means by which a debased stage-realism is produced and flourishes. No longer would there be a living figure to confuse us into connecting actuality and art; no longer a living figure in which the weakness and tremors of the flesh were perceptible.[8]

The actor must go, and in his place comes the inanimate figure – the Über-marionette we may call him, until he has won for himself a better name. Much has been written about the puppet, or marionette. There are some excellent volumes upon him, and he has also inspired several works of art. To-day in his least happy period many people come to regard him as rather a superior doll – and to think he has developed from the doll. This is incorrect. He is a descendant of the stone images of the old temples – he is to-day a rather degenerate form of a god. Always the close friend of children, he still knows how to select and attract his devotees.

* * *

Am I mistaken, or is it not the old Greek Traveller of 800 B.C. who, describing a visit to the temple-theater in Thebes, tells us that he was won to their beauty by their "noble artificiality"?

* * *

And who knows whether the puppet shall not once again become the faithful medium for the beautiful thoughts of the artist. May we not look forward with hope to that day which shall bring back to us once more the figure, or symbolic creature, made also by the cunning of the artist, so that we can gain once more the "noble artificiality" which the old writer speaks of? Then shall we no longer be under the cruel influence of the emotional confessions of weakness which are nightly witnessed by the people and which in their turn create in the beholders the very weaknesses which are exhibited. To that end we must study to remake these images – no longer content with a puppet, we must create an Über-marionette. The Über-marionette will not compete with life – rather will it go beyond it. Its ideal will not be the flesh and blood but rather the body in trance – it will aim to clothe itself with a death-like beauty while exhaling a living spirit. Several times in the course of this essay has a word or two about Death found its way on to the paper – called there by the incessant clamouring of "Life! Life! Life!" which the realists keep up. And this might be easily mistaken for an affectation, especially by those who have no sympathy or delight in the power and the mysterious joyousness which is in all passionless works of art.

* * *

To speak of a puppet with most men and women is to cause them to giggle. They think at once of the wires; they think of the stiff hands and the jerky movements; they tell me it is "a funny little doll." But let me tell them a few things about these puppets. Let me again repeat that they are the descendants of a great and noble family of Images, images which were indeed made "in the likeness of God;" and that many centuries ago these figures had a rhythmical movement and not a jerky one; had no need for wires to support them, nor did they speak through the nose of the hidden manipulator.

* * *

Did you think, ladies and gentlemen, that these puppets were always little things of but a foot high?

Indeed, no! The puppet had once a more generous form than yourselves.

Do you think that he kicked his feet about on a little platform six feet square, made to resemble a little old-fashioned theater, so that his head almost touched the top of the proscenium? and do you think that he always lived in a little house where the door and windows were as small as a doll's house, with painted window-blinds parted in the centre, and where the flowers of his little garden had courageous petals as big as his head? Try and dispel this idea altogether from your minds, and let me tell you something of his habitation.

In Asia lay his first kingdom. On the banks of the Ganges they built him his home, a vast palace springing from column to column into the air and pouring from column to column down again into the water. Surrounded by gardens spread warm and rich with flowers and cooled by fountains; gardens into which no sounds entered, in which hardly anything stirred. Only in the cool and private chambers of this palace the swift minds of his attendants stirred incessantly. Something they were making which should become him, something to honour the spirit which had given him birth. And then, one day, the ceremony.

In this ceremony he took part; a celebration once more in praise of the Creation; the old thanks-giving, the hurrah for existence, and with it the sterner hurrah for the privilege of the existence to come, which is veiled by the word Death. And during this ceremony there appeared before the eyes of the brown worshippers the symbols of all things on earth and in Nirvana. The symbol of the beautiful tree, the symbol of the hills, the symbols of those rich ores which the hills contained; the symbol of the cloud, of the wind, and of all swift moving things; the symbol of the quickest of moving things, of thought, of remembrance; the symbol of the animal, the symbol of Buddha and of Man – and here he comes, the figure, the puppet at whom you all laugh so much. You laugh at him to-day because none but his weaknesses are left to him. He reflects these from you; but you would not have laughed had you seen him in his prime, in that age when he was called upon to be the symbol of man in the great ceremony, and, stepping forward, was the beautiful figure of our heart's delight.

Do you see, then, what has made me love and learn to value that which to-day we call the "puppet" and to detest that which we call "life" in art? I pray earnestly for the return of the image – the Über-marionette to the Theater; and when he comes again and is but seen, he will be loved so well that once more will it be possible for the people to return to their ancient joy in ceremonies – once more will Creation be celebrated – homage rendered to existence – and divine and happy intercession made to Death.

FLORENCE: *March* 1907.

"Gentlemen, the Marionette!" (1908–1920) from
The Theater Advancing

He has been waiting so long in the servants' hall that I am sure you will not find fault with me for having called him upstairs and brought you together.

Yes, he has a capacity for waiting – a talent not without charm in so humble a creature.

Humility is only an assumption in men.

Let me begin by saying a word on the nature of the Marionnette.

He will wait anywhere for any length of time – hidden in a box – in a cellar – or even in a century. But he will wait – and when he is brought forward and is made to feel at home he will still wait; then he waits upon you and all of us like a true servant.

There is only one actor – nay, one man – who has the soul of the dramatic poet, and who has ever served as true and loyal interpreter of the poet. This is the Marionnette. So let me introduce him to you.

Some of you will think you have met him before. But how is that possible? For once to meet him is never to forget him – whereas you and he are strangers.

Yet I am not entirely just. There are times when you have come across him unawares. He has many disguises, and he impersonates known heroes and despised persons equally well.

You have come across him in some deserted cathedral in Italy or even in England – for cathedrals are free and "open to the public," and are therefore deserted. There you will have seen him hanging upon the Cross. And many Christians love him; he is interpreting the Drama of the Poets – Man and God.

Or you have caught a glimpse of him in some temple in the Far East, enacting a more serene drama – seated before incense – hands folded – very calm.

Or in the arms of a child you have seen him, interpreting the little hearts and the larger dreams of love!

These attempts of his to reach you have not entirely failed; but still for all this until now you have actually and unconsciously kept him waiting in the servants' hall.

Gentlemen – the Marionnette!

Yet silently he waits until his master signals him to act, and then in a flash, and in one inimitable gesture, he readjusts the injustice of justice, the illegality of the law, the tragic farce of "Religions," the broken pieces of philosophies, and the trembling ignorance of politics.

And what other virtues can I name beside these two of silence and obedience? I think these are enough.

For his chief virtue springs out of these. Because of them he has been able to avoid that appalling crime of exhausting the stock. Born of wood, of ivory, of metal or what you will, he is content to obey his nature – their nature. He does not *pretend* to be flesh and blood. Others can be as great as he – true, he always leaves much to be desired; a great being therefore – greater than Wagner and the other celebrated men who leave nothing we long to have any longer.

After Richard Wagner, after Michael Angelo, after Shakespeare – what? Blanks! They exhausted their gift, they squandered their talent; nothing was left. They did everything, suggested nothing; and their sons inherited empty purses, empty veins; instead of thinking of their responsibilities these great exhausters thought only of themselves. They were all fullstops to short sentences.

This is not the ideal of the artist, nor the ideal of mankind.

The ideal is more companionable, more paternal, gentler. It ends nothing; it will not go alone; it takes its sons with it; and it has somthing more priceless than all else to hand out to them at the end of the journey.

Leonardo was such an ideal. The Marionnette is another.

The Marionnette, through his two virtues of obedience and silence, leaves to his sons a vast inheritance. He leaves to them the promise of new art.

The Marionnette is a little figure, but he has given birth to great ones who, if they preserve the two essentials, obedience and silence, shall preserve their race. The day that they hunger for further power they shall surely fall.

These children of his I have called Über-Marionnettes, and have written of them at some length.

What the wires of the Über-Marionnette shall be, what shall guide him, who can say? I do not believe in the mechanical, nor in the material. The wires which stretch from Divinity to the soul of the poet are wires which might command him. Has God no more such threads to spare – for one more figure? I cannot doubt it.

I will never believe anything else.

And did you think when I wrote five years ago of this new figure who should stand as the symbol of man – and when I christened him the Über-Marionnette – to see real metal or silken threads?

I hope that another five years will be long enough time for you to draw those tangleable wires out of your thoughts.

PARIS, 1912.

I see now it will run into ten – or eleven.

SAN PANTALEO, 1920.

ALEXANDER HEVESI ON MARIONNETTES

To the pupils in my Dramatic College I put the following question yesterday: "Do you consider the Marionnette natural?" "No," they answered with one voice.

"What!" I replied indignantly. "Not natural? All its movements speak with the perfect voice of its nature. If a machine should try to move in imitation of human beings, that would be unnatural. Now follow me: the Marionnette is more than *natural*; it has Style – that is to say, *Unity of expression*; therefore the Marionnette Theatre is the true theatre."

BUDAPEST, 1908.

Final Bow – In Retrospect

**A Play for Marionettes from *The Scene* (1914),
unpublished script – HRC**

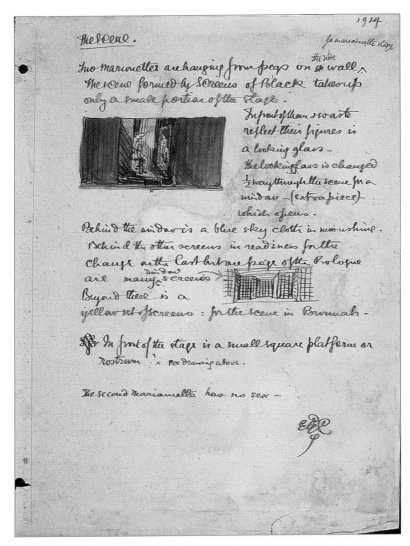

Craig's title page of a play for marionettes. Courtesy of HRC.

"Many meet the Gods, but few salute them" The second puppet is "John Bull"
a clock is ticking slowly and loudly – the hour strikes – several bells in chime.
It is taken up by all the bells of the city. One after another – and some together –
a very few rays of pale light creep in to the room – a cock crows – another
answers then: –

1st PUPPET: (*whispering*) Wake up! It's time to be moving.
2nd PUPPET: Hush – Hush – Don't disturb me. I'm thinking.

The clock continues to tick. 1st Puppet waits a moment, then descends and moves
to a small square platform and begins his morning's exercises:...begun without
music, finished with drums and fifes. During these exercises which he performs to
the rhythm of the ticking of the clock he puts out his hand to it causing it to change
its beat – from 1.2.1.2 to 123.123 to 1.2.3.4.1234. His exercises consist of all the
movements which a marionette is easily capable of and none other. These exclude
all the movements which are called useful or realistic, such as scratching the head,
blowing the nose and wiping the eyes with a handkerchief...and so forth. The
Light increases during his exercises. When the exercises are over, and as the drums
and fifes seem to go away into the distance he returns to his original position
hanging on his peg. He speaks:

1st PUPPET: Are you still thinking? (*whispered*) That sort of thing was not
   tolerated in my day. (*pause*) You are not listening to me. That is well. He
   does not hear – so much the better. You came here only forty odd
   years ago and you brought with you a lot of little badly printed books
   in a cracked black varnished leather bag...monstrous things... You
   have hung next me for all that time and I've read your thoughts day
   by day...all angular and thin thoughts...
      Once upon a time I with my fellows performed miracles and your
   coming amongst us has *prevented* any further miracles.
      That is your achievement...the result of having IDEAS. These *Ideas*
   have made you sick. Wake up, there! Wake up! and when you wake look
   into the glass there and see how sick you are! Look at your yellow cheeks
   and your real hair...look at your costume...look at your boots...
   black. That's all the result of thinking. (*Louder*) are you still thinking —?
2nd PUPPET: (*turning his head*) speaking in a loud voice. What do you
   mean? Isn't it good to think?
1st PUPPET: Hush – not so loud only you will wake the showman and
   then we shall not be able to escape today and see the new world you
   promised to show me.
2nd PUPPET: (*Whispering*) but say – is not it good to think.
1st PUPPET: (*loud whispering*) No.

2nd PUPPET: Isn't it?...what, not to think,...to be a fool all one's life,...to do as you're told,...to be positively a slave...do you hear...a slave... Why, you must be mad...mad, (*shrieks*) Do you mean to say that when I get up in the morning.

1st PUPPET: But you don't get up.

2nd PUPPET: Well, you know what I mean...

1st PUPPET: Go on...

2nd PUPPET: Well... I start thinking at once. I dress myself...

1st PUPPET: You don't.

2nd PUPPET: Well, you know what I mean... I think about what I put on, or, as you would sneeringly remind me, what is put on me. I think about it carefully.

1st PUPPET: And then?...

2nd PUPPET: ...then I ...(*growing faintly sentimental*) I think about something else.

1st PUPPET: Oh, what do you think about then?

2nd PUPPET: Well now I'll tell you... I'll tell you because I *like* you. (*drops his voice*) I then think about God. (*in an awful whisper and with a tendency to weep and gurgle*), (*pause*) *movement* (*long pause*) *movement* (*longer pause*) Well, why don't you say something about that?

1st PUPPET: Go on...

2nd PUPPET: I suppose you never thought about God and the Creation and the Arts and Sciences and Learning and Commerce?... I think about all of 'em; but I think about God first... Why first? (*confidentially and churchy*) why, because he made me...no better than I am, that I am (*the cockney voice*)...still HE made me. (*slight break in his voice*)

1st PUPPET: Indeed.

2nd PUPPET: Yes:...let me tell you how I know. I read it in a book. This is what it said: "And God formed man of the dust of the ground and breathed into his nose the breath of Life and man became a living soul". You don't believe in the soul, If you did you'd be like me. With a soul one can do anything; (*whispers*) one can become as God, knowing good and evil.

1st PUPPET: Really?...what is *good*?

2nd PUPPET: What, you don't know what *good* is?

1st PUPPET: How should I?

2nd PUPPET: But aren't you good?

1st PUPPET: How can I tell if I don't know what it is?

2nd PUPPET: Well, good's the opposite of evil.

1st PUPPET: But I don't know what evil is; tell me.

2nd PUPPET: You really are the limit!... You're enough to drive me mad with your ignorance.

1st PUPPET: But tell me, what is Good?…what is Evil?…I want to know.

2nd PUPPET: Are you serious?… Now, surely you know what Good and Evil are. You have a soul too, haven't you?… God surely gave you a soul when he made you?

1st PUPPET: I really don't know what you are talking about. Certainly God never made me. A man made me…o…h how many hundred years ago no one can remember. I have no "soul" so far as I know, for I do not know what it is…

2nd PUPPET: Then of course that explains it. *That's* why you don't know what Good and Evil are… Now shall I tell you?

1st PUPPET: I have been asking you that.

2nd PUPPET: Well, Good is the possessing of desirable qualities… Evil is having qualities tending to injury and mischief. If you don't believe me you can come with me one day to Mr Webster, an old friend of mine, and he'll tell you that what I say is true and exact.

1st PUPPET: And what do you derive by knowing that?

2nd PUPPET: Pouf! (*makes noise with his teeth and tongue*) Why, first of all as you see I have the advantage of you.

1st PUPPET: Ah, I forgot that.

2nd PUPPET: Besides, knowing that, d'ye see, I am able to order my life so much better than if I was in utter ignorance as so many poor souls are.

1st PUPPET: Is it possible to have a poor soul as well as a rich soul?

2nd PUPPET: Oh yes.

1st PUPPET: Yours is…?

2nd PUPPET: Mine is a rich soul…(*pause*) of course if God never made you you can't have a soul.

1st PUPPET: Has God then got all the souls?

2nd PUPPET: Why Yes,…do you mean to say you didn't know *that*? (*almost shrieks*)

1st PUPPET: Forgive me… I didn't know it.

2nd PUPPET: Why, of course I forgive you. Why, I pity you… Would you mind moving the string of my left arm?…it's making my wrist numb… Thank you… (*begins to wave his left arm and gesticulates a great deal now that it is free*) I can't tell you what an advantage it gives a man to have a soul:…it makes all the difference…one becomes *absolutely* self-dependent. Will you do me a favour?

1st PUPPET: Certainly. What is it?

2nd PUPPET: Untie the strings of my head and shoulders for me and lower me into the sitting position. Ah!…(*sign of relief*) that's better. Why don't you come down too?

1st PUPPET: I was down early today while you were thinking…but I like my situation up here

2nd PUPPET: Now really, do you?...that's queer...(*repeat*) but that's because you haven't got a free soul...(*he lies prone back*) "where Ignorance is bliss", they say, you know.

1st PUPPET: What do they say?

2nd PUPPET: Why,..."it's folly to be wise".

1st PUPPET: (...*he passes one hand slowly over the prostrate figure*)

2nd PUPPET: (*Continuing and sitting up*) It's not foolish of me to be wise; you mustn't think I think that, Tell me...I never asked you this before... What do you think of me as an actor?

1st PUPPET: Why, I think you are just like an actor.

2nd PUPPET: (*Springing to his feet and posing like actor, with outstretched hands grasping the hanging hand of the other figure*) Thank you!... thank you!...thank you for those words! O, thank you, thank you, my friend.

1st PUPPET: Just like one. (*2nd Puppet almost sobs with gratitude*).

2nd PUPPET: (*ruminating and poses like Shakespeare.*) Apropos as Napolean used so often to say. What is Inspiration?...what is this mysterious something by which we recognise the true actor of genius,...something *in* us, (*correcting himself*) in me?...something which...which... which gives me an appetite. (*suddenly*) Were you ever in Love? (*Sentimental music begins*) *he looks round and round and then at the first Puppet.* Hark. Is that music that I hear?

1st PUPPET: Music?...music? where?

2nd PUPPET: Curious, that's often so with me. When my thoughts turn towards love I always hear strange music i' the air. You hear nothing...and I hear it... Extraordinary! –

1st PUPPET: That's because you are a poet as well as an actor...but it is more than that:...it is because, as you have so well explained to me,...I who did not understand at first...that you are a man with a soul which is the gift of God... Don't interrupt me...

You are the very man I've been looking for all these years. But answer me one more question.

If God made you I cannot understand how it is you have strings attached to you shoulders and your hands.

2nd PUPPET: It is...(*whispers*) so that when I want anything I can pull one of the strings and... God is very obliging, you know.

1st PUPPET: But just now when you wanted to sit down you asked me to lower the strings for you.

2nd PUPPET: (*Looking round cunningly*) That was because... I wonder if I ought to tell you...well, why not?... (*coming nearer*) if I tell you will you promise that it shall go no further...no, no, no, no, no, on your word of honour as a gentleman,...I think I can trust you, but, (*hypocritically*) you don't know how many have promised to retain my confidences...and I am utterly unsuspicious...and how many have deceived me, inventing lies, lies...

But I will trust you...

Well then,

   (*the following spoken frightfully seriously and like Truth itself*)

the reason why I had to ask your help to get down just now, is, that God has become helpless lately...he cannot help himself, and so I prefer not to ask him anything: In fact,...but I tell you this trusting in your honour as a gentleman...in fact God has lied to me and he has lied about me.

(*spoken with devilish indignation, like a mad cat as Bourienne and Murat spoke in the Champ-Elyses in vol. 3 memoirs page. 222 as the little always speak of that which they cannot cosperhead*)

1st PUPPET: *Is it possible...*

Here Elaborate. The question whether and how there can be more gods than *his* one god – the god he has just abused.

2nd PUPPET: So you can well understand I prefer to ask nothing from him...in fact I wish to have nothing to do with him. (...*an awful pause...*)

   Let us change the subject, my dear friend, the whole thing is so distasteful to me; let us speak of other things.

   Tell me about yourself a little,...what is *your* part...your role, you know... I remember in England there were several divisions such as Heavy Father, Heavy Lead, Juvenile Lead, Walking-on-Gentleman,... numbers of different groups, don'tcher know. I suppose, now, you would be a Juvenile Lead?...

1st PUPPET: I am Buddha.

2nd PUPPET: You're what?

1st PUPPET: I am a God. (*2nd Puppet falls prone*) Don't be distressed... I will lift you up. (*raises him*).

2nd PUPPET: ....(*gasping faintly*) Air!...sir! !!!!!

1st PUPPET: (*pushes open a window and lodges 2nd Puppet in the window frame*)

   I did not wish to upset you, my old friend. Now let me explain a thing to you which you will easily understand and which anyone may be excused from not knowing unless it be explained first.

2nd PUPPET: (*still prostrate with amazement*) Go on,...you speak very very reasonably...for a God.

1st PUPPET: I come from the East...that is only a chance. I might as easily have come from the West. I come from India – from Burmah.

2nd PUPPET: Indeed East or West its all the same to me. Have it which way you like-o-oh – the room seems to be going round and round.

1st PUPPET: I am an Image...the Image of a God... I am therefore a God to those who believe in me.

2nd PUPPET: I believe in you, my friend,...I believe in you.

1st PUPPET: Of course,...but then your intelligence is of a superior order....and now and again I believe I have been of some slight assistance to you...

2nd PUPPET: (*sobbing*) my friend...my friend!...

1st PUPPET: Now by virtue of being a God I am enabled to serve...

2nd PUPPET: Yes indeed, only yesterday you served me to a wing of the best partridge I ever tasted.

1st PUPPET: And shall hope to do better.

2nd PUPPET: (*weeping*) My friend...my best friend...my great friend.

1st PUPPET: Now we are beginning to understand each other.

A few words more and I am done.

I am, as I told you, able to serve: this is because I am privileged to obey.

You see my strings,...eight strings, and a ninth that is invisible; (some day I will show you even that).

When I was made by a man, whom all call my creator for he made me out of his vision, he put the best that was in him into shaping my body, and so I at once became an Idol or an Image of the Godhead.

2nd PUPPET: (*tearfully*) Ah, tell me, dearest friend, did God treat you as shamefully as he has treated me...what?...

(*hoping he will answer "he did".*)

1st PUPPET: I know nothing about God. My duty is to be solely the Image of God...to do that knowledge is not requisite: obedience only is required.

I am an illusion and a Reality.

2nd PUPPET: ...(*gasping*) My dear friend, my dearest only friend...do you think you could open the window a bit wider...

1st PUPPET: It is already wide.

2nd PUPPET: Then could you do something to the room – it seems stifling –

1st PUPPET: Let us enlarge it – so – (*he presses back the walls which extend in all directions forming a large room with many windows –*) anything more

2nd PUPPET: Open all the windows – air – air –

1st PUPPET: (*Does so*) and now –

2nd PUPPET: Oh would you be so kind as to open the landscape?

1st PUPPET: Certainly. (*He raises a rope and pulls it and the backcloth with the sky and moon on it. The sun and moon and stars either hasten their*

coming and going or delay it – It is as the wire puller holder wishes – Thus
where as it was morning a short while ago the sun has come and gone and the
moon is high when it is rolled up. Goes up and discloses a sunny scene
depicting the open loggia of a house in Burmah on which an old white-haired
man is seated surrounded by his family who are singing sweetly. Under the
loggia hang three or four beautiful Puppets).
2nd PUPPET: (*cheerfully at once*) Oh, my friend, I do like that! who is the
old boy, and what's he doing?
1st PUPPET: "The old boy" as you call him was my creator. He is dying.
(*The chanting sinks lower*)

Curtain Call – Looking Forward to the Future

Foreword I (1919) from *Towards A New Theatre*

IT seems there is still very much to explain about the Theater, and the
Art of the Theater, before the world will understand rightly.

The danger of pointing in a new direction, even towards a familiar
object, is very great. It is even greater where the object is strange to us.
Everyone cries out "Where, where?" and is content when his eye alights
upon the very first object that it chances upon. The difficulty he finds is
to see far enough, and then, at that distance, to see in perfect detail.

If I point, for instance, to a mountain at a great distance from us,
a child, sitting on the grass, will look up to see the tall grasses in front of
his nose, and what he hears me say about the distance he will apply to
the tops of these grasses. A women standing by me, instead of looking in
the direction to which I point, will probably look at me pointing. A man
will probably look as far as he can. It is a thousand to one that his eye
will be caught by something a hundred yards off, or even a thousand
yards off, or it may be that a bird springing up from the bushes and
floating off will catch his eye, and all interest in the mountain will be
gone. It may be that he will take a castle on a hill to be the mountain; or
there may be some who, looking as far as they can, searching the horizon,
will finally deny that any such mountain exists.

It is a mountain that I am pointing towards – a high place; that
mountain is the Theater. If it were something else, I would call it
something else. As yet I know no other name for it. Let it then remain the
Theater, and please believe me when I tell you it is A MOUNTAIN. It is not
a hill, nor group of hills, nor any mirage of hills – it is the largest
mountain I have seen. No one has yet been able to scale its heights,
because there is something evidently very strange about this mountain.
Had it been easily accessible, it would have been climbed long ago. Now,

tell me, don't you consider there is something very strange about this? People have wandered about its base for thousands of years, and no one has ever one to the top, and many there are who refuse to believe that it has a top; but as I have seen the top, I wish flatly to contradict the many. I have seen the top from the distance; Fuji is not crowned more beautifully.

It is towards that mountain that I am attracted, and since I began to move in its direction, I find that I have come a little nearer to it than I was when I set out twenty-five years ago.

On my journey I have come across some curious people. I have met some who went past me and back to the place from whence I started, and who in passing told me they were going in the direction of that mountain. Some I met with backs turned to it who assured me they had just been there; "it wasn't very much to see after all." They had a disappointed look on their faces. Others there were who described it to me, saying, "It is just six thousand and fifty-two and a half feet high; it is an extinct volcano, and the middle class inhabit the summit. The climate is very dry; the trade in cinders is very brisk." These people have been looking at the wrong mountain. Others who profess to have come from there say that it is ruled by ladies – and the rest of their story is too ridiculous to repeat.

Now this is all very well for use as paragraphs in the Press, but it isn't the truth. Nobody has scaled those heights; nobody's report concerning those heights is correct. Everybody lies about it, for everybody is talking of something else.

I do not lie about it. I don't tell you that I have discovered the place: I tell you I am moving towards it. I do not tell you I am moving towards a new temple, for that also would be a lie. I am moving towards a new Theater, and this book is one of my contributions towards a new Theater. All that I have put in the book now lies behind me. I found it in the level plains, not even on the rising ground, far less in the heights, and therefore you must not get too excited about the little discoveries – for now the larger and finally the great discoveries await us.

There will be many theaters before the Theater comes, just as there are many plateaus in the mountain. It is for this reason that I call this book "Towards *a* New Theatre" instead of "Towards *the* New Theatre." If I were to speak of *the* new Theater, some of you would be sure to think I spoke of the new theater which is to be opened in three or four years, and as I write in the English language, you would be sure to think I meant the new English theater, and to say to yourselves, "The English theatre is *the* theatre." One of the first things the English have to do is to get out of their heads a belief that the theater exists in England only, and to remember that there is a theater in France, a theater in Germany, theaters in Russia, Italy, Spain, Hungary, Sweden, Norway, Denmark, and even in Switzerland and Finland, and then don't let them think that they have thought of all the theaters, for there is a theater beyond the Caucasus, a theater in the East, and there is even a theater in America and in Africa.

To which of them is my contribution made? To none of them, for there is still another new Theater being founded.

* * *

An Idea is only of value because of the life *which gives it birth*, and nothing but original vibration can ever give life to it again. Even then, when recreating it, it will come out a little different, and it will not therefore be the same idea; so that when an Autolycus of the modern European theater takes one of my ideas and thinks that he puts it into practice, he has done nothing of the kind, for there is a great difference between a reflection in a mirror and the thing reflected. The difference is all a matter of life, and it is so contemptible too to copy an idea when by a little activity of soul and body you can give birth to an idea yourself and so add life to life – and if you have no ideas, don't be ashamed of admitting it.

What we do not want is these dead ideas, these copied things, and everyone should protest against the obvious hoax being practised month after month in the theater of England of passing off unoriginal ideas as though they were original. One of the faults I find with English criticism is, that even the best critics enthusiastically chase after some copied idea, ignorant of the fact of the existence of the original, or, if conscious of it, criticising the copy in the same terms as they would use towards the original.[9]

Finally, this book represents my preliminary efforts in *one division* of a phase of theatrical art which I have passed through. As I have written in my book "On the Art of the Theatre," the artist of the Theater of the future will create his masterpieces out of action, scene, and voice. That was in 1905, and the future to which I referred is still before us, and therefore anybody, who can go into the matter more thoroughly than I did, is still free to alter that and to show that it can be created out of something different...something finer, simpler. My reason for mentioning it here, is to call your attention once more to something which some of you at times overlook when speaking of my work. That is to say, I am not concerned alone with what is called the "scenic" part of the art. I would like you to remember that I have clearly stated that action and voice are the other two parts which I am studying. Action and voice cannot be satisfactorily treated by means of the written word or diagrams, whereas scene to some extent can be so treated.

EDWARD GORDON CRAIG, 1872–1966:
A THEATRICAL CHRONOLOGY

THE ACTOR

1878   Appears on stage in a nonspeaking part in *Olivia* at the Court Theater at the age of six.

1881   Makes a brief, nonspeaking appearance in *Charles I* at the Alexandra Theater, Liverpool.

1884   Plays nonspeaking roles with the Lyceum Company on tour in America in *Hamlet, Much Ado About Nothing, Twelfth Night*, and *Charles I*.

1885   Acts in his first speaking role in the Lyceum Company's performance of *Eugene Aram* in Chicago.

1889   Joins the Lyceum Company and makes his London debut as Arthur de Saint Valéry in *The Dead Heart*.

1890   Plays Moses in *Olivia*, Caleb Deecie in *Two Roses*, and Henry Ashton in *Ravenswood* for the Lyceum. Tours with the Haviland and Harvey Company in *Two Roses, The Day After the Wedding, The Taming of the Shrew, and The Lady of Lyons*, acting in roles selected by Henry Irving.

1891   Plays the Messenger and one of the Watch in *Much Ado About Nothing*, Alexander Oldworthy in *Nance Oldfield*, and Abel Quick in *A Regular Fix* at the Lyceum. Plays Charles Surface in *School for Scandal* in summer stock for Sarah Thorne's Company, then tours as Malcolm in *Macbeth* and Lorenzo in *The Merchant of Venice* with the Lyceum Company.

1892   Plays Cromwell in *Henry VIII* and Oswald in *King Lear* at the Lyceum, Ford in *The Merry Wives of Windsor* and Petruccio in *The Taming of the Shrew* at the Margate Theater, then returns to the Lyceum to play Oswald in *King Lear*.

1893   *The Merchant of Venice* is revived at the Lyceum with Craig again as Lorenzo. This is followed by Tennyson's *Becket*, in which he plays the Youngest Knight Templar. This role marks the end of his regular association with the Lyceum. Directs Alfred de Musset's *No Trifling with Love (On ne badine pas avec l'amour)* for his own company in Uxbridge, designing scenes and costumes as well as playing the lead role.

1894   Joins the W. S. Hardy Shakespeare Company to tour as Romeo, Hamlet, Charles Surface, Cassio in *Othello*, Gratiano in *The Merchant of Venice*, and Richmond in *Richard III*.

1895   Joins the Evelyn and Leigh Company as Cavaradossi in *La Tosca*. Plays lead roles in *The New Magdalen, The Streets of London, La Dame aux Camélias, The Lady of Lyons*, and *Hamlet* at Paisley. Tours Aberdeen and Dundee in *François Villon*.

1896   Plays Petruccio in *The Taming of the Shrew* and the title roles in *The Corsican Brothers, Macbeth*, and *Hamlet* with Sarah Thorne's Company in Chatham before rejoining the Lyceum Company at Liverpool in his old parts.

THE ACTOR-MANAGER

Directs and plays the title role in *Romeo and Juliet* with his own company at the Parkhurst Theater, then returns to the Lyceum to play Arviragus in *Cymbeline* and Edward IV in *Richard III*.

1897   Directs and plays leading roles in *François Villon* and *The New Magdalen* with his own company at the Theater Royal in Croydon, but returns to play Edward IV in the Lyceum revival of *Richard III*, then takes over the title role in *Hamlet* (wearing Irving's costume) at the Olympic Theater. Plays Young Marlow in *She Stoops To Conquer* (with Granville-Barker) at the Kingston-on-Thames Theater, and puts on an impromptu performance of *François Villon* (with James Pryde) plus a Pierrot show. Resigns from the Lyceum Company and ceases to act.

1898   Writes and publishes the first four issues of *The Page* and devises *What the Moon Saw* (a Pierrot show based on a Hans Andersen story).

1899   Publishes *The Page*, and also *The Gordon Craig Book of Penny Toys*, and *Woodcuts and Some Words* (Hackbridge, at the Sign of the Rose), as well as sketches of leading British actors for newspapers and journals, nineteen of which were reproduced in *Henry Irving, Ellen Terry: A Book of Portraits* (Chicago). Begins to design scenes for imaginary dramas.

THE DIRECTOR

1900   Publishes volume 2 of *The Page* and a booklet, *Bookplates*. Directs and designs *Dido and Aeneas* for the Purcell Operatic Society at the Hampstead Conservatoire with Martin Shaw.

1901   Directs and designs *The Masque of Love* (adapted from Purcell's masque for *Dioclesian*) at the Coronet Theater, together with a revival of *Dido and Aeneas*. Breaks off publication of *The Page* (vol. 4, no. 2).

1902   Directs and designs Handel's *Acis and Galatea* together with a revival of *The Masque of Love*, at the Great Queen St. Theater. Directs and designs Laurence Housman's *Bethlehem* at the Imperial Institute. Starts to devise original masques with *Harvest Home*, which was advertised but never produced, and holds the first major exhibition of his drawings and woodcuts in London.

1903   Directs and designs Ibsen's *The Vikings at Helgeland* and Shakespeare's *Much Ado About Nothing* for Ellen Terry's company at the Imperial Theater. Designs costumes and three of the scenes for R. G. Legge's *For Sword or Song* at the Shaftsbury Theater. Devises an "Alhambra Masque" and begins to make designs for *The Masque of Hunger, The Masque of London*, and *The Masque of Lunatics*. Advertises a "London School of Theatrical Art," and holds his first exhibition of theatrical designs.

THE AUTHOR AND DESIGNER

1904   Designs scenes, which are only partially realized, for Hofmannsthal's version of Otway's *Venice Preserved* (produced by Otto Brahm at the Lessing Theater in 1905), and meets Isadora Duncan. The first exhibition of Craig's designs is mounted in Berlin.

1905   Prepares designs for *The Tempest* and Bernard Shaw's *Caesar and Cleopatra* for Max Reinhardt, though these never reach the stage because Craig demands complete control of the productions. Designs Hugo von Hofmannsthal's *Electra* for Eleonora Duse (unproduced, though the costumes and scenery were completed under Craig's direction) and illustrates *The White Fan* for Hofmannsthal. Publishes *The Art of the Theatre* in German and English (translated into Dutch and pirated in Russian in 1906, issued in Japanese in 1912 and in Hungarian and Danish in 1963). Exhibits his theatrical designs in Cologne, Dresden, Dusseldorf, Munich, Vienna, Weimar, and Zurich.

1906   Publishes *Isadora Duncan: Six Movement Designs*. Designs Duse's production of Ibsen's *Rosmersholm* (first staged at the Pergola Theater in Florence) and issues "A Note on Rosmersholm." Writes "The Actor and The Über-Marionette" (published in vol. 1 of *The Mask* and in *On the Art of the Theatre).* Develops *The Masque of Hunger.*

1907   Writes "The Artists of the Theatre of the Future," and "Motion" (later republished in vol. 1 of *The Mask* and inserted as a preface in *Scene).* Constructs his first model theater to experiment with his screens, and begins the first of his series of Black Figures.

1908   Starts to design screen scenes and costumes for *Hamlet* at Stanislavski's invitation. Publishes his first *Portfolio of Etchings* (the *Oresteia* and *King Lear)* and the first volume of *The Mask,* a monthly journal of the Art of the Theatre. Presents Ellen Terry with a set of screens and designs arrangements for their use in *The Merchant of Venice* (unproduced). Prepares designs of settings and choreography for a projected ballet of *Psyche,* and exhibits "Designs for Motion" in Florence.

1909   Publishes vol. 2 of *The Mask.* Presents W. B. Yeats with a set of screens for the Irish National Theater and designs scenes (unused) for Beerbohm Tree's production of *Macbeth.* Discusses designing a production of *King Lear* (abortive) for Reinhardt.

1910   Publishes vol. 3 of *The Mask* and a second *Portfolio of Etchings.* Travels to Moscow to work out the interpretation of *Hamlet* with Stanislavski and to begin the production process.

1911   Publishes vol. 4 of *The Mask* and the English edition of *On the Art of the Theatre* (translated into French in 1920, into Italian in 1924, and subsequently into Hungarian, Spanish, Polish, and Russian). Yeats's *The Hour Glass* and Lady Gregory's *The Deliverer* are produced at the Abbey Theater in Dublin with Craig's screen-arrangements. (The screens influence Yeats in revising *Dierdre* and are still in use for *On Baile's Strand* in 1914.)

1912   Publishes vol. 5 of *The Mask.* Craig's production of *Hamlet* (as interpreted by Stanislavski) is staged at the Moscow Art Theater using the screens. Mounts an exhibition of his stage designs, including those for *The Vikings, Macbeth,* and *Hamlet,* in London (transferred to Manchester, and in 1913 to Liverpool, Dublin, and Leeds).

THE THEORIST

1913   Publishes *Towards A New Theater,* and vol. 6 of *The Mask.* Opens the School for the Art of the Theater at the Arena Goldoni in Florence, and issues "A Living Theater," which, describes the school's aims and activities.

1914 Builds the large model stage for Bach's *St. Matthew Passion* and begins writing marionette plays, including *The Scene*. Publishes vol. 7 of *The Mask*.

1915 Breaks off publication of *The Mask* with the August issue, vol. 8, and closes the school.

1916– Writes marionette plays, including *School, The Gordian Knot, Once*
1917 *Upon a Time, and Mr. Fish and Mrs. Bones* (published in 1918 and 1919 under the pseudonym of Tom Fool).

1918 Begins publishing *The Marionette* as a monthly journal in March; *The Mask* reappears in April.

1919 Breaks off publication of *The Mask* once more after the March issue, vol. 9. Ceases to issue *The Marionette* with the twelfth issue in August. Publishes *The Theater Advancing* in the United States (reprinted in England in 1921 and translated into French in 1964). Advises Lovat Fraser on designs for *The Beggar's Opera* (performed at the Lyric Theater in 1920).

1921 Publishes *Puppets and Poets* (London).

1922 Shows work at the International Theater Exhibit in Amsterdam.

1923 *The Mask* reappears as a single issue. Publishes *Scene* with Oxford University Press (incorporating etchings from the portfolios of 1908 and 1910 together with the essay entitled "Motion" from 1907 and a foreword by John Masefield).

1924 Publishes vol. 10 of *The Mask* as a quarterly. Also publishes *Woodcuts and Some Words* (London).

1925 Publishes vol. 11 of *The Mask, Books and Theaters,* and *Nothing, or the Bookplate* (London).

1926 Publishes vol. 12 of *The Mask*. Designs Ibsen's *The Crown Pretenders* for Johannes and Adam Poulsen, and collaborates on the production at the Royal Theater in Copenhagen. Receives the Order of the Knights of the Danneborg for his services to the Danish theater.

1927 Publishes vol. 13 of *The Mask*, and exhibits work at the Deutsche Theater-Ausstellung at Magdeburg. (Craig was the only non-German invited.)

1928 Publishes vol. 14 of *The Mask*. Designs and outlines a production of *Macbeth* (signed C.P.B. for "Craig Pot-Boiler") for George Tyler in New York, and exhibits the designs for *Macbeth* in New York and for *The Pretenders* in London.

1929 Ceases to issue *The Mask* with vol. 15. Publication of the Cranach Press edition of *Hamlet* with seventy-five woodcuts by Craig (reprinted in England in 1930). Approached by Norman Bel Geddes to design productions for a theater festival planned as part of the Chicago World Fair, and exhibits stage designs at the International Theater Congress and Exposition in Barcelona.

1930 Publishes *A Production, 1926* (Oxford) and *Henry Irving* (London).

1931 Publishes *Ellen Terry and Her Secret Self* in a limited edition (reprinted in ordinary editions in Britain and the United States, 1932).

1932 Receives an invitation to direct the Habima Company in Jerusalem.

1934 Contributes "settings for an Ideal Theatre" to the International Exhibition of Theater Art at the Museum of Modern Art in New York, and attends the convention on theater of the Foundazione Alessandro Volta (together with Yeats, Tairov, Maeterlinck, and Pirandello).

1935 Travels to Moscow to discuss the possibility of setting up his own workshop theater, and proposes a production of Bach's *St. Matthew Passion* (as an alternative to a suggested production of *Quo Vadis*) for the Coliseum in Rome.

1946 Elected a member of the French Syndicat des metteurs en scène.

1951 Presents fourteen talks about theater on the BBC.

1956 Made a Companion of Honour by Queen Elizabeth in recognition of his services to the theater.

1957 Publishes *Index to the Story of my Days* simultaneously in London and New York.

1961 Made an honorary member of the United Scenic Artists in New York.

NOTES

To save confusion and to avoid repetition, initials have been used for those names that recur frequently: EGC for Edward Gordon Craig, ET for Ellen Terry, ID for Isadora Duncan, MFS for Martin Fallas Shaw, and WBY for William Butler Yeats. In addition, the titles of certain books are referred to in a shortened form after their first appearance: for example, *Index* for Gordon Craig's *Index to the Story of My Days*, and *Gordon Craig* for Edward Craig's *Gordon Craig: The Story of His Life*. In each case in which Craig's notebooks, daybooks, or other unpublished material is first referred to, the collection in which the work is to be found has been indicated in parentheses: BL for the British Library in London, BN for the Bibliothèque Nationale in Paris, Bledlow for the Edward Craig Collection in Bledlow, HRC for the Humanities Research Center of the University of Texas at Austin, Rood for the Arnold Rood Collection in New York, LC for the Museum of the Performing Arts at Lincoln Center in New York, UCLA for the Rare Books Collection of the University of California at Los Angeles, and V & A for the Enthoven Collection of the Victoria and Albert Museum in London (now in the London Theatre Museum).

1. Prologue: The argument

1. MFS, *The Observer*, November 29, 1931; Helen Chinoy, *Directors on Directing*, ed. Toby Cole and Helen Chinoy (Indianapolis, 1976), p. 45; (First published 1953).
2. ID, *My Life* (New York, 1927), p. 185, and EGC's marginal annotation, dated 1945 (BN).
3. *The Times* (London), July 30, 1966.
4. Lee Simonson, "The Case of Gordon Craig," *Theater Guild Magazine* (February, 1931), pp. 19f. For comparison, see Chinoy, *Directors*, pp. 41f., where Craig is referred to as an "evangelist...[and] an effective propagandist" whose "own productions were few and never completely successful," whose "sketches were basically impractical as scene designs," and whose "manifestoes were contradictory and often illogical."
5. Letter to MFS, May 20, 1905 (HRC).
6. EGC, "14 Notes on 8 pages from *The Story of the Theater* by Glenn Hughes," ed. Glenn Hughes (University of Washington Press, 1931), pp. 8 and 11; Daybook 2, 1910–11, p. 63 (HRC).

7. Theatre Designs. Notebook 1904–5–6, p. 106 (HRC); "Books on the Theatre, II," TS, n.d. (HRC).
8. Daybook 6, 1933, p. 15 (HRC).
9. For a full description of *The Pretenders* production, see Frederick and Lise-Lone Marker, *Edward Gordon Craig & The Pretenders* (Carbondale, 1982).
10. EGC, *Index to the Story of My Days* (New York, 1957), p. 213.

2. Scene changes: Victorian theater, an acting career, and points of departure

1. Cf. EGC, *Henry Irving* (New York, 1930), p. 186, and EGC, "14 Notes," p. 9: "You must add that my master...was IRVING; my tutors, self-chosen – Walt Whitman, William Blake, Shakespeare – no realists."
2. EGC, *Henry Irving*, pp. 96 and 49. (Craig was not relying on memory, for his descriptions of Irving's productions. Although this study was published in 1930, it is based on notes made in 1901 or earlier.)
3. Quoted in Bram Stoker, *Personal Reminiscences of Henry Irving* (London, 1906), vol. 1, p. 147.
4. EGC, *Henry Irving*, p. 74.
5. Ibid., p. 54; Henry Irving, *The Drama: Addresses* (London, 1893), pp. 55f. and 157.
6. EGC, *Henry Irving*, pp. 55 and 59; Ellen Terry and Bernard Shaw, *A Correspondence*, ed. C. St. John (London, 1931), p. 228, and Felix Emmel, *Das ekstatische Theater* (Prien, 1924), p. 37. For a full discussion of expressionist acting, see my book, *Avant Garde Theatre* (Routledge 1994), pp. 56f.
7. EGC, *Henry Irving*, pp. 56–8. For a more objective description of this performance, cf. David Mayer, ed., *Henry Irving and The Bells* (Manchester, 1980), pp. 22, 45, 47, 83.
8. William Archer, *Henry Irving, Actor and Manager* (London. 1883), pp. 67–8; EGC, *Henry Irving*, p. 61.
9. EGC, *Index*, p. 154.
10. Ibid., pp. 156, 216, 159–60; Daybook 6, 1933, p. 46.
11. *The Era*, July 25, 1896; *The People*, July 26, 1896.
12. EGC, *Henry Irving*, pp. 74 and 32. For EGC's criticism of Irving's "egotistical" productions, see p. 84 of *Henry Irving*; also see EGC, *On the Art of the Theater* (London, 1962), p. 173.
13. EGC, *Henry Irving*, p. 91. Cf. also EGC, *Index*, p. 61.
14. ET, cit. George Taylor, *Henry Irving at the Lyceum* (Cambridge, 1980), p. 38.

15. EGC, *Henry Irving*, p. 113.

16. Handwritten note (d. 1948) in his program for *No Trifling with Love*, Uxbridge Town Hall, December 13/14, 1893; promptbook, pp. 148, 166, 172 (UCLA).

17. *Middlesex and Bucks Advertiser*, December 16, 1893; promptbook, p. 145 and an interleaved note.

18. EGC, *Index*, p. 149; promptbook for *A Midsummer Night's Dream* (unperformed) 1896 (UCLA).

19. Theodore Child, "A Christmas Mystery in the Fifteenth Century," *Harpers New Monthly* (1888–9), vol. 78, pp. 59f.

20. EGC, Daybook 5, 1930–3, p. 26 (HRC); Thomas A. Janvier, "The Comédie Française at Orange," *Century Magazine* (June, 1895), vol. 50, no. 2, pp. 165f.

21. Daybook 5, p. 26.

22. E. W. Godwin, *The British Architect*, May 29, 1874, p. 342.

23. Program, Prince of Wales Theater, April, 1875; *The Illustrated Sporting and Dramatic News*, April 24, 1875 and January 3, 1881.

24. Cit. J. C. Trewin, *Shakespeare on the English Stage, 1900–1964* (London, 1964), p. 14.

25. Advertisement for *Helena in Troas*, April, 1886 (Handbill, V & A); *The Illustrated Sporting and Dramatic News*, May 29, 1886, *Life*, 1886, p. 943, and *The Pall Mall Gazette*, May 18, 1886.

26. John Todhunter, *Helena in Troas* ("as adapted for the stage and produced by E. W. Godwin") (London, 1886), p. 15; *The Daily Telegraph*, May 18, 1886. The plot of Todhunter's play verges on the ludicrous. Paris alone can defend the city, and when he is wounded by a poisoned arrow only his discarded wife Oenone can save him. She will only do so if Paris will return to her, but Paris would rather die than renounce Helen, and her resulting suicide provides a melodramatic climax (p. 21):

    > OENONE: Death, Death, hail Death!
    > CHORUS: O mighty love, self-slain in slaying her!
    >   O furious passion strangled suddenly!
    >   For dead she is, having with piteous shriek
    >   O'leaped the battlements, and crushed and dead lies;
    >   Her wild soul shrill in the shrieking air.

27. EGC, letter to MFS, September 6, 1904 (HRC); *The British Architect*, October 15, 1886. (As EGC remarked, "A *mise en scène* is childs-play when one has had an architect for a father and Irving for a master," and he wrote of Godwin that his own "vocation" could "easily seem to be his – architecture," EGC, *Index*, p. 101.)

28. "Professor Herkomer's School," *The Art Annual* (1892), n.p. Hubert v. Herkomer, *The Magazine of Art* (July, 1889), p. 316. (For a contemporary evaluation of Herkomer's influence, particularly on Irving, see Edwin Sachs, *Stage Construction* [London, 1898], cit. Herkomer, *My School and My Gospel* [London, 1908], p. 205.)
29. Cf. EGC, *Index*, pp. 100, 122, and 131.
30. *The Magazine of Art* (May, 1892), p. 261.
31. Ibid, p. 319.
32. Cf. Edward Craig, "Gordon Craig and Hubert von Herkomer," *Theatre Research*, vol. 10, no. 1 (1969), pp. 9–10.
33. Herkomer, *My School and My Gospel*, p. 203; *The Magazine of Art* (July, 1892), pp. 316, 320.
34. *The Magazine of Art* (May, 1892), pp. 261, 259, and 262; EGC, *On the Art of the Theatre*, p. 161; Herkomer, *My School and My Gospel*, pp. 151 and 140.

3. A rising action: Design and movement

1. Notebook 1904–5–6, p. 106.
2. Daybook 6, p. 120 (d. 1949), and EGC, *Index*, p. 210.
3. Haldane Macfall, *The Studio* (1901), no. 102, p. 255, and *Review of the Week*, August 11, 1900.
4. EGC interview, *The Daily News*, April 15, 1903.
5. EGC MS. Book 13, p. 25 (BN).
6. EGC, *Towards A New Theatre* (London, 1913), p. 29.
7. Nahum Tate and Henry Purcell, *Dido and Aeneas* (London, 1887), pp. 6f., and EGC, souvenir program for *Dido and Aeneas* (May, 1900 and March, 1901), n.p.; EGC, cit. Edward Craig, *Gordon Craig: The Story of His Life* (New York, 1968), p. 121.
8. Souvenir Program, and *Dido and Aeneas* promptbook (1901, EGC's personal copy), p. 38 (BN).
9. WBY, *The Saturday Review*, March 8, 1902; *The Speaker*, May 11, 1901 (where the style of performance was also referred to as "a new and legitimate art, appealing to a taste formed by itself and copying nothing but itself"); *The Hampstead Annual* (1900), p. 138.
10. *Dido and Aeneas* promptbook, p. 38.
11. *The Hampstead Annual* (1900), p. 138; WBY, *The Saturday Review*, March 8, 1902.
12. Notebook – Dido (1900), n.p. (UCLA), and *Dido and Aeneas* promptbook, p. 24.
13. Reported by *The Musical Standard*, March 30, 1901, and by George Sampson in a letter to *The Times* (London), March 21, 1926.

14. *The Daily Chronicle*, April 1, 1901; *The Hampstead Annual* (1900), p. 138; *Review of the Week*, August 11, 1900.
15. *Dido and Aeneas* promptbook, pp. 1 and 5.
16. Edward Craig, "Gordon Craig and Hubert von Herkomer," *Theatre Research*, vol. 10, no. 1 (1969), p. 10–to which I am indebted for many of the details of this performance – and W. B. Yeats, letter to Nora Dryhurst, d. April 2 (HRC).
17. Letter to MFS, cit. Craig, *Gordon Craig*, p. 118.
18. Notebook – Dido n.p.; EGC, *On the Art of the Theatre*, p. 21 (1907); *The Musical Standard*, March 30, 1901.
19. All stage directions are taken from the *Dido and Aeneas promptbook*, pp. 16–17, 21, 26–7, 32–3, 36, and from Notebook – Dido (n.p.).
20. Notebook – Dido, n.p., and annotated copy of the souvenir program for *Dido and Aeneas* (BN).
21. Notebook – Dido, n.p., and MFS, *Up to Now* (London, 1929), p. 28.
22. Program, *Dido and Aeneas* and *The Masque of Love*, 1901.
23. EGC, *Index*, p. 235; and EGC, MS annotation to a "Biographical Note" Craig issued in 1919 (Bledlow), on which he drew a graph in 1948. The line on the graph rises from *Dido to The Masque*, then falls to *Acis* and *Bethlehem* (both ranked half-way between the preceding productions), and shows *Vikings* descending to the low point occupied by *Much Ado*, which leads in the direction of commercial theater and Craig's bête noir, the cinema.
24. *The Artist*, NS, vol. 1, no. 1 (May, 1902), p. 27; *Sphere*, vol. 8, no. 113, March 22, 1902, p. 291.
25. Cf. Craig, *Gordon Craig*, p. 152.
26. Graham Robertson, preface to *The Art of the Theatre*, 1905, cit. Craig, *Gordon Craig*, p. 151, and Max Beerbohm, *Saturday Review*, April 5, 1902 (reprinted in *Around Theatres* [New York, 1930], vol. 1, p. 257).
27. EGC, promptbook for *Acis and Galatea*, sketch 3 (BN), and Robertson, preface, p. 151.
28. Henry Nevinson, notebook, cit. Janet Leeper, *Edward Gordon Craig: Designs for the Theatre* (Harmondsworth, 1948), p. 7, and Craig, *Gordon Craig*, p. 136.
29. MS instructions on the costume designs (BN).
30. *The Artist*, NS, vol. 1, no. 1, p. 57.
31. MFS, *Up to Now*, p. 28, and Haldane MacFall, letter to EGC, March 13, 1902. The triple bill of *Nance Oldfield* (ET's very short curtain raiser), *Dido* and *The Masque* stretched performances from 8:00 p.m. to well after midnight with the long intervals between each scene. As a result, much of the audience had left before the work that Craig regarded as his masterpiece began.

32. Notebook – Acis and Galatea (1901–2), n.p. (HRC).
33. Program, *Dido and Aeneas* and *The Masque of Love*, 1901; Daybook 6, p. 120.
34. Christopher St. John, "The Masque of Love" (undated: BN), and note in the program for *Dido and Aeneas* and *The Masque of Love*, 1901.
35. *The Musical Standard*, March 30, 1901, p. 194.
36. Robertson, preface; Craig, *Gordon Craig*, p. 147. The advertisement was privately published by EGC in London in 1904.
37. *The Playgoer*, vol. 2 (April–September 1902), p. 31; Notebook – Acis and Galatea; promptbook for *The Masque of Love* (BN).
38. Arthur Symons, *The Monthly Review* (June, 1902) (reprinted in *Studies in the Seven Arts* [London, 1906], pp. 349–50).
39. EGC, *On the Art of the Theatre*, p. 52; Symons, *Monthly Review* (Craig's marginalia are in his scrapbook of press clippings – BN).

4. Problem drama: Texts and performers

1. Purcell, preface to *The Prophetess, or the History of Dioclesian* (London, 1691); MFS, *Up to Now*, p. 27.
2. EGC, note (dated 1943) in promptbook, *The Masque of Love*, p. 2; MFS, *Up to Now*, p. 26.
3. MFS letter to EGC, n.d. (1902: HRC).
4. *The Critic*, vol. 42 (February, 1903), p. 140; *The Times* (London), February 24, 1903. Cf. also Craig, *Gordon Craig*, p. 164.
5. Promptbook, *Bethlehem*, pp. 11 and 14 (BN).
6. *The Critic*, vol. 42 (February, 1903), p. 140.
7. Daybook 1, 1908–10 (HRC), p. 159. Cf. also EGC, *Towards A New Theatre*, p. 9.
8. Laurence Housman, letters to EGC, undated, August 24, and July 7, 1902 (UCLA).
9. Housman, letters to EGC, September 8 and 10, 1902; EGC, Sketchbook 1902, n.p. (BN); Housman to EGC, August 28 and undated; EGC, promptbook, p. 24; notes by Nora Dryhurst in her copy of *Bethlehem* (HRC).
10. For details about the reuse or rediscovery of these ideas by Artaud, Barrault, Schechner, and Piscator, see my books, *Avant Garde Theatre*, pp. 137f. and 195f., and *Modern German Drama* (Cambridge, 1979), p. 172.
11. Promptbook, *Bethlehem*, pp. 26–7 and 29–30; notes by Nora Dryhurst; Laurence Housman, "In Spite of the Censor," *The Critic*, vol. 42 (February, 1903).
12. EGC, note on title page of the promptbook (1915); undated letter to MFS (HRC).

13. Housman, letter to EGC, June 4, 1902; *The Critic*, vol. 42 (February, 1903); letter to EGC, July 1, 1902. Paradoxically, the example Housman recommended that Craig follow here was equally out of sympathy with the theme of the play and echoed Craig's approach precisely in substituting aesthetic effects for religious content. According to William Poel, "An acted religion is all insincere...and the tendency of such plays is towards sentimentalism and claptrap. I did not myself produce *Everyman* as a religious play. Its theology is indefensible...but the whole story, Eastern not Catholic in its origin, is beautiful as a piece of art; it offers a hundred opportunities from the point of view of beauty" (*Daily Chronicle*, September 3, 1913).

14. Housman, letters to EGC, July 8, undated, and August 24, 1902 (UCLA).

15. Housman, letter to EGC, November 24, 1902; Charles Ashbee, journal, December, 1902 (Kings College, Cambridge); EGC, letter to ET, November, 1902 (UCLA).

16. EGC, *Towards A New Theatre*, p. 51.

17. EGC, letter to MFS, August, 1902. Cf. also *The Star*, April 16, 1903.

18. *Pall Mall Gazette*, April 16, 1903; EGC, *Towards A New Theatre*, p. 73.

19. Cf. Craig, *Gordon Craig*, p. 169, and J. G. Buckle, *Theatre Construction and Maintenance* (London, 1888); EGC, interview in *The Tatler*, no. 98, May 13, 1903, p. 260.

20. *The Saturday Review*, April 28, 1903.

21. Cf. Craig, *Gordon Craig*, p. 171; EGC notes on construction appended to sketches of props; *The Vikings* promptbook, p. 164 (BN).

22. *Lady's Pictorial*, April 25, 1903, p. 884; *The Saturday Review*, April 28, 1903; James Huneker, *Iconoclasts: A Book of Dramatists* (London, 1905), p. 31. Similarly, in Craig's production of *Much Ado* the church was suggested by a backing of gray curtains, two of which were gathered in the foreground to suggest great columns, and decorated with patterns of "dirty yellow – like old ivory – varnished all over" (EGC, promptbook: B.N.) to catch the dim light. Yet one critic gave a detailed description of "arched mosaic columns" and "Byzantine splendour." (Cf. Craig, *Gordon Craig*, pp. 175–6.) See also *Black and White*, April 25, 1903, p. 566.

23. Huneker, *Iconoclasts*, p. 32; *The Saturday Review*, April 28, 1903.

24. EGC, letter to MFS, November 11, 1903; *The Saturday Review*, April 28, 1903, and *The Playgoer*, vol. 4, no. 19 (May, 1903), p. 397.

25. EGC, *On the Art of the Theatre*, pp. 11, 35–6, and 82. Cf. also WBY, *Essays and Introductions* (London, 1961), p. 224 (1916).

26. ET, interview in *The Daily Telegraph*, April 6, 1903; Huneker, *Iconoclasts*, p. 31, and MFS, *Up to Now*, p. 35; *The Daily Chronicle*, April 16, 1903, and *The Playgoer*, vol. 4, no. 20 (June, 1903).

27. EGC, interview in *The Daily News*, April 15, 1903, and letter to MFS, November 11, 1903.
28. EGC, *On the Art of the Theatre*, p. 53 (1907); *Theatre Arts Monthly*, vol. 11, no. 4 (April, 1927).
29. William Rothenstein, *The Saturday Review*, May 9, 1903; EGC, holograph note in the program for *The Vikings*, Imperial Theater, April 15, 1903 (BN), and letter to ET, March 8, 1903 (UCLA).
30. Cf. EGC, *Index*, p. 241. The costs for *Dido* were £373.10.6, of which 61 percent went to scenery, costumes, lighting and programs. For each performance the orchestra was paid £10.10.0, hairdressing and makeup cost £2.7.0, and the hire of the hall £9.10.0. If the actors and chorus had been paid 2 pounds and 1 pound respectively each week for six performances, their total salary for one performance would have been £8.12.0, and the total cost per performance £30.19.0. The sale of tickets brought in an average of £44 at each performance. (The total income for three nights was £192.15.6, out of which £60 were subscriptions to the Purcell Society; the remaining deficit was made up by donations from the cast and Ellen Terry.) The actual profit per performance would therefore have been £13.1.0, and it would have taken forty performances to clear the true cost of £513.15.6: £305.15.6, representing the actual amounts laid out on staging and advertising together with the running costs for that number of nights, plus £208 for the actors' salaries over the rehearsal period. (For a breakdown of the actual costs, see Craig, *Gordon Craig* p. 126.) In a regular theater the time needed would have been even longer, despite larger houses. EGC's correspondence with E. G. Saunders about the rental of the Coronet Theater (BN) shows that the management customarily took 50 percent of box-office receipts, though on that occasion they settled for 35 percent but only because Ellen Terry would be appearing in *Nance Oldfield*.
31. ET, letter to EGC, March 24, 1903; MFS, *Up to Now*, p. 36; EGC, letter to MFS, cit. Craig, *Gordon Craig*, pp. 176–7. (For comparison see Peter Brook's comments on the way his *King Lear* production changed during the RSC tour of Eastern Europe and the United States in *The Empty Space* [Harmondsworth, 1972], pp. 25f.)

5. A play of ideas: Principles, theory, and an Übermarionette

1. Lee Simonson, "The Case of Gordon Craig," p. 21.
2. Janet Leeper (*Edward Gordon Craig*, p. 9) attributes this Greek design to *The Vikings*, an error that could have come about only through

Craig himself associating it with that production, as Leeper consulted with him in preparing her book and the one identifiable piece of costume is clearly not Nordic.

3. EGC, *Towards A New Theatre*, p. 18.
4. Promptbook for *The Pretenders* (Everyman ed., no. 659) pp. 54–5 (BN). "X" indicates points in the text at which these movements occur. EGC, Scenes 1, pp. 46 and 47 (BN). Cf. also a list of designs in EGC, Notebook 1904–12 (HRC).
5. EGC, *Index*, pp. 243 and 40–1.
6. "The Artists of the Theatre of the Future," *The Mask*, vol. 1, nos. 3–4 (May–June 1908).
7. EGC, holograph notes on margins of designs for *Macbeth* (BN).
8. EGC, letters to MFS, September 7 and November 25, 1904; *Vossische Zeitung*, January 23, 1905; *Berliner Börsen-Courier*, January 22, 1905; and *Vossische Zeitung*, January 22, 1905.
9. Morton Eustis, cit. Cole and Chinoy, *Directors* p. 51; EGC, letters to Reinhardt (cit. Craig, *Gordon Craig*, p. 199) and to ET, n.d. (UCLA).
10. EGC, letter to ET, 1909; marginal annotation on a letter from Brahm, September 30, 1904; correspondence between EGC and Johannes Poulsen, August, 1926 (published in EGC, *A Production*, 1926 [Oxford, 1930], pp. 4 and 5).
11. Cit. Craig, *Gordon Craig*, p. 198.
12. EGC, *On the Art of the Theatre*, pp. 138, 140–1; Daybook 1, 1908–10, pp. 165–6 (HRC). Cf. also EGC, *Towards A New Theatre*, p. 41.
13. Daybook 1, 1908–10, p. 85; EGC letter to MFS, 1905 (cit. Craig, *Gordon Craig*, p. 199); Daybook 2, 1910–11, p. 165 (HRC).
14. WBY, *Plays for an Irish Theatre* (London, 1911), EGC's copy, pp. 80 and 85 (BN); and Daybook 1, 1908–10, p. 209.
15. EGC, "Dancing Is Not Flying." MS, n.d. (cit. Arnold Rood, *Gordon Craig on Movement and Dance* [New York, 1977] p. xxii); *The Mask*, vol. 6, no. 1 (July 1913). Cf. also The Mask, vol. 5, no. 1 (July, 1912), and ID, letter to EGC, February 14, 1920: "The Russian Ballet are hopping madly about in Picasso pictures . . . epileptic gymnastics with no thought or centre."
16. EGC, letter to MFS, May 20, 1905, and "Memories of Isadora Duncan," BBC radio, reprinted in *The Listener*, June 5, 1952. (The central importance of this memory for Craig is indicated by the way he repeated this passage in *Index*, pp. 261–2.) Cf. also ID, *My Life*, p. 21, and EGC, Daybook 5, 1930–3, p. 88 (HRC).
17. EGC, Daybook 2, 1910–11, p. 302 (HRC).
18. ID, *My Life*, p. 75.

19. Ibid., p. 165, and ID, *The Art of the Dance* (New York, 1928), p. 102; EGC, *Index*, pp. 263–4.
20. EGC, "Motion. Being the Preface to the Portfolio of Etchings" (originally published as a pamphlet, Nizza-Firenze, 1907), *The Mask*, vol. 1, no. 10 (December, 1908.) For further details on the relationship between Isadora Duncan's dancing and EGC's concept of Scene, see Craig, *Gordon Craig*, pp. 234–5.
21. Ursula Bridge, ed., *W. B. Yeats & T. Sturge Moore: Their Correspondence, 1910–1937* (New York, 1953), p. 156; Duse cit. Arthur Symons, *Studies in Seven Arts* (New York, 1907), p. 336.
22. Thomas A. Janvier, "The Comédie Française at Orange," pp. 169f.
23. EGC, *Towards A New Theatre*, p. 6.
24. WBY, letter to EGC, March 10, 1902; EGC note (1906), reprinted *Index*, p. 289, and *Towards A New Theatre*, p. 11.
25. EGC, Daybook 1, 1908–10, pp. 79 and 77. Cf. also EGC, *Towards A New Theatre*, p. 6, and a letter to MFS, February 18, 1906: "The people thought I was reckless – see how cautious my recklessness was. I threw overboard their old machine first – then their scenes – then their methods of moving the figures – then the play-wright – then speech – now, last of all, the figures – real or pasteboard – over they go, trumpery and unworthy" (cit. Craig, *Gordon Craig*, p. 227).
26. *The Times* (London), May 24, 1900, and EGC, *The Mask*, vol. 35, nos. 4–6 (October, 1910).
27. *The Mask*, vol. 1, no. 1 (March, 1908).
28. Ibid., and Daybook 1, 1908–10, pp. 41–3. Compare Jean-Louis Barrault, who described the aim of his acting as "striving towards a purely animal state where the face becomes a natural mask" (*Cahiers Renaud–Barrault*, vol. 71, p. 22), or Peter Brook and Charles Marowitz, who discovered in their 1964 LAMDA experiment that "facial expressions, under the pressure of extended sounds, began to resemble Japanese masks" (*The Drama Review*, vol. 11, no. 2, p. 156).
29. *The Mask*, vol. 1, no. 2 (April, 1908) (reprinted in EGC, *On the Art of the Theatre*, p. 55).
30. Ibid.; *The Mask*, vol. 1, no. 1 (March, 1908), and letter to MFS, February 15, 1906. In some ways the intellectual quality that Craig wanted in acting anticipated Brecht. It is therefore quite in line that one of the few modern dramas he should mention with complete approval should be *The Threepenny Opera*, though at first glance it might seem very far from his symbolist ideals. Cf. *The Mask*, vol. 15, no. 2 (April–June, 1929).
31. EGC, "Puppets & Poets" in *The Chapbook*, no. 20 (February, 1921), pp. 28 and 22 and *The Mask*, vol. 3, nos. 4–6 (October, 1910).

32. EGC, *Index*, pp. 34 and 24; EGC, "The Rarest Dancing in the World," *The Dancing Times* (January, 1932); Daybook 2, 1910–11, pp. 83–5 (HRC). Cf. also EGC, *On the Art of the Theatre*, p. 295.
33. "Alassio Notebook" (1911), n.p. (HRC). Cf. also EGC, *Index*, p. 293.

6. Toward a new theater: Masques, Screens, and a *Hamlet*

1. Daybook 2, 1910–11 (HRC), and EGC, *Towards A New Theatre*, p. 2.
2. Henry Irving cit. Cole and Chinoy, *Directors on Directing*, p. 25; EGC, *On the Art of the Theatre*, p. 143 (1905).
3. EGC, *Index*, p. 99; Daybook 2, 1910–11, p. 51.
4. EGC, marginal annotation to "Beauty's Awakening," in his copy of *The Studio* (Summer, 1899), pp. 12–13 (Rood); "Beauty's Awakening," pp. 5f.
5. Paul Hentzner, *Travels in England during the Reign of Queen Elizabeth*, trans. Horace Walpole (London, 1797), p. 55, quoted by EGC in "A Masque: The Harvest Home" (prospectus), *The Green Sheaf*, no. 3 (1903), p. 3. For details of EGC's claim relating to Hone's *Ancient Mysteries* (London, 1823), see Craig, *Gordon Craig*, p. 166 – though in a letter to me (November 4, 1981) he indicates that the passage is intended only to convey "that it was there that [EGC] got the idea."
6. *The Green Sheaf*, no. 3, p. 3; EGC, Notebook 3, 1902–3, pp. 4–6 (BN); and EGC, Notebook 1, n.p. (HRC).
7. *The Mask*, vol. 5, no. 3 (January, 1913).
8. EGC, cit. Leeper, *Edward Gordon Craig*, p. 43; letter to MFS, November 11, 1903 (HRC); Notebook 1904–12, n.p. (HRC); and EGC, *Towards A New Theatre*, p. 27. (At the end of this description Craig noted that "the hunger of the poor was put down right enough, but the hunger of the rich has not been fairly treated...it is as tragic." "Theatre. Shows and Motions. 1905–1909" follows this up with a sketch for a drama in which "the poor men go down on their knees and begin to gild the chains of the rich men.")
9. EGC, "Theatre. Shows and Motions. 1905–1909," n.p. (HRC).
10. Ibid. Cf. also Leeper, *Edward Gordon Craig*, p. 45.
11. EGC, letter to MFS, May, 1905; EGC, *On the Art of the Theatre*, pp. 46–7.
12. EGC, *On the Art of the Theatre*, pp. 144 and 139.
13. EGC, Daybook 1, 1908–10, p. 89; cit. Leeper, *Edward Gordon Craig*, pp. 17–18. (Edward Craig dates the first notes toward *The Steps* as 1902 – *Gordon Craig*, p. 162 – but the concept only took shape in 1905.)

14. EGC, *Towards A New Theatre*, pp. 43 and 47.
15. Ibid., p. 83; EGC, *On the Art of the Theatre*, p. 50.
16. EGC, MS Book 12, p. 35 (BN). Cf. Edward Craig, *Gordon Craig*, p. 239, where Craig also suggests that the screens derived from EGC's concept of a three-dimensional, vertically moving Scene. The sketches that exist in fact show that he was formulating these ideas simultaneously. It therefore seems more logical to view Scene, with its greater complexity and abstraction, as a progression from the screens, which in turn clearly developed out of curtains; Craig's notes demonstrate that he only began to work out ways of using Scene later. To some extent he regarded both staging techniques as equal alternatives and – confusingly – he also called his screens "the Scene," with the result that the 1907 notebook (MS 12) that describes them is footnoted by Bablet and listed in the catalog of the Bibliothèque Nationale as referring to Scene.
17. EGC, note dated 1940 in MS Book 12, p. 51.
18. EGC, patent application A.D. 1910, Jan. 24, no. 1771, p. 2.
19. MS Book 12, p. 34. (This is a point he returned to in an address to the Theatre Worker's Guild on June 18, 1920; "If each artist will feel and think for himself, we can have four or five examples of mobility of scene within a year.")
20. WBY, *Plays for An Irish Theatre* (London, 1911), p. 221.
21. *The Music Review*, vol. 1, no. 2 (1912), and *The Dublin Times*, February 16, 1912 (my emphasis); WBY cit. EGC, MS Book 12, p. 40, and J. B. Yeats, letter to EGC, March 18, 1912.
22. *The Daily News*, September 19, 1911; EGC, undated letter to MFS (1911). To some extent this change of attitude was also due to Craig's realization (having taken out the patent on advice from a lawyer friend, Gilbert Cannan) that the screens could provide a source of continuing income if their use in productions was kept in his control.
23. Henry Irving, MS notes on *Hamlet* (in EGC's collection) n.p. (BN). For EGC's comments on *Hamlet* as a play in which "talk suits the whole situation so well," see *The Dancing Times* (July, 1932).
24. EGC, letter to Stanislavski, July 14, 1910; Daybook 2, 1910–11, pp. 168–9 (HRC); undated letter to MFS (1910?).
25. Stanislavski, letter to EGC, June 21, 1910, and EGC's reply, July 14, 1910 (HRC).
26. Serafima Birman cit. Lawrence Senelick, "The Craig–Stanislavski 'Hamlet' at the Moscow Art Theatre," *Theatre Quarterly*, vol. 6, no. 22, p. 108; EGC, notes on sketches for *Hamlet* (Moscow, 1908); EGC, *Towards A New Theatre*, p. 81; Stenogramme des entretiens concernant la préparation de la mise en scène d'Hamlet, pp. 4–5 (BN); and Daybook 1, 1908–10, p. 225.

27. "The characters must be King, Queen and Hamlet. The rest are only a background of vileness, wealth and density... The problem is to show the throne, the three characters and the retinue, the courtiers, merge into one generalized background of gold. Their mantles flow together, and they cannot be perceived to have individual faces." Stanislavski, rehearsal notes, cit. Senelick, "The Craig–Stanislavski 'Hamlet,'" *Theatre Quarterly*, p. 62.

28. EGC, "Theatre. Shows and Motions. 1905–1909;" Sulerzhitski, cit. Senelick, "The Craig–Stanislavski 'Hamlet,'" *Theatre Quarterly*, p. 80. (Senelick also reproduces the sketch in question on p. 75.)

29. Stenogramme, pp. 3, 7, 18–19; and EGC, *Towards A New Theatre*, p. 81.

30. Stenogramme, pp. 22, 12, 7, 11–13. (See also EGC, *Index*, p. 290.)

31. Stenogramme, pp. 1 and 4f.

32. Stanislavski cit. Craig, *Gordon Craig*, p. 246; Sulerzhitski and Valery Bryusov, cit. Senelick, "The Craig–Stanislavski 'Hamlet,'" *Theatre Quarterly*, pp. 99 and 120 (my emphasis).

33. MS. note in EGC's copy of Constantin Stanislavski *My Life in Art*, p. 522, (London, 1924); Daybook 2, 1910–11, pp. 321, 322.

34. MS. note on typescript of "Hamlet," EGC radio talk for the BBC, 1956; Stanislavski, *My Life in Art*, pp. 509, 513, and EGC MS. notes; Daybook 2, 1910–11, p. 27.

35. David Magarshak, *Stanislavski: A Life* (Westport, Conn. 1975), pp. 328, and 299–301.

36. *The Times* (London), January 9, 1912.

37. Cf. Craig, *Gordon Craig*, pp. 250–1, and Brian Arnott, *Edward Gordon Craig & Hamlet* (Ottawa, 1975), p. 37. (Arnott, for instance, argues that the screens could not be moved because the MAT stage was raked. As Senelick has pointed out this was not the case.)

38. EGC, "Alassio Notebook" (1907), n.p. (HRC), into which the letter from Stanislavski (1935) is pasted, and MS. note to *My Life in Art*, p. 521.

39. Production notes, reprinted by Senelick, "The Craig–Stanislavski 'Hamlet,'" *Theatre Quarterly*, p. 69; Stenogramme, p. 9.

40. EGC, draft for an article entitled "Stage Scenery," 1910 (UCLA). (Details of the quarrel with Stanislavski are given in EGC's MS. notes to Isadora Duncan, *My Life*, pp. 253f., and in Senelick, "The Craig–Stanislavski 'Hamlet,'" *Theatre Quarterly*, passim).

41. Stanislavski, *My Life in Art*, p. 519; EGC, Daybook 1, 1908–10, p. 117.

42. EGC, "Alassio Notebook" (1911).

43. EGC, *Towards A New Theatre*, p. 77; letter to MFS, 1911.

44. Daybook 1, 1908–10, pp. 150–1.

7. The theater of the future: Scene, puppets, and a religious festival

1. EGC, *Towards A New Theatre*, p. 17; Daybook 5, 1930–3, p. 88 (HRC).
2. EGC, *Scene* (Oxford, 1923), pp. 5, 22.
3. EGC, "Stage Scenery," TS, 1910 (UCLA). The "eidophusikon," little more than a curiosity in the history of the theater, was invented by de Loutherbourg, David Garrick's designer.
4. MS Book 12, 1907, p. 1; letter cit. Leeper, *Edward Gordon Craig*, p. 16, and EGC,"Catalogue of Etchings being designs for Motions by Gordon Craig, Florence 1908," pp. 1 and 6.
5. EGC, MS notes in the cover pages of Sebastiano Serlio, *Architettura*, vol. 2, p. 1545 (BN); letter to *The Times* (London), October 7, 1907.
6. EGC, *Scene*, pp. 15, 14, and 20; letter to ET, March 8, 1903 (UCLA); Daybook 1, 1908–10, p. 183.
7. EGC, cit. Maurice Magnus, unpublished TS, 1907 (HRC). For a full analysis of expressionist acting, see my *Avant Garde Theatre*, pp. 53f.
8. Daybook 3, 1911–18, p. 25; EGC, *Towards A New Theatre*, p. 48.
9. Letter from Edward Craig to the author, September 15, 1981. (For the reason why EGC never used this model to develop his theory through experimentation, see Craig, *Gordon Craig*, p. 317.)
10. Arnold Rood, (ed.), *Craig on Movement and Dance* (New York, 1977), p. 166; EGC, "Puppets and Poets," *The Chapbook*, no. 20 (February 1921), pp. 17 and 30–1; EGC, *On the Art of the Theatre*, p. 62.
11. Alfred Jarry, *Selected Works of Alfred Jarry*, trans. Roger Shattuck and Simon Watson Taylor (London, 1969), pp. 86 and 83; Paul Margueritte, *Le Petit Théâtre* (*Théâtre de Marionettes*) (Paris, 1889), pp. 7–8.
12. EGC, *The Scene*, TS, 1914 (HRC); and EGC, *The Art of the Theatre*, p. 48.
13. EGC, interview in *The Washington Post*, December 1, 1907.
14. EGC, "Puppets and Poets," p. 30; Daybook 2, 1910–11, p. 310.
15. Notes to designs for *Macbeth* (BN). See also Daybook 1, 1908–10, pp. 129 and 179, and Daybook 2, 1910–11, p. 203.
16. Adolphe Appia, "Comment reformer notre mise en scène," *La Revue*, vol. 50, no. 2, June 1, 1904, pp. 344f.
17. Daybook 3, 1911–18, p. 147 (HRC); EGC, *Scene*, pp. 20 and 23.
18. EGC, TS draft for *Scene*, pp. 3 and 19 (HRC); EGC, *On the Art of the Theatre*, p. 123.
19. Daybook 1, 1908–10, pp. 198–9; Daybook 2, 1910–11, pp. 315f; Notebook on Movement, 1907–20, n.p. (UCLA).
20. ID to EGC, June, 1913 (CD no. 231, LC).

21. EGC to ID, undated. See also EGC, *On the Art of the Theatre*, pp. 74 and 89.
22. EGC, TS draft for *Scene*, p. 19; and MS note in Craig's copy of Serlio, vol. 2. See also EGC, *Towards A New Theatre*, p. 77.
23. Notebook 26, "Notes for Bach's *Passion*, 1912. 1913. 1914," pp. 6 and 7 (BN).
24. EGC, TS, "The Stage a Sport," 1922, p. 11 (HRC). See also EGC, *Towards A New Theatre*, p. 33, and EGC, *On the Art of the Theatre*, p. 80.
25. Daybook 2, 1910–11, p. 78.
26. It could also be pointed out that the central bridge construction at the rear of the main acting area corresponds very closely to Copeau's Vieux Columbier stage.
27. For the reconstruction of the imagined action of *The St. Matthew Passion*, I am indebted to Edward Craig, and to his article in *Theatre Notebook*, vol. 26, no. 4 (Summer, 1972), pp. 148f. I have taken the liberty of departing from his interpretation in one significant respect. He places the Evangelist "out in the auditorium, where one might perhaps expect to find a conductor on a podium," and the solo singers also outside the stage area on either side (p. 149). Quite apart from the fact that this arrangement would reduce a performance to a conventional concert piece (albeit with illustrative action in the background), several of Craig's designs specifically place a gesticulating figure on the central column at the base of the upper flight of steps. This column shows up clearly in the photograph of the lower stage area.
28. Further details of performance come from Daybook 3, 1911–18, pp. 180f., Notebook 26, pp. 12f., "Proposal for the production in Roma of Bach's St. *Matthew Passion*," TS, n.d. (HRC), Notebook 26, pp. 4 and 25, and Notebook 27, p. 5 (BN).
29. EGC, *Index*, pp. 298–9.
30. Arthur Kahane cit. Cole and Chinoy, *Directors on Directing*, p. 52. See also Daybook 3, 1911–18, pp. 39 and 55.
31. Daybook 3, 1911–18, p. 171; *A Production*, p. 5; "Proposal for the production in Roma of Bach's St. Matthew Passion."
32. Daybook 1, 1908–10, p. 183.

8. Final bow: A school and the printed word

1. Annotation in EGC's copy of the program for *Dido and Aeneas* (BN).
2. EGC, cit. Craig, *Gordon Craig*, p. 181, and letter to MFS, November 26, 1903 (HRC).
3. EGC, *On the Art of the Theatre*, pp. 163–78, 257, 239–40, 242.

4. Daybook 2, 1910–11, pp. 324, 181.
5. Cf. "Society of the Theatre," minute book, 1912–13 (UCLA).
6. EGC, "Advertisement for the School for the Art of the Theatre," London, 1912, pp. 1 and 3 (BN). See also Daybook 1, 1908–10, p. 187 (HRC).
7. EGC, "A Living Theatre," Florence, 1913, pp. 35 and 31 (BN).
8. Ibid., p. 44.
9. EGC, "Rules for the School for the Art of the Theatre," Florence, 1913 (BN).
10. EGC, holograph note on p. 53 of "A Living Theatre," d. October, 1914; Daybook 1, 1908–10, p. 54; "Alassio Notebook" (1911), n.p.; Daybook 2, 1910–11, p. 325.
11. Daybook 1, 1908–10, p. 53, and EGC, *Index*, p. 268.
12. EGC, "A Living Theatre," p. 18.
13. EGC, *On the Art of the Theatre*, pp. 45–6; EGC, undated letter to ET (1909?) (UCLA).
14. Harley Granville-Barker, *The Daily Mail*, September 26, 1912
15. Jean-Louis Barrault, cited on the cover of the 1943 edition of EGC, *De L'Art du Théâtre*; EGC letter to MFS, 1922.
16. Undated annotation in Craig's copy of the program for *Dido and Aeneas*.
17. EGC, *Henry Irving*, p. 187.

9. Curtain call: Craig's vision and contemporary theater

1. In this the French were only partly successful. The government had paid only a fraction of what Craig had reportedly been offered by an American library. Resenting this forced sale, Craig sold or gave away various items to visiting admirers – the Arnold Rood collection, now in the London Theater Museum, being one example – while a great deal of Craig's own work (as distinct from the historical artifacts he had collected) was smuggled out of France on the day immediately following his death and reached various institutions in America, primarily the Humanities Research Center in Austin, Texas.
2. For a discussion of Craig's influence on Copeau, see John Rudlin, *Jacques Copeau*, Cambridge 1986, pp. 36ff.
3. *The Unknown O'Neill*, ed. Travis Bogard, Yale 1988, pp. 406–411.
4. Peter Brook, Program note to *The Tempest*, CIRT 1968, and interview, *The Drama Review*, vol. 17, no. 3 (1973), pp. 47 & 50.
5. EGC, Daybook 2, 1910–11, p. 324.
6. Robert Wilson, *Practice*, vol. 5, no. 2 (1987), p. 116 & Heiner Müller, Program note for *CIVIL warS*, ART 1985 (p. 23).
7. For full descriptions of Wilson's productions, see Arthur Holmberg, *The Theatre of Robert Wilson*, Cambridge 1997.

10. Programme notes: Craig on theater
(Notes by Gordon Craig)

1. You will say, perhaps, that Irving seems to have explained so much to us that the other characters in the play were daft not to notice too; that a hundred times, by eavesdropping they might have caught him giving us a full explanation that he was the culprit.

   You are quite right. Irving followed the most ancient and unshakable tradition, which says that the Dramatist is to take his audience into his confidence. The actor who fails to observe this fails as an actor. I have seen such actors recently in London. The villain of the play comes on the stage smiling: he is quite alone; and though he remains alone for five minutes, he does not dare to tell us that he is "the villain " – has not dared to let any tell-tale look escape him, and he fails to explain anything to us. It is called realism – it is no such thing: it is merely incompetence – an incapacity to understand that *everything* has to be clearly explained to the spectators, and little or no thought paid to whether the other characters on the stage overhear or see. If they overhear, if they see, they too have failed in the simplest rudiments of their craft.

2. At Letchworth, in the autumn of the year 1912, I was fortunate enough to be present at a performance practically in the open air, where artificial light was banned. England is quite an ideal country for open-air and daylight performances. In the south of Europe it is uncomfortably hot – here in England it is cool; and the rain is always a natural legislator which prevents an exaggerated number of unnecessary festivals. Festivals are for the spring-time; one month is enough.

3. Remember here the derivation of the word "theatre." According to Professor Skeat, a French word, derived from Latin; the Latin word from Greek. Middle French, *theatre*; Cotgrave's Dictionary, ed. 1660. Derived from the Latin *Theatrum*, derived from the Greek θέατρον, a place for seeing shows, derived from the θεάομαι, I see. Compare θέα, a sight; see Prellwitz. Note: Not a word about it being a place for *hearing* 30,000 *words babbled* out in two hours.

4. "The central and most solemn rite of the Christian worship was the Mass, an essentially dramatic commemoration of one of the most critical moments in the life of the Founder." – E. K. Chambers, *The Mediæval Stage*, vol. ii. bk. iii. p. 3.

5. I think it was this which went far towards persuading people that Irving was an *intellectual* actor. He never pretended to more intellect than a great actor need possess: a millionaire hardly ever bothers to parade his possessions, and Irving was rich in all that is necessary to an actor – nothing more than that.

6. "Why waste time talking to so stupid a man as this 'Playgoer'?" asked a charming lady – and would not wait for an answer. The reply is obvious: one does not talk to wise people – one listens to them.

7. Of Sculpture Pater writes: "Its white light, purged from the angry, bloodlike stains of action and passion, reveals, not what is accidental in man, but the god in him, as opposed to man's restless movement." Again: "The base of all artistic genius is the power of conceiving humanity in a new, striking, rejoicing way, of putting a happy world of its own construction in place of the meaner world of common days, of generating around itself an atmosphere with a novel power of refraction, selecting, transforming, recombining the images it transmits, according to the choice of the imaginative intellect." And again: "All that is accidental, all that distracts the simple effect upon us of the supreme types of humanity, all traces in them of the commonness of the world, it gradually purges away."

8. From another point of view, and one not lightly to be either overlooked or discussed, Cardinal Manning, the Englishman, is particularly emphatic when he speaks of the actor's business as necessitating "the prostitution of a body purified by baptism."

9. This seems to me to be a little fault which might easily be prevented if English critics were *given the opportunity* to study what is being done in the other cities of the British Isles and in the other cities on the Continent. The English critic should be sent by the rich English journals to Paris, to Berlin, to Krakau and to Budapest. The public deserves to know what is being done in these and other places. Who had heard of Strindberg, for instance, until he died – and had it not been for Mr. William Archer, who so often went to Norway, who in England would have heard of Ibsen? Then, just lately, were we informed by the journals about the revival of the art of improvisation under Hevesi in the theatres of Italy and Hungary? Does anyone know about Wyspiansky and his school? But who is there that does not know of the third-rate imitators of these people? The London Press gets hysterical about third-rate imitators when it is the duty of the editors to see that we are given sound information about the origin of these imitations.

SELECT BIBLIOGRAPHY

Gordon Craig's own publications are listed in the chronology. Bibliographic details of both his major articles and the reviews of his works are to be found in the Notes.

Arnott, Brian. *Edward Gordon Craig and Hamlet*. Ottawa, 1975.

Bablet, Denis. *Edward Gordon Craig*. Paris, 1962.

Barshay, Bernard. "Gordon Craig's Theories of Acting," *Theatre Annual* (1947), pp. 55–63.

Craig, Edward. "Gordon Craig and Bach's *St. Matthew Passion*," *Theatre Notebook*, vol. 26, no. 4 (1972), pp. 147–51.

—— "Gordon Craig and Hubert von Herkomer," *Theater Research*, vol. 10, no. 1 (1969), pp. 7–16.

—— *Gordon Craig: The Story of His Life*. New York, 1968.

Duncan, Isadora. *My Life*. New York, 1927; London, 1928.

Fletcher, Ifan Kyrle, and Arnold Rood, *Edward Gordon Craig: A Bibliography*. Society for Theatre Research, 1967.

Gorelik, Mordecai. *New Theatres for Old*. New York, 1962.

Guidry, Lorelei. *Introduction and Index to The Mask*, vol. 16. New York, 1968.

Hewitt, Barnard. "Gordon Craig and Post Impressionism," *Quarterly Journal of Speech*, vol. 30, no. 1 (1944), pp. 75–80.

Housman, Laurence. *The Unexpected Ideas*. London, 1937.

Huneker, James. *Iconoclasts: A Book of Dramatists*. London, 1905.

Hyllestod, Morgens. "The pretenders: Copenhagen 1926," *Theatre Research*, vol. 7, no. 3 (1966), pp. 117–22.

Ilyin, Eugene. "How Stanislavski and Gordon Craig Produced *Hamlet*," *Plays and Players* (March, 1957), pp. 6–7.

Leeper, Janet. *Edward Gordon Craig: Designs for the Theatre*. Harmondsworth, 1948.

Loeffler, Michael. *Gordon Craig's frühe Versuche zur Ueberwindung der Bühnenrealismus*. Bern, 1969.

Macfall, Haldane. "Some Thoughts on the Art of Gordon Craig," *The Studio*, vol. 22, no. 2 (1901).

Marker, Frederick and Lisa Lone. *Edward Gordon Craig and The Pretenders*. Carbondale, Ill., 1982.

Marotti, Ferrucio. *Edward Gordon Craig*. Bologna, 1961.

Newman, Lindsay. *Gordon Craig Archives: International Survey*. London, 1976.

Rood, Arnold. *Gordon Craig on Movement and Dance*. New York, 1977

——and Donald Oenslager. *Edward Gordon Craig: Artist of the Theater*. New York, 1967.

Rose, Enid. *Gordon Craig and the Theatre*. London, 1931.

Senelick, Laurence. "The Craig–Stanislavsky *Hamlet* at the Moscow Art Theatre," *Theatre Quarterly*, vol. 6, no. 22 (1976), pp. 56–122.

Shaw, Martin Fallas. *Up to Now*. London, 1929.

Simonson, Lee. *The Stage is Set*. New York, 1932.

——"The Case of Gordon Craig," *Theatre Guild Magazine* (February 1931), pp. 18–23.

Stanislavski, Constantin. *My Life in Art*. London, 1924.

Symons, Arthur. *Studies in Seven Arts*. London, 1906.

INDEX

Other titles in the Contemporary Theatre Studies series: